EXPLORING STUDIO MATERIALS

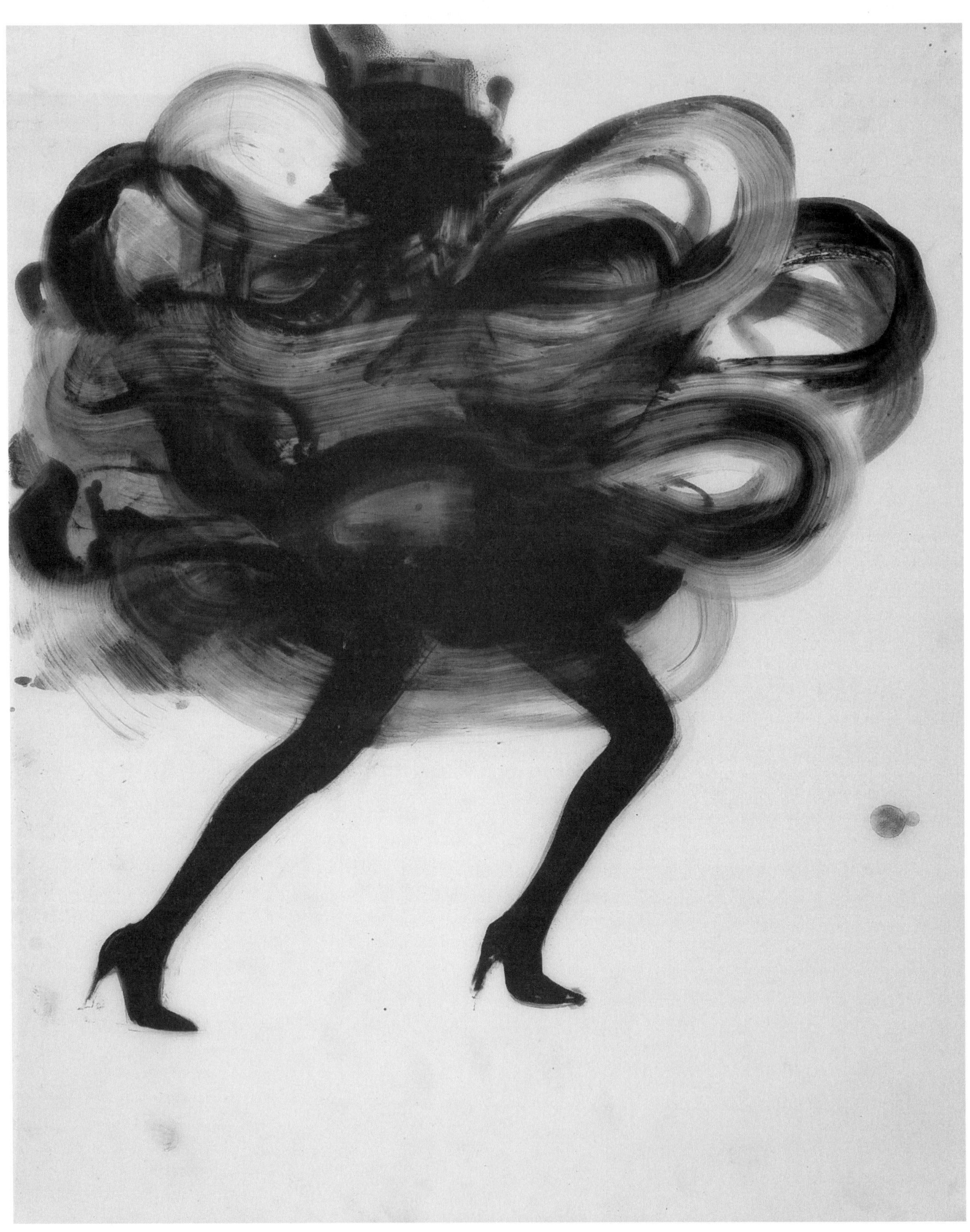

Cathy Daley, Untitled, 2007, pastel on vellum, 24″ × 19″

EXPLORING STUDIO MATERIALS

Teaching Creative Art Making to Children

MARY HAFELI

Teachers College, Columbia University

New York | Oxford
OXFORD UNIVERSITY PRESS

Oxford University Press is a department of the University of Oxford.
It furthers the University's objective of excellence in research,
scholarship, and education by publishing worldwide.

Oxford   New York
Auckland   Cape Town   Dar es Salaam   Hong Kong   Karachi
Kuala Lumpur   Madrid   Melbourne   Mexico City   Nairobi
New Delhi   Shanghai   Taipei   Toronto

With offices in
Argentina   Austria   Brazil   Chile   Czech Republic   France   Greece
Guatemala   Hungary   Italy   Japan   Poland   Portugal   Singapore
South Korea   Switzerland   Thailand   Turkey   Ukraine   Vietnam

For titles covered by Section 112 of the US Higher Education
Opportunity Act, please visit www.oup.com/us/he for the
latest information about pricing and alternate formats.

Published in the United States of America by
Oxford University Press
198 Madison Avenue, New York, NY 10016
http://www.oup.com

Oxford is a registered trade mark of Oxford University Press.

Library of Congress Cataloging-in-Publication Data
Hafeli, Mary Claire.
   Exploring studio materials : teaching creative art making to children / Mary Hafeli,
Columbia University, Teachers College. -- First Edition.
      pages cm
   Includes bibliographical references and index.
   ISBN 978-0-19-997555-6 (alk. paper)
   1. Art--Study and teaching (Elementary) 2. Artists' materials. I. Title.
   N350.H15 2014
   372.5'044--dc23
                                                                2014028735

Printing number: 9 8 7 6 5 4 3 2 1

Printed in the United States of America
on acid-free paper

Table of Contents

Chapter 3   **Working Wet:**
Tempera, Watercolor,
Gouache, Acrylic,
and Oil Paints 69

Chapter 5   **Collecting, Altering, Layering, and Attaching: Collage** 147

Chapter 6   **Forming and Building: Sculpture** 177

Chapter 7 Articulating Studio Learning Outcomes and Planning for Meaningful Instruction 221

Preface

WHAT IS A MATERIAL LIKE TO TOUCH? How does it smell and what kind of sound does it make? Beyond visual qualities, young artists respond to multiple sensory properties of materials. In their experimentation with studio media, they discover that the stickiness and pliability of clay, for example, leads to physical forms and visual effects that are different from those of fluid and creamy paint or stiff and slick-surfaced paper. Young people come to understand that the varied forms they create with materials can *mean* different things as well. Deciding to tear or cut paper in collage involves a choice between a wispy, feathered, and soft edge and a sharply crisp and even one. Each means something different. And it is within this assigning of meaning to both different materials and the visual and communicative effects they afford that young people *transform* materials into media, or suggesters of meaning.

This book is for people who teach beginning and experienced young artists and who want to encourage imaginative and inventive work with studio art materials, by exploring them in depth and in open-ended ways. It is intended for anyone who uses materials with young people—art teachers in schools and other settings, classroom teachers, teachers of subjects other than art, and parents and caregivers. The book is meant for those who want to help kids approach making art through the challenge of ongoing exploration and experimentation, through imaginative and divergent thinking, through openness to discovery and possibility, and through recognizing and valuing ideas, meaning, and learning that emerge through the studio process.

The focus of the book is on tactile, touch-based materials and not on new media or digital and computer-based technological processes for artmaking. This is simply a limitation of space and not, in any way, a political or philosophical stance. In fact, I hope that this book will be followed by another that takes a similarly in-depth approach to exploring the richness and diverse potential of digital materials and forms. As adult artists do, young people should have opportunities to develop expertise in all sorts of traditional and new media, and should be guided to consider the many ways in which these approaches can complement one another in ongoing studio practice.

Throughout the chapters on materials, you will not find recipes for lessons with steps to follow toward predictable, uniform, overly teacher-directed outcomes. Rather, my goal in writing the book is to at least temper, and at best eradicate, that kind of deterministic studio teaching. Studio projects that rely primarily on simply following someone else's directions or adopting a teacher's singular aesthetic sensibility do not reflect the myriad ways in which artists approach making work in the studio. Instead, the book is predicated on the surprise and possibility that characterize what actually happens when people work intensely and experimentally to make things of their own invention and with their own meanings. The process is not neat, tidy, linear, and certain. It's often messy and full of questions, ambiguity, and challenges.

One trick for any good art teacher is to understand the complexity that meaningful artmaking entails, and to know firsthand how working with materials in particular ways—with students of various ages, backgrounds, and abilities—brings this "real world" studio practice and learning about. Experimentation, pushing materials in different directions, understanding possibilities and limitations, and exploring novel approaches while gaining expertise in a medium are paramount to artistic practice, no matter what the age of the artist. Many art teachers have never been invited to get to know the materials they themselves use as artists with these considerations in mind. Many also have not had the opportunity to study the artistic lives and practices of children, who bring to their studio experiences essential ideas for what their works may mean, or be about. Without these insights, it is difficult for teachers to "teach for" divergent approaches to working with studio media, and to set up the instructional circumstances for students to create meaningful art through materials.

Exploring Studio Materials addresses the need in the field of art teacher education for teachers to understand the properties of various media, the divergent effects that can be produced, the skills that can be gained through experimental exploration, and the expressive potential of those technical effects for meaning in young people's artwork. Hopefully, the book offers readers different types of experiences with materials and their expressive possibilities, practical knowledge about how to use various media with young people, and an intimate understanding of how to encourage in young people a sense of divergent, independent studio thinking and practice.

Beyond examining my own studio work and teaching over many years, in writing this book and forming ideas about the role of materials in studio practice I recognize the profound shaping impact of my own teachers, including Sherri Smith and Judy Burton. I also appreciate the wonderful conversations around materials that many of my students have fueled, and thank those who gave permission for me to use images of them and their work in the publication. I have been fortunate to work with colleagues who share my deep interest in studio thinking and practice—my ideas have further crystallized in these ongoing friendships and conversations. Seventy artists generously contributed images of their works and reflections on their studio practices, and I am heartened that so many found the book's philosophy and approach to studio teaching to be resonant and needed. Their contributions give life to the book's spirit and purpose.

I am grateful for the editorial guidance and assistance of Richard Carlin, Emily Schmid, and Cindy Sweeney at Oxford University Press and thank the art educators who reviewed the manuscript, including Susan Brewster (Michigan State University), David Burton (Virginia Commonwealth University), Stacey McKenna (Maryland Institute College of Art), and Sydney Walker (Ohio State University). A special thanks to Tony Venne (Maryland Institute College of Art), whose early design of the book inspired its completion.

At home, my husband—Hal Abeles—was, as always, a source of inspiration, encouragement, and good humor. This book is dedicated to him.

Mary Hafeli

April, 2014

EXPLORING STUDIO MATERIALS

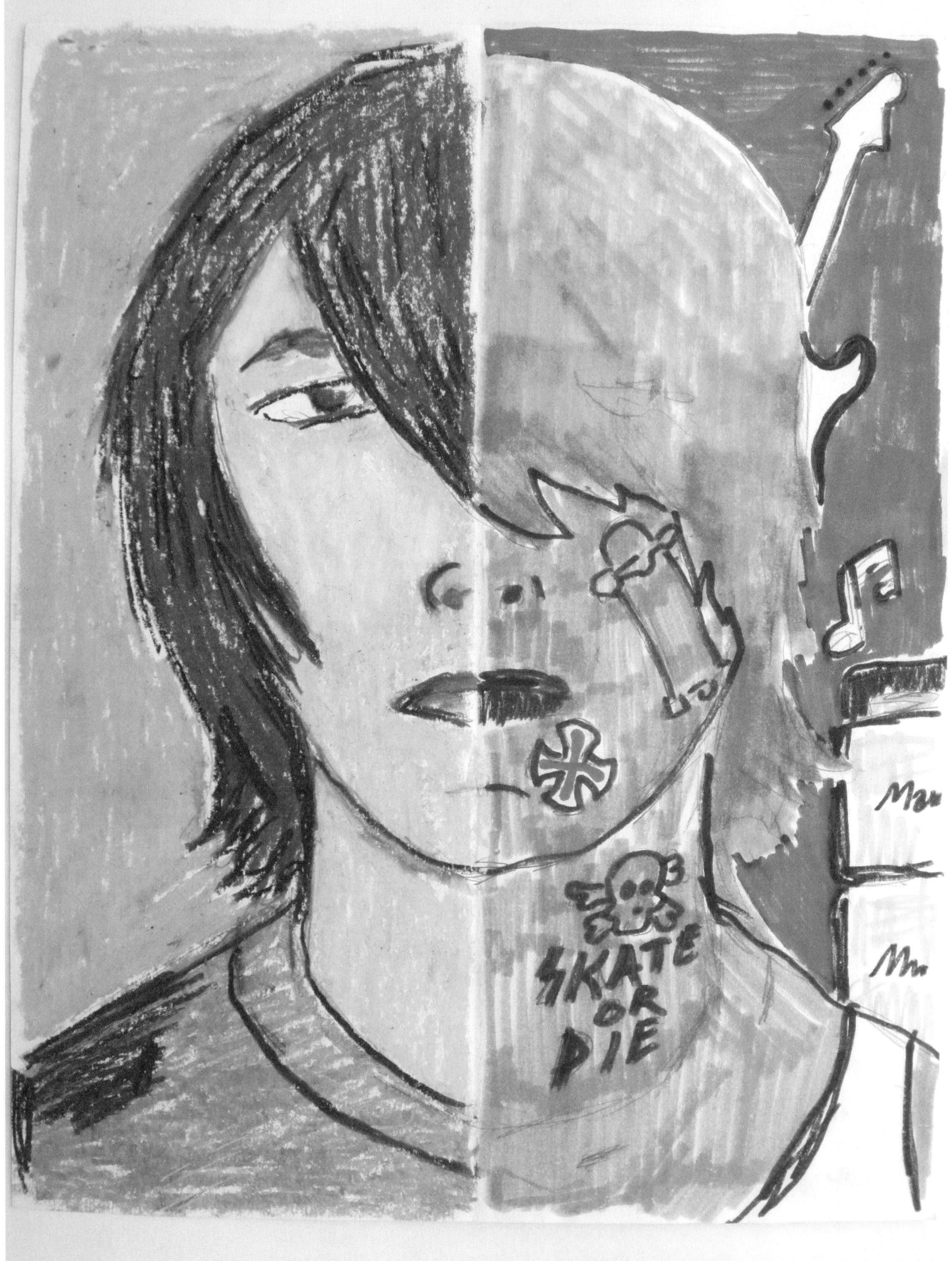

Portrait Stereotype Drawings

1

Rethinking the Role of Materials in Studio Practice

I think you have to learn by procedure. Half of the most interesting things in the world are the result of spilling the water and turning around. Moments of recognition.

—**Richard Wentworth**[1]

WHAT IS IT THAT ARTISTS actually do as they work with materials to create art? What are their individual processes like and what kinds of thinking and action happen as they work with materials in the studio? Whether or not you are an artist, and whether or not you are a teacher yet, this chapter and those that follow ask you to consider young people as artists—independent thinkers and doers who experiment with ideas, imagine possibilities, take risks, make messes, form meaning, veer from initial expectations, and succeed and fail according to their own internal sense of rightness—as they invent ways of working expressively

---

[1] S. Horodner (2001), The Language of Stuff: An Interview with Richard Wentworth, *Sculpture Magazine*, 20(3). Retrieved August 29, 2013, from http://www.sculpture.org/documents/scmag01/april01/went/went.shtml.

with materials to make artworks. You'll be encouraged to move beyond your prior experiences with art making in and out of school, and expand your thinking about what an art making experience entails—especially if you did not engage in the kind of open-ended, exploratory materials investigation you'll be invited to do throughout the book.

Understanding Studio Practices

Below are some contemporary artists' views that, taken together, describe a set of concepts, attitudes, and behaviors that define processes of studio thinking and action (Table 1.1).[2] While this collection of statements is not exhaustive, it does suggest a range of considerations that play into the ways in which artists understand the role of materials in the development of their work. As you read through these reflections and the discussion that follows, compare the artists' views to your own assumptions about how young people are or should be taught using studio materials in the classroom.

THINKING LIKE AN ARTIST

For these artists, working with art materials is not just about perfecting studio techniques or following preconceived models (such as a teacher's step-by-step directions). Instead, individual, expressive ideas and themes emerge in actions on the materials with which artists choose to work. Mona Hatoum describes a fluid relationship between ideas and materials, a condition that allows the artist's ideas to emerge from materials during the process of making the work, or conversely, to "have an idea first" and then find the right materials to create the work.[3] James Elkins wonders about the kinds of ideas that "happen in" materials—paint, for example—and what "thinking in a painting" might mean.[4] Richard Wentworth describes how ideas are related to the suggestive meanings of individual materials and to their juxtaposition in an artwork. To Wentworth, artistic thinking involves recognizing and acting on these relationships.[5] For sculptor Martin Puryear a high level of technical perfection in and of itself isn't "so important." An artist's preoccupation with trying to make things perfect can be, for Puryear, a "real trap for anybody who makes things" because it hinders the flow and germination of ideas.[6]

Whether the topic is technique and materials or how and in what sequence ideas are formed, these artists' comments describe a general sense of sustained belief or trust that is essential in a sometimes overwhelmingly uncertain process. For Tim Hawkinson, trust in the studio process leads to the ability to "keep the

---

[2] The analysis of artists' comments about their studio thinking and processes is taken from Hafeli (2008), "What Happened to Authenticity? 'Assessing Students' Progress and Achievements in Art' Revisited," in R. Sabol & M. Manifold (Eds.), *Through the Prism: Looking into the Spectrum of Writings by Enid Zimmerman*, Reston, VA: National Art Education Association.

[3] Steiner & Herzog (2004), p. 22.

[4] Elkins (2000, p. 3).

[5] Horodner (2001), p. 17.

[6] *Art: 21* (2005c), par. 28.

Table 1-1

Artists' Perspectives on Studio Thinking and Practice

I started using patterns, but I shouldn't have. . . . It broke the ideas I had in my head. I should have stayed with my own ideas.

—Nettie Young

I put my trust in the materials that confront me, because they put me in touch with the unknown. It's then that I begin to work . . . when I don't have the comfort of sureness and certainty.

—Robert Rauschenberg

I just take my cues from putting the color down and seeing how it works.

—Elizabeth Murray

I don't start with a color order, but find the colors as I go.

—Helen Frankenthaler

And for an artist, it just seems to me it's not so important to have that level of technical perfection. It's important to have a flow and have things be able to germinate and not get caught in the trap of perfection—because that can be a real trap for anybody who makes things.

—Martin Puryear

I love Minimalist work, but . . . I need texture, surface, and different kinds of materials.

—Patricia McKenna

By having things in the studio, and if there's enough of them, it raises it to the level to which they might tap me on the shoulder and go, "Psst. Did you notice that I've been sitting next to so and so? And when you were out of the room, I spoke to so and so." I need that.

—Richard Wentworth

What kinds of problems, and what kinds of meanings, happen in the paint? Or as one art historian puts it, what is thinking in a painting, as opposed to thinking about painting? These are important questions, and they are very hard to answer using the language of art history.

—James Elkins

I don't come to this work through books. And I don't make this work in response to other people's theory. And I don't think about what the piece means and then make it.

—Jessica Stockholder

There's an organic aspect in much of my work that maybe has to do with keeping the rules really open. There's this hand held, hand made aspect. . . . It's not something I'm really trying to go after—it's sort of a by-product I think.

—Tim Hawkinson

When you work with ideas . . . the form the work takes also depends on the material that is available to me. Sometimes it's the other way around, I have an idea first and then search for the material with which it can best be realized.

—Mona Hatoum

There are a lot of tricks you have to keep playing on yourself to keep at it because every time you hit a problem you want to walk away.

—Janet Fish

It seems I have learned to bear the anxiety of uncertainty. Now I accept that one can't know ahead of time what is on the other side.

—Anne Truitt

rules open."[7] For Robert Rauschenberg, trust is placed in the materials themselves: "sometimes it works and sometimes it doesn't, but I would substitute anything for preconceptions or deliberateness."[8] Similarly, Ann Truitt points out that making art is a "patient business,"[9] not a sure thing. She notes that artists have to "accept that one can't know ahead of time what is on the other side."[10]

This belief in the process stems in part from the ability to constantly adapt and shift directions in the fluctuating world of relationships between the effects the artist creates with a material—like marks, mixtures of colors, and textures. For example, Elizabeth Murray describes how she takes her "cues from putting the color down and seeing how it works."[11] Murray's words echo those of Helen Frankenthaler who says she finds colors "as I go": "There are no rules . . . that is how art is born, that is how breakthroughs happen. Go against the rules or ignore the rules, that is what invention is about."[12] For Frankenthaler, as well as for Richard Wentworth and Bob Ross, belief in the process extends to thinking differently about and recasting the traditional negative perception of "mistakes." In these artists' works, "spills"[13] and "happy accidents"[14] lead not necessarily to failure but rather to improvisation, reenvisioning, editing, and new directions.

To sustain belief and to trust in their work and its at times unpredictable evolution, artists must be willing to not only take on the risk of failure but also persevere through periods of ambiguity and nonclosure. For Joan Mitchell, considering what to include and what to leave out leads to "not know[ing] what to do with it" as the work takes shape, and of being "afraid of ruining what I have."[15] Trust in the process comes more easily for artists like Patricia McKenna when they can use the materials and forms that "speak" to them and with which they can speak.[16] Despite the discomfort of not knowing how things may turn out, artists like quilter Nettie Young trust that their own ideas are better than any patterns or models they might find to follow. As Young says, "I started using patterns but I shouldn't have. . . . I should have stayed with my own ideas."[17]

FROM MATERIAL TO MEDIUM

The scratchy, dry grinding of soft pastel on paper and the powdery residue that remains, the fluid, slippery, pooling of wet ink and its velvety intensity when dry— how is it that the sensory qualities of materials contribute their own ideas to the meaning of an artwork (see Figure 1-1)? Elliot Eisner described this kind of transformation from technical effect to expressive meaning over 40 years ago:

> *The distinctive feature of those who express themselves is their ability to inform matter in ways that reveal the qualities they have seen, felt, or conceptualized. The material that they employ properly functions as a medium,*

---

[7] Hawkinson, in *Art: 21* (2005f), par. 25.
[8] Thomas (1987), p. 2.
[9] Meyer (2002), p. 80.
[10] Munro (2000), p. 324.
[11] Kino (2005), p. 30.
[12] Babington (2006), p. 1.
[13] Wentworth, in Horodner (2001), p. 1.
[14] As host of the PBS series *The Joy of Painting* on PBS from 1983 to 1994, Bob Ross regularly proclaimed the creative potential of "happy accidents."
[15] Stiles & Selz (1996), p. 33.
[16] Barlow (2001), p. 10.
[17] Beardsley, Arnett, Arnett, & Livingston (2002), p. 156.

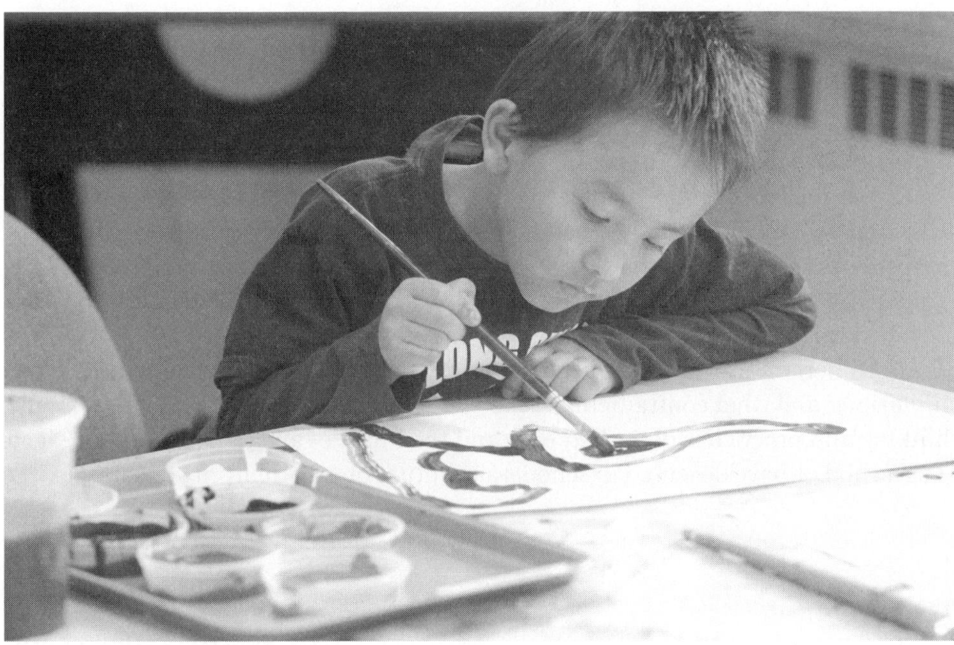

F 1-1: Painting with tempera

a vehicle, for carrying their ideas, images, or feelings forward. The material as medium comes to embody these ideas, images, and feelings only after the artist has exercised intelligent control over the material.[18]

Today we might say that whether intended or not, and whether "intelligently controlled" or not, the visual outcomes of artists' selections and uses of materials suggest ideas, and these ideas may be interpreted in various ways by different people who view the work. Contemporaneously, along with Eisner's own writing on the topic over time, inquiry by other scholars into the thinking and practices of artists has built on the idea of material-as-medium. Collectively, these studies provide insights into the expressive capacities of materials as seen in the art making practices of artists of various ages, historical periods, cultural backgrounds, and levels of experience.[19]

---

[18] See Eisner (1971, p. 5), "Media, Expression, and the Arts," *Studies in Art Education 13*(1), 4–12. Eisner (1978, 2004) evolved and nuanced along the way descriptions of multiple studio thinking practices, such as flexible purposing (borrowed from Dewey, 1938), a practice in which ideas, actions, and intentions are not fixed but instead shift according to what's happening at any given time in the artwork in progress. He also described how materials "inscribe," or capture or preserve, representational ideas that in themselves are fleeting until they are formed and made visible through material substance (see Eisner [2004], *The Arts and the Creation of Mind*, p. 6). Earlier theorizing of artists' interactions with materials (see, for example, Scheffler in Lancaster, 1973–1974) assumed that artists' principal aims were to "dominate" their materials and that the tension caused by their inability or failure to do so, Scheffler's "stubborn interaction" (p. 41), if grappled with repeatedly, could lead to skilled control and knowledge of what a material could and could not do.

[19] Along with John Berger (1974) and Margaret MacIntyre Latta (2001), I document studio process in a firsthand, close-up, "real time" account of this shifting of goals and directions with materials (Hafeli, 2011). Graeme Sullivan (2005) and James Elkins (2000) both explore the concept of artists "thinking in" particular materials. Judith Burton's (2000, 2005) research on children's artistic thinking and development, particularly her ideas about "sensory logic," addresses these issues with the assumption that children are artists in their own right, with ideas, intentions, and responses that are as authentic and essential as those of their adult counterparts. Lee Emory (1989) examined the state of "believing" in the process as a necessary practice and Nelson Goodman's (1978) writing about "rightness of fit" has been applied to the kind of refined judgment that an artist uses to determine what's working and not working in an artwork, and when a piece is deemed complete (Eisner, 2004; Hafeli, 2000, 2001).

The artists' statements above describe specific attitudes and actions—like problem finding and solving, flexible purposing, originality, perseverance, risk taking, tolerance of ambiguity and uncertainty, belief in the process, and willingness to delay closure—that characterize the process by which artists transform materials into expressive media. By taking into account what artists say about their work processes and recognizing the complexity of thought and action that studio work entails, and by understanding what needs to be considered, grappled with, and overcome as artists create their work, art teachers have the opportunity and the responsibility to translate these "real world" ways of thinking and action into classroom experiences for the young people they teach. How do the artists' views discussed here reinforce or challenge your assumptions about teaching art? What similarities, and what contradictions, can you find between the ways in which studio thinking and practice is described here and the kinds of art activities you engaged in as a child or have observed in schools as a future or practicing art teacher?

Material Memories

This is a useful comparison to consider, as art teachers analyzing our own prior experiences with art materials. Try to remember one of the first things you ever made, outside of school. Did you draw on paper—or table, floor, or wall—with crayon, pencil, pen, chalk, or marker? Did you color in a coloring book, or make something from a kit? Paint juicy colors with brush or fingers? Did you mush, roll, and poke holes in Play Doh or sticky clay? Did you use other materials to make marks or build forms? Lipstick? Ketchup? Mud? Sand? Rocks? What was it like to discover what you could do with these materials? What else did you make on your own, outside of school, as you got older?

Now think back on one of your first art class or school art experiences. What's your memory of what you were asked to make, to think about, and do? How does this memory of art making in school compare to what you did on your own? What other school art experiences can you recall? What kinds of art teaching have you observed as a current or future teacher?

Ask others about their memories of making art—classmates, roommates, partners, family members, friends, children, teens—and begin to map out a range of what kids did and still do, made and still make, with art materials in schools and on their own (see Figures 1-2 and 1-3). As you think about how these activities relate to your own sense of what it means to "make art," consider the following questions:

- To what degree do you think students' independent thinking and decision making should be encouraged as they use materials to make artwork?
- How much should students be invited to infuse their own meaning into the materials they use, and invent their own forms to express personal ideas, narratives, and insights?
- What does it look like, and feel like, in an art class where they are invited to do just that?
- What does it look and feel like in classrooms where students are *not* invited to imagine and express their own ideas as themes for artwork, take risks and experiment with materials and tools, and develop artistic independence to judge the success of their artwork?
- What *should* be the teacher's role in young people's art making experiences?

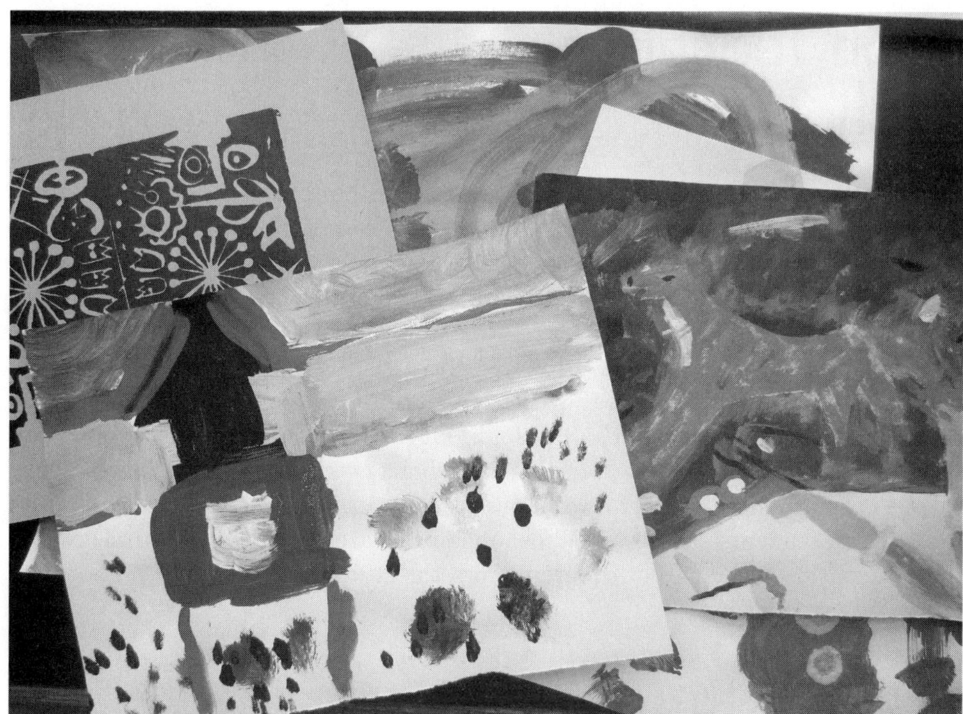

F 1-2: Paintings and prints

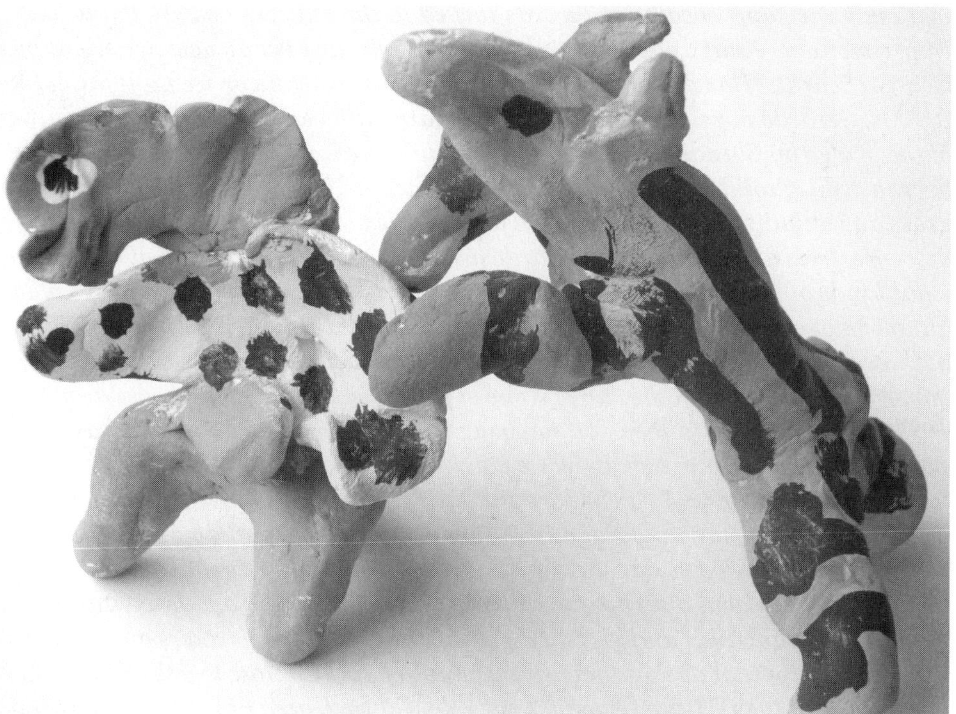

F 1-3: Clay animals painted
with tempera

Studio Materials in Teaching: Classroom Snapshots

The following four art class scenarios are fictitious but based on elements of real life art classes I've experienced as a student, taught myself, or observed as an art teacher educator who spends many hours in schools researching what goes on in art classrooms. As you read these stories, see how your findings and reflections compare to the different instructional approaches taken by the teachers— Ms. Gerardo, Mr. Cooley, Mrs. Brooks, and Mrs. Angelino—as they focus kids' work with materials. What are the different learning outcomes that result in each scenario? What is the teacher's philosophy-in-practice with regards to how kids should use and think about materials? In each art class, who has made the essential decisions about how and for what purposes materials are to be used to express meaning in students' artwork? Whose meanings are being expressed? How are these scenarios similar to or different from the studio thinking and practices of artists described earlier?

SEUR-DOTS! WITH MS. GERARDO

"Okay everybody, let's gather here on the rug," Ms. Gerardo calls to us as we walk into the art room. We're starting something new today, because behind Ms. Gerardo is a big poster and vocabulary words tacked to the bulletin board—Pointillism, Impressionism—and under the Artist of the Week card is our new artist's name, Georges Seurat. "Has anyone ever seen this painting before or seen anything like it?" Ms. Gerardo asks. Hands shoot into the air—it looks a little like the painting of the bridge by Claude Monet we looked at last year, with little dabs of paint all over instead of solid colors. We first talk about what we see—people relaxing on the grass and standing with umbrellas. A dog, a little monkey, water with boats in the distance, trees all around. Ms. Gerardo asks us how the artist applied his paints, what kinds of brushes he had to use to get his dots so small. "We're going to make our own dot artwork today, just like Georges Seurat did," she says, and this is met with everyone's excited "oooooooh." "You can decide whether you'd like to make yours just like his, with the entire scene of people in the park, or choose a smaller part of his painting to focus on for your work. Each table has postcards of the painting you can use to look at while you work."

Next, with all of us in a ring around the front table, Ms. Gerardo tells us that we can either use tempera paint and Q-Tips or markers to make our dots. First she shows us how to sketch out the main part of our scene on small paper, with a pencil. "To fill in, you can choose whatever colors you need from the containers at your tables," she says, "and we're only using the tips of the markers or the Q-Tips dipped in paint to make our dots. They have to be really close together, like this— see how I'm doing it? I can either use one color for each area or I can use two colors together and make my dots create new colors. Either way, today is all about dots. Now, who can guess what this style of art is called? I'll give you a hint, it has to do with the part of the marker we're using."

The rest of the class we work on our park scenes. Some of us use paint, but mostly everyone loves working with the "smelly" markers, all the tapping on paper sounding like fast raindrops. It's fun making dots with markers, and relaxing, and the finished pictures look good—all bright and cheerful, and just like Ms. Gerardo's example (see Figures 1-4 and 1-5). As we finish, she hangs our work on the wall that says "Fourth Grade Seur-DOTS!" and talks about how neatly we did our work today, how well we followed directions. As we line up for lunch, she says, "Next week, I'm going to show you how to use watercolor to make abstract circle ring designs just like Kandinsky! Who remembers what abstract means?"

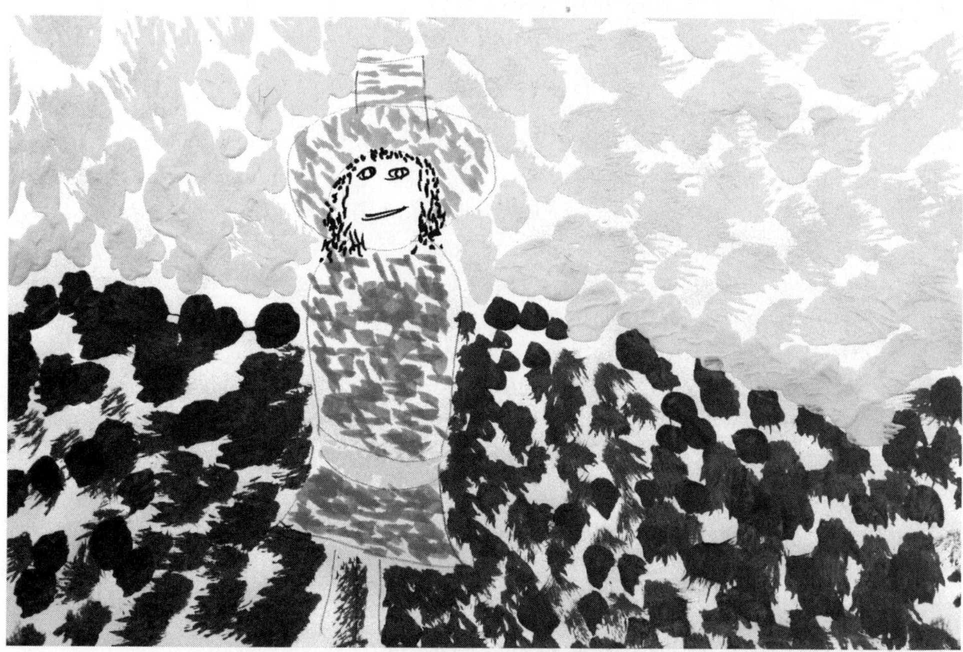

F 1-4: Seur-dot paintings

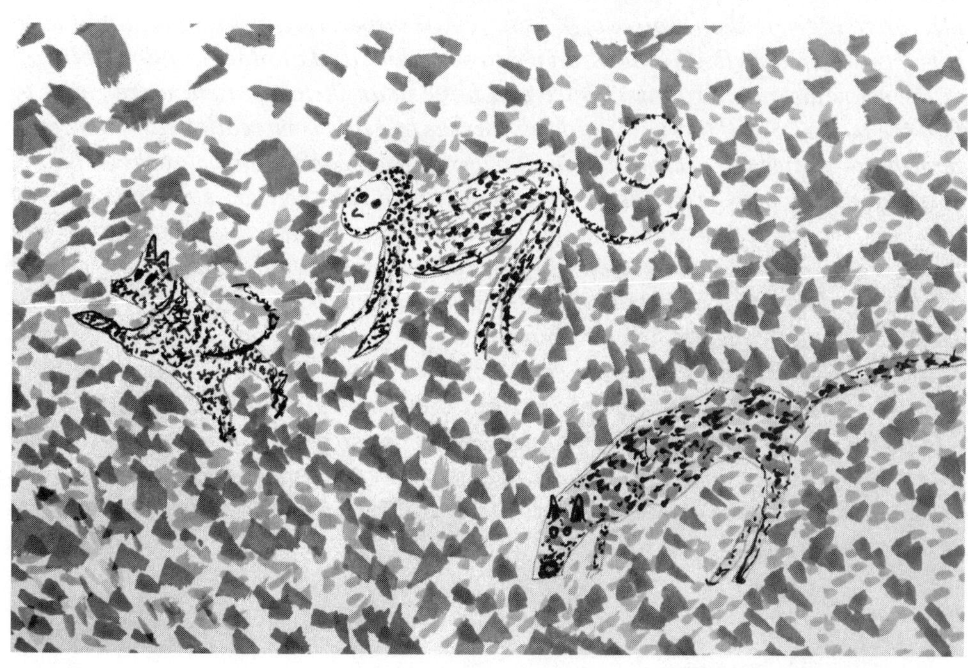

F 1-5: Seur-dot paintings

PORTRAIT STEREOTYPES WITH MR. COOLEY

The fall semester freshman Art 1 course is filled with all different kinds of people. In our first class, Mr. Cooley asks everyone to tell about our "life before Eastern High," and we make lists of all of the places people were born and where they lived before we got here. Mr. Cooley tells us to make more lists for "each culture or race we can think of" and then make lists for different school groups—jocks, brains, goths, and all of that. "What kinds of ideas and characteristics do people associate with these different groups? Let's tape your lists to the walls, and then as you walk around the room write down things on sticky notes that you've heard people say about people in these groups, even if you don't believe these things yourself or think they're fair."

The next day we talk about how damaging stereotyping can be, even when we don't know we're doing it. Without signing our names, we each write a paragraph about a time that we've been discriminated against. Mr. Cooley shuffles our papers and passes them out so that no one has to read their own. There are lots of stories about being stereotyped—for a person's looks, gender, skin color, body shape, grades, views, things they do like sports or band or things like that, or their social group. We talk about how visual stereotyping works, how we "read" people and make assumptions about them just based on how they look. "See if you can find some real examples of what we're talking about," Mr. Cooley says as he puts a pile of magazines on the front table by the door. "For homework take one of these and find an ad with a person or group of people, and pay attention to what is in the picture and how things are arranged and presented. What is emphasized? What might these things symbolize or suggest about these people and the products they're trying to sell? What messages are communicated, what stereotypes are presented or reinforced?"

At the beginning of the next class we share the ads we found. Mr. Cooley brings us all up to the demo table. "We're making our own artwork today," he says, "and what I want you to do is a self portrait of how you really look and how you think the world sees you, based on what we've discovered about stereotypes." He demonstrates how to do a quick, light sketch of his own face from observation with a mirror, using pencil on a piece of 9" × 12" white paper. He gives us a handout with correct proportions for the face, and we go over that, and another handout with all of the steps for our portraits. "Once you have your sketch drawn, we're going to fold the paper in half like this, and color in the left side very realistically using oil pastels. You'll need to press hard, we don't want any washed out colors here. I don't want to see any part of the paper showing through. On the right side, with colored markers, I want you to draw symbols, kind of like tattoos, that symbolize how you think the world sees you because of stereotyping you've experienced. Color in the background with the bigger markers—you'll find the skin colors you need in the packets at your tables. When all of that is done and you've gotten my OK, grab a thick black Sharpie and outline each part your face—the eyes, nose, lips, ears, hair, everything. Then draw a bold pattern in the background that communicates something about you that most people don't know. Now I want you to really take your time and do a good job on these, because next week we're going to hang them in the main entrance as the art exhibition for Diversity Month" (see Figures 1-6, 1-7, and 1-8).

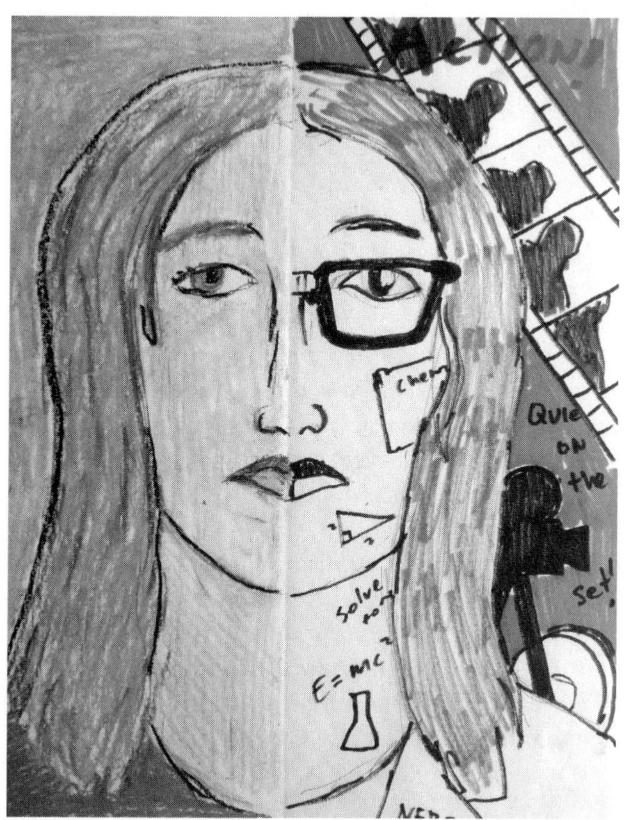

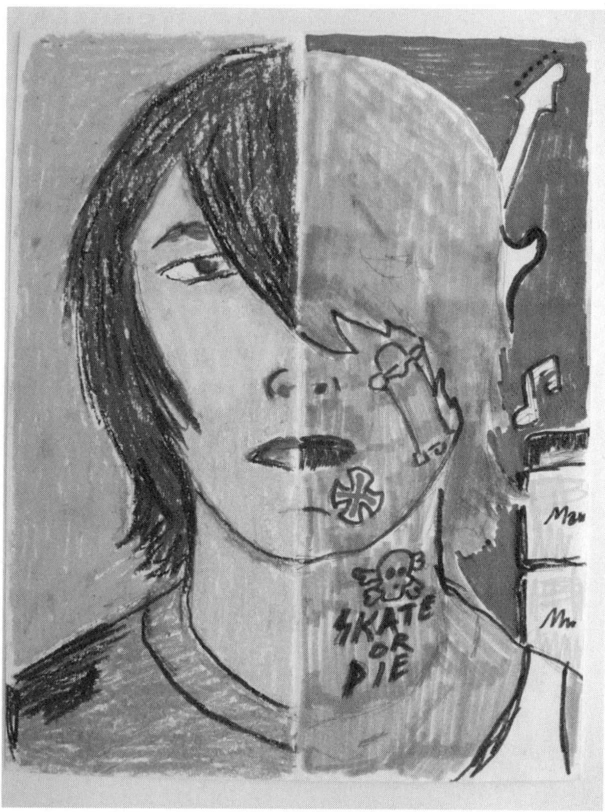

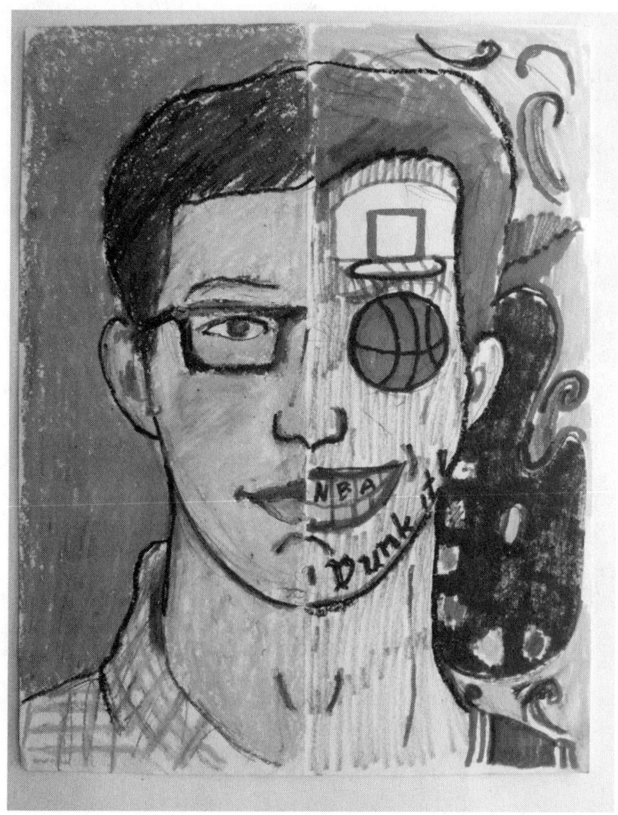

F 1-6: Portrait stereotype drawings. (above, left)

F 1-7: Portrait stereotype drawings. (above, right)

F 1-8: Portrait stereotype drawings

WINTER WONDERLAND WITH MRS. BROOKS

It's second grade, the week before Christmas, and Mrs. Brooks is standing in the front of the room showing us the steps for making these long, red and green chains from paper strips. We couldn't believe it—our finished chains were going to be strung all across the classroom for holiday decoration!

"You take your first strip," Mrs. Brooks says, "and make a circle so that the ends overlap just a little, just this much, and dab some glue all the way across there and press . . . and count one, two, three, four, five. There, you see?" She shows us how to thread the next strip through the paper link she'd just made and repeat the process, alternating red and green strips as she goes along. We're squirming as we watch from our desks. We can't wait to get to work on this enticing task, all of us buzzing about who is going to make the longest chain.

The next morning we arrive to find our finished handiwork festively looped and draped from the corners of the room, four long identical chains meeting in the center of the ceiling and cascading down like a majestic, construction paper chandelier. Hurrying to hang our coats, we delight in our new environment. It feels like a giant party. As we settle in to morning math, Mrs. Brooks says that if we are good boys and girls that day we'll have a surprise. And sure enough, right after reading that afternoon she presents another magnificent project, showing us from the front of the room how to fold and cut white paper into crisp, intricately patterned snowflakes. "When you're finished we'll hang those around, too," she says gaily, and again we can't wait to get started. But there is more, and this next part is too much to handle just sitting in our seats and watching her from afar. In a stampede to the front of the room as if she had unveiled a jar of candy and invited us to have some, we surround the two large shakers of glitter

F 1-9: Paper chains and snowflake

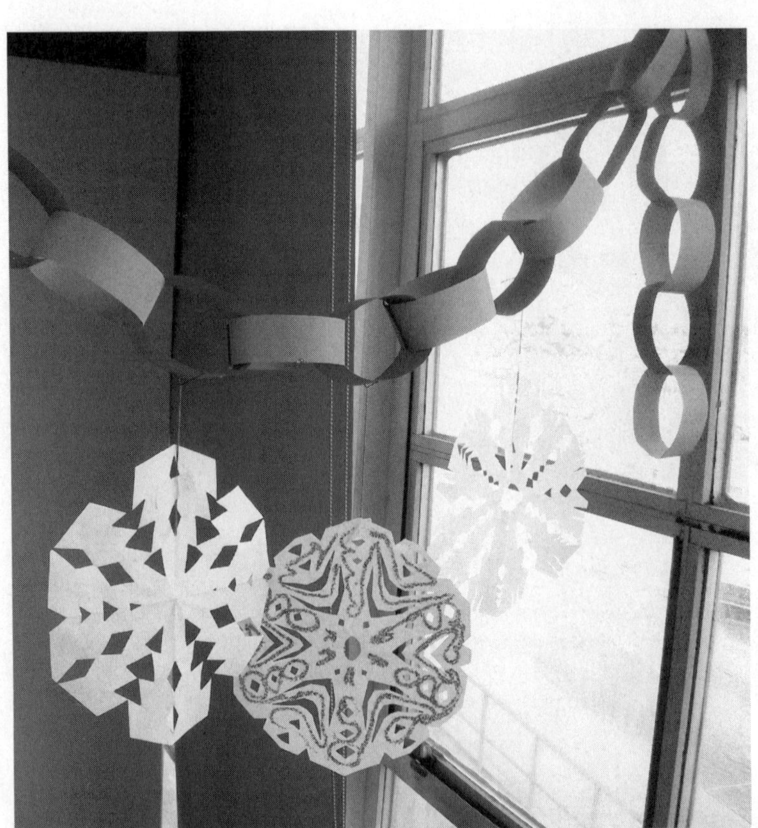

Mrs. Brooks set out on her desk. As we crowd in close, she shows us how the glitter is to be spread out in an even layer on a piece of paper, then transferred neatly to a design of wet glue drizzled in lines and dots on the front of the snowflakes. For everyone in Room B-2 these tiny, shiny specks are magical as fairy dust, as intoxicating as the sparkly colored sugars we sprinkle on cookies at home before baking. For the rest of the afternoon, we make the most beautiful snowflakes imaginable, and hang them one by one on the walls and door, each of us saving our prettiest to hang from the paper chains (see Figure 1-9).

EXPRESSIVE PAINTING WITH MS. ANGELO

On the first day of art class in seventh grade, one of the things Mrs. Angelo has us do is fill out a survey about what why we think artists make art, along with some other questions—What kinds of projects would you like to do, maybe that you've never done or haven't done in a while? What would you like to get better at doing as an artist? When we come in the next morning she says, "There's a lot of agreement here about why you think artists create artworks. Many of you mentioned things like to express an idea, or tell a story, or give a point of view about an issue that's important to you. And you also said that you wanted to get better at drawing things realistically, especially people, and that you'd like to get into some painting. So that's going to be our first project this quarter."

For the next few days we start the class off sketching two students standing or sitting in poses on desks pushed together in the middle of the room. Everyone volunteers, so different people model each day. Mrs. Angelo asks each pair to pose like they're "relating or not relating." After drawing for the first half of each class, we experiment with tempera paints, something a lot of us haven't really used in a long time. Mrs. Angelo writes some questions on the board for us to think about as we work:

1. *What kinds of marks can you make with these brushes? What happens when you move each brush different ways?*
2. *What new colors can you make from the paints?*
3. *What happens when you use a lot of paint? What happens when you use just a little?*
4. *What happens when you use a lot of water on your brush? What happens when you use just a little?*
5. *Can you make the paint look fast? Slow? Quiet? Angry? Intense? Loud? Energetic?*
6. *How many ways can you find to arrange marks you make with the brush? What happens when you put marks close together? Far apart? How else can you do it?*
7. *How does the same paint color look on different background colors of dried paint?*

The day we talk about beginning our big painting, Mrs. Angelo has us put all of our sketches and paint experiments up on the wall. We talk about how the figures in the sketches look different depending on where the artist was drawing from, above or below or from different sides. Mrs. Angelo says these are "vantage points" and writes it on the board. Next we look at our painting experiments, and talk about how different ways of using paint can make things look really different on the paper. "Can you find some places where the paint looks thin and watery and flowing and see-through? What kinds of ideas might those areas suggest if you were to use them in a painting? How about some colors and combinations that make you think of certain ideas? Who can find an area where bits of one color are peeking through another? Right, that's called scumbling," she says as she writes on the board. "Where do you see colors next to each other that seem to jump or vibrate? Why do you think that is? Who knows what that color relationship is called?" Mrs. Angelino shows us some examples of artists who paint people in scenes and settings, and we talk about how they position the figures, use different vantage points, and use color and apply paint in ways that communicate different ideas beyond just the people and surroundings themselves. At the end of class she says, "Think about a time in your life when you and another person were relating, or not relating. Who has some ideas?" We discuss playing sports, going to the mall, getting into arguments with friends or family, or feeling part of or separate from a group. Mrs. Angelo tells us to think about a scene involving ourselves and at least one other person, doing some kind of activity. "Who will you be with? What will you be doing? Where will you be and what details about the place will you want to include in your painting? What colors will you use to communicate the feeling in your story and how will you use the paint to create the effects that suggest that?" We work on some small idea sketches for a while and then she says that tomorrow we're going use charcoal to lightly draw in the large parts of our final painting on big paper. As we get ready to leave, we're excited, talking with our friends about what everyone's paintings might be about (see Figures 1-10, 1-11, and 1-12).

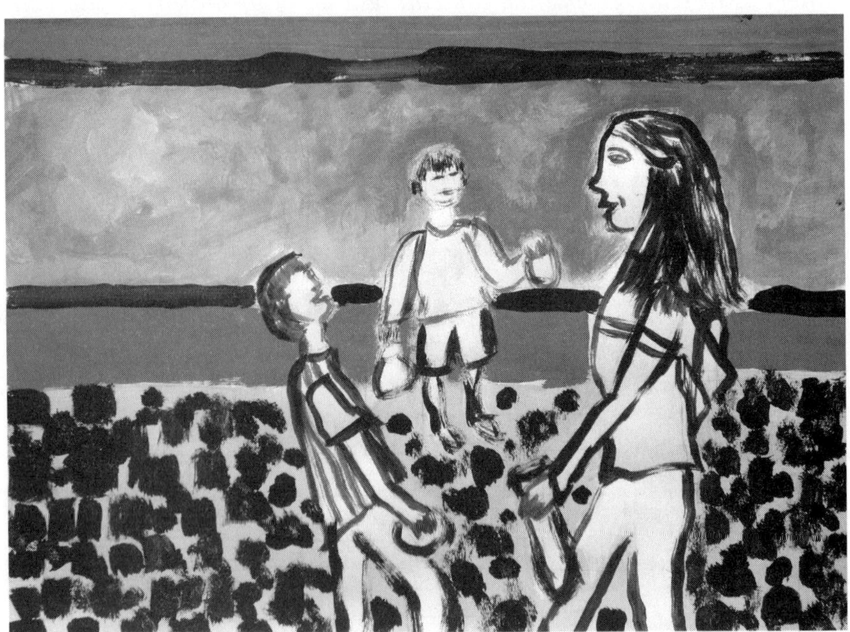

F 1-10: Expressive paintings

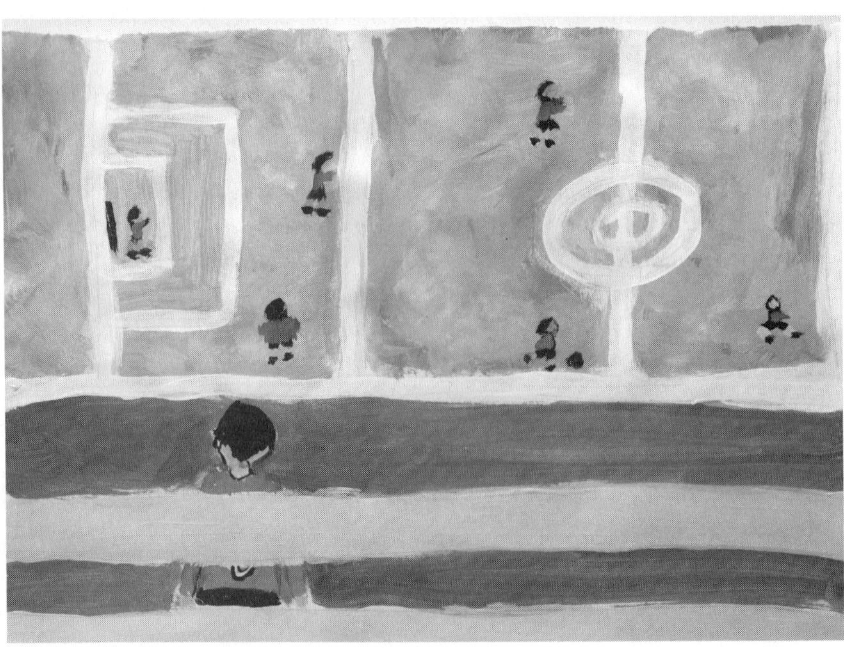

F 1-11: Expressive paintings

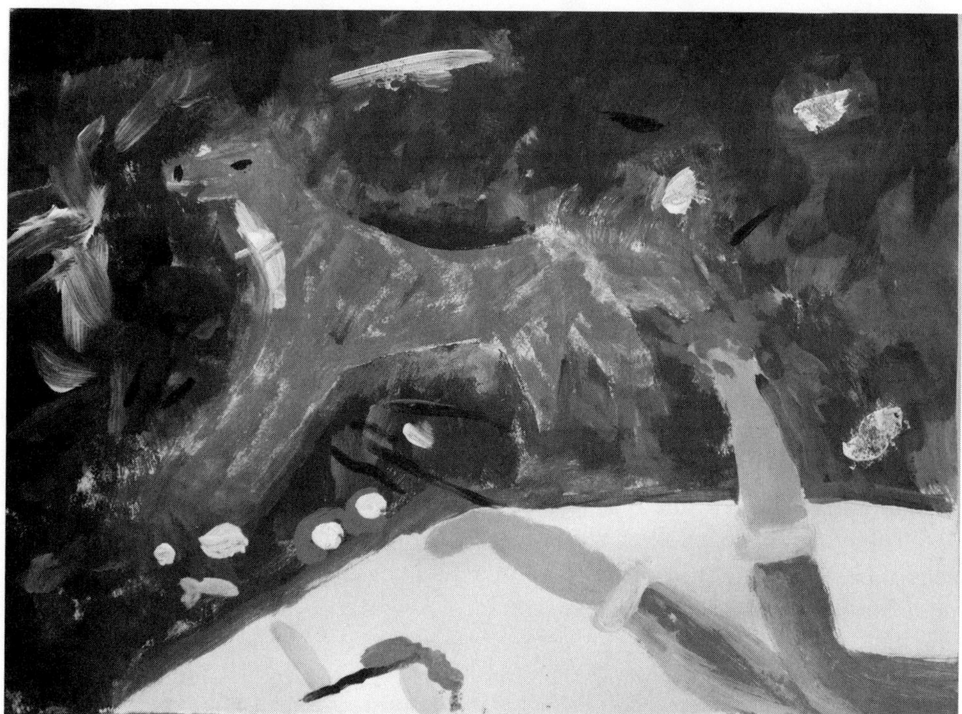

F 1-12: Expressive paintings

ENCOURAGING INDEPENDENT ARTISTRY

As you reflect on these scenarios of studio art teaching and learning, how would you describe each teacher's assumptions about young artists and the teachers' views of their own roles in students' art making? To what degree are uniform ways of thinking and doing and the visual results of students' artworks dictated by the teacher? In which classrooms are kids invited to not only develop their own themes and ideas but also be inventive, experimental, and imaginative as they work with materials to find unique forms for their expression? Which teachers may have had intriguing, valuable, and personally relevant lesson content yet failed to provide experiences that parallel what real artists do and how they think in the studio with regards to materials? Again, to what degree do you think students' independent thinking and decision-making *should* be encouraged as they work with materials to create art? To what degree *should* art experiences push students to explore and experiment, move beyond boundaries, take risks, and arrive at finished works that don't look stylistically identical or express ideas similar to everyone else's?

Exploring Materials as an Artist-Teacher: Getting Started

In this chapter we've examined the dissonance and disconnect, as well as the similarities, between examples of instructional approaches some art teachers take and the kinds of thinking and practice that artists actually engage in as they make studio work. What implications can you see for teachers who wish to create the kinds of learning environments that will encourage students to explore materials experimentally and in open-ended ways, as artists do? Understanding how artists describe their thinking and practice is important, but it is not enough. As teachers who aim to guide the artistic and expressive development of students, we need to experience for ourselves working with a variety of art materials in ways that transform them from mere substances and tools to expressive *media*, or carriers of meaning.

The chapters that follow are designed for you to experience first-hand how school-based art materials can be approached not in formulaic ways but in open-ended and divergent ways. By experimenting with and exploring many materials yourself and creating myriad effects with each, you'll see how working in this way leads artists to expressive ideas. The materials-based chapters—on media related to drawing, painting, printmaking, collage, and three-dimensional construction—are designed to provide you, regardless of your present level of experience as an artist, with a series of studio explorations featuring the kinds of materials you will be using with kids of different ages in art class settings. By experimenting as an artist yourself you'll be focusing on divergent ways of using each material and tool, pushing them in different directions to invent and discover your own techniques for achieving a variety of effects. You'll reflect on these materials experiments to identify and interpret expressive ideas and meanings the visual effects you create may suggest. The goal is for you to document your learning and discoveries as you produce a personal studio notebook of materials explorations (see Figure 1-13).

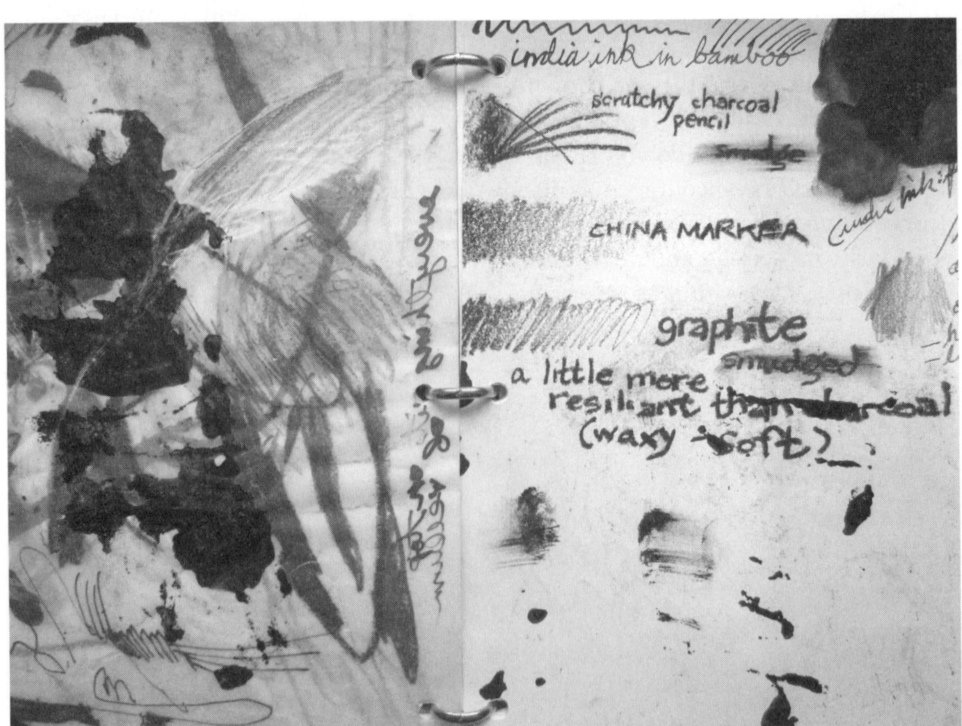

F 1-13: Test pages, mixed media

In the final chapter you'll look back on your studio experiments and use your understanding of how materials become expressive media to design open-ended, thematic art experiences for your own students—studio experiences that help young people develop individual voices and independent judgment as artists. You'll be asked to analyze your personal exploratory processes from the materials chapters to recreate this same experimental atmosphere around materials in your own present or future classroom setting. You'll also be invited to design studio-based lessons in which kids explore materials to construct artworks based in their intentions, their inventions, and their meanings. Based on your own studio insights, you'll be able to choose appropriate materials and identify concepts, skills, and themes that stand as practical alternatives to recipe-type, formulaic projects derived from overly teacher-imposed directives. The goal is to eradicate those kinds of art projects that can't help but lead to visually and conceptually uniform outcomes, and replace them with art experiences you design in which the essential artistic thinking and doing is placed in the minds and hands of the artists themselves, your students.

OPENING UP POSSIBILITIES AND BECOMING EXPERIMENTAL

Comparing the artists' reflections on their studio practices to different aspects of the class scenarios described earlier, it's clear that just because a lesson or project involves special art materials and making things doesn't mean it's an optimal creative experience for the artist. Similarly, even when kids are highly motivated to do something and are pleased with the results, it doesn't necessarily mean that the studio experience reflects artistically and educationally sound instructional practice. Missing from all but one of the art class scenarios (the exception, of course, was Mrs. Angelo's class) was open-ended exploration of materials, in which students were challenged to experiment with and push studio media in ways that diverged from the teacher's predetermined set of expectations for the subject and visual appearance of works to be produced. Moving away from this overly directed style of teaching requires a great deal of a specific kind of activity that is missing from many teaching environments—play. Play in the studio context, as the above artists make clear, has in part to do with materials experimentation, with figuring things out as you go along, and with discovering on your own through exploration what materials do and can't do and how they can be used to create different effects that suggest different kinds of meanings.[20]

If your early or prior experiences of "art class" are primarily of the overly teacher-directed kind, it may take you a little while to get used to this idea of play in materials exploration. Even if you are an artist, you may not be used to really

---

[20] The lack of imaginative and open-ended play in the lives of children today, and the detrimental effects this condition has on their overall learning and development, is widely acknowledged in the contemporary literature. See, for example, David Elkind's (2007) *The Power of Play: Learning What Comes Naturally*, Singer, Golinkoff, and Hirsh-Pasek's (2007) *Play = Learning: How Play Motivates and Enhances Children's Cognitive and Social-Emotional Growth*, and Vivian Paley's (2004) *A Child's Work: The Importance of Fantasy Play*. Purposeful and interpretive play that comes from experimenting with art materials is a natural antidote to the current shortage of imaginative play in the day-to-day lives of young people.

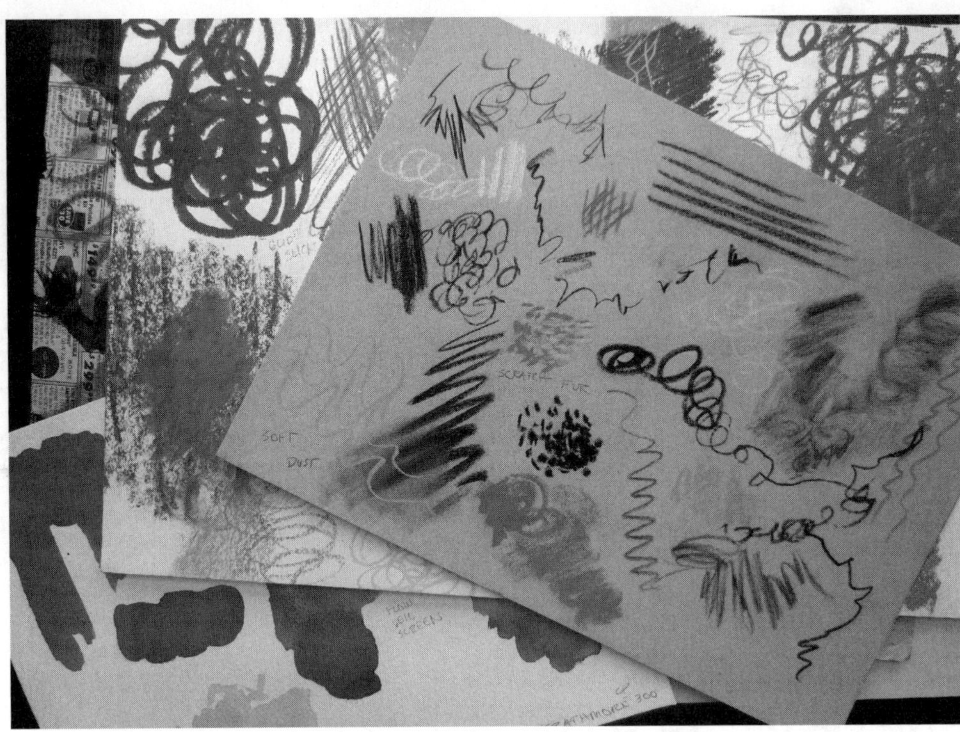

F 1-14: Test pages, mixed media

pushing materials around in innovative ways to see what they can do, beyond traditional techniques and conventions. There are two things to keep in mind as you begin the open-ended studio process—first, that experimenting with art materials is purposeful play, testing each medium and tool out and using them in different ways to see how many different effects you can achieve. The second idea to consider is that the goal of purposeful play with materials is not merely to achieve a variety of visual effects but to understand how this variety of effects you create can suggest different meanings in an artwork. This is interpretive play, and leads to understandings of the ways in which different materials themselves—paint, clay, charcoal, and other media—and what comes from how they are used can contribute their own expressive ideas to artwork (see Figure 1-14).

DOCUMENTING MATERIAL INSIGHTS: SETTING UP YOUR STUDIO JOURNAL

In each chapter you will find a description of the materials used for the studio explorations, including some specific tools and media that may be unfamiliar to you. All of the materials called for in this book meet the safety and health guidelines for use with children and teens.[21]

---

[21] Two legal documents specifically pertain to the proper use of materials in educational settings (Bain, 2009). The first, the Fourteenth Amendment, guarantees children's right to a safe school environment. The second is Public Law 100–695, the Labeling of Hazardous Materials Act (LHAMA), which dictates that hazardous materials must be clearly labeled as such by the manufacturer. The Art and Creative Materials Institute (ACMI), an international association of over 200 art material manufacturers, has two certification designations. The first, AP (Approved Product) Non-Toxic Seal, identifies art materials that are safe and that are certified in a toxicological evaluation by a medical expert to contain no

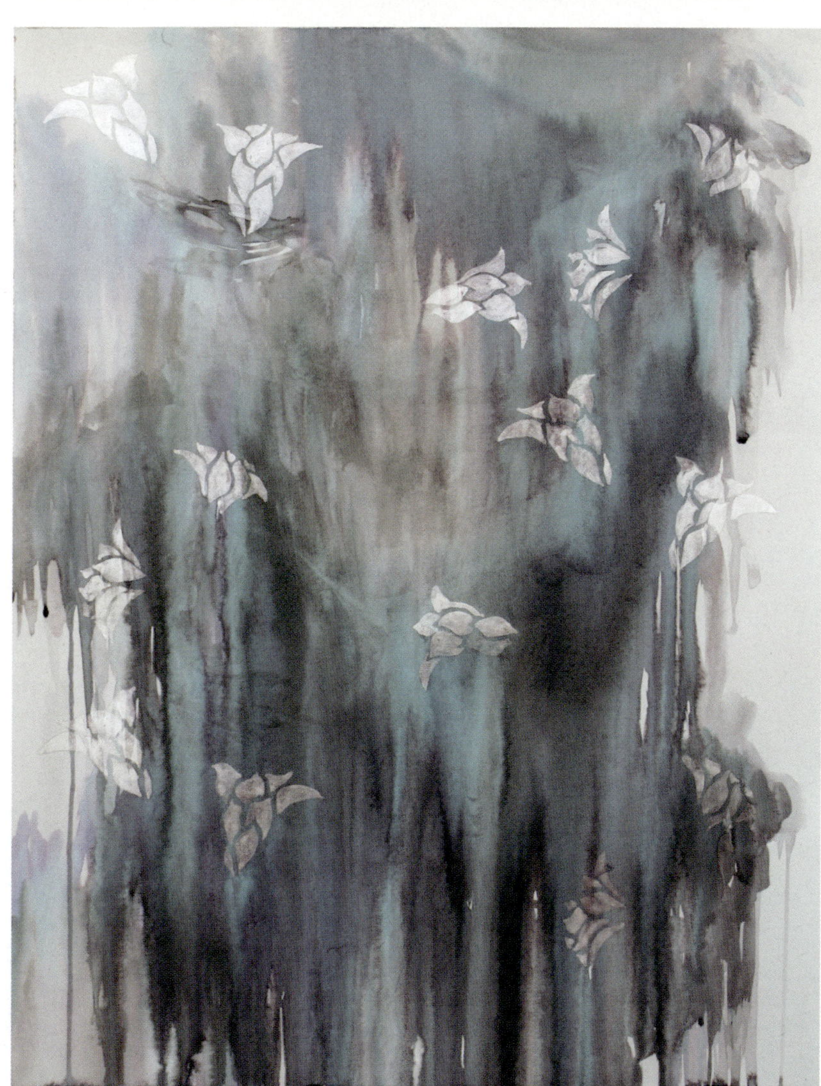

F 1

Kelly Sturhahn, Nouveau Marsh, 2013,
ink and wash on paper, 20″ × 15″.
© Kelly Sturhahn. Courtesy the artist.

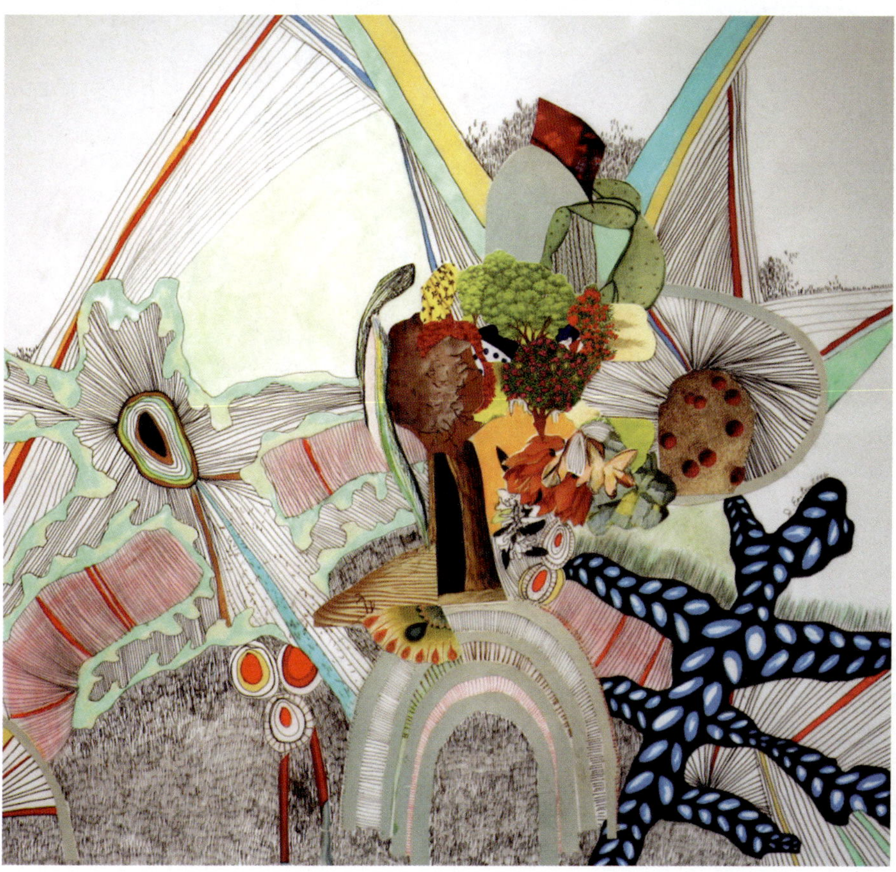

F 2

Janae Easton, Zealot Rock Den, 2006,
mixed media, 27″ × 27″ × 1″.

F 3
Sid Garrison, October 13,
2005, colored pencil on
paper, 28″ × 28″. Photo by
Ira Schrank. Courtesy the
artist.

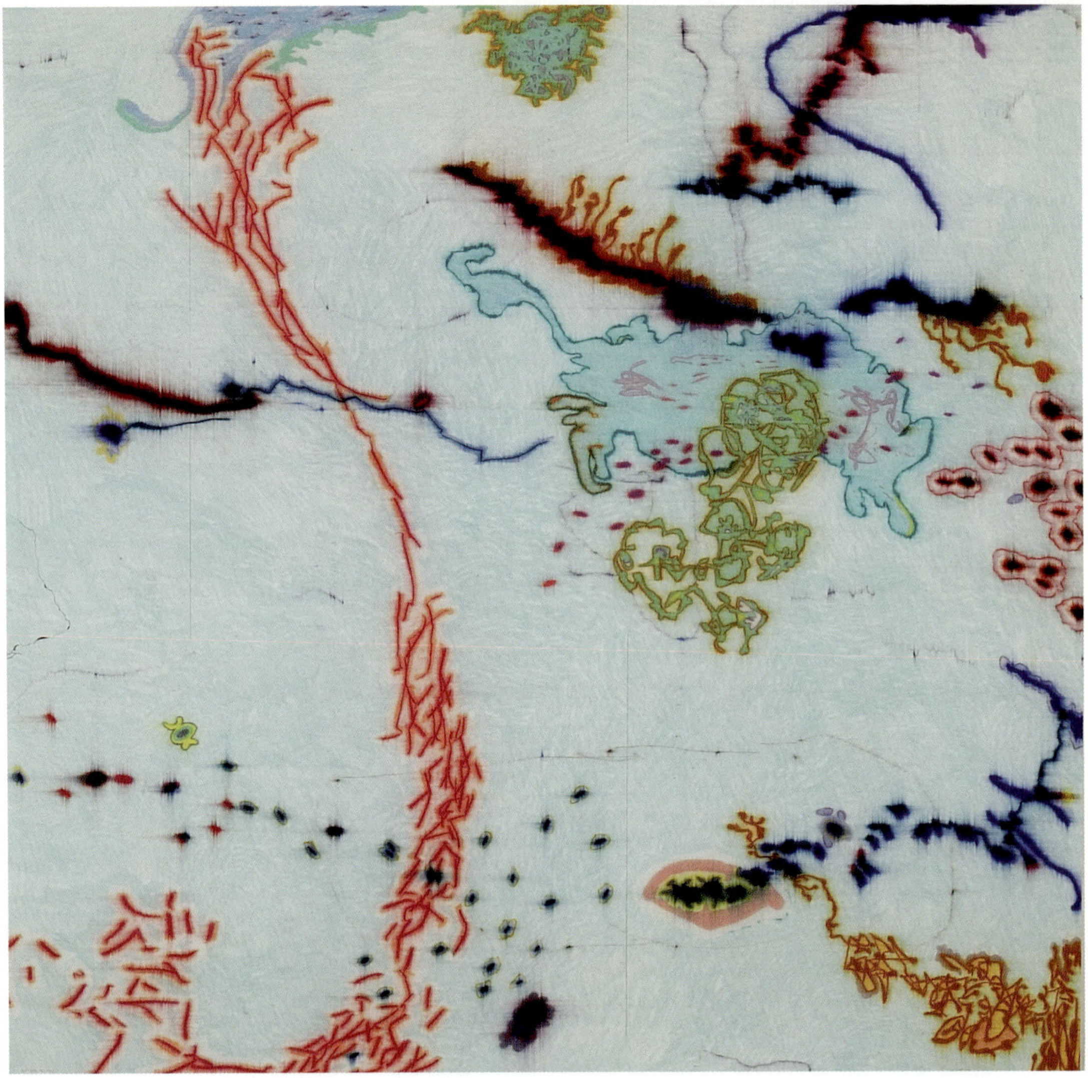

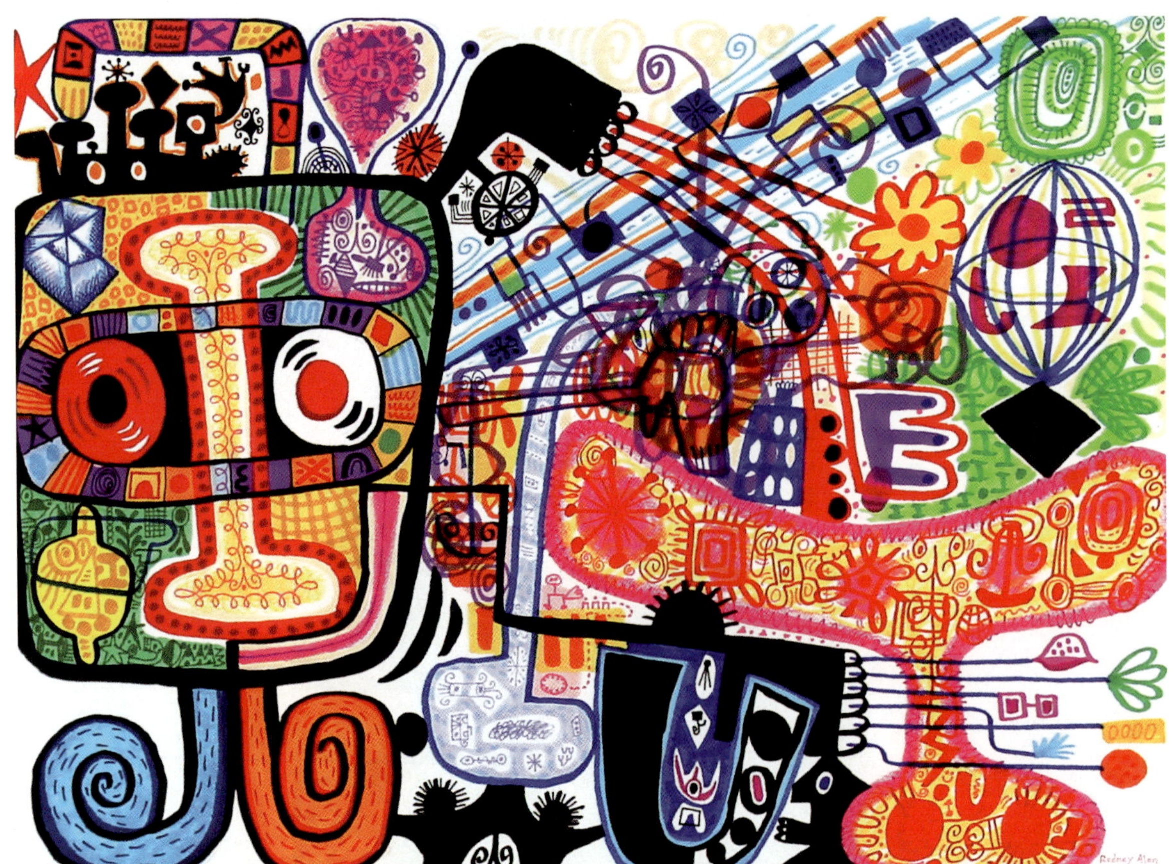

F 4
Rodney Alan
Greenblat, Action
Very Reaction, 2003,
colored marker on
paper, 15″ × 20″.
© 2003 Rodney
Alan Greenblat.

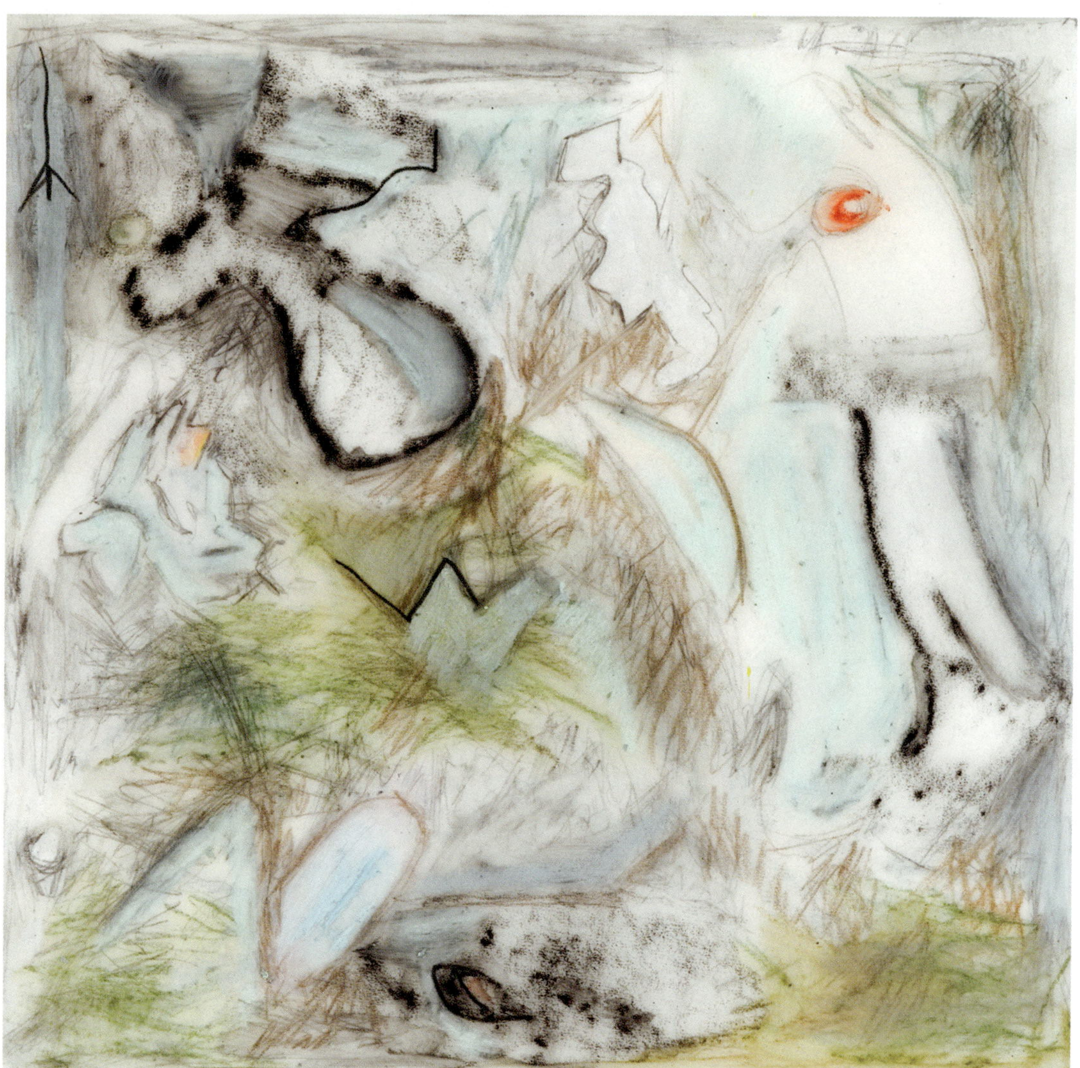

F 5
Mary Hafeli, Untitled (from Saint in Any Form series), 2004, graphite, colored pencil, and oil pastel on vellum, 6″ × 6″.

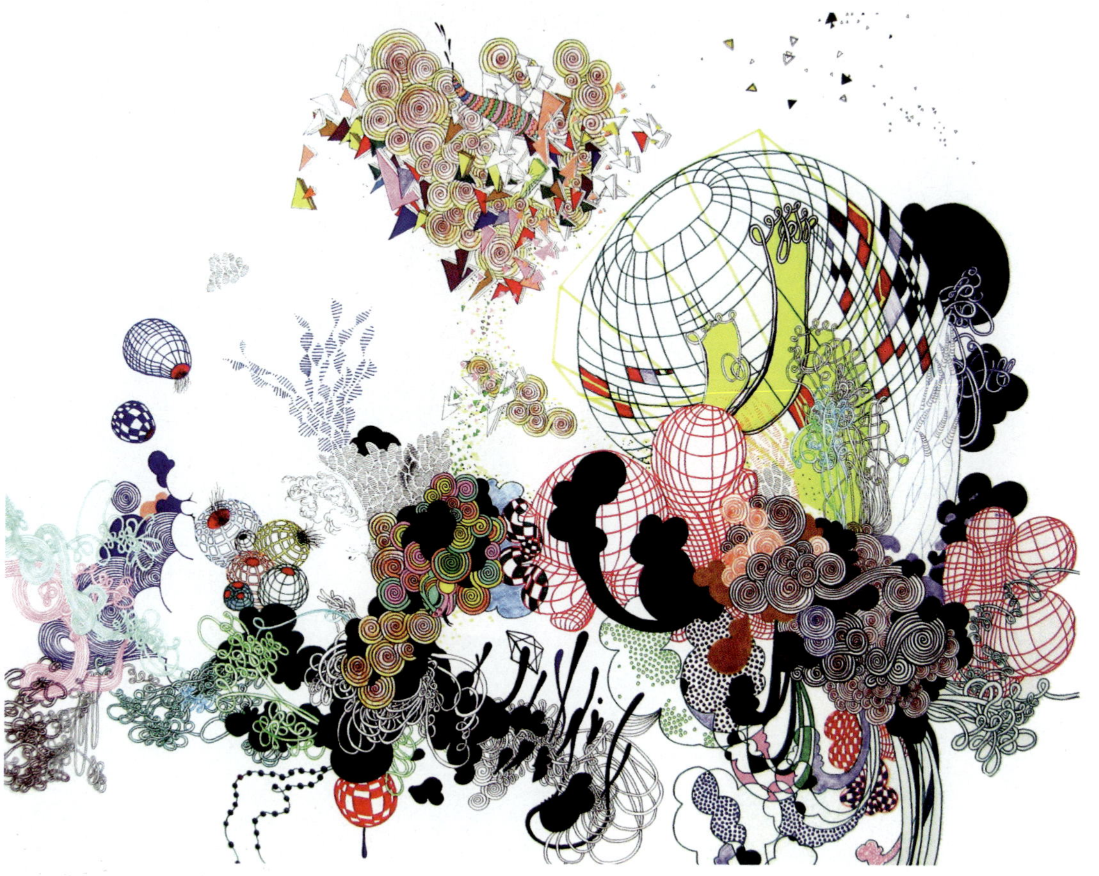

F 6
Jen Stark, A Night Over: Collaboration with Alvaro Ilizarbe, 2006, mixed media on paper, 19″ × 24″. Photo by Harlan Erksine.

Elizabeth Gilfilen, Tether, 2011, oil on canvas, 72" × 64".

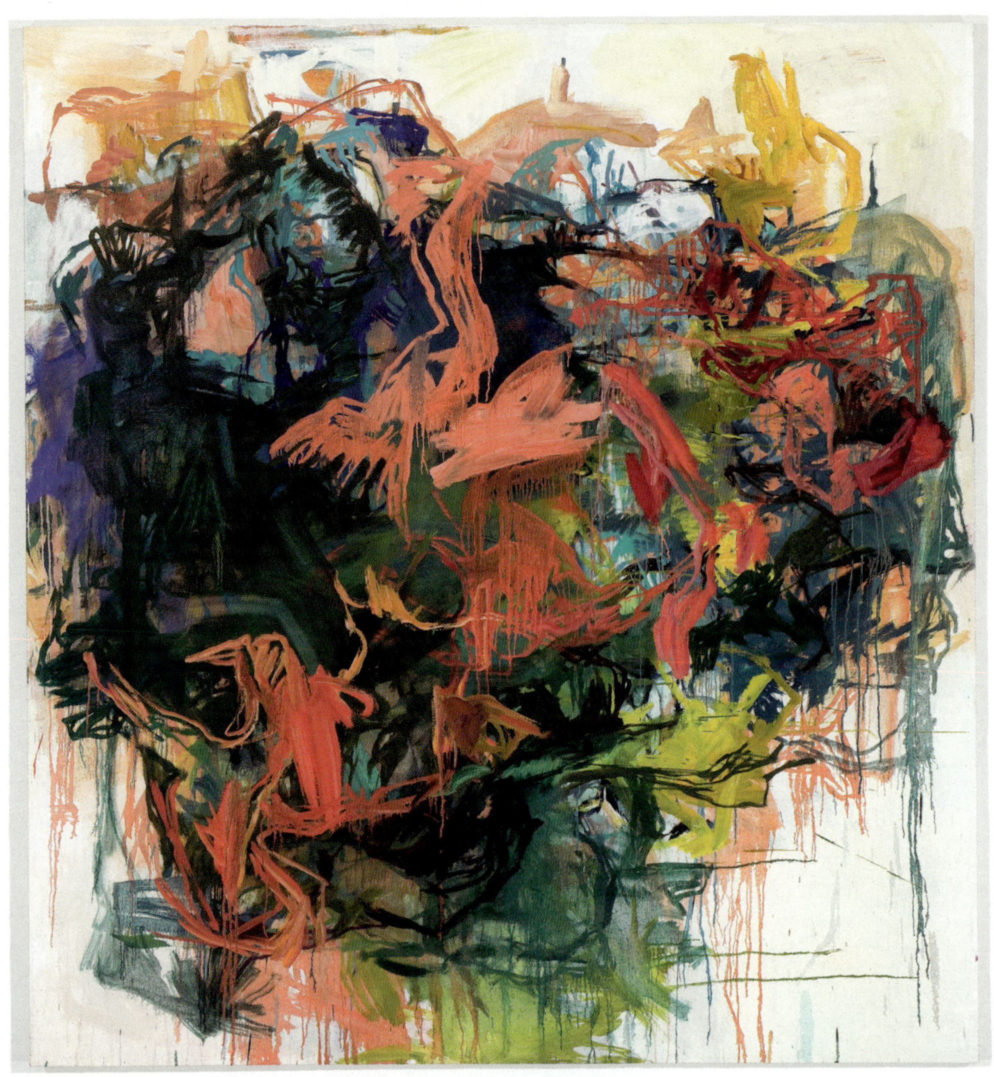

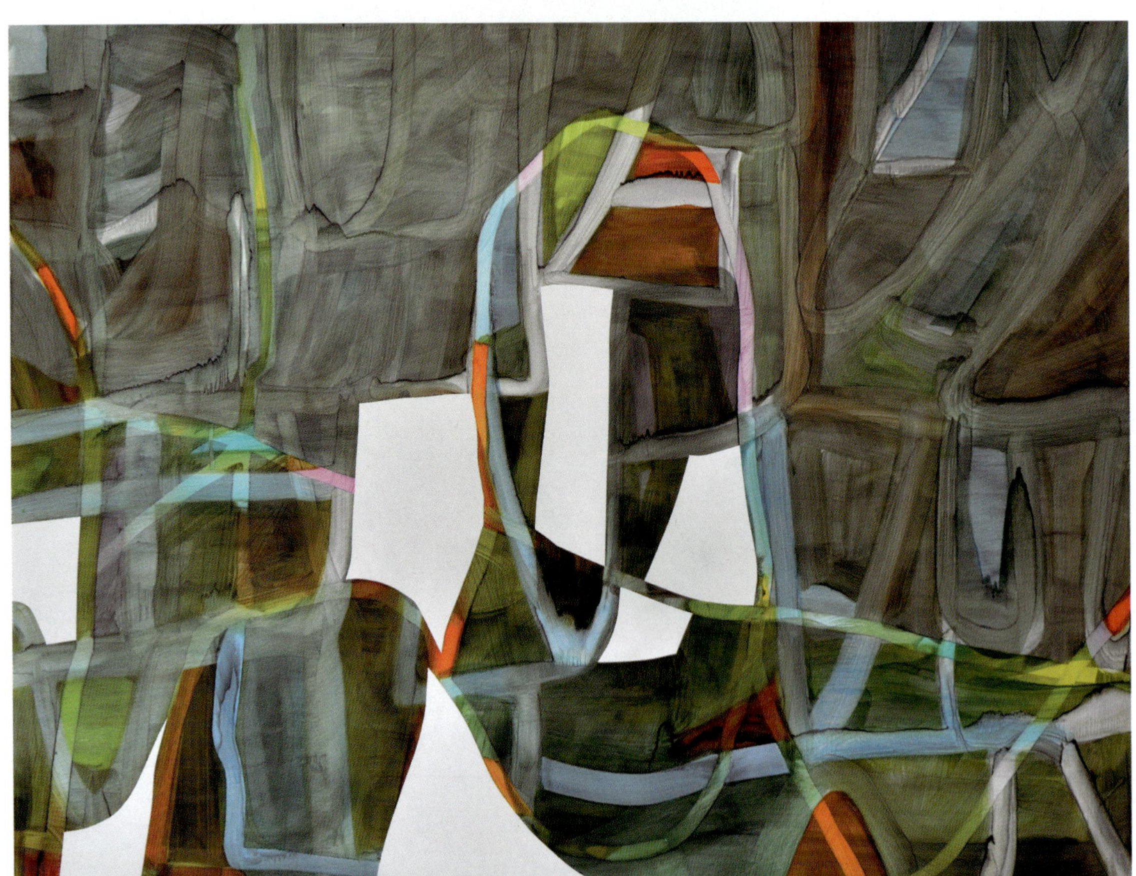

Stephanie McMahon, Crystal Visions, 2013, oil on canvas, 47" × 59".

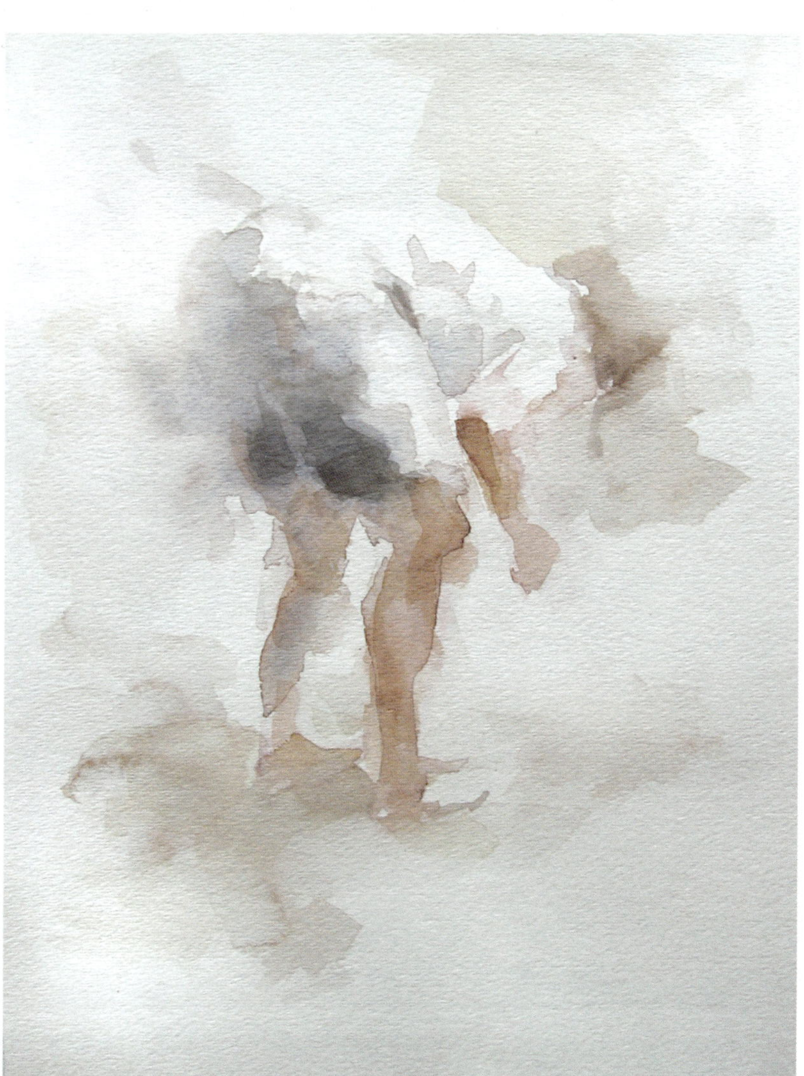

F 9
Anne Petty, The Bend, 2009,
watercolor on paper, 8″ × 10″.

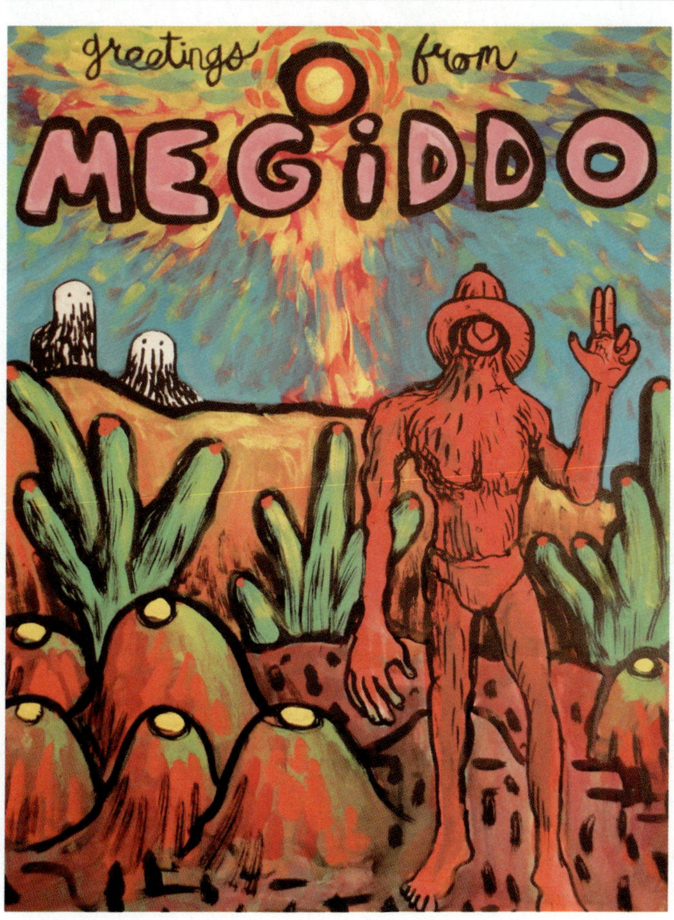

greetings from
MEGiDDO

F 10
Ben Campbell, Greetings From
Megiddo, 2012, gouache, ink, and
watercolor on paper, 22″ × 30″.
Original work © Ben Campbell, 2012.

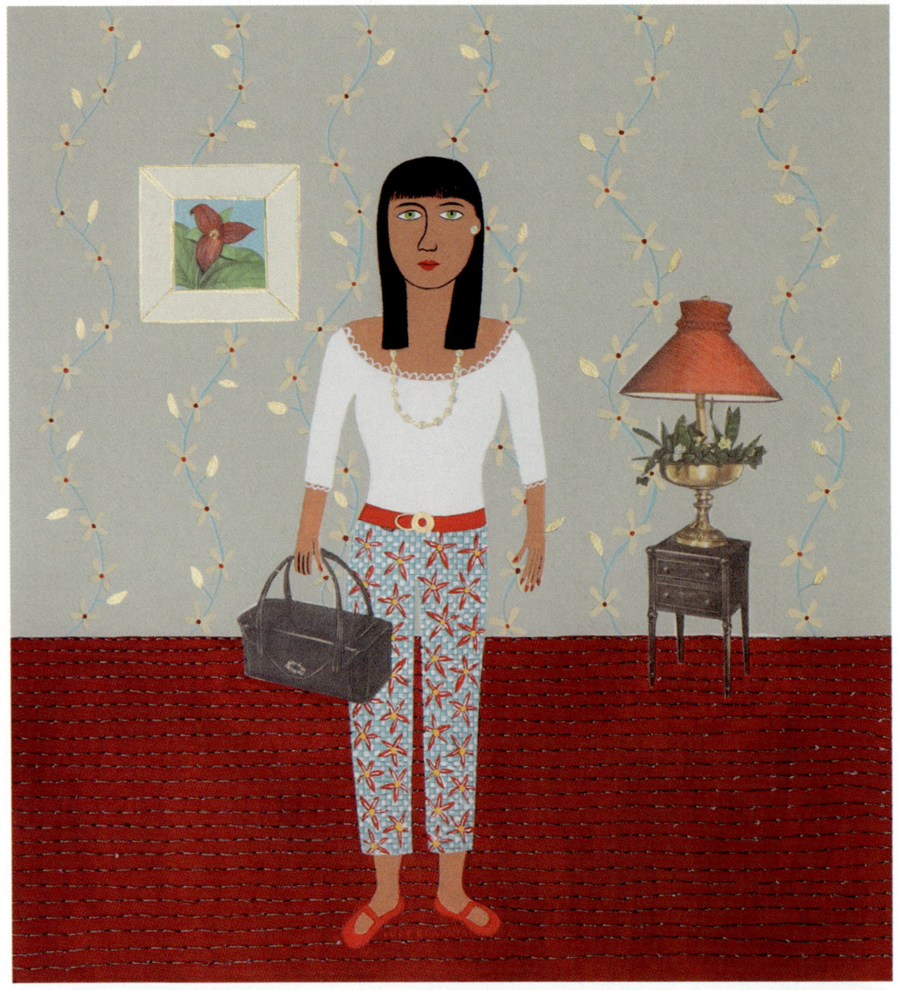

F 11
Lucy Fradkin, What Becomes of the Brokenhearted, *2013, acrylic gouache on paper with collage, metallic thread, and pencil, 11" × 10". Courtesy the artist.*

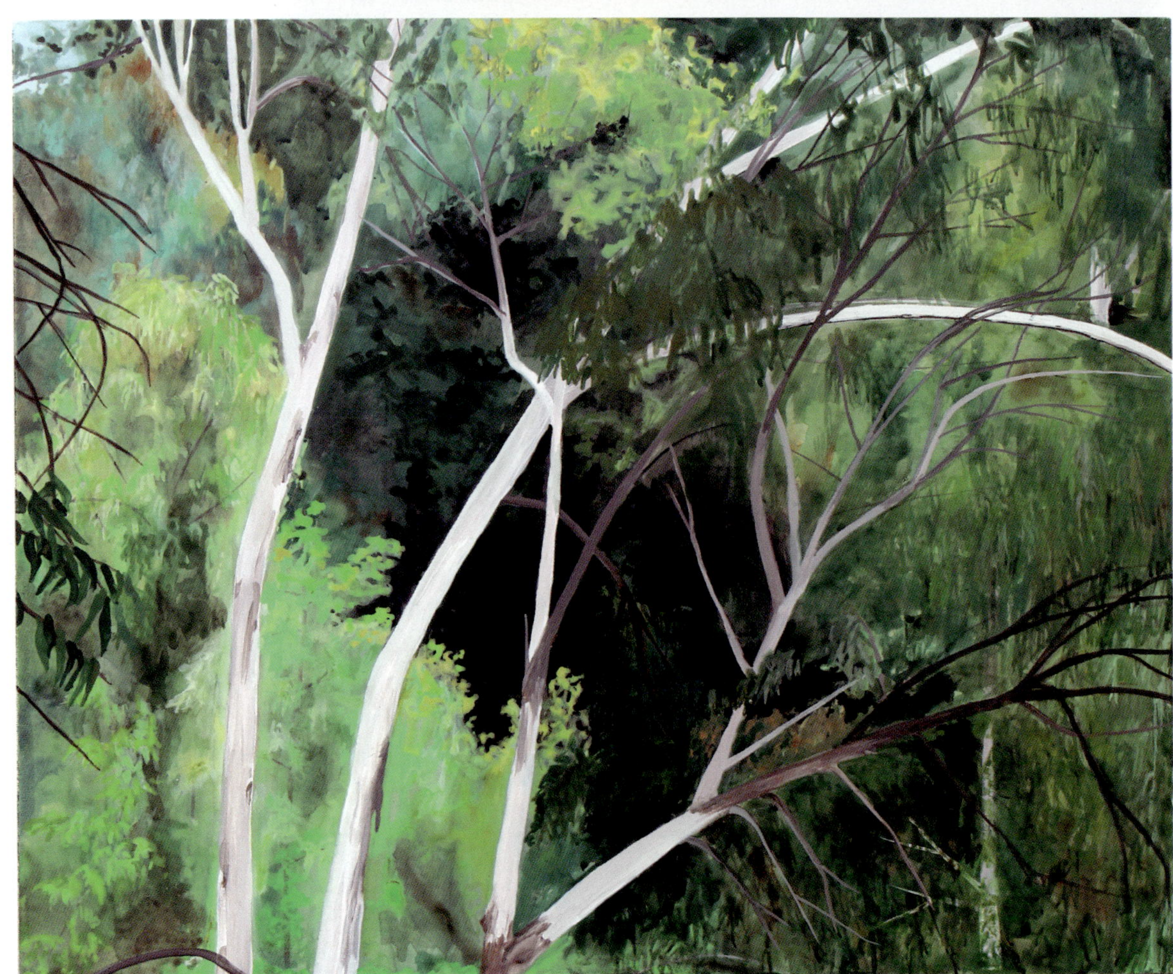

F 12
Wendy Heldmann, Were There When There Were, *2006, acrylic on canvas on panel, 20" × 24". Courtesy the artist.*

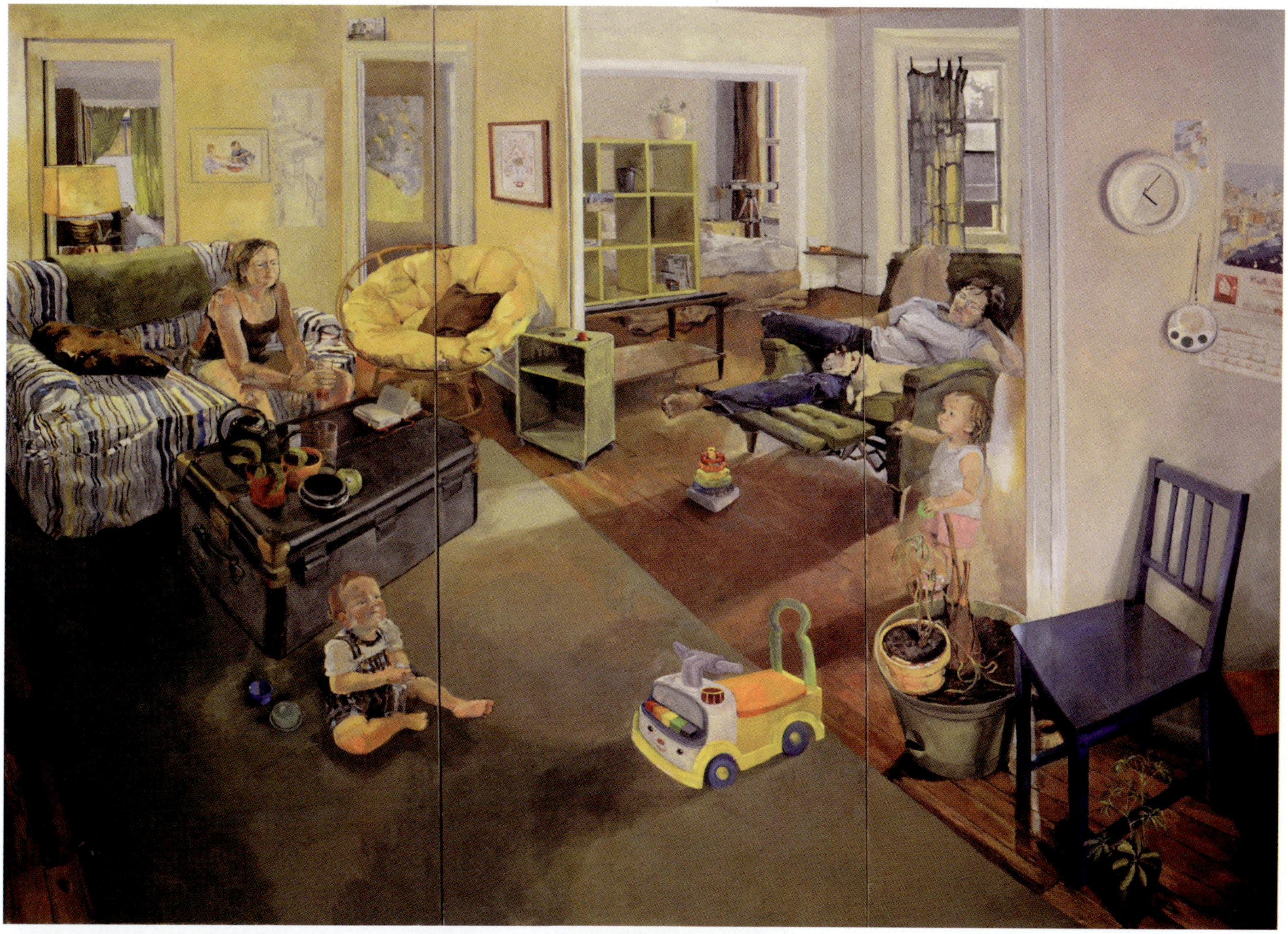

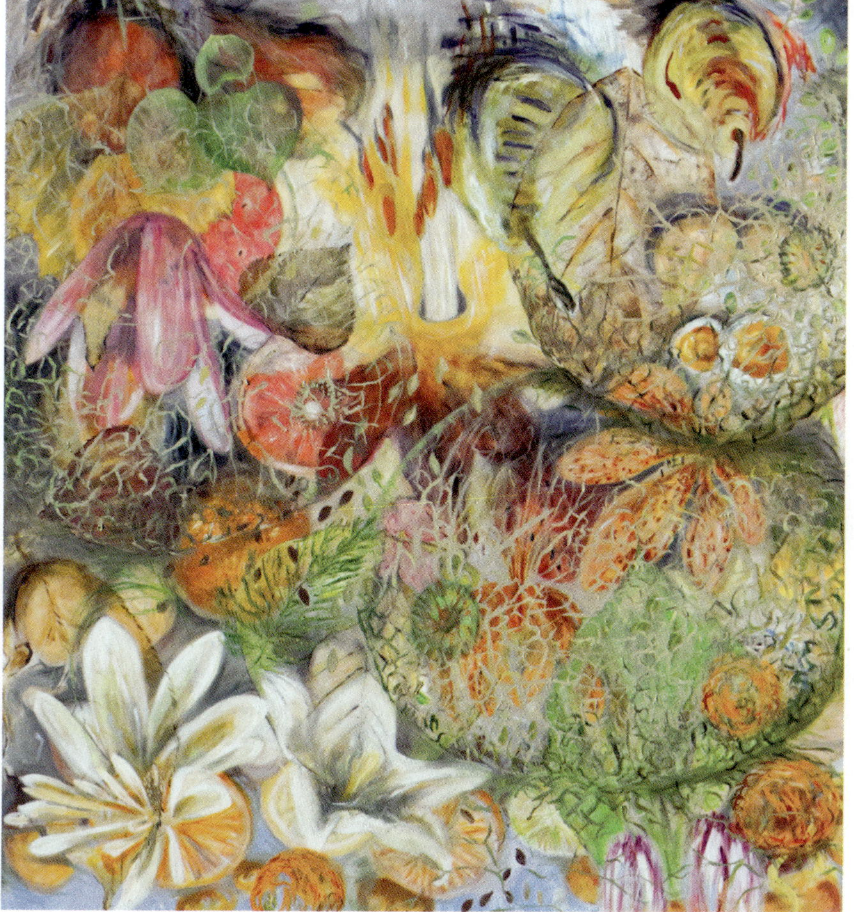

F 13
*Amber Carky, Transitions II,
2008.2009, oil on canvas, 10.5′ × 8′.*

F 14
*Robin Arnold, Compost, 2013, oil
and wax on canvas, 72″ × 63″.*
© 2013 Robin Arnold.

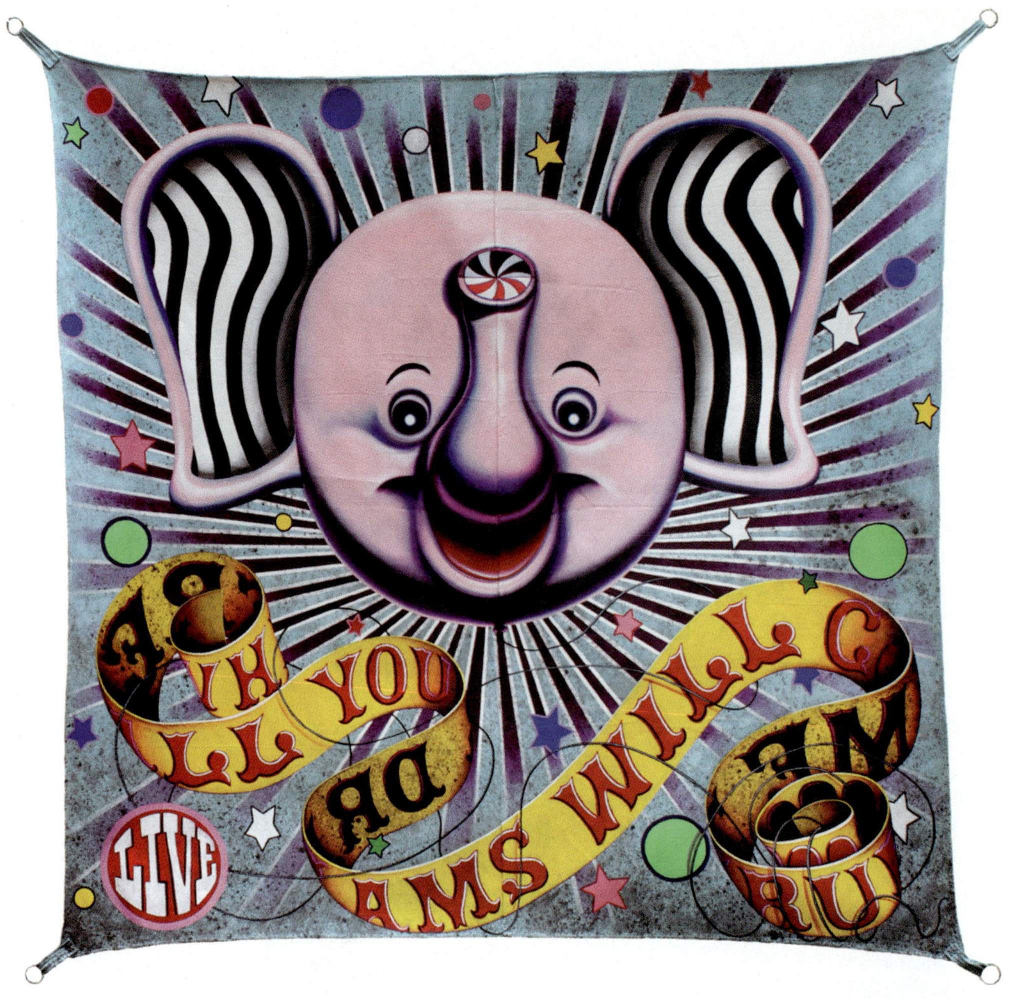

F 15

Seamus O'Brien, Here it comes
hippity, hoppity (Where All Your
Dreams Will Come True!!!), *2011,
acrylic on canvas, 7′ × 7′.*

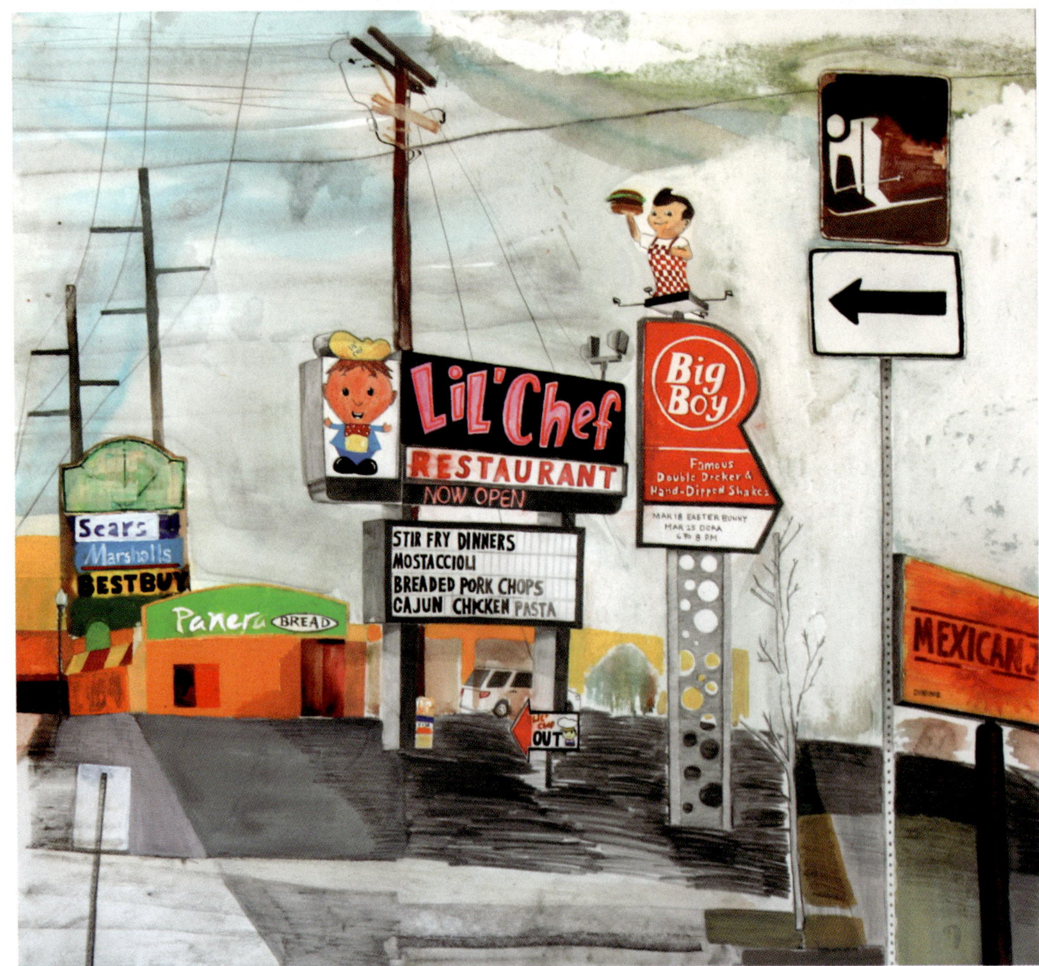

F 16

Karla Wozniak, Lil' Chef, Brighton,
MI, *2008, mixed media on paper,
28.5″ × 30.25″. Collection of
Daniel & Hilary Goldstine.*

In setting up your studio journal, decide whether you'd rather take a paper-based sketchbook or scrapbook approach—in which all of your materials experiments are collected and organized in a binder or sketchbook—or document your studio explorations using digital technology. In the paper-based approach, a binder works well for keeping all of your actual drawing, painting, collage, and printmaking work; you can punch holes in your test sheets and note pages, and easily change the organization of the book if necessary at any time in the process (this is difficult to do in a bound notebook format).

In either case, whether you use a binder or build your journal digitally, you will need access to a camera to document the three-dimensional work you produce in the chapters that follow (or, if you like drawing, you can document that way). If you are using this book as a course text, you'll also want to document the work of other students in your class, to expand your learning and examples of the potential of each material you work with.

To begin, refer to the materials and tools lists in each chapter, gather the supplies you will need for the different explorations, and start experimenting. Your goal is to work with each material extensively and in a variety of ways so that you understand the range of possible effects that can be achieved. As you are working, keep notes about the qualities and properties of each material, the various ways each can be used and the visual effects that result, and the different meanings that can be suggested through these effects. Record your responses to the materials and techniques, make notes on lesson ideas you may want to develop, and research contemporary and historical artists whose work relates to the materials for each section of your journal. This research will be carried forward in the planning of lessons and structuring of curriculum in the final chapter.

---

materials in sufficient quantities to be toxic or injurious to humans, including children, or to cause acute or chronic health problems. The second, CL (Cautionary Labeling) Seal, identifies products that are certified to be properly labeled in a program of toxicological evaluation by a medical expert for any known health risks and with information on the safe and proper use of these materials. Some manufacturers, like Amaco—which makes glazes for ceramic ware—deem their CL-rated glazes as suitable for use with students in grades 7 and up with adult supervision (and not for use in grades PreK–6). Many schools and districts have their own regulations regarding allowable materials and tools. In choosing materials for use in your own teaching setting, good rules of thumb are to (1) understand and abide by existing local policies, (2) use AP certified materials, and (3) communicate with parents about any CL certified materials in advance of using them with students, so that accommodations can be made for individual students whose medical conditions may warrant them.

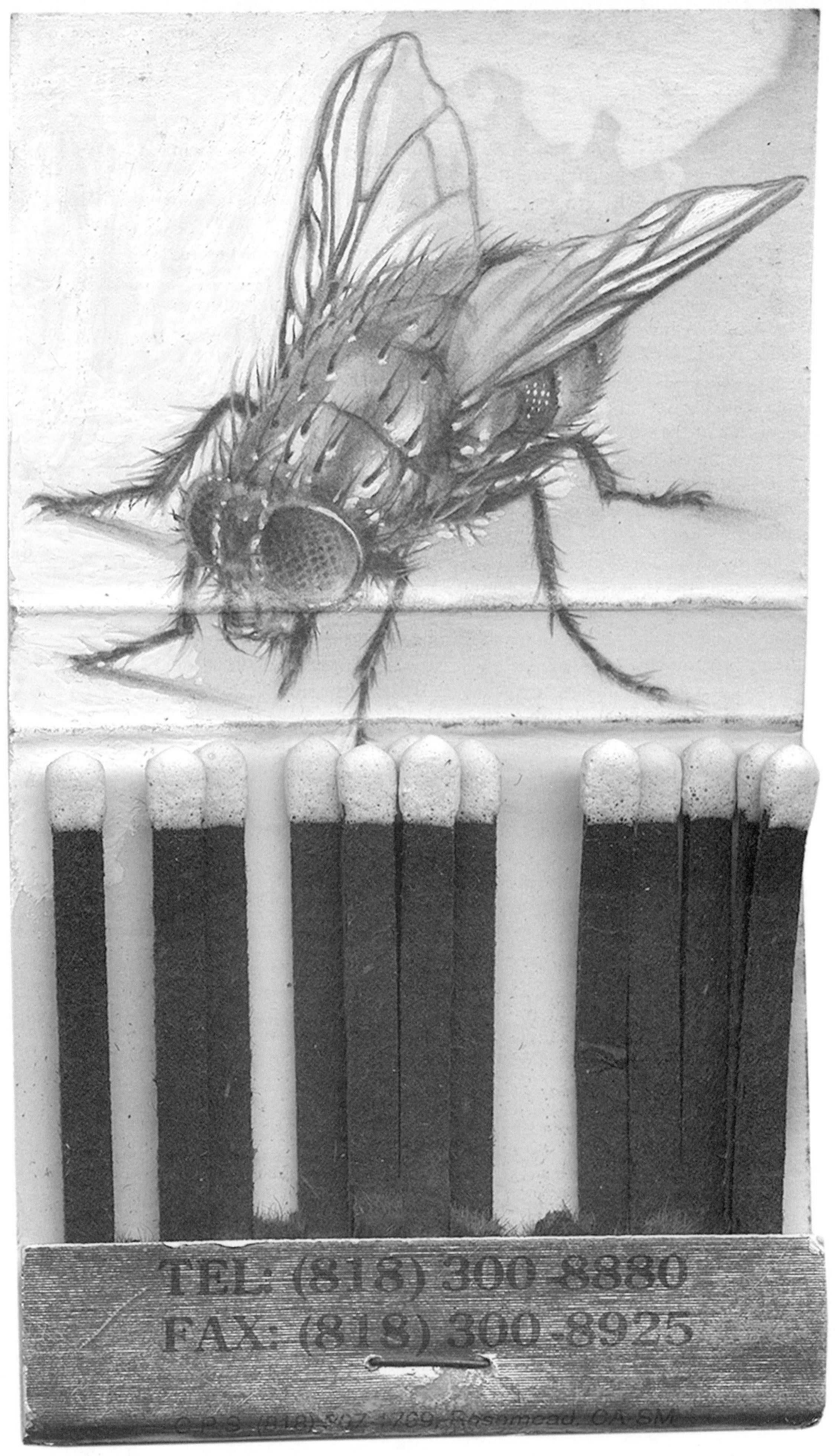

Jason D'Aquino, Black Fly, 2006

2

Working Mostly Dry

Graphite, Charcoal, Pastels, Crayons, Ink

*When my daughter was about seven years old, she asked me one day
what I did at work. I told her I worked at the college—that my job was
to teach people how to draw. She stared back at me, incredulous, and
said, "You mean they forget?"*

—**Howard Ikemoto,** *Art and Fear*

WHAT DO VARIOUS DRAWING MATERIALS DO? How can they be used
to create different effects? How might the qualities of charcoal, or ink or oil pastel,
suggest ideas and create meaning in a drawing? And what are some approaches
for encouraging in students the curiosity and experimentation that lead to thinking in a material, and the analysis, judgment, and interpretive reflection that are
part of this practice?

The best way for teachers to approach these questions is to get our hands in
materials—to understand for ourselves how divergent ways of working can
broaden the expressive potential of pencils, charcoal, pastels, ink, or any other
material we plan to present to kids. Engaging in materials exploration is purposeful play, open-ended but systematic. The goal is to push each material or tool to
get as many different "looks" and effects as possible. What kinds of marks can you
make with the tip of an oil pastel? The edge? The side? What happens to the line
when you press harder or more lightly with a piece of charcoal? What happens
when you twist your wrist as you go along? Investigating materials in this way is

something artists do. And it's what we need to do ourselves, as teachers, to be able to encourage in our students the curiosity, divergent thinking, and artistic autonomy that come with realizing the power of materials to communicate ideas.

Figuring out What Materials Can Do

CHOOSING MATERIALS, SUPPORTS, AND DRAWING TOOLS

How might the ashiness of charcoal suggest something different from the silvery, metallic sheen of graphite? How does black ink used one way suggest ideas that are different from those expressed through an alternate approach or application? Look carefully at the three drawings below (Figures 2-1, 2-2, and 2-3) and make a list of descriptive words that come to mind for each. How do the artists' approaches to working with materials and the effects they create suggest these ideas? How have the artists taken a material—ink—and used it as a medium to convey ideas?

Getting started in teaching for open-ended exploration of materials can be daunting. Just browsing the drawing materials section of an art supply store,

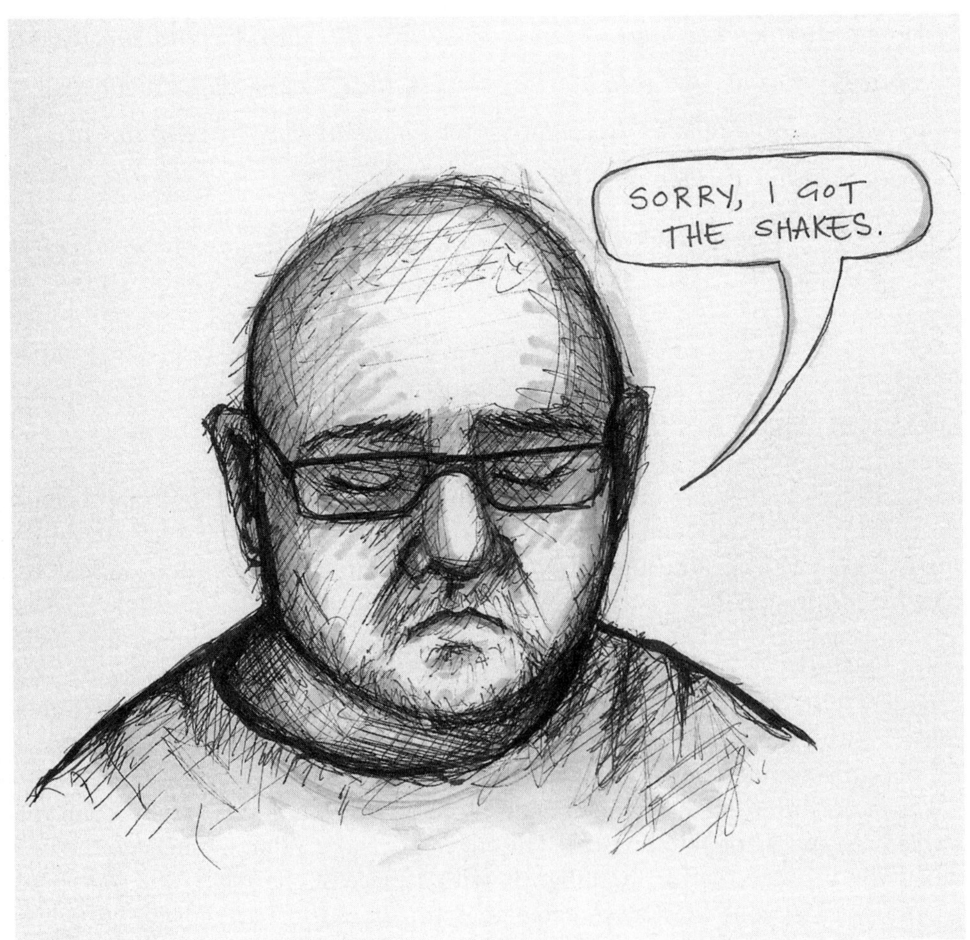

F 2-1
Jeannette Langmead, Dan Nolan Portrait, 2007, ink on paper.

online or in person, can be overwhelming even for teachers who are experienced artists. What kinds of pencils will be best for five-year-olds? For middle school students? What kind of paper is good to use with ink? With pastels and charcoal? Will these materials wash out of clothes? What do different erasers do?

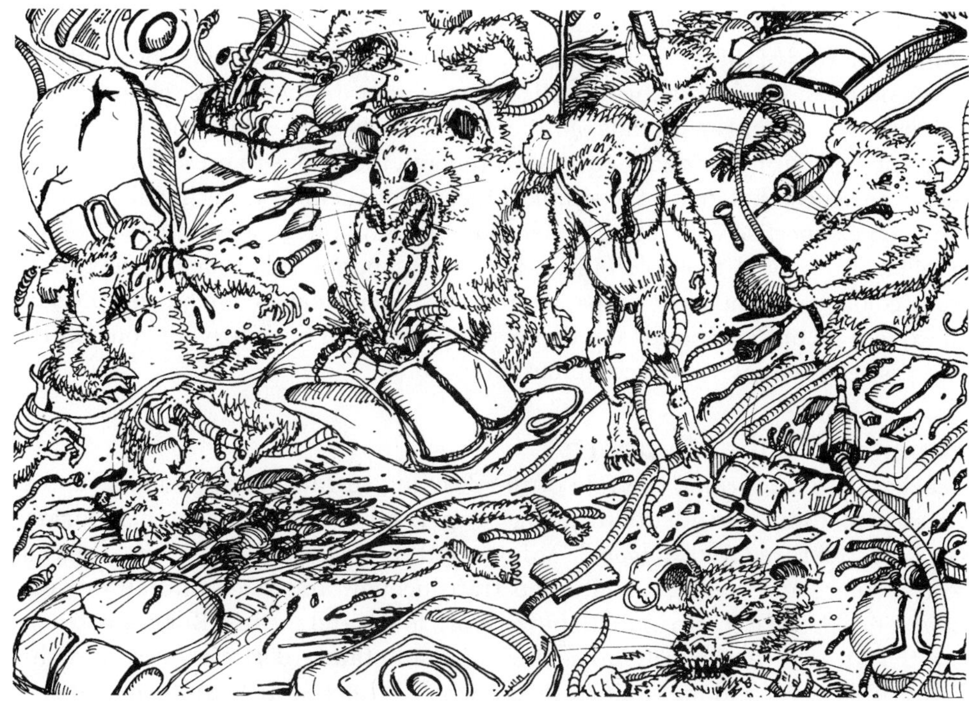

F 2-2
Ernest Concepcion, Mice vs. Mice, 2008, ink on paper.

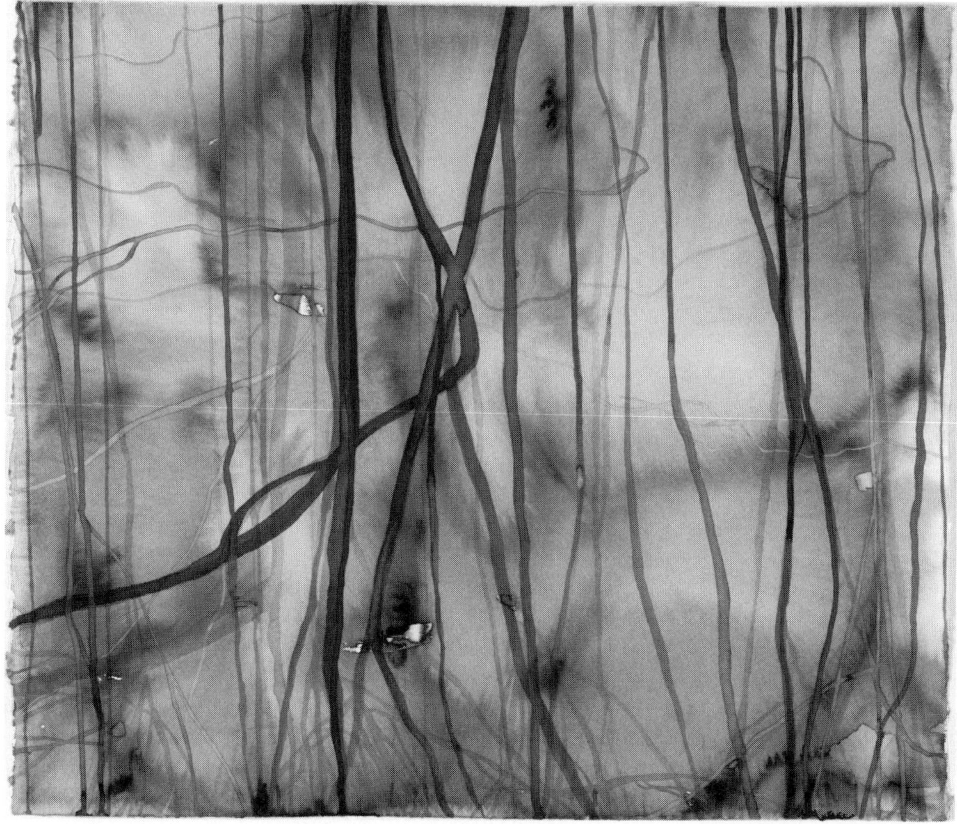

F 2-3
Kelly Sturhahn, Untitled (Lake), 2007, ink and wash on paper, 19 ½" × 22", © Kelly Sturhahn.

For the studio explorations that follow, groups of materials are presented separately with accompanying historical and technical information (the kids I teach are interested to hear the stories behind the media) and suggestions for experimentation. Beginning with limited color and ending with a full range of color, explore the materials for yourself using the open-ended prompts in each section. Keep a running documentation in your studio journal of the expressive effects that different materials, tools, and drawing surfaces create and the concepts, skills, and ways of thinking that can be taught with them. It will also be helpful to make notes about the practical applications of your discoveries for choosing and using these materials with kids of different ages. My suggestions throughout can be combined with your own findings. In general, the goal is to present younger or less experienced kids with the simplest means for them to experiment with and gain some expertise with a single material, to create the greatest range of effects possible. To extend the possibilities for more experienced students, new tools, more colors, and other types of paper or other supports can be introduced. Be sure to explore all of these options in depth so that you can inventory for yourself the expressive potential of each combination.

Paper and Other Supports

Teachers often overlook the role of the drawing surface, or support, as an expressive medium in students' drawings. Papers for drawing vary in their surface (smooth, textured [with *tooth*], shiny, matte), weight, color (whites/blacks/ grays, colors and tones), opacity and translucency, and size—and all of these characteristics can contribute to how a work looks and means. But many teachers tend to rely exclusively on white paper in standard ream sizes, and this limits kids' work and makes it look, as a whole, unnecessarily uniform. An easy way to avoid teacher-dictated visual uniformity in students' works is to let kids choose what size, color, and opacity/translucency of paper they would like to use for drawing.

Student-grade and professional-grade papers differ according to their durability, permanence, and lightfastness. With younger or less experienced kids, student-grade sulphite (wood pulp) papers can be used with dry and wet media (for wet media use a heavier paper, such as 80 lb., to reduce buckling). Cut assorted sizes of squares and long rectangles and have these available for students. As a class, brainstorm other surfaces that could be interesting—used brown paper grocery bags trimmed into sheets, patterned paper, transparent acetate sheets or translucent vellum[1] sheets all are possibilities. For more experienced students and special projects, if your budget allows, introduce artist-grade papers made from a combination of wood and cotton rag (Strathmore and Canson each make a variety of colors and weights). As much as possible, without making the number of choices overwhelming, let kids select, as artists do, the kind of surface they prefer or a new one they would like to explore.

For many artists working today, the hunt for alternative supports and surfaces is a key conceptual and aesthetic part of the drawing process (see Figure 2-4). Found things bring with them their own connotations and stories from past lives. Matchbooks, seed packets, pages from used ledgers and scrapbooks, vintage wallpaper, and printed

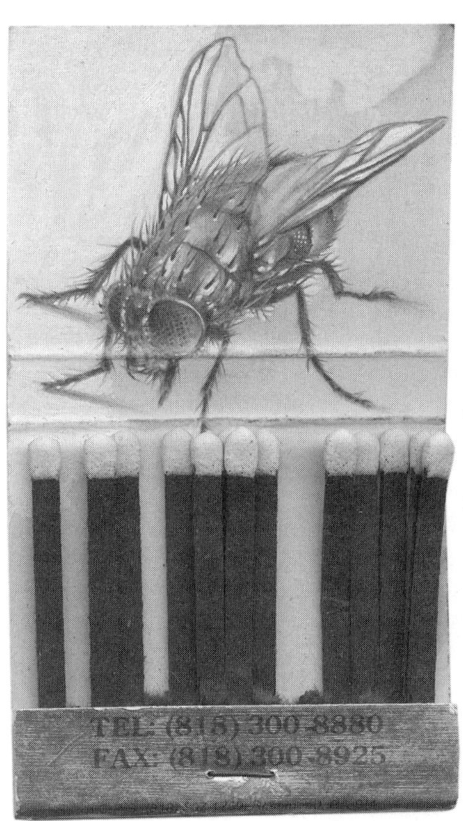

F 2-4

Jason D'Aquino, Black Fly, 2006, graphite on matchbook, 1" × 1".

---

[1] Translucent vellum sheets in pads are sold at art supply stores.

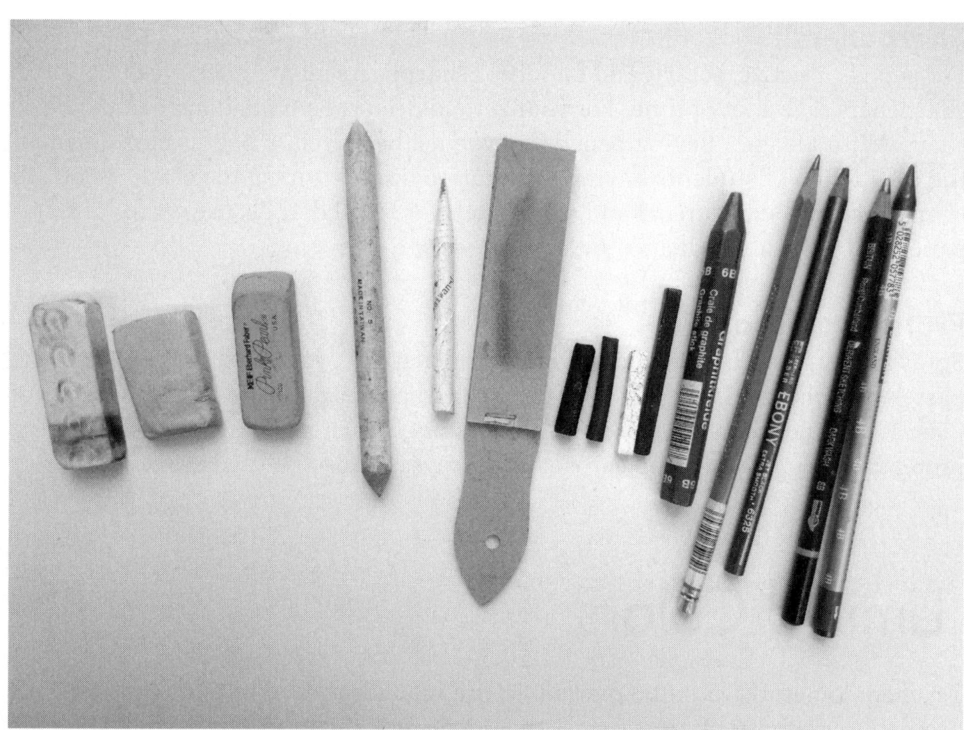

F 2-5: Assorted drawing materials and tools, including tortillon, stump, and kneaded rubber and plastic/vinyl erasers

wrapping paper and book pages are just some nontraditional surfaces used by contemporary artists. In addition to looking at the world around them as a source for searching out interesting two-dimensional surfaces, students may also be interested in using some of the drawing materials on collages (see Chapter 5), on fired clay pieces, and on the surfaces of other three-dimensional objects they build (see Chapter 6).

Tools

Tools like rolled paper tortillons[2] and paper stumps[3] (see Figure 2-5) are good for blending charcoal and soft pastels, but scraps of paper towel, Q-tips, and fingers work as well. Erasers can be used not just for getting rid of unwanted parts of a drawing but also as tools for making lines and other marks in a built up area of graphite or charcoal. Pink Pearl erasers work for pencil on most paper surfaces, and white plastic and vinyl erasers are effective on both vellum and plastic surfaces. For charcoal and soft pastels, use kneaded rubber erasers (these can be formed into different shapes to get at small areas). Small pieces of soft bread pinched into different shapes are also good blotters for charcoal and pastels.

---

[2] Also called tortillion, a tortillon is a tool with a point on one end for blending dry drawing materials on a surface. It's made from a small piece of paper rolled tightly around itself in a spiral and fastened. Art teacher Pete Sotello in Yakima, Washington, suggests this approach for making your own tortillon: "Take a piece of scrap paper and trim it into a $6'' \times 3''$ rectangle. With the paper laid out horizontally, make a mark on the top edge that's $3\frac{1}{2}''$ from the left edge, then make a mark on the right edge that's $1''$ up from the bottom edge. Remove the right top corner by cutting from one mark to the other. Fold the bottom corner up on an angle to create a point at the $1''$ mark on the right edge, fold again, and begin to roll tightly on a steep angle so that there is a point on one end. Secure with tape when done."

[3] A paper stump is similar to a tortillon but is denser and pointed on both ends. Stumps are available in larger sizes than tortillons, and stump points can be cleaned with sandpaper.

Sharpeners

For pencils, electric, rotary, and handheld sharpeners all are effective but electric sharpeners save a lot of time. For younger children the points don't need to be as sharp. With all ages, having pencils sharpened before class begins cuts down on the distraction of students having to get up to do this during the class period. To shape and sharpen charcoal and soft pastels for small details, use scraps of sandpaper or handheld sandpaper pads.

Protective Sprays

Spray fixatives can be used to seal materials that are prone to smudging, like soft pastels and charcoal, but these sprays are not approved for use in the presence of kids. Read and follow all directions and safety warnings carefully when using protective sprays. Nonpump aerosol hairsprays can also be used as fixatives.

Drawing with Limited Colors

Teachers sometimes assume that, in art, giving kids a lot of options to work with promotes creativity. But often just the opposite is the case. Presenting students with a single material or limited colors and asking them to invent as many different ways as possible of working within those limitations presents opportunities for developing flexible and divergent thinking, fluency of ideas, risk taking through in-depth experimentation, and resourcefulness. These qualities play into any kind of creative work and they lead to a kind of intimate, artistic knowledge, insight, and familiarity, an expertise called *thinking in a material*. I tell my students that we are going to be "experimenting scientists" to see how many different ways we can invent to work with just black, white, and grays, in charcoal, pencil, or India ink. We share our results and talk about how these ways of working and the marks and effects they create might suggest different ideas in an artwork. I've found that when they're presented with too many options at once, or multiple materials they haven't encountered before, students are less likely to sustain in-depth exploration in any one of them.

Once students have fully explored a material, for example, graphite—for very young children a single pencil and one type of paper, for older kids a few pencils with varying degrees of softer and harder lead—new papers and other supports can be added as options for experimentation, and new materials can be introduced. The trick is to balance studio experiences so that kids can develop expertise through repeated encounters with the same materials *and* gradually become familiar with a range of options. At this point, offering choices for what to draw with and on allows students to make thoughtful, informed choices instead of continually choosing whatever is novel or convenient and using it in a limited way. The materials themselves need to have the kind of flexibility that can accommodate divergent uses and applications. For the most part, gimmicky drawing materials like glitter pens or pencils with multicolored composite leads are too front-loaded with a single, built-in special effect to afford much in the way of diverse approaches and outcomes.

Using the activities that follow, working first with dry materials and then with wet ones, keep notes as you work with various drawing materials. This will allow you to plan for similar kinds of open-ended investigations with your students, tailored for their ages and prior experiences. In Chapter 7 there are suggestions for how to carry forward the media-based discoveries you make, by articulating specific learning outcomes for students and identifying open-ended themes and approaches for sparking and focusing their studio work. The materials explorations here are sequenced for you to experiment one by one with a range of drawing materials and supports to create a variety of visual effects. Each exploration begins with an investigation that mirrors how students experience art materials not only visually but also through touch, sound, and smell. Beyond visual qualities, artists (and children) respond to materials even before they start using them to make something (remember the smell of Playdoh, the sticky feel of clay)? These initial experiences can influence how we select media, our ways of working with them, and what the work and the experience of making it might mean.

Note: Table 2-1 contains some ideas for focusing your work once you have explored in depth the different materials featured in this chapter.

Table 2-1 Ideas for Focusing Drawing

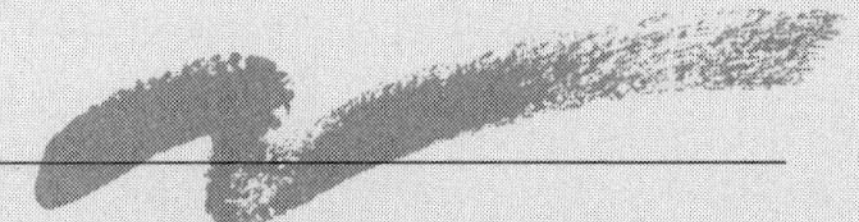

- A drawing based on a part of something—a cropped portion of another drawing or an object, a part removed from or attached to a larger object, figure, etc.
- A drawing that uses lines and textures to document the close observation of a stuffed animal or toy.
- A drawing that focuses on qualities of lines to express different kinds of information and meanings.
- A group of drawings that show a single object from multiple vantage points—up close, further away, top view, side views, bottom view.
- A group of drawings that portray a single object using different materials to change its meaning.
- A drawing that extends the image or ideas from a previously created painting, collage, print, or sculpture.
- A drawing of a place that uses color and other design elements to communicate a feeling about that place.
- A drawing that features an unusual placement of marks or image on the paper.
- A drawing that explores what on object is like on the inside.
- A drawing that visually translates a common sound.
- A drawing that combines multiple sensory qualities of a place or an event at once—smell, sound, appearance, feel, etc.
- A drawing that translates and/or builds upon the instrumentation, melody, and tempo of a piece of music.
- A drawing that is based on building up areas of marks, or removing and erasing them.
- A drawing that uses light and dark areas to create a sense of drama.
- A drawing that responds to a poem, or an excerpt from a poem.
- A drawing that transforms a wall.
- A drawing that is about an action or movement—bolt, bounce, dart, flee, flick, hurl, ram, propel, rush, scamper, scramble, scurry, spin, streak, swerve, swoop, whisk, zoom, etc.
- A drawing that uses no lines.
- A drawing that moves from one place to another.
- A drawing that plays with scale—substantially enlarging a tiny object or detail, or miniaturizing a massive one.
- A drawing that shows a scene or subject from an unusual vantage point—looking down from above, looking up from below, close up, far away, through a keyhole, etc.

WORKING DRY

Graphite Pencils and Crayons

Although rod-shaped pieces of the metal lead were used as pencils in ancient times, what we now commonly call lead when talking about pencils is the mineral graphite (a form of carbon) mixed with clay. This paste is formed into strips, dried, and fired in a kiln, then enclosed in a shaft of cedar wood.

Different pencils have different ratios of graphite to clay, making some leads harder (more clay) or softer (less clay). Twenty grades of wooden drawing pencils—coded by "H" for hardness, "F" for fine point, and "B" for blackness—reflect this range, from 10H or 9H (hardest lead, finest and lightest marks) to HB and F (mid range—HB is like a standard #2 pencil) to 8B and 9B (softest lead and roughest, darkest marks). Ebony pencils contain a particularly soft, silvery lead that offers a wide range of possibilities for mark making (see Figure 2-6). There are also woodless pencils made entirely of soft lead, and these have a larger marking surface that can be used for broader strokes to cover bigger areas. Paper-covered graphite crayons have a larger diameter still. For drawing on nonpaper surfaces, Stabilo makes a graphite pencil (Stabilo "All") that works on plastic and other surfaces that are too slick for regular pencils. All of this means that you can create a great variety of visual effects and in turn suggest—just through the kind of graphite material you use and how you use it—different kinds of ideas and meanings.

Exploring Graphite

From the unassuming, yellow "Number 2" with the pink eraser to graded drawing pencils that produce a full range of mark making possibilities, what do they all do? Explore as many graphite materials as possible on different papers and other surfaces, and note the ways of working that each lends itself to. What kinds of effects can you create? For what ages and purposes would these different forms of graphite be useful and practical? Keep working notes in your studio journal about your discoveries.

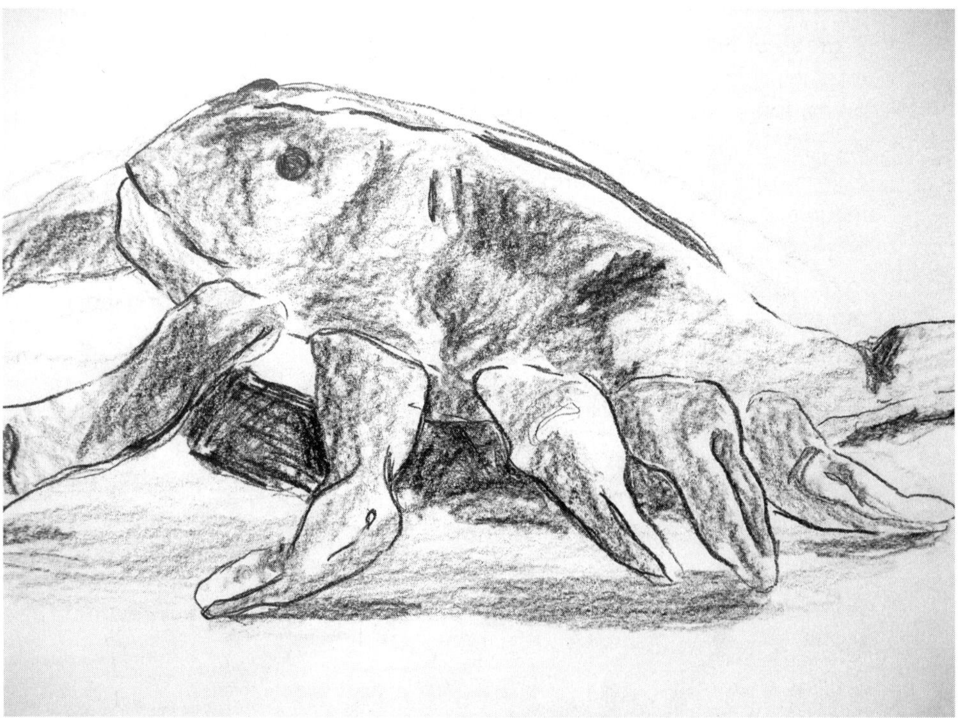

F 2-6: Jean Marie Holmes, a student in a course I taught, used Ebony pencil for this drawing of a stuffed animal toy. What are some different ways of using just one pencil, as seen in this drawing? What kinds of ideas, qualities, or other information about the object are suggested and through what means?

Materials:

Assorted graphite materials—common #2 pencil, graded pencils (at least three to compare, a high numbered H, like 7H, an HB, and a high numbered B), Ebony pencil, woodless pencil, graphite crayon, Stabilo "All" graphite pencil (works on paper, plastic, metal, etc.)

A selection of papers and other surfaces—plain newsprint (rough and smooth), plain copier paper, other textured or toothed papers, brown butcher paper or sheets cut from brown paper bags, colored and toned paper (construction paper, Strathmore or Stonehenge drawing paper in various colors), printed or patterned paper, translucent vellum, tracing paper, clear acetate

Erasers (pink rubber, white vinyl)

Getting Started:

1. Note the different qualities of the graphite and drawing surfaces you use in the investigations below. What are the materials' visual qualities? What do they feel like to touch? What sound does the drawing surface itself make when it comes into contact with the table, or when you shimmy it around in front of you? What sounds does the graphite make when it comes into contact with different drawing surfaces?

2. Use each type of graphite in as many different ways as you can think of, first on a piece of white paper, then on a variety of colors, textures, and opacities (see Figure 2-7). Use the following questions as starting points in your experiments: How can you create different marks and effects by varying the pressure of the graphite on the drawing surface? What happens when you twist your wrist or arm as you're working, or change the angle? What marks can you make with small movements? With large ones? With straight back-and-forth motions versus curving or circular movements? What kinds of marks can you make with the tip of the lead?

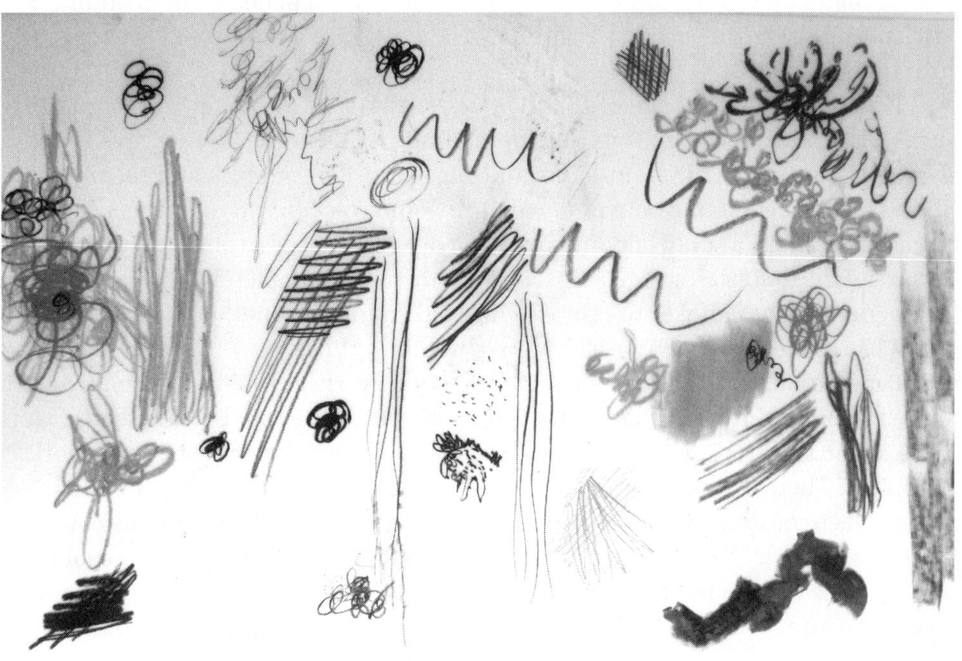

F 2-7: Experimenting with graphite

The sides? The edges? How many different ways can you change the look of one continuous line? What textures can you make? How does changing your way of holding the pencil affect what you can do?

Note: For young children just learning how to write, it's good to know how they are being taught to hold a pencil. At times, or for some children, you may want to reinforce these hand positions for writing so they are not confused. When children have achieved the hand-eye coordination for writing, make sure to model and encourage other ways of holding the pencil while drawing.

3. Invent different ways of covering larger areas of the drawing surface. How can you do it with lines? Patches? Dots? Layers? Can you make a large area that looks very smooth? Rough? What are different ways to make an area go from light to dark? How can you combine a variety of tones (varied grays, black, white)?
4. Try drawing with the erasers on some of your built up areas—what kinds of lines and marks can you make by removing the graphite?
5. Make sure to try all of the papers and other surfaces. How does the surface you draw on—color, size, texture, degree of transparency—change the effects you're able to achieve? How do you respond differently to the look and feel of various drawing supports?

Charcoal Sticks and Pencils

Charcoal's use as a drawing material can be traced to prehistoric times (think cave drawings). In its simplest form, charcoal is *charred* wood, made by heating twigs of willow or vine in an airtight kiln—the lack of air ensures that the wood will not turn to ash. There are different formulas of drawing charcoal and different forms, and they each produce a range of marks and effects. Vine sticks come in different degrees of hardness, from extra soft to hard, and willow sticks come in varied widths. Compressed charcoal, made from a mixture of ground charcoal powder and clay binder pressed into stick form, comes in both various degrees of hardness and a range of sizes. Compressed charcoal is a stronger, less fragile substance than vine and willow charcoal. It comes in wood pencil form in addition to sticks. And there are carbon pencils as well, which are a mixture of charcoal and graphite.

Beyond the wide range of tonal values (lights and darks) in lines and other marks, charcoal easily lends itself to spreading and blending (see Figures 2-8 and 2-9). You can create different looks and suggest different ideas and meanings in your drawing depending on how you do this—and you can use your finger, a paintbrush, a chamois, a scrap of paper towel, a paper stump, or a rolled paper tortillon to spread the material, soften areas, or wipe them out completely. You can also use a kneaded (rubber) eraser to remove charcoal from the paper, not just to fix mistakes but as another way of creating marks, like highlights.

Papers that have a textured surface (tooth) work well with charcoal, as the material embeds into the paper instead of sitting on the top. Because charcoal is such a soft material, it needs to be fixed to the paper surface when the work is complete. There are no art fixatives that are approved for use with or by kids, so this needs to be done when students are not present (read the directions carefully regarding health hazards and proper ventilation). Some inexpensive aerosol hairsprays, ones that do not contain oils or plant products, can also be used as a fixative, but again, you will need to follow the product's safety guidelines for use.

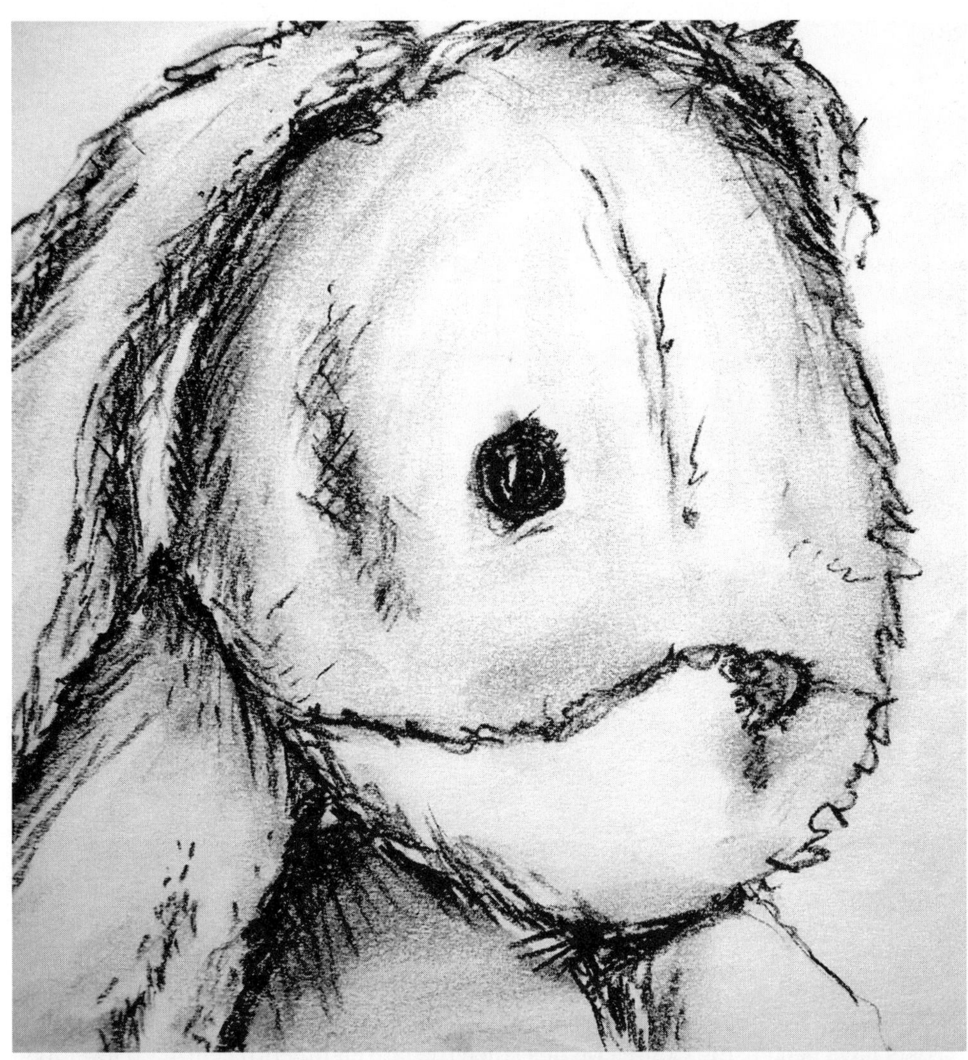

F 2-8
*Melissa Schmid, 2007, charcoal
pencil on paper.*

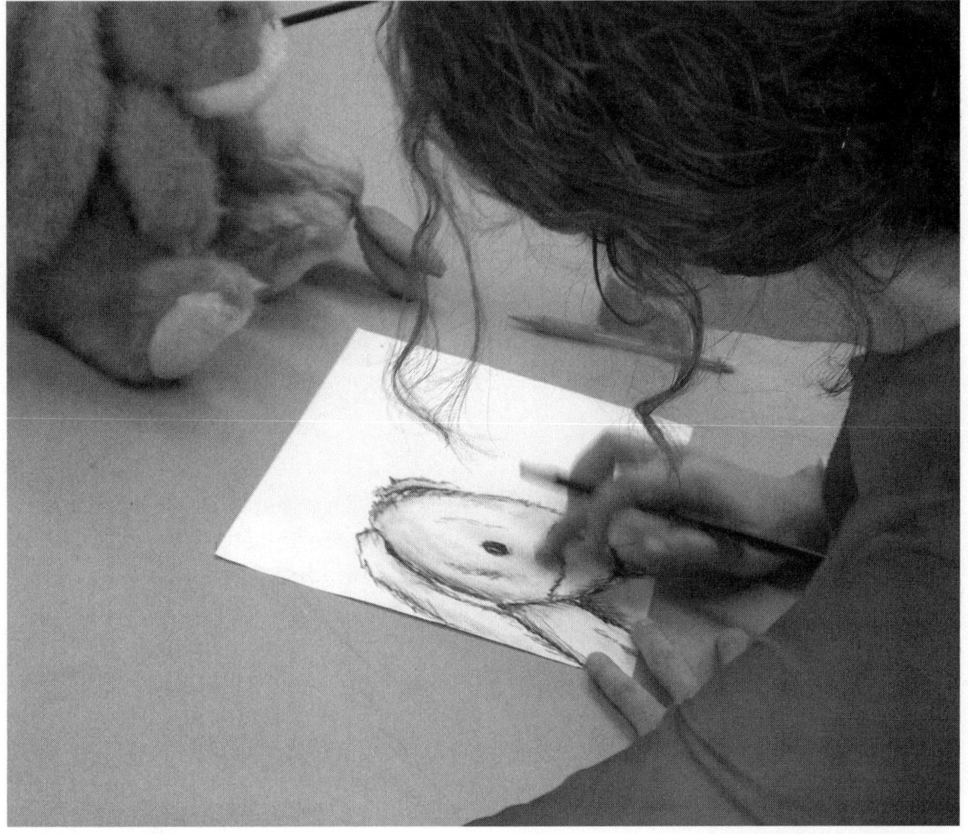

F 2-9: Melissa Schmid smudges
and blends charcoal pencil to
suggest the soft and fuzzy feel
of the stuffed animal's fur. She
used the point and side of the
charcoal pencil to create
scratchy, jagged, and layered
lines—suggesting areas of
shadow and the rougher
texture of all-over clumps of fur.

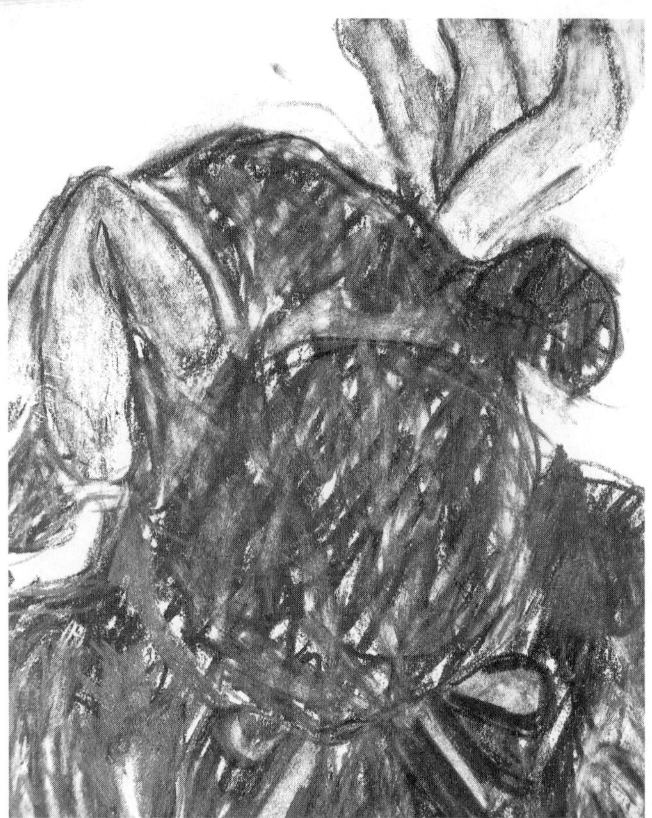

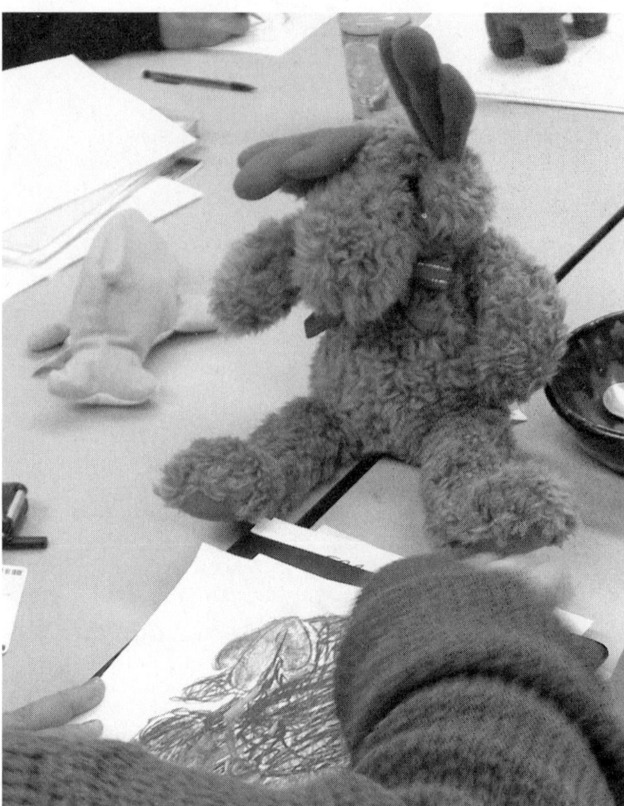

F 2-10
Vanessa Viruet, 2007, Conté crayon on paper. (above, left)

F 2-11: Vanessa Viruet uses the Conté crayon's versatility to produce the smooth, soft feel of the moose's antlers contrasted with heavy lines and dense layering for the matted fur. (above, right)

Conté Crayons

Artists have been using Conté crayons since the late eighteenth century. Developed in France by Nicolas-Jacques Conté, the drawing sticks were made from carbon black (a pigment derived from charcoal), graphite, and/or iron oxide, mixed with clay. Traditional colors include black, white, gray, different versions of sanguine (red orange to warm brown), and bistre (cooler brown). You can now find Conté crayons in 48 colors in the United States and in 70 colors elsewhere. Some colors come in varying sizes, and black and white are available in different degrees of hardness.

Generally, the firm and dense consistency of the standard Conté crayon produces crisper marks and sharper lines that appear slightly glossy when compared to the more matte look of charcoal or chalk pastels. Marks can be layered to build up a dense surface as well (see Figures 2-10 and 2-11). As with charcoal, coarser papers trap the pigment better than papers with a smooth surface, and finished artwork can be sprayed with fixative for protection.

Pastels

Pastels come in two basic forms, dry and oil-based. Dry pastels have varying consistencies, from soft and powdery to hard and dense. Soft pastels, available in full sticks, half sticks, and pans, are made of pure ground pigment, a chalk or clay extender, and a binding medium of gum. This paste is then cut and formed into sticks (rectangular or round) that harden when dry. Medium and hard pastels are made in a similar way but contain more extender and binder and less pigment than soft pastels. The dense consistency of harder pastels generally results in less vivid colors—the material is also less fragile and able to produce sharper lines and marks compared to soft pastels. Pastel pencils are made from a thin pastel stick inserted into a wood shaft, and can be used alone or in combination with hard, medium, and soft pastels.

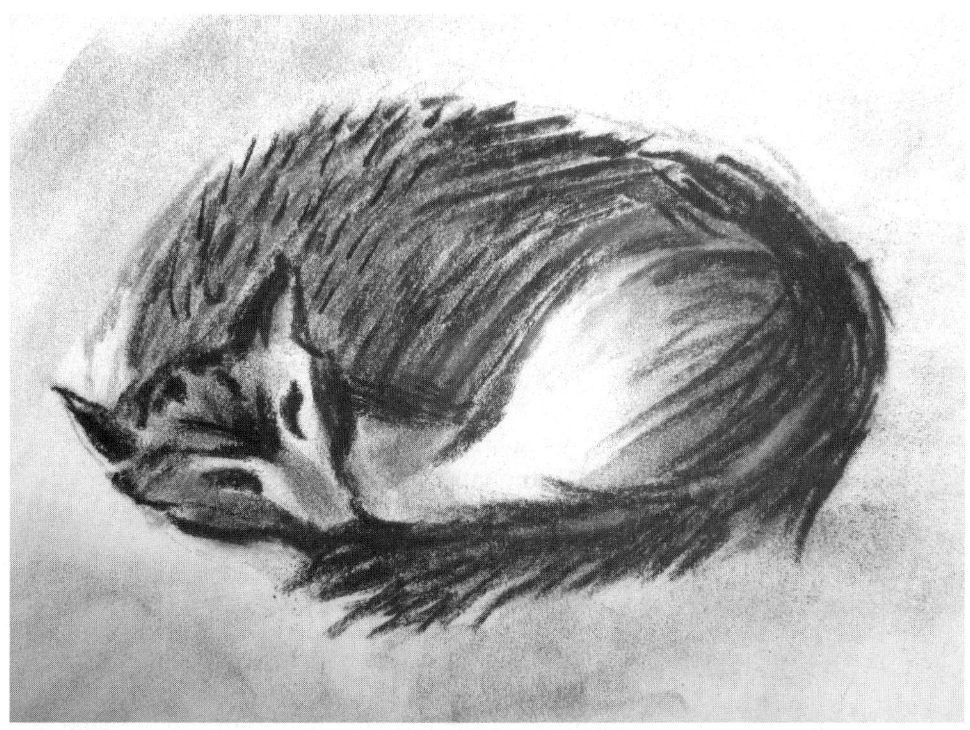

F 2-12: Dry pastel on paper

Oil pastels have a different chemistry—instead of using chalk or clay as extender and gum as binder, oil soluble wax is mixed with the pure pigments. Like dry pastels, different proportions of color pigment to extender/binder produce different material qualities—some oil pastels are more buttery and soft while others are more stiff. Also, oil pastel brands and even different colors within a single brand can vary in color intensity or density, with some more opaque and others more transparent. And oil pastels generally do not dry completely—again, results can vary across brands and across colors within a single brand. It can be harder to blend different colors on your paper using oil pastels as opposed to dry pastels, and oil pastels do not require a spray fixative for protection.

Depending on the type of pastel you use and the quality of the drawing surface (more textured or more smooth), dry and oil pastels can produce a wide range of visual effects that in turn can suggest different ideas and meanings in a drawing. Working monochromatically you can use black, white, and a range of grays—to this you can add one other color blended in different amounts to create a range of tints and tones (see Figure 2-12). Many pastel manufacturers offer tints and tones for single colors, and these pastel groupings can be used for monochromatic work as well. While oil pastels are difficult to erase, dry pastels can be removed from small areas with kneaded rubber erasers, special "black" erasers, and small kneaded pieces of bread.

Note: When dry pastels come in contact with one another, or are applied in layers, the sticks themselves can become marked up with other colors. For an easy way to remove unwanted markings scrape single pastels on textured drawing paper or fine sandpaper. For cleaning several at once fill a container with rice, add the pastels, and gently shake until the pastels are clean.

Exploring Charcoal, Conté Crayon, and Pastels

Explore various types of charcoal, Conté crayons, and black, white, and gray dry and oil pastels on different papers and other surfaces. What kinds of effects can you create with each material? What ideas can you suggest with these different approaches? How is working with these media different from using graphite? As you did previously, note the approaches that each material lends itself to and the ages and purposes for which each would be useful and practical.

Materials:

Charcoal in a variety of grades and forms (vine sticks, compressed sticks, pencil)
Conté crayons in black and white, sanguine, and/or bistre
Dry and oil pastels in black, white, assorted grays, and one additional color
A selection of papers and other surfaces—plain newsprint (rough and smooth), smooth papers, white, black, neutral and colored textured or toothed papers (construction paper, Strathmore or Stonehenge drawing paper in various colors), brown butcher paper or sheets cut from brown paper bags, printed or patterned paper, sandpaper, translucent vellum, clear acetate
Kneaded eraser, Factis Soft Black 18 or Factis Extra Soft White eraser, and a small piece of soft bread
Paper towel, chamois, tortillons or paper stumps for blending

Getting Started:

1. Notice the different qualities of the drawing materials, their visual and tactile characteristics. How are they different from graphite?
2. As in the graphite exploration, push each material in a variety of ways on white paper and on other surfaces. Explore each drawing material separately, then try different combinations of colors and types. Make sure to try the white Conté crayon and pastels on dark and black papers. How can you create different marks and effects by varying pressure, moving your arm in different ways, changing how you hold the charcoal or pastel, and using different parts of it? What lines and textures can you make?
3. Try multiple ways of covering larger areas to create lighter and darker tones. How can you do it with lines, patches, and layers? How can you do it by spreading and blending the material into the paper? Experiment with blending using your finger, a tortillon, or stump (for charcoal and dry pastel), and a scrap of paper towel. Try this in smaller areas, too. Try different ways of combining black, white, and gray with one other color.
4. Experiment with different ways of removing charcoal, Conté crayon, and dry pastel—use the kneaded eraser on some areas. Knead a clump of bread until it's moist and sticky and experiment with using it as a blotter on another area.
5. Explore using the more textured papers and the translucent vellum with the dry materials and oil pastels. Also try the oil pastels on smoother paper and on clear plastic. Try using some colors on one side and others on the reverse. Note how the drawing surface affects what kinds of marks and effects you're interested in making, and the look and feel of the finished work.

ADDING WATER

The point at which drawing becomes painting is debatable, and with drawing such an open concept among contemporary artists these boundaries seem irrelevant in the classroom. Adding water through the use of washes can extend the expressive effects of graphite, charcoal, and dry pastels, and working in ink creates an additional array of possibilities for meaning in mark making. As you experiment with these approaches keep notes about ideas suggested by the new effects you're able to produce. How does the fluid nature of the material change your response to it and the kinds of marks and meanings you create?

Water-soluble Graphite Pencils, Crayons, and Pastels

Water-soluble graphite drawing materials use a binder that dissolves in water, offering a simple way to transition from dry to wet work. You can apply the material in dry form to paper and add a wet brush for wash and other painterly effects. You can also use the material dry on wet or damp paper, or dip the material in water and apply to dry, dampened, or wet paper. Like other forms of graphite, water-soluble graphite pencils and crayons are available in different grades of hardness for light, medium, and darker marking effects. Using more or less water and a softer or stiffer brush will contribute to the range of potential effects.

Charcoal and Dry Pastel Wash

You can create a charcoal wash by using a soft brush dipped in water over compressed charcoal (other kinds as well) that you've applied to paper. The same can be done with dry pastel. This action doesn't dissolve the charcoal and pastel particles but it does mix them into a fluid, spreadable form. The residue on the brush can be used to add additional marks and areas to the drawing.

Exploring Water-soluble Graphite and Charcoal/Pastel Washes

Use water-soluble graphite pencils and water-soluble crayons or pastels, compressed charcoal sticks and pencils, and dry pastels to build up lighter and darker areas on your paper—single lines and masses of lines and other marks, solid shapes, and patches. Use different parts of each material—tip, side, edge— and experiment with varying the pressure as you draw with each material.

What happens when you add a wet brush to different areas of the paper? How does working this way change the mood or feeling of the work? What new ideas can be expressed just in the way a dry material is transformed, made fluid, and spread across the surface of paper?

Note: Erasers are usually not as effective on dried graphite and charcoal washes. Factis Soft Black 18 or Factis Extra Soft White erasers (made by General) will remove, though not entirely, some dried pastel washes.

Materials:

Charcoal in a variety of grades and forms (vine sticks, compressed sticks, charcoal pencils in a range from harder to softer)
Dry pastels in black, white, assorted grays, and one additional color
Water-soluble graphite in assorted softer and harder grades, water-soluble crayons/pastels in black, white, assorted grays
Container of water
Soft hair brush (as opposed to a stiff bristle brush)
A selection of heavier papers (at least 80 lb.) and other surfaces—white textured or toothed papers, colored paper (common construction paper, Strathmore or Stonehenge drawing paper in various colors), translucent vellum, brown butcher paper or sheets cut from brown paper bags, printed or patterned paper, fine sandpaper

Artist Profile: **CATHY DALEY**

Cathy Daley works with black dry pastel on vellum and adds liquid to create a wash effect (see Figures 2-13 and 2-14). How does her use of vellum as a support, as well as the transformation of dry pastel into a wash, suggest different actions, movements, and qualities in the figures and clothing in her drawings?

F 2-13
*Cathy Daley, Untitled, 2007,
pastel on vellum, 24" × 19".
(below, left)*

F 2-14
*Cathy Daley, Untitled, 2007,
pastel on vellum, 24" × 19".
(below, right)*

I work primarily in the medium of drawing and almost exclusively with black pastel on translucent vellum. This medium with its potential for overwriting offers me the possibility of a spontaneous and direct working process. I use black pastel for its depth and wide range of tonality. The drawings often have an almost sculptural presence as a sense of volume is produced. I also use black pastel because it is an elemental drawing material. The vellum has a very smooth surface which I enjoy working on. I use solvent to liquefy the pastel as I am working, so the process is very fluid. I can create transparent washes as well as very dense blacks. I like how the vellum in its transparency conducts the light.

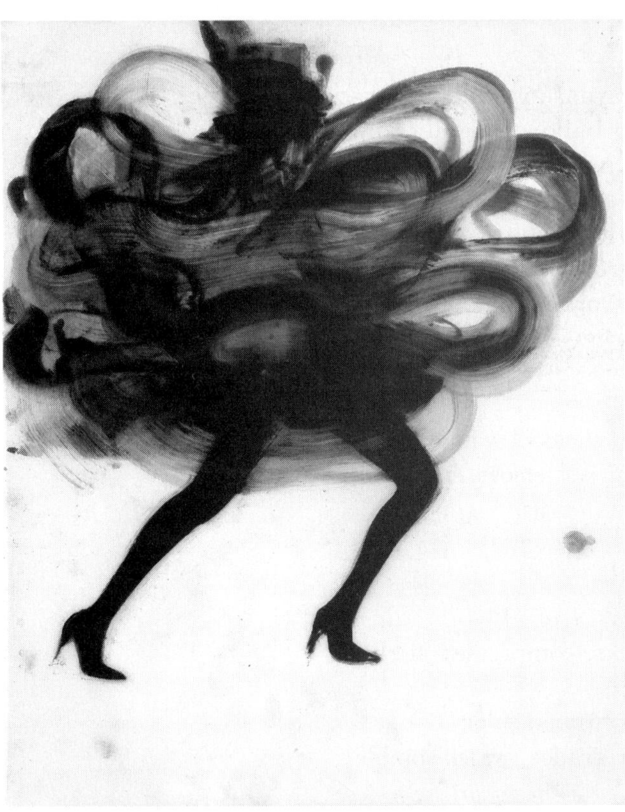

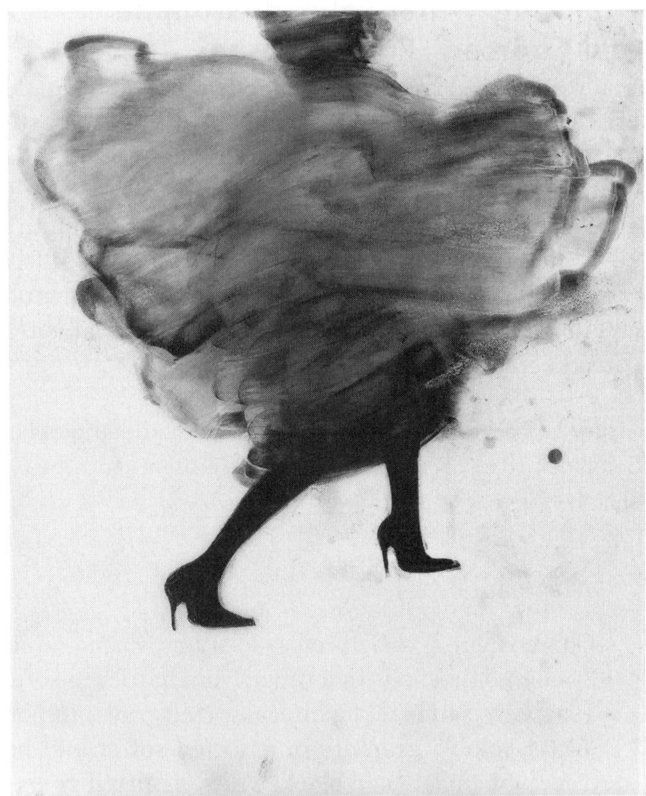

Getting Started:

1. Use the water-soluble graphite pencils, crayons, and pastels, and compressed charcoal and dry pastels, to make a variety of marks on a piece of white paper. Create lines, patches, and shapes in different areas. Vary the pressures and use the different parts of each stick. Create a variety of values and tones—lighter areas, midtone areas, and darker areas where the material is built up heavily on the paper.
2. Dip your brush in water and apply to the different parts of the paper. Experiment with using just a little water and then using more, on light, medium and darker areas of the paper. How do the water-soluble materials change with the addition of water? How are the areas of charcoal and dry pastel transformed? What kinds of visual effects are created? What kinds of ideas or feelings might these effects suggest?
3. Draw back into some of the wet areas of the paper with the charcoal and pastels. How does working this way change the look and feel of the material? What new ideas might be suggested through the visual effects you've created?
4. Explore all of the above actions in the same way but this time using the colored papers and the translucent vellum. Again, note how the drawing surface affects the kinds of marks and effects you're making, and the look and feel of the finished work. How does working on vellum compare to using these approaches on brown butcher paper, or colored drawing papers?

Ink

Ink for drawing and writing hails from China and Egypt and was developed around 2500 BC. Today there are basically three kinds—India ink, sometimes called Chinese ink (which is black and comes in waterproof and nonwaterproof forms), waterproof colored inks, and nonwaterproof colored inks. Both the waterproof and nonwaterproof inks, in liquid form, can be diluted with water to lighten their color intensity.

It is thought that "India" ink was developed in China and first imported to Europe in the sixteenth century. India inks are made largely from lamp black, a type of carbon derived from the soot of burning substances like resins, fat and oils, and paraffin. The carbon is mixed with binders that are either nondissolvable (nonsoluble) with water when dry, like shellac, or dissolvable with water once the ink has dried. The nonsoluble form is waterproof while the soluble form is not. Water-soluble ink also comes in solid bars known as sumi ink. The sumi bar is ground on a suzuri, or ink stone, and the ground powder is mixed with water to form the liquid ink.

Waterproof and nonwaterproof colored inks are made from either dyes or pigments. Typically, dye-based inks are less permanent, or lightfast, than pigment inks. You can also find acrylic inks (waterproof) and liquid concentrated watercolors (nonwaterproof), which behave like ink when applied to paper. Both waterproof and nonwaterproof inks can be diluted with water to produce a variety of intensities, and single colors can be mixed together to form new colors. Ink ingredients and consistencies vary across manufacturers and across multiple brands from the same manufacturer, so combining products from different lines is not recommended.

Pens to Use with Ink

Nib pens (often called dip pens), bamboo pens, reed pens, and quill pens are some of the tools available for working with ink. Each has its own character and feel, and creates different marks and effects. Nib pens have a handle made from wood or plastic, with a metal tip (nib) that is split to allow the ink to flow. Nibs are available in assorted sizes and shapes, and many dip pens take interchangeable nibs. Bamboo and reed pens are made by cutting short stalks of the dried plant, making an angled cut on one end to form a tip, and then splitting the tip a short distance lengthwise to form a connecting pathway for the ink to flow. Used since the Middle Ages for writing, quill pens are made from a flight feather of a large bird. The tubular base of the feather's shaft is cut at the end and the tip is slit in the center, similar to bamboo and reed pens. All of these pens can be used with different types of waterproof and nonwaterproof inks. To control the amount of ink intake, some artists use eyedroppers instead of dipping to ink the pen.

Brushes to Use with Ink

Although both softer and stiffer brushes can be used with ink, soft hair brushes tend to work best for smooth application and coverage. These brushes hold more ink and there is less resistance than with a stiffer brush. I like to use Japanese bamboo brushes with kids, both for working in line and texture with undiluted India ink and adding diluted ink washes. Smaller brushes are good for finer lines and textures with undiluted ink, and wider "wash" brushes are good for applying ink washes evenly to larger areas.

Exploring Ink with Dip Pens and Brushes

Experiment with ink using assorted dip pens and brushes (see Figure 2-15). Using undiluted ink with these tools, what kinds of lines, other marks, and textures can you create? What happens when you layer over these areas darker and lighter washes of ink diluted with water?

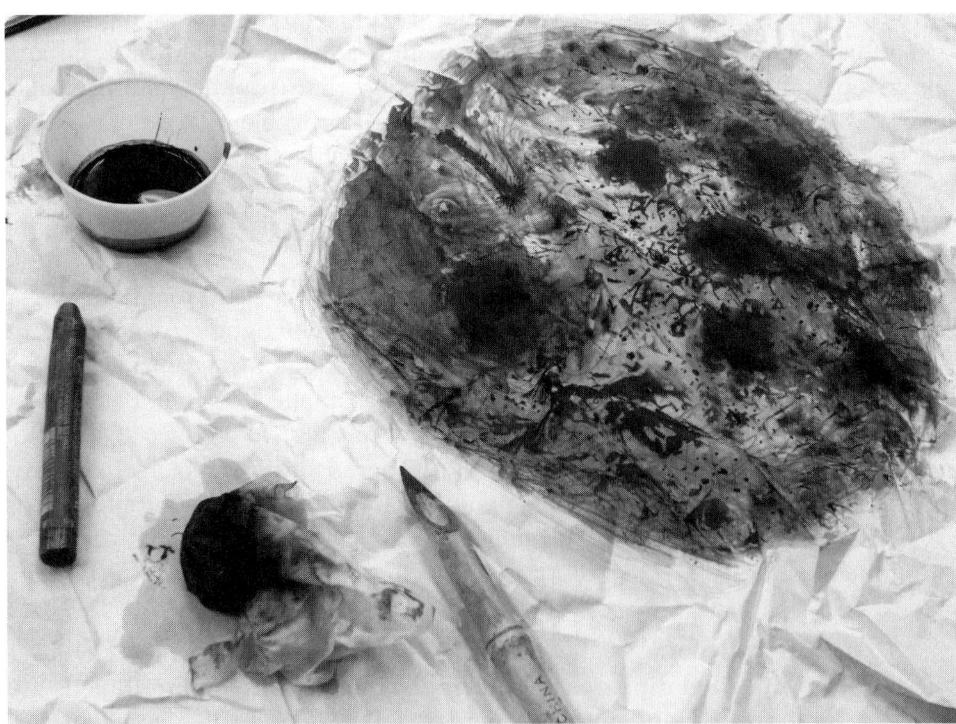

F 2-15: Experimenting with India ink and washes

Materials:

India ink
Small cups for ink and washes
Bamboo pens
Dip pen with assorted metal nibs
Bamboo or soft watercolor brushes
Container of water for rinsing pens and brushes
A selection of heavier papers (at least 80 lb.) and other surfaces—white tex-
   tured or toothed papers, colored paper (common construction paper,
   Strathmore or Stonehenge drawing paper in various colors), translucent
   vellum, brown butcher paper or sheets cut from brown paper bags, printed
   or patterned paper

Getting Started:

1. As you prepare for working with the ink, note the characteristics of the
   material itself—its visual qualities and its smell. How do these qualities
   compare to those of the dry materials you've been experimenting with so
   far? While you are exploring the ink with pen and brush below, note its
   characteristics as a material on different drawing surfaces. How does it
   behave differently from the other materials you've explored? What is it
   like to work with? What effects can you create that are different from
   those achieved working dry?
2. Using undiluted India ink in a small container, work with one pen at a time
   on white paper to make as many kinds of lines, other marks, and textures
   as you can. Move the pen side to side, up and down, and in other ways, and
   experiment with using different amounts of ink. Vary the pressure of tool
   on paper. Use the tip and edges of the tools to create different effects.

Note: Rinse pen nibs and brushes in water immediately after use to prevent ink from
drying in them.

3. Try out the brush with undiluted ink. Use the tip and side, and experiment with different angles and pressures. Try dragging and twisting as
   you go along. What kinds of lines and other marks are possible? How can
   you layer marks to create textured and built-up areas?
4. On the same paper, once the undiluted ink is dry, try out the pens and
   brushes with different grades of washes—light, medium, and darker. To
   make the washes pour small amounts of water into separate cups and add
   ink sparingly until you have three graded (lighter, medium, darker) values.
   Explore making lines and marks with the brush and diluted inks.
5. Once all of the above areas on the paper are dry, apply the graded washes
   over different areas of dried undiluted ink and diluted ink. What kinds of
   layering are possible? What visual effects are created and what ideas/feelings
   might those effects suggest?
6. Try the reverse process on a new piece of white paper by using your brush
   to apply light and medium washes in different areas, blending in some
   places. Once the paper is dry, use pens and brushes to draw over the dried
   wash areas with undiluted inks. Also try working in this sequence but
   while the wash layer is still wet or damp. What different effects can you
   create experimenting this way?

Artist Profile: **KELLY STURHAHN**

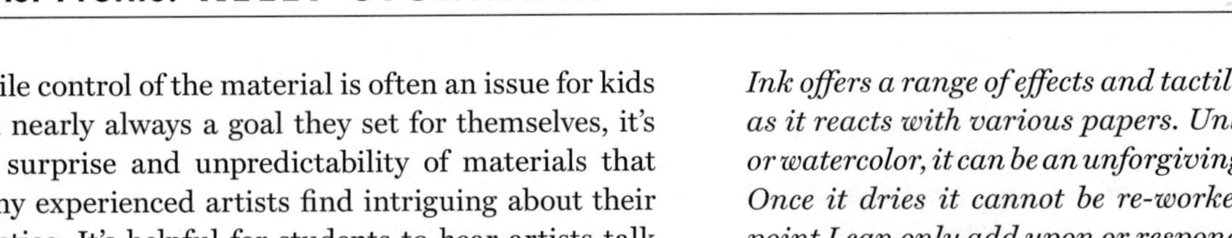

While control of the material is often an issue for kids and nearly always a goal they set for themselves, it's the surprise and unpredictability of materials that many experienced artists find intriguing about their practice. It's helpful for students to hear artists talk about this aspect of studio work, to understand that control of the medium need not always be a primary concern. For Kelly Sturhahn, whose work appears in Figure 2-3 and Figure 1 of the color insert, the balance between "the nature of the material" and what she "can and cannot control" plays a large part in the imagery itself. She comments,

Ink offers a range of effects and tactile qualities as it reacts with various papers. Unlike pencil or watercolor, it can be an unforgiving medium. Once it dries it cannot be re-worked; at that point I can only add upon or respond to the existing marks. In this sense, working with ink is often unpredictable. It requires an open negotiation between what I can and cannot control about the nature of the material. This notion is reflected in the imagery, as the drawings trace a direct, organic process. When things work out it seems like magic.

---

7. Experiment with undiluted ink and ink washes as above but using the colored papers and translucent vellum. As in previous explorations, how does the drawing surface affect the look and feel of the finished work? What new ideas are possible just through the suggestions of different ink solutions on various surfaces?

Markers and Other Drawing Pens

Markers and other fiber tip pens come in a wide range of colors and in many tip sizes and shapes. Across brands, inks vary in terms of color intensity and permanence, as well as type (waterproof, nonwaterproof). Waterproof markers have inks that contain alcohol or spirits, and these may bleed through certain types of paper. Waterproof markers also can be layered one color over the other without the underlying color showing through. Nonwaterproof markers have water-soluble inks that mix more transparently when colors are layered—these inks do not tend to bleed through paper.

Marker and drawing pen tips may be made of fiber, nylon, plastic, resin, or other materials. Different tip materials offer different degrees of flexibility, producing a range of lines and marks. Brush markers, for example, have flexible tips that are very responsive to varying pressures, angles, and manipulations (twisting, dragging, tapping, etc.). More rigid tips offer considerably less variation of lines and marks. Different tip shapes (bullet nose, fine, chiseled) also offer an assortment of possibilities for creating different marks and effects. Regardless of type, markers and drawing pens are great for building up areas through repetition and layering of lines (see Figures 2-16a and 2-16b) and other marks.

Exploring Markers and Other Drawing Pens

Using the prompts below, invent ways of working with ink pens to achieve a range of interesting results. Instead of relying on how you usually use these kinds of pens, as for writing, be artistically innovative and really push yourself to imagine alternative approaches. Try holding the pens in different ways, vary the pressure and angle as you draw, and find other approaches that maximize the visual and expressive outcomes you can achieve. Change the scale of your explorations by experimenting with working large, and vary your usual distance from the drawing surface by using extenders.

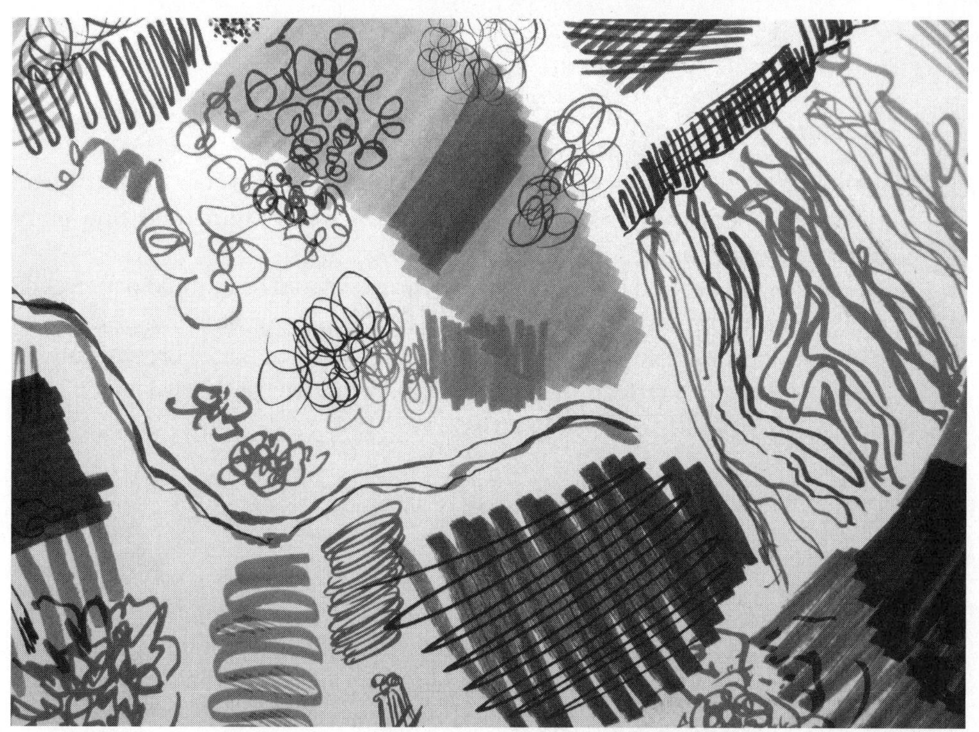

F 2-16a: Experimenting with drawing pens and markers

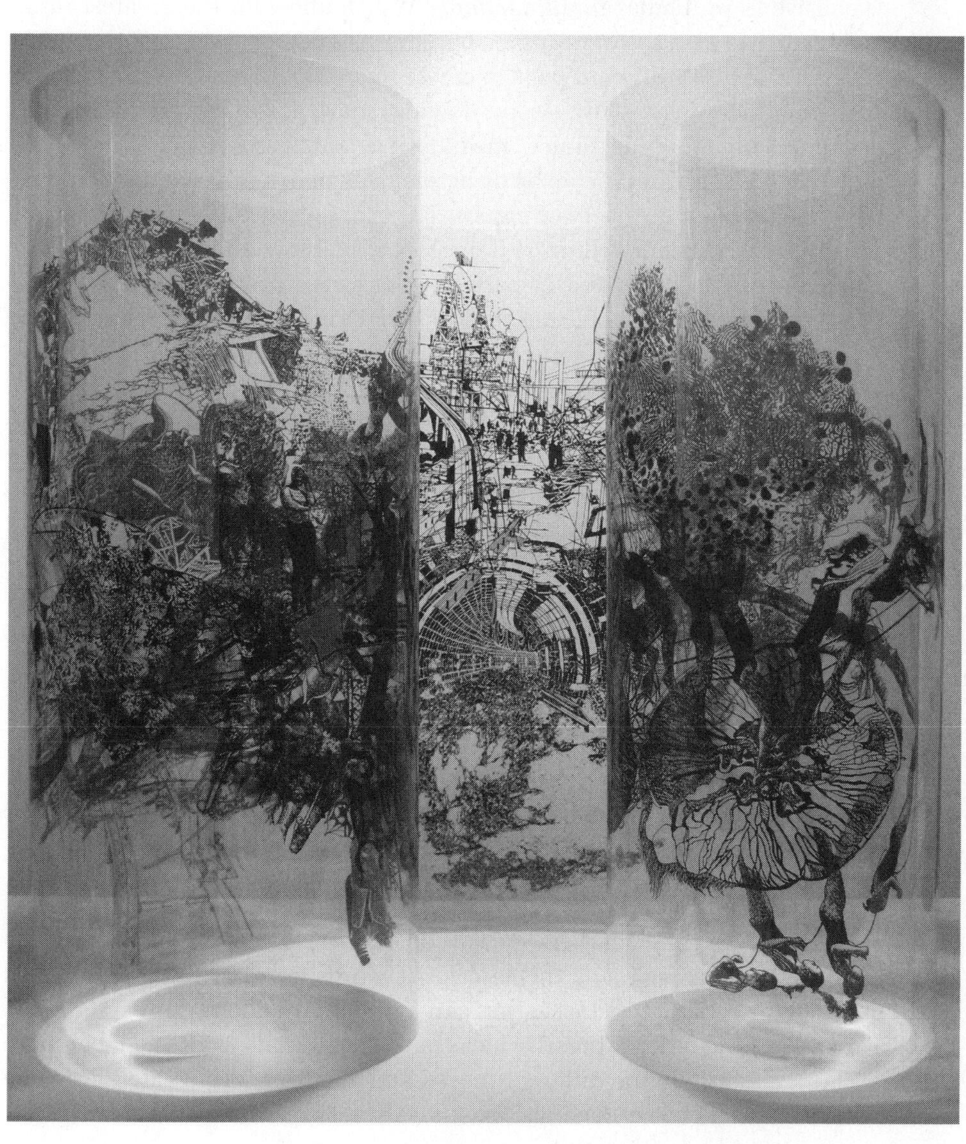

F 2-16b
Joomi Chung, Leap, 2008, ink drawing on acetate, 24" × 36" × 20"; 20" × 100" fully open.

Materials:

Black and gray permanent and water-based ink markers in a variety of tip sizes and shapes (Sharpies, brush tip markers, medium and fine point drawing pens, jumbo/magnum tip markers)

A selection of papers and other surfaces—white textured or toothed papers, colored paper (common construction paper, Strathmore or Stonehenge drawing paper in various colors), translucent vellum, clear acetate, brown butcher paper or sheets cut from brown paper bags, printed or patterned paper

Round wood dowels of various lengths

Masking tape

Getting Started:

1. On a piece of white paper, experiment with an assortment of pens and markers and push each as far as possible to create different lines and marks. Use different parts of the pen, twist your arm slightly as you draw, and vary your pressure. Layer marks to build different textures in selected areas of the paper, and create lighter and darker areas. Which pens are most responsive to particular manipulations? Which allow for the greatest range of results? Which are most uniform in the visual appearances of the marks they create? Use different pens to create lines and marks that may suggest different meanings—slow, sleepy, flowing, snarled, soft, prickly, searching, caffeinated, swooping, quiet, meandering, zingy, zooming. What other ideas can you communicate by using the pens in inventive ways?

2. Try each pen on a variety of papers. Experiment with the permanent ink pens on translucent vellum and clear plastic. How do the color, texture, opacity/translucency, and/or pattern of assorted drawing surfaces influence the effects you're able to achieve? What kinds of ideas or meanings do these different visual effects suggest?

3. Using masking tape, attach a jumbo/magnum-tip marker to one end of a wooden dowel. With a large piece of paper taped to a wall, stand at a distance from the drawing surface as you experiment making and layering lines and marks. Try this with different marker tip sizes, and lengths of extensions, varying your distance from the paper. How do these approaches affect your response as an artist working with these tools? How do they contribute to the visual effects you're able to create? What new meanings come into play as you alter the scale and distance aspects of the mark making process?

STUDIO REFLECTIONS: DRAWING WITH LIMITED COLORS

Looking at all of your experiments so far—graphite, charcoal, Conté crayon, water-soluble materials, ink, and markers—where do you see different expressive ideas emerging in certain areas? Using the descriptive words listed in Table 2-2, find as many qualities and characteristics as you can and note them on your explorations (see Figure 2-17). Find other expressive ideas in your materials work and label those as well. Think about how the different marks and effects you've created could be used to express specific ideas, feelings, moods, states, or qualities in a drawing.

Table 2-2   Expressive Ideas from Drawing Materials

strong	sheen	sheer	plush	stinging
harsh	shadow	veil	velvety	flat
intense	crevice	noisy	billowy	even
loud	light	film	airy	smooth
delicate	dappled	shaky	puffy	scratchy
frail	mottled	blanket	heavy	dry
quiet	solid	calm	stark	fluid
animated	crisp	serene	cloudy	moving
awake	sagging	edgy	muddy	pooling
fast	wilted	nervous	bumpy	runny
sleepy	snarl	playful	poke	thick
slow	menace	serious	pointed	lumpy
shimmery	fierce	soft	sharp	prickly

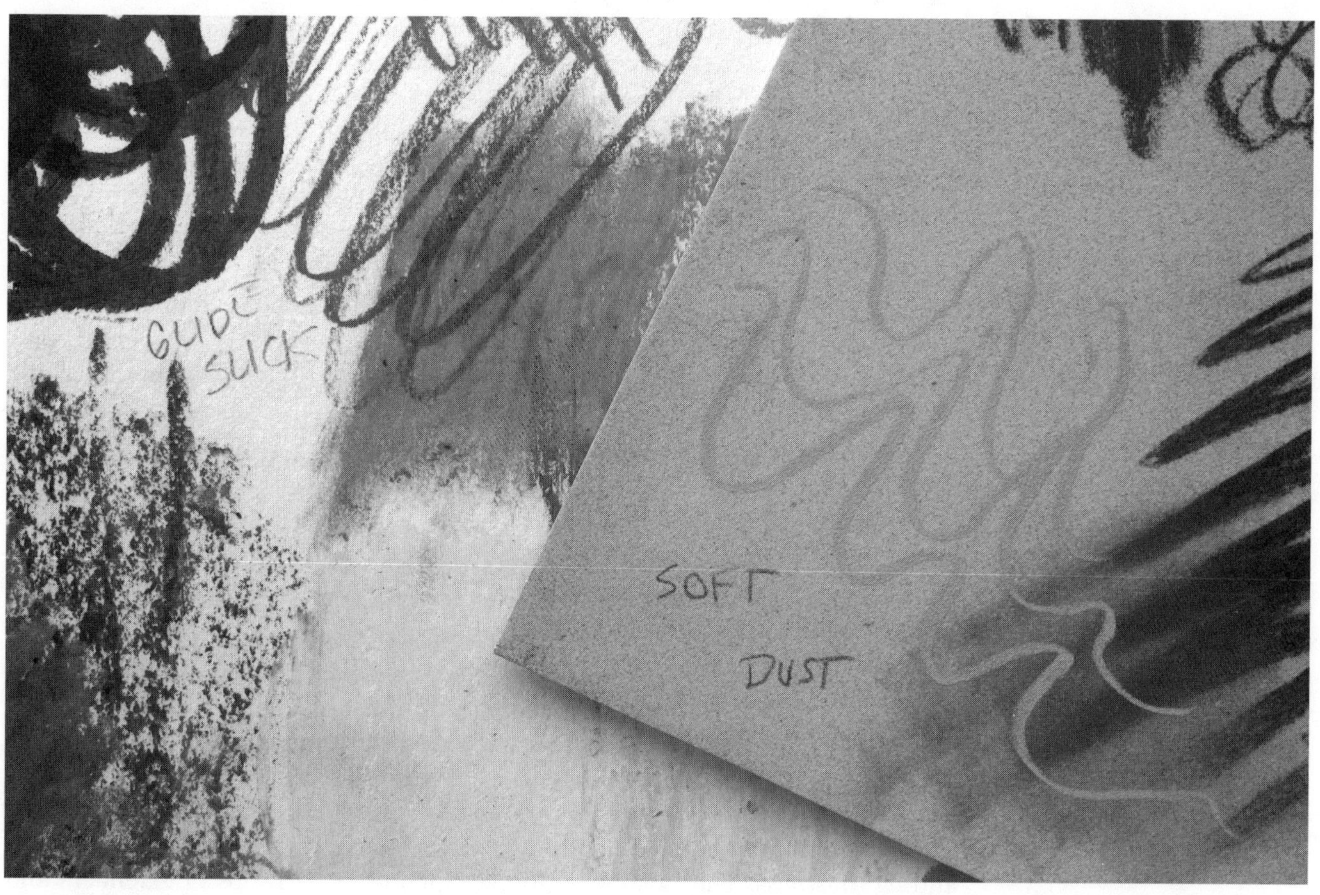

F 2-17: Exploring limited colors with a variety of materials

Reflecting on your written observations and looking at your test pages, what combinations of materials and drawing surfaces do you find most interesting? Most versatile? Most expressive? Most fun to work with? Most challenging? Most disappointing? Most surprising? Why? Compare your responses to what the artists featured at the end of this chapter have to say about their choices and use of materials.

Using what you understand about the processes of working with these materials and their potential for expressing ideas, consider how you might both introduce and revisit them in art lessons with young people of different ages. In Chapter 7, you will be asked to develop exploratory and thematic lesson ideas with these materials in mind. As you begin that work, you'll want to return to the notes and reflections you document here.

Drawing with Many Colors

Moving from a limited color selection in black and white and monochromatic work to using a full range of colors opens up an array of possibilities for creating ideas and meaning with materials (see Figure 2 in the color insert). Now, in addition to encouraging kids to think in a material—keeping in mind the physical and sensory properties of, say, dry soft pastel and the marks and effects pastel affords—we're asking them to think in color. How does that blue look when it's next to that yellow? What happens if we mix the two? What are different ways we can find to blend them? How many variations of the colors can we get? What things or ideas, or moods, could we represent or suggest in a drawing by using these colors?

There are many ways to structure opportunities for kids to experience working in color, and these approaches may isolate different color groupings so that students learn the relationships among the groups and their member colors (primary colors, secondary colors, etc.). While these concepts may be important, even mandated by school or district curriculum demands, they can be taught through students' open-ended exploration with color. Just as important, students can select and use color and color relationships for expressive purposes in their work, without the teacher having to dictate the exact colors to be used and where and how they are to appear in the students' artwork. It's important to remember that artists may never use the words primary, secondary, and tertiary in describing how they consider color and its role in their work.

WORKING DRY

Colored Pencils

The process for making colored pencils is similar to that of graphite pencils. But instead of graphite, pigment is mixed with the clay extender and gum binder, and generally there is no kiln firing involved. Wax is also added to make the material less brittle—this makes for a smooth application on the drawing surface. Generally with the wood-encased colored pencils, the thicker the lead, the softer the material.

Colored pencils vary widely across manufacturers in quality and color selection. Different brands use different qualities of pigment in terms of permanence and lightfastness. They also use different qualities and ratios of extenders and binders. Aside from traditional wood pencils with colored leads, you can find woodless colored pencils and sticks—both expand the possibilities for creating a variety of effects and for covering large areas and layering colors in a drawing.

Some brands, like Prismacolor, now offer lightfast colored pencils and these solve the problem for many artists who may have avoided the medium previously because of its potential for fading over time.

Note: Many of the kids I've worked with, especially older students, like colored pencils because of the fine detail they can get with them, the sense of control they feel they have with them as a material, and the lack of mess involved in working with them. For kids of all ages, colored pencils are a great means for clearly depicting narratives and stories (see Figure 2-18). I've found, though, that since colored pencils are often something students work with regularly on their own outside of class they have not done much in-depth experimentation with them as a medium—they tend to use colored pencils in limited ways as they would use a graphite pencil for writing. Getting them to revisit colored pencils in an experimental way and introducing new forms of the material (sticks, woodless pencils) opens up new possibilities for expression and meaning in their ongoing drawing in and out of school.

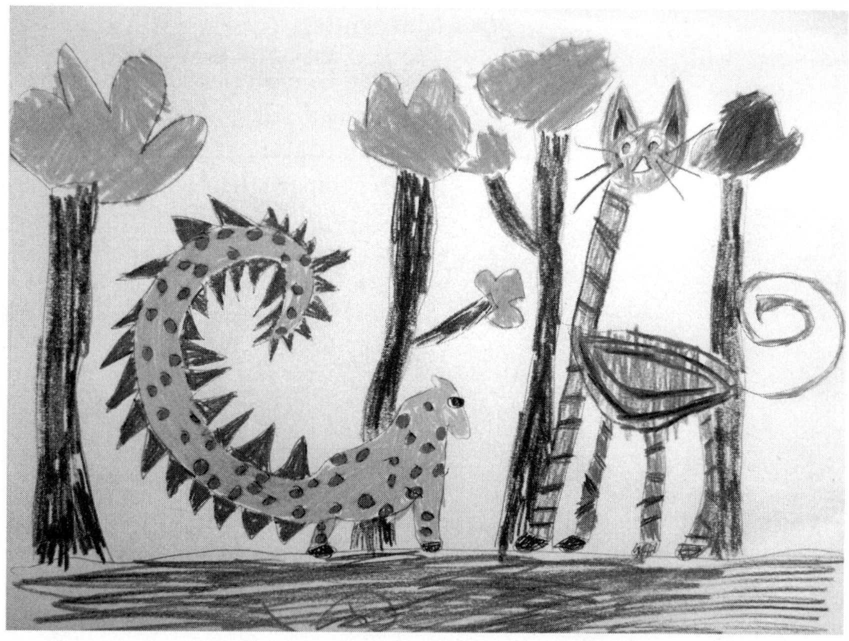

F 2-18: Colored pencil on paper

Exploring Colored Pencils

Use the prompts that follow to explore colored pencils on different papers and other surfaces, and note the ways of working that each approach provides. What kinds of effects can you create? For what ages and purposes would colored pencils be useful and practical? Keep working notes in your studio journal about your discoveries.

Artist Profile: **SID GARRISON**

For Sid Garrison, an artist who has long used colored pencil in his drawings (see Figure 3 in the color insert), working in color "provides a feedback loop that sustains me and that I don't find without color." After painting on leather for some time, he began to focus on colored pencil, a medium he considered to be "underutilized." Garrison explains,

I wanted to see if I could push it in a way that I had done, to some degree, with the painted leather works. I have always drawn and it is very natural to me, which is a big attraction. Operating in a zone that is not too crowded is also a plus in my mind. After basically twenty *years of exploration with this medium I am still amazed yearly to find new modes. Sometimes I consider them as minting new "words." To contribute new words, or even sentences, through the totality of my drawings, to the art dialogue is also a goal. Orson Wells once said, "The enemy of art is the absence of limitations." This quote is attractive to me and I feel like my chosen limitations are the colored pencil, paper in a square format and abstraction. I work flat and thus size is also a limitation in that I can only reach so far. This keeps the work intimate and I am very comfortable with that limitation and find my challenges elsewhere in the work.*

Materials:

Assorted colored pencils and, if available, woodless colored pencils and colored lead sticks—if possible try a range of colors from a less expensive, standard student grade as well as an assortment from another brand so you can compare their characteristics.

Note: To encourage young children and less experienced older students to experiment with layering and mixing colors, limit the color selection at first. When you see that they are being inventive with using the pencils by varying marks and layering color you can gradually introduce new colors.

A selection of papers and other surfaces—plain newsprint (rough and smooth), plain copier paper, white drawing paper, brown butcher paper or sheets cut from brown paper bags, black, colored, and neutral tone paper (construction paper, Strathmore or Stonehenge drawing paper in various colors), printed or patterned paper, translucent vellum
Erasers (pink rubber, white vinyl)

Getting Started:

1. Use the pencils in as many different ways as you can think of, first on a piece of white paper then on a variety of colors, textures, and opacities. Make sure to experiment with the colored pencils on dark colors and black paper. As you did with graphite, vary your pressure, angle, and arm movement as you experiment.

    What kinds of marks can you make with the tip of the lead? The sides? The edges? What textures can you make? Change your way of holding the pencil or stick. How does that affect what you can do?

2. Invent different ways of covering larger areas of the drawing surface. How can you do it with lines? Patches? Dots? Layers? Can you make a large area that looks very smooth? Rough? What are different ways to layer two to three colors? How can you do it with layering lines? How else can you do it?

3. Make sure to try all of the papers and other surfaces. How does what you draw on—color, size, surface texture, transparency—change the effects you're able to achieve? How do you respond differently to the look and feel of various drawing supports?

Crayons

The first wax crayons for drawing were introduced by Binney and Smith in 1903. Wax crayons are made from, primarily, a mixture of pigment and paraffin wax—in the form of either a hot liquid which is poured into molds then cooled and set (molded), or a paste that is forced through a die and dried till solid (pressed). You can also find crayons made from soybean oil (a sustainable resource) instead of paraffin wax (a petroleum by-product). Crayons come in a variety of colors, sizes, and shapes (stick, stump, round, flat-sided) and all of this allows for teachers to consider the specific needs of their students when choosing types and brands. For example, larger crayons are easier for small or weak muscled hands to grip, and flat-sided crayons will not roll off the table.

Molded crayons can be more brittle and may break more easily than pressed crayons. Pressed crayons are more like oil pastels in that the colors go on bold and saturated and with less flaking than molded crayons. Pressed crayons can also be blended on the paper more easily than molded crayons.

Dry Pastels and Oil Pastels

Pastels offer vivid and rich colors that can be used to create lines and cover large areas in both heavy and lighter applications (see Figure 2-19). Both dry and oil pastels are available in a vast range of colors sold singly and in sets. Deciding not only on the brand to get but also about the number and types of colors can be overwhelming (for example, in the Rembrandt soft pastel line for artists there are 14 different yellows and 22 blues). As with other materials, it's important to offer students a limited number of colors to begin with and encourage them to explore blending those colors to make new ones. If they are given too many colors at once they may be less likely to experiment and instead simply use the given colors without exploring different kinds of mark making and color mixing. A good starting range for working in color is red, yellow, blue, black, and white—with green, orange, purple, and other colors easily added when students have fully explored the previous colors. The goal is to get kids to push the available materials and to be inventive. With pastels, in addition to mark making, a major part of this is exploring the creation of new colors. How can you make your vivid red go to lightest pink? How many different greens can you make from a yellow and a blue pastel?

As discussed previously, the different consistencies of oil pastels (creamy and slick) and dry pastels (chalky and powdery) influence their blending capabilities on the drawing surface. With dry pastels it's easy to blend colors by rubbing and smearing the edges of adjacent color patches or layering one color over another and using a Q-tip, tortillon or stump, finger, or other blending tool. For oil pastels, colors can be layered but are more difficult to blend by hand (tortillons and stumps are not effective here). Color mixing can be done "optically" by creating small, repeating marks (like dashes) of more than one color side by side and keeping them separate (not manually blending). Alternately, patches of lines in one color can be layered on top of patches of lines of another color. When you stand away from the paper, your eyes seem to mix the colors for you.

Exploring Crayons, Dry Pastels, and Oil Pastels

Experiment with ways to work with each material—wax crayons, dry pastels, oil pastels—separately to achieve a broad range of results. As with other explorations,

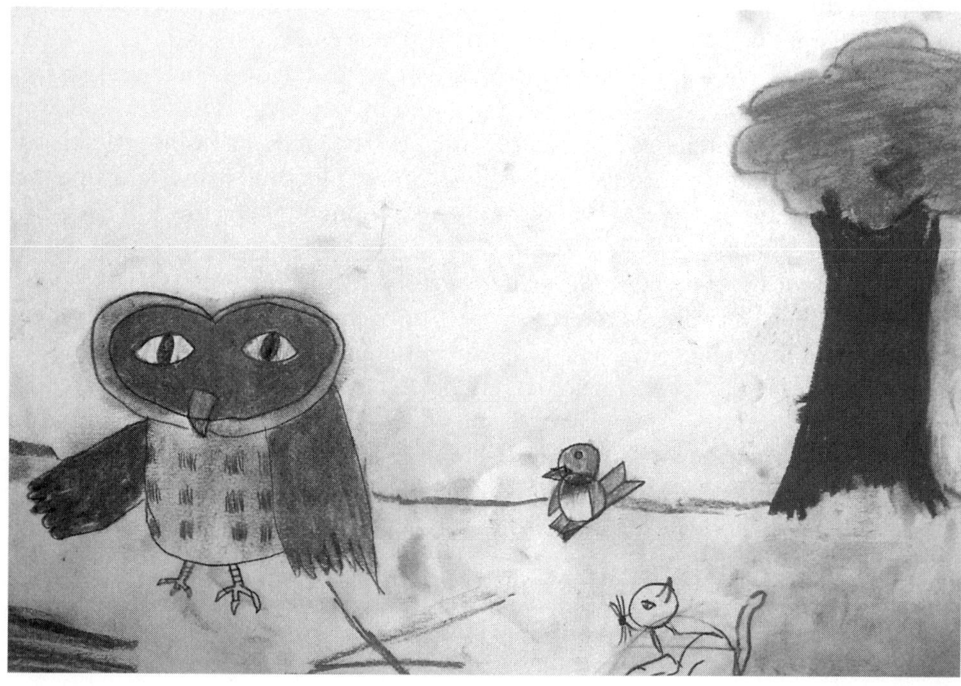

F 2-19: Pencil and dry pastel on paper

use different parts of the crayon or stick, vary the pressure and angle as you draw, and invent a variety of approaches to maximize the range of possible outcomes. Explore different ways to mix the colors you have to create new ones.

Materials:

Assorted wax crayons (an assortment of brands if possible, including Crayola Construction Paper crayons), as well as dry (harder and softer) pastels and oil pastels. Include primary colors (red, yellow, blue), pairings that are close in hue (like blues and greens, reds and oranges), and combinations that offer more contrast (yellow and purple, blue and orange). Also include black, white, and gray.

A selection of papers and other surfaces—plain newsprint (rough and smooth), smooth papers, white, black, neutral and colored textured or toothed papers (construction paper, Strathmore or Stonehenge drawing paper in various colors), brown butcher paper or sheets cut from brown paper bags, printed or patterned paper, sandpaper, translucent vellum, clear acetate

Kneaded eraser, Factis Soft Black 18 or Factis Extra Soft White eraser, and a small piece of soft bread

Paper towel, chamois, tortillons or paper stumps for blending

Getting Started:

1. Note the different characteristics of the drawing materials—their visual qualities and other properties. How are they different from what you've used so far?

2. Push each material in a variety of ways on white paper and on other surfaces. Explore each separately, then try different combinations of colors and types. Try the pastels on a variety of surfaces as well. Test each group of materials separately (wax crayons, hard and soft dry pastels, and oil pastels) so that you can see how the colors can be blended. How can you create different marks and effects by varying pressure, moving your arm in different ways, changing how you hold the crayon or pastel, and using different parts of it? What lines and textures can you make?

3. Try multiple ways of covering larger areas to create lighter and darker tones, and blocks of various straight and mixed colors. How can you do it with lines, patches, and layers? How can you do it by spreading and blending the material into the paper? Experiment blending using your finger, a tortillon or stump (for dry pastel), and a scrap of paper towel. Try this in smaller areas, too.

   Try different ways of layering colors by feathering (with short, repeating lines of two to three colors next to each other, like blades of grass), scumbling (where you apply a thin veil of color or short, broken lines or scribbles over another color so that both show at once), and cross hatching (with a group of short parallel lines in one color layered over and at an angle to a group of short, parallel lines in another color).

4. Try out different ways of removing the dry pastel—use the kneaded eraser and black and white vinyl erasers on some areas and a clump of bread on another area.

5. Explore using the more textured papers and the translucent vellum with the dry materials and oil pastels. Also try the oil pastels on smoother

paper and on clear plastic, using some colors on one side and others on the reverse. Make sure to try the construction paper crayons on dark colors of paper and compare the effect to that of regular crayons on the same surfaces. Note how the drawing surface affects what kinds of marks and effects you're interested in making, and the look and feel of the finished work.

ADDING WATER

As with the monochromatic media explored above, adding water through the use of washes and inks can extend the expressive effects of colored drawing materials (see Figure 2-20). Keep notes in your studio journal about ideas suggested by the new effects you're able to produce. How does the fluid nature of the material and the new color possibilities change your response to it and the kinds of marks and meanings you're able to produce?

Water-soluble Colored Pencils, Crayons, and Pastels

Like water-soluble graphite, water-soluble colored pencils, crayons, and pastels use a binder that dissolves in water. You can apply the colored materials dry to paper and add a wet brush for wash effects and color mixing, use the materials dry on wet or damp paper, or dip the materials in water and apply to dry, dampened, or wet paper. Again, using more or less water and a softer or stiffer brush will contribute to the range of potential effects.

Colored Pastel Wash

Standard (non-water-soluble) colored dry pastels can also be used to create washes, similar to the washes above made with charcoal and black and gray pastels. You can create pastel color washes in the same way, by using a soft brush dipped in water over the dry media applied to paper. Experiment with spreading the material, using more and less amounts of water to create lighter and darker areas. Explore mixing layered and adjacent colors to create new ones.

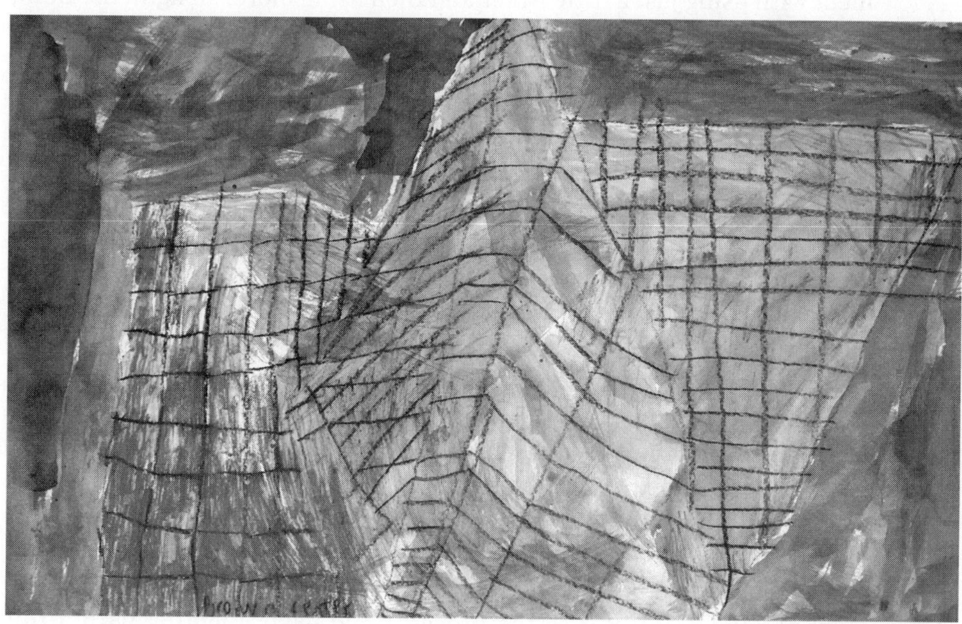

F 2-20: Drawing with water soluble pencils and crayons

Exploring Water-soluble Colored Pencils, Crayons, Pastels, and Pastel Wash

Use water-soluble colored pencils, crayons, and pastels in inventive ways to create a variety of lines and other marks. Build up darker areas on selected parts of your paper and contrast single lines and masses of lines with other marks, solid shapes, and texture patches. Also experiment with standard dry pastels to create areas of varied colors and marks. What happens when you add a wet brush to parts of your work? How does this approach suggest new information or change the mood or feeling of the work?

Materials:

Water-soluble colored pencils, crayons, and pastels in assorted colors
Dry pastels in assorted colors
Container of water
Soft hair brush (as opposed to a stiff bristle brush)
A selection of heavier papers (at least 80 lb.) and other surfaces—white and black textured or toothed papers, colored and toned paper (construction paper, Strathmore or Stonehenge drawing paper in various colors), printed and patterned papers, translucent vellum

Getting Started:

1. Make a variety of marks in small and larger areas on a piece of heavy weight white paper, experimenting with the water-soluble materials and dry pastels. Vary your pressure with the material on the paper as you work, and use different parts of the sticks. Create a range of values and tones—light areas, mid-tone areas, and darker areas where the material is built up heavily on the paper. Create spaces where different colors are placed adjacent to one another, so that you can see what happens when you add water to blend them into new colors.

2. Dip your brush in water and apply to selected parts of the paper. Experiment with using just a little water and then using more, on light, medium, and darker areas of the paper. Explore different approaches to mixing colors to see what kind of range you can get.

3. Draw into some of the wet areas of the paper with the water-soluble materials in different colors and with the dry pastels. Use this same approach of drawing dry into wet on areas of the paper brushed with clean water. How does working this way change the look and feel of the material and expand the visual effects you can create? What new ideas might be suggested through these new visual effects?

4. Using a new piece of white paper, try a different approach by dipping the water-soluble pencils, crayons, and pastels in water first and then drawing with them on dry paper. Contrast lighter and more built up, layered areas. Add a wet brush to selected areas for further blending and spreading. Try the same approach with the dry pastels.

5. Explore all of the above processes using the colored papers, translucent vellum, and printed/patterned papers. As you have throughout each exploration, note how different drawing surfaces affect the kinds of marks and effects you're able to make and the look and feel of the finished work. How does adding water to the process—and experimenting with a full

range of color drawing media and surfaces—open up possibilities for new expressive effects and ideas?

Colored Ink, Ink Pens, and Markers

Expanding the range from black to a fuller array of ink colors, both in liquid ink and in pens and markers, introduces opportunities for new approaches in layering, color mixing, and meaning of materials and the marks they create in a work (see Figure 4 in the color insert). When choosing colored inks and ink pens, keep in mind that many are not fade proof and will lighten over time. If this is an issue for the kinds of work your students will be creating then make sure to get lightfast ink materials.

Exploring Ink with Dip Pens and Brushes

Experiment with colored inks, dip pens with assorted metal nibs, and brushes. Using undiluted ink with these tools, how many kinds of lines, other marks, and textures can you create? What happens when you layer darker and lighter washes of ink diluted with water over dried parts of your paper?

Materials:

Colored drawing inks in red, blue, yellow, black, white, and other colors if available
Small cups for ink and washes
Dip pen with assorted metal nibs
Bamboo brushes or soft watercolor brushes
Container of water
A selection of papers and other surfaces—white textured or toothed papers, colored paper (common construction paper, Strathmore or Stonehenge drawing paper in various colors), translucent vellum, brown butcher paper or sheets cut from brown paper bags, printed or patterned paper

Getting Started:

1. While you are exploring the ink with pen and brush below, note its characteristics as a material. How does it behave differently from the other colored materials you've been experimenting with? How is it different from black India ink? What new possibilities does it open up for expressive marks and effects?
2. Using undiluted ink in a small container, work with one pen nib at a time on white paper to make as many kinds of lines, other marks, and textures as you can. Move the pen side to side, up and down, and in other ways.
3. Try layering lines and marks of different colors. Clean your pen nib by swishing in water each time you change colors.
4. Try out the brush with undiluted ink. Use the tip and side, trying out different angles and pressures. By dragging and twisting as you go along, what kinds of lines and other marks are possible? What kinds of marks can be made with just the tip of the brush? What happens when the brush is loaded with ink? What effects can you create by using less ink? What are different ways you can invent to layer marks, to create dense or textured areas?

Note: Remember to rinse pen nibs and brushes in water immediately after use to prevent ink from drying in them.

5. On the same paper, once the undiluted ink is dry, try out the brush with lighter and darker washes (as with the India ink washes, pour small amounts of water into separate cups and add ink sparingly until you have different values). Explore making lines and marks with the brush and diluted inks and apply the washes over some dried areas of undiluted ink.

6. Try the reverse process on a new piece of white paper—use your brush to apply light and medium colored washes in different areas, blending in some places. Once the paper is dry, use pens and brushes to draw over the wash areas with undiluted inks. Also try working in this sequence but while the wash layer is still wet or damp. What different effects can you create by experimenting this way?

7. Work with the ink and washes as above but using the colored papers, translucent vellum, and printed and patterned surfaces. How does the drawing surface affect the visual effects and suggested meanings of the finished work?

Exploring Colored Markers and Other Drawing Pens

Invent ways to work artistically with ink pens and markers to achieve a range of results. Again, be innovative and push yourself to imagine alternative approaches to using these tools. Try holding the pens in different ways, vary the pressure and angle as you draw, and think of other approaches to maximize the range of possible visual and expressive outcomes. If you wish, experiment again with the scale of your explorations by working large, varying your usual distance from the drawing surface by using extenders.

Materials:

Permanent and water-based ink markers in a variety of tip sizes and shapes, and colors (Sharpies, brush tip markers, medium and fine point drawing pens, jumbo/magnum tip markers)
A selection of papers and other surfaces—white textured or toothed papers, colored paper (common construction paper, Strathmore or Stonehenge drawing paper in various colors), translucent vellum, clear acetate, brown butcher paper or sheets cut from brown paper bags, printed or patterned paper
Round wood dowels of various lengths
Masking tape

Getting Started:

1. On a piece of white paper, experiment with the pens and markers in various ways. Push each pen as far as possible to create different lines and marks. As you did in the exploration with limited colors, use different parts of the pen, twist your arm as you draw, and vary your pressure. Layer marks to build different textures in selected areas of the paper. Create lighter and darker areas. Which pens are most responsive to varied manipulations? Which allow for the greatest range of results? Which markers are best for layering transparent areas of color to create new colors? Which are least alterable in the marks and effects they create? Use different pens and colors to create lines, marks, and combinations that may suggest distinct meanings—noisy, crisp, sparkling, electric, rushing, flowing, dense, complicated, fuzzy. What other ideas can you communicate by using the pen nibs and colors in inventive ways?

2. Try each pen on a variety of papers. Experiment with the permanent ink pens on translucent vellum and clear plastic. How do the color, texture, opacity/translucency, and/or pattern of assorted drawing surfaces influence the effects you're able to achieve? What kinds of ideas or meanings do these different visual effects suggest?

3. As you did previously, use masking tape to attach a jumbo/magnum-tip marker to one end of a wooden dowel. With a large piece of paper taped to a wall, experiment making and layering lines and marks. Try this with different colors, marker tip sizes, and lengths of extensions, varying your distance from the paper. How do these approaches affect your response as an artist working with these tools? How do they affect the visual effects you're able to create? Again, what new meanings come into play as you vary the scale and distance aspects of the mark making process, this time using color?

Mixing Media

Combining materials—for example graphite, colored pencils, and oil pastel—in a single drawing is another approach to expanding the possibilities for creating new effects and meanings (see Figure 2-21 and Figure 5 in the color insert). Many artists work in this way, using an assortment of media simultaneously. For kids, I offer a choice of two or three different media for optional combining only after they have experimented in depth with each material separately. This is a good way to encourage them to think about materials from the standpoint of the narrative ideas they're interested in making artwork *about*. With their thematic ideas in mind, we talk about choosing materials whose qualities and capabilities will be good matches for the overall subject or components and details of each student's drawing. At the same time, ideas come from materials themselves. As you've seen in your own explorations, the fluidity of ink suggests concepts that may be different from the powdery, dustiness of charcoal and dry pastel. The creaminess and density of oil pastels suggest different ideas still. For many kids, narrative ideas for the drawing emerge as the work itself takes shape, as the artist responds to the qualities and effects of the materials—another example of thinking in materials and media.

F 2-21
Mary Hafeli, Untitled (from Saint in Any Form series), 2004, graphite, colored pencil, and oil pastel on vellum, 6" × 6".

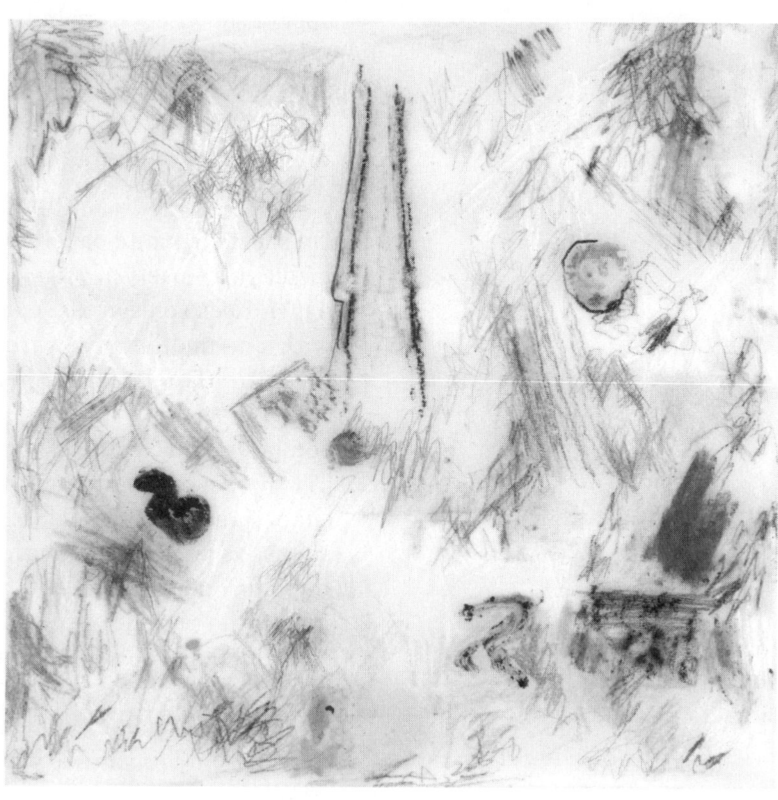

Exploring Mixed Media

From all of the materials you've worked with so far, select different groupings to combine on different surfaces. How might graphite, colored pencils, and oil pastels be used together? How might ink be combined with oil and/or chalk pastels? What kinds of surfaces offer interesting possibilities (color, texture, transparency/opacity, etc.) for these mixtures? As in all of your other explorations, push the materials to see what kinds of new effects you can create, and note these discoveries and their potential for expressive ideas in your studio notebook.

Materials:

Graphite pencils and sticks

Colored pencils

Charcoal in a variety of grades and forms (vine sticks, compressed sticks, pencil)

Conté crayons in black and white, sanguine and/or bistre

Kneaded eraser, Factis Soft Black 18 or Factis Extra Soft White eraser, and a small piece of soft bread

Paper towel, chamois, tortillons or paper stumps for blending

Dry and oil pastels in black, white, assorted grays, and colors

Permanent and water-based ink markers in a variety of tip sizes and shapes, and colors (Sharpies, brush tip markers, medium and fine point drawing pens, jumbo/magnum tip markers)

Water-soluble graphite in assorted softer and harder grades, water-soluble crayons/pastels in black, white, assorted grays and colors

Black India and colored drawing inks in red, blue, yellow, white, and other colors if available

Small cups for ink and washes

Bamboo pen

Dip pen with assorted metal nibs

Bamboo brushes or soft watercolor brushes

Container of water

A selection of papers and other surfaces—white textured or toothed papers, colored paper (common construction paper, Strathmore or Stonehenge drawing paper in various colors), translucent vellum, clear acetate, brown butcher paper or sheets cut from brown paper bags, printed or patterned paper

Round wood dowels of various lengths

Masking tape

Getting Started:

1. On sheets of white paper, experiment with your selected combinations of media in a variety of ways, playing with placement of each material on the paper. Keep some areas separate, and note how they relate to and contrast with one another just through their positioning on the page. In other areas, overlap, layer and juxtapose marks created with different materials. Find as many approaches as you can for divergent ways of using and combining materials on white paper.
2. Try these media combinations on other papers and surfaces. Try different shapes and sizes of surfaces. How do the materials combinations themselves, as well as the character of the different surfaces you've applied them to, create new effects and suggest new ideas and meanings?
3. Play with the scale of your drawing surfaces and alter your distance from the action as you work with various media. How does size and distance affect your working process and the effects you're able to create working with mixed media? What new ideas are suggested as you vary your approaches and as you see what happens in the visual results?

STUDIO REFLECTIONS:
DRAWING WITH MANY COLORS

Gather all of your color media experiments and spread them out in front of you (see Figure 2-22). As you study your results, look for different media effects you were able to create through your marks and color mixtures and relationships, and note the variety of expressive ideas these media effects suggest. Find as many qualities and characteristics as you can and label them. Think about how the different marks and effects you've created could be used to suggest specific ideas, feelings, moods, states, or qualities in a drawing—note these different ideas right on your exploration pages.

Reflecting on your written observations and experiments with media, what combinations of materials and drawing surfaces do you find most interesting? Most expressive? Most fun to work with? Most challenging? Most disappointing? Most surprising? Why?

How does working with many colors compare to working with limited colors? Do you prefer one over the other? Why or why not? What instances can you think of for which working in a limited range of colors would be more effective for communicating certain ideas than a full range of colors? What new considerations does working with many colors bring into the studio thinking process? Compare your responses to what the artists below have to say about their choices and use of materials.

Using what you now understand about the processes of working with a full range of color materials, begin to consider how you might alternate between working with limited colors and a range of colors, and between working dry and working wet, in art lessons with young people of different ages. See Chapter 7 for ways to get started with planning lessons with the materials featured in this chapter.

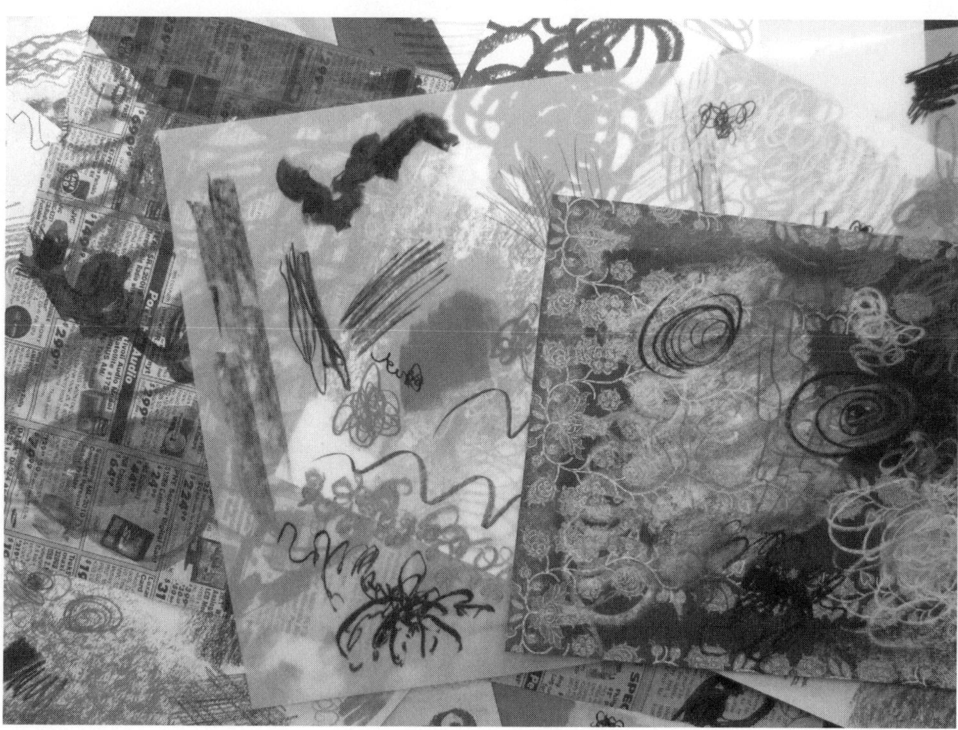

F 2-22: Exploring expanded color options with a variety of materials

More Artists on Media

From the standpoint of art materials and their use, selecting artists' works to share with kids is a matter of finding examples of artworks that collectively exemplify a range of approaches that students can both learn from and be inspired by. When I share artists' works with kids, along with interpreting narrative and other content ideas I get them to look closely at how the artists select and use materials. Looking at artworks together, we notice how the materials and the artists' particular ways of working with them create certain visual effects (such as light and dark tonal contrasts, as shown in Figure 2-23) that in turn can suggest specific ideas and meanings in an artwork. While sometimes we look at artists' works before we begin our own, I often initiate these discussions after my students have been working on their own drawings so that they don't simply copy the artists' techniques. With students' immediate experiences with materials in mind, and with their in-process artworks displayed for the group to see, the conversation is more about how "other artists are doing and communicating some of the same things we are." This creates a sense of community in which experiences are shared among artists rather than a hierarchical deference to external experts for the "right" way to do things. In this artist community environment, my students are just as likely to find great ideas to borrow from each other as they are to incorporate the approaches they admire in adult artists' works.

Older students are adept at and enjoy finding irony in artists' works, and are interested in playing with these relationships in their own artwork. Getting them to consider how a material like graphite can help other artists in this pursuit gives them the chance to be more purposeful in their own selections of media.

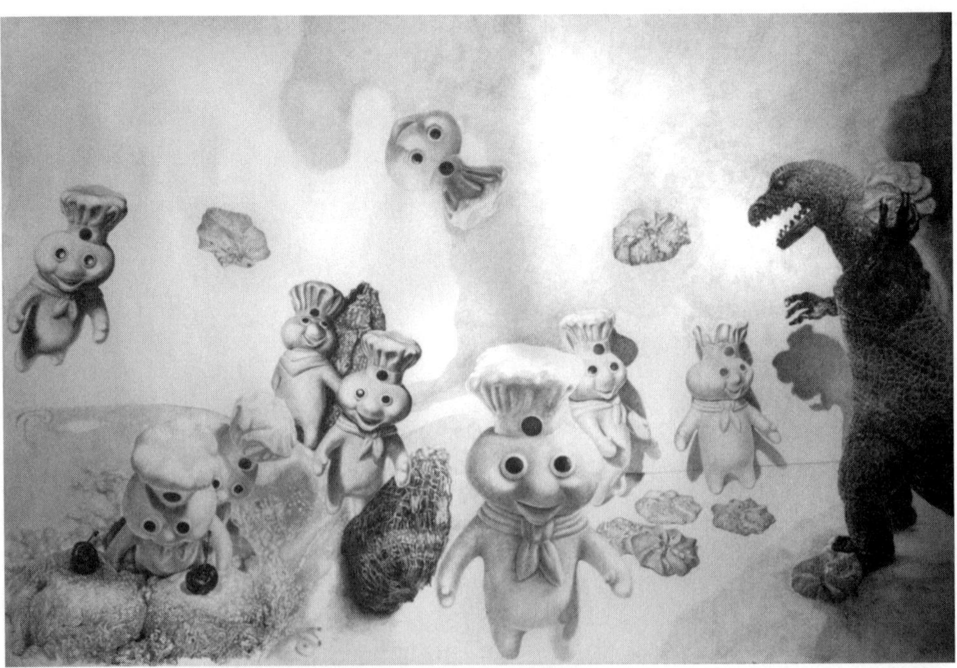

F 2-23
Monika Malewska, Desert Storm, 2006, graphite on paper, 47" × 56".

Artist Profile: **REBECCA CLARK**

Rebecca Clark works in graphite, drawing natural ephemera that she finds on the ground (see Figure 2-24). To her, the drawings are "tributes to the beauty and dignity of things separated from their whole and in a state of transition." Her works are inspired by Joris Hoefnagel's sixteenth century illustrations of "natural minutiae," Andy Goldsworthy's "collaborations with nature," and the drawings of Vija Celmins.

What would these plant forms be like to touch? How did the artist use graphite to make some parts of her drawing look smooth? Dry? Rough? Sharp? Rounded?

What feeling or sense do you get from this drawing? Is it loud and audacious? Secretive? Unadorned? Overly accessorized? What do you think the artist is intent on communicating? What is she focused on showing? How does the choice and use of graphite as a medium contribute to your interpretations? Clark comments,

When I draw roots, leaves, seed pods, etc., I want to emphasize their individuality by focusing on the tiniest details. By depriving them of color (often their most distinguishing characteristic,

at least to the casual human observer), the viewer is forced to really look. Color also tends to "prettify" nature and my intent is to look beyond the superficial to where things really get interesting! Drawing with graphite allows one to see things in black & white, so to speak.

Working with graphite is so ancient, so fundamental, so direct. There's also a purity, a naked honesty, to simple graphite that I appreciate. I like to listen to music while I draw and have often thought that pencil drawings are like acoustic compositions, stripped down to their pure, "unplugged" essence, unadorned.

I enjoy the intense introspection of working at a level of detail (hairline cracks, veins, delicate tendrils, soft fur, gentle folds) that would be hard to achieve with another medium. I tend to be obsessive-compulsive and derive a certain pleasure out of making millions of tiny circles and cross-hatches that make up multiple layers of graphite in my drawings. I love the velvety, luxurious quality of graphite when it is built up in blankets, layer upon layer! I also like the relatively clean practice of working with graphite pencil (as opposed to water or oil-based media, sculpture, or mixed media). I like working in an uncluttered environment, surrounded by basic tools: pristine white paper, a set of graphite pencils (B, HB, 5B, 9H), X-Acto knife, sandpaper block, and kneaded eraser. Shutting out the clutter of the outside (and inside!) world, my studio becomes a sanctuary and I approach my drawing with zen-like discipline and patience. Working with lean graphite pencils reinforces that purity of mind and spirit. And lastly, there are practical benefits of working with graphite. I can draw anywhere. I can take my drawing materials outside, on the road, or anywhere else. And drawing supplies are relatively inexpensive. I feel a certain amount of freedom working in such a low-maintenance medium!

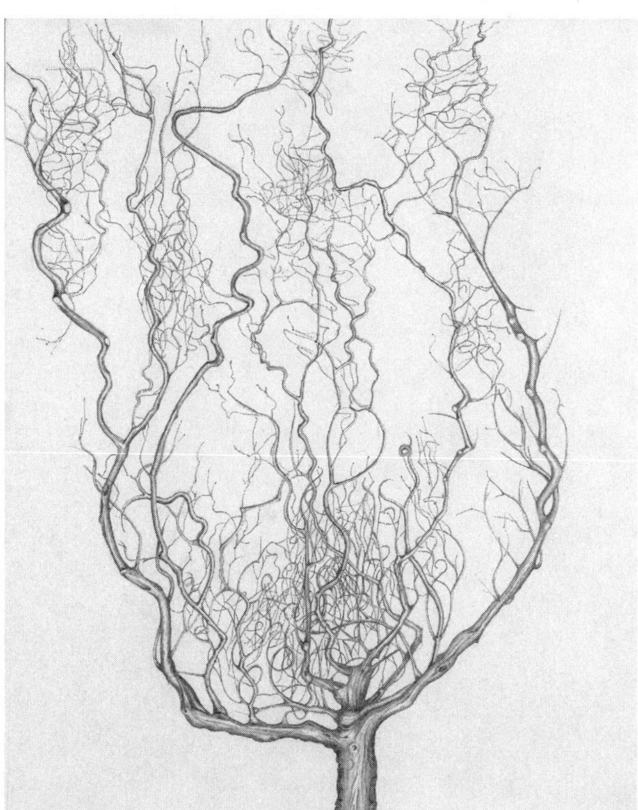

F 2-24
Rebecca Clark, Boxwood Roots, *2006, graphite on paper, 12" × 9".*

Artist Profile: **MONIKA MALEWSKA**

Like Rebecca Clark, Monika Malewska works in graphite to realistically depict individual objects, but the juxtapositions of subjects she portrays are often anything but natural (see Figure 2-25). Dolls, toys, and corporate icons merge kitsch and high art by, according to the artist, "alluding to the theme of Vanitas in seventeenth-century Dutch still-life paintings." The scenes themselves may at first appear playful and innocuous. For Malewska, the works use "the conventions of the historical still-life genre in relation to contemporary consumer culture in America." Her aim is to "manipulate the representation of objects to deconstruct the aesthetics of commercial ads and the politics of a world constituted by material desire."

How does the artist's use of graphite contribute to the feeling and mood of the drawings? What qualities and characteristics of the objects is she able to suggest or convey? Malewska says,

I work in a range of different media but I mostly consider myself a painter who also creates drawings. I do not use drawing as preliminary sketches for my paintings. Rather, I see drawing as a medium of choice that is complete in itself. From the beginning, I envisioned the Pillsbury Doughboy series in black and white, using graphite to give a rich tonal range to my compositions. I wanted the dough to appear perceptually convincing and somewhat unappetizing. I also wanted to emphasize certain textural qualities of the dough and did not think I could do this as effectively in another medium. I used a fairly extensive range of graphite, from H2 to B6, to manipulate the tonal range and create the illusion of tactile properties (from dry to sticky and gooey). This texturally rich, realistic rendering of physical properties provides a contrast with the absurd, surreal depiction of this popular commercial icon to suggest a darker or mischievous side.

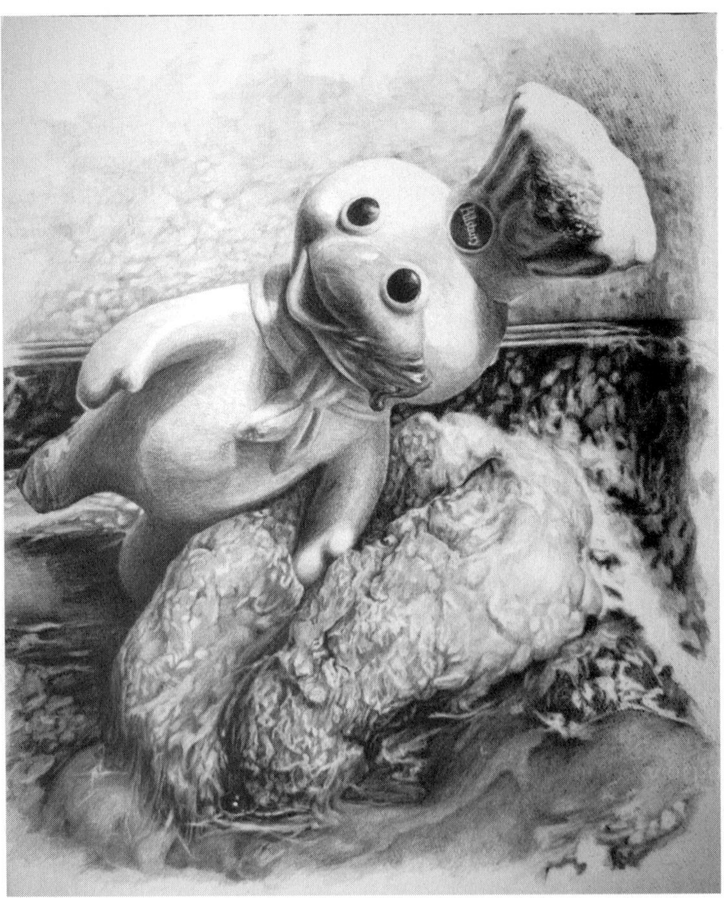

F 2-25
Monika Malewska, Pillsbury Doughboy #3, 2005, graphite on paper, 22″ × 18″.

Artist Profile: **ELAINE KAUFMANN**

According to Elaine Kaufmann, the series *International Design* is meant to "appropriate the layout and text of articles about home design" (see Figures 2-26a and 2-26b). Her use of graphite suggests the soft, grainy texture and unremarkable, unassuming informality of printing ink on newsprint. Kaufmann's work is another example of how drawing and the materials used to create it can produce visual irony through juxtaposition of opposites. Here, by using graphite to mimic the look of newspaper ads, Kaufmann invites us to skim the ad and turn the page as we would in reading a newspaper. Instead, her contradicting images and text stop us. We look harder, drawn in, unable to skim. Says Kaufmann,

F 2-26a
Elaine Kaufmann, Kid.Centric Condos, 2007, graphite on paper, 12" × 9.5". (below, left)

F 2-26b
Elaine Kaufmann, Kid.Centric Condos, 2007 (detail). (below, right)

In each drawing, I replace the article's original photograph with an image of housing in the developing world. By juxtaposing luxury with conditions stemming from rapid urbanization in the global south, I connect the fantasies of first-world affluence with the production of third-world poverty. This relationship reveals how newspapers and magazines promote the extremes of wealth and poverty as natural and unproblematic.

Since the magazines that were the source for many of the project's texts are typically glossy and colorful, I wanted to use a medium that would counter this standard format. I chose graphite for its modesty, directness, and low cost. I was also attracted to graphite because of how it can be layered on itself, the image slowly emerging with each subsequent layer. The labor required for the time-consuming drawings supports a re-evaluation of how the media assigns value.

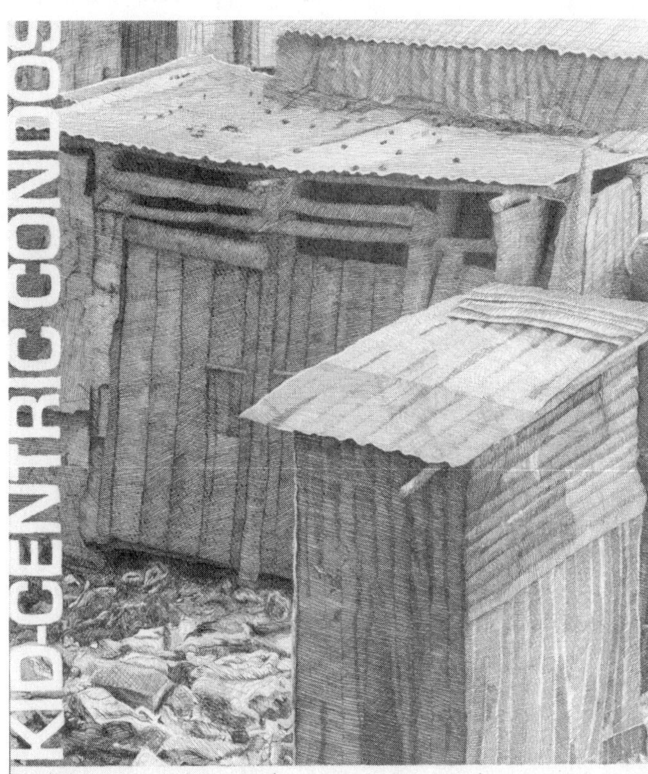

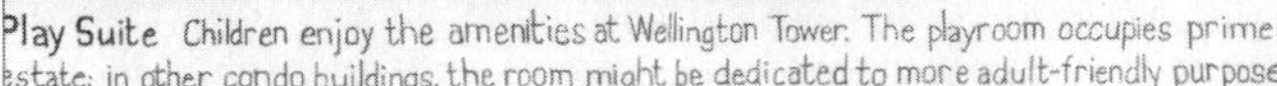
Play Suite Children enjoy the amenities at Wellington Tower. The playroom occupies prime estate; in other condo buildings, the room might be dedicated to more adult-friendly purposes

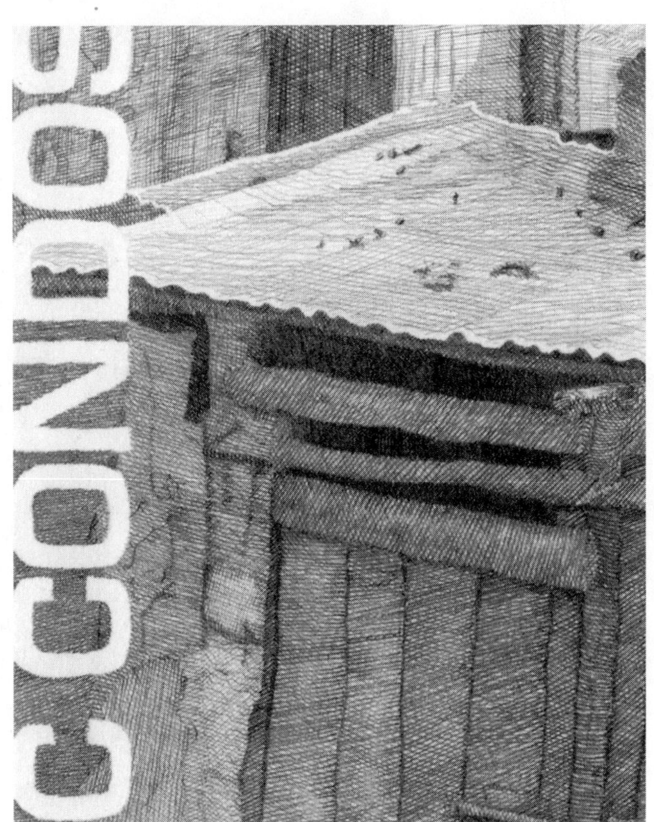

Artist Profile: **JASON D'AQUINO**

Jason D'Aquino is a miniaturist who works in graphite on found surfaces (see Figure 2-27). His drawings have been described as "bizarre children's book illustrations" and are inspired in part by the work of Maurice Sendak, Wayne Anderson, Henry Darger, and Hans Bellmer. According to D'Aquino, "just about anything I could possibly use as a drawing surface" is suitable for his work, but graphite and found surfaces are his media of choice because virtually anywhere he "can pick up a scrap of worn paper, be it a paper bag, or a cigarette pack, and with only a pencil be able to create a work of art." The hunt for and discovery of surfaces goes beyond mere convenience. He works on an assortment of materials—parchments, ledgers, maps, matchbooks, manuscripts, notebooks, letters—some of which "have come from some pretty outrageous locations." For example, he "recently exhibited a drawing which was accomplished on an original piece of Gestapo letterhead and one on a surface retrieved from a (documented) haunted house."

How might drawing surfaces themselves influence the technical approaches taken in the work and the images that emerge in the process? For D'Aquino:

Finding surfaces is half the work because the surface usually dictates what I am going to create on it. Usually things are created in miniature with high concentration on detail, obviously the matchbook renderings are about 1 inch square. I never artificially age anything, never try to make it look as if it's old. It's all about finding an object that has already aged and has a history to it—there is something more interesting to me in that. Like the work is already instilled with this additional layer. It has a depth to it, a mystery to it. To age something artificially would be cheating and it wouldn't hold my interest.

While the drawn images themselves may appear to be done in one sitting, with only the humblest of materials—the pencil—the process of creating the images is actually quite complex. D'Aquino is also a tattoo artist (something older kids would be interested to know) and he likens his drawing process to the "one shot" he has at getting it right in a tattoo: "If you're going to respect your customers, they have only one skin and the tattoo needs to be ready to go, needs to be right, you need to know what you're doing before you begin." D'Aquino says,

I sketch something out one way, then light box it, do it again backwards and I'll take elements of the drawing that I think need to be pushed or pulled and I'll blow them up bigger or smaller, collage it back together, photocopy it, reverse it back to the original size, do it again. Then shrink it down to the size of the paper I want to put it on, transfer it with the graphite, erase the dark lines, draw it all over again. It's redundant but I have surfaces that I've worked on that were one-of-a-kind. There is no second chance. You have one piece of paper, one surface. You need to have it right before you put it down.

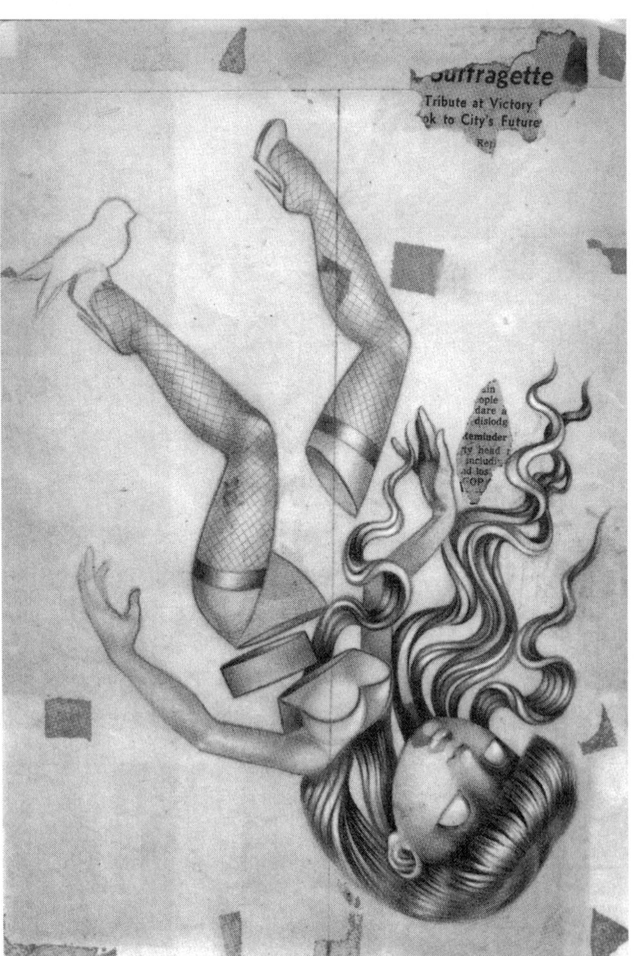

F 2-27

Jason D'Aquino, Suffragette, graphite on page from a New York senator's scrapbook, 10" × 8".

Artist Profile: **ERNEST CONCEPCION**

Ernest Concepcion says about his work (Figure 2-28):

From tables vs. chairs to cowboys vs. aliens and cookies vs. milk, The Line Wars *began as a series of over 100, 9 × 12 inches, ink drawings that emerged from sketches and doodles—the most rudimentary expression of visual thinking. The images are based on the entertainments of childhood and adolescence: Video games, action figures, strategy board games—always two forces opposing one another.* The Line Wars *is a celebration of making impulsive, nonchalant drawings, as well as a personal journey into nostalgia and an homage to geekdom.*

Like other contemporary artists who have recently engaged themes from childhood and adolescence in their work, Concepcion's subject matter is a revisiting and memorializing of the kinds of thinking and impulsive action that we associate with youth and miss as grownups. He uses ink "because it's just so immediate and accessible. It's a kind of a bring anywhere, anytime kind of tool. It's inconspicuous, too, tiny and unnoticeable to bring but can do so much damage to property or to any surface once I start drawing. Though I don't really vandalize and I don't really use any other color except black and white markers, I just like the fact that it's capable of doing that." He writes:

Specifically for The Line Wars *series, ink is just the best medium I can think of using to bring my visions directly on paper. When I was doing the series, I would draw them on the subway, on the streets, on a park bench, etc. I draw on the fly with no prior sketching and so when I make mistakes, they either turn into blood, or a crater, or a piece of rock, debris maybe—remnants of war, and only ink can somehow achieve the blackness I want. Though I could have used brush and ink, they're just too messy. I prefer ink in containers like markers and pens.*

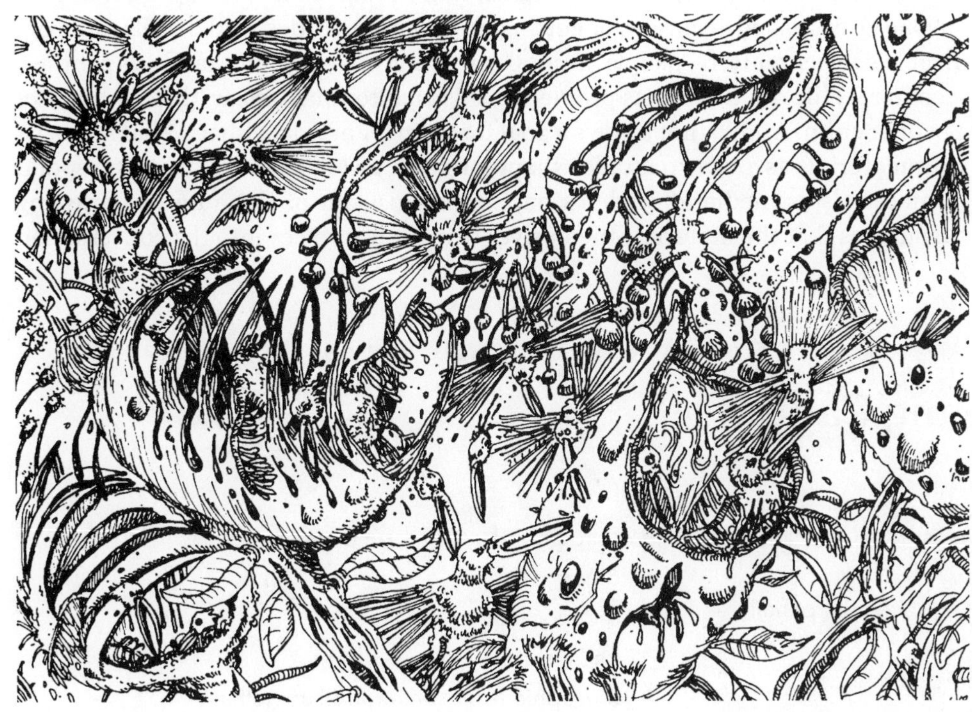

F 2-28
Ernest Concepcion, Hummingbirds vs. Venus Fly Traps (from the Line Wars series), 2005.06, ink on paper, 9" × 12".

While the drawing in Figure 2-28 was done in black Sharpie pen, Concepcion's "weapon of choice" these days is the Rapidograph pen with different sized nibs "because of the varying gauges I can use and the assurance of India ink." In this drawing, how does Concepcion manipulate and maneuver the Sharpie pen—commonly thought to offer little in the way of potential variation of marks—to create distinctive effects and areas of intense movement and action?

Thoughts about Drawing as a Studio Practice

Why do people draw? What is drawing, to you? What was it when you were seven? Twelve? Seventeen? What kinds of goals and intentions can you find for drawing in the artists' comments throughout this chapter?

Drawing is such an open concept in art today that it's hard to say with any certainty what makes something a drawing as opposed to some other art form (see Table 2-3). As we've seen, artists make drawings using traditional and alternative materials on all kinds of surfaces. They build them three-dimensionally in space (see Chapter 6) and create them digitally and on objects. For many artists drawing is more a state of mind than a defined outcome. It's an unrestricted and flexible *place* to play with not only ideas and questions but also the sensory and expressive qualities of materials and the effects that can be gotten from experimental and open-ended work with them. Some artists, like Jen Stark, find drawing to be a creative site and practice that is well suited for collaboration with other artists (see Figure 6 in the color insert, and Figure 2-29).

Younger children and teens approach drawing in artistically divergent ways, too. At times they may endlessly experiment with pencils, crayons, pastels, and pens to discover the range of marks and effects they can create, and then use particular actions repeatedly in their work. Sometimes they may think it necessary to show in their drawing only the bare essentials that serve to communicate an idea, story, or feeling. At other times they may be absorbed with capturing minute detail, or presenting multifaceted narratives with symbolic nuance.

Teachers and other adults often think that the sole aim of drawing for kids or anyone else is visual accuracy, or getting the forms, qualities, and details of recognizable subject matter—people, animals, and objects—to look exactly as they are seen in real life. As the artists profiled in this chapter make clear, this is often *not* a primary aim. And it's not always a goal for younger artists, either. What happens with materials as a drawing takes shape—that is, as artists think in and respond to materials as media and what's happening in front of them on the drawing surface—is that the materials themselves bring other voices into the conversation

---

Table 2-3   A Drawing Can Be

- a quick visual study of the essential structures or qualities of something
- an image made on a flat surface with pencil, pastels, charcoal, or ink
- a mapping of components and their relationships to a thing, place, or idea
- a preliminary plan for a more "finished" work
- a visual narrative or story
- a place where real life issues or problems can be explored, debated, resolved
- a tracing of action or movement
- a comic
- a decoration or ornament
- an illustration
- a graphic representation of something observed, experienced, or imagined
- a precise rendering, like architectural plans, diagrams, or scientific illustrations

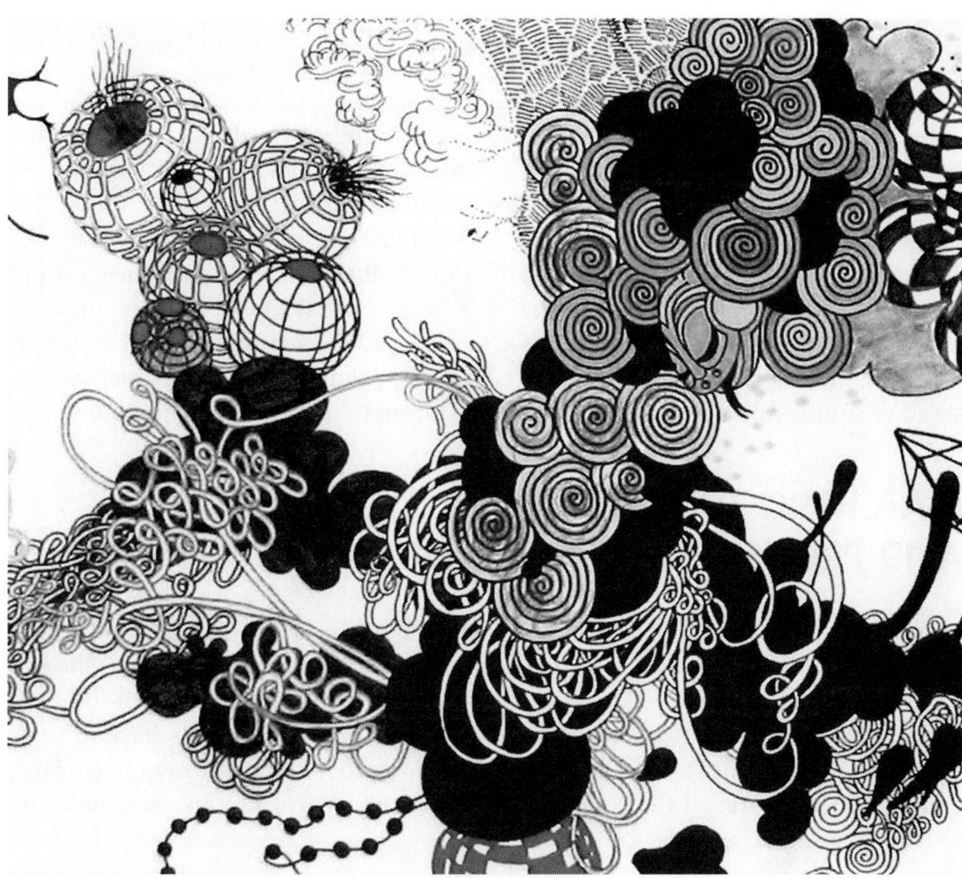

F 2-29
*Jen Stark, A Night Over.
Collaboration with Alvaro
Ilizarbe, 2006, (detail).
Photo by Harlan Erksine.*

and push ideas in new directions or suggest new meanings. In experimenting with a variety of materials yourself, you've seen how this can happen even when you're not working on something formal or finished.

In the final chapter of this book, you will revisit the discoveries made here about drawing media as you apply what you've learned to identifying concepts and skills to teach, choosing approaches, and designing lessons for kids of different ages. You will learn how to set up classroom experiences in which students have opportunities to draw from observation, imagination, and narratives of their own experiences and research, using a variety of media. In what follows are practical considerations for presenting to kids the kinds of materials for drawing featured in this chapter.

Setting up for Working with Drawing Materials

ESTABLISHING A CLIMATE OF EXPERIMENTAL INQUIRY

Establishing a climate of experimental inquiry around studio materials means that as teachers we need to resist the kinds of instructional approaches that discourage divergent thinking. Instead of showing students single techniques to master with materials, through teacher demonstration, the idea is to invite kids to discover their own varied ways of working with different media and to share techniques discovered in their explorations with others in the class. In this way, all students benefit from each individual's special discoveries.

I often invite student volunteers to lead the media demonstrations for the whole class, and my students are eager to participate. At the demonstration table with everyone gathered around, I ask students to think of different things we could do and approaches we could take with certain materials and tools, like brush and ink. I invite those who wish to demonstrate to create different marks and effects on paper, and together we imagine what those marks and effects could be used for in a drawing. The emphasis is on getting students to come up with ideas, as many as they possibly can, for working with each material. This is how they learn to really experiment, take risks, and push media in new directions instead of simply following directions or continuing to use a single approach.

MATCHING TIME ALLOTTED AND PROCESSES OF WORKING WITH MEDIA

Matching time allotted for working with particular media is a second consideration—to fully explore materials and to reflect on and share what was accomplished in the process takes time. Coordinating the sizes of drawing surfaces with the sizes of mark making tools and materials according to the time students have to work is also essential. For example, hurrying kids along to fill a large drawing surface, using a tool or material that makes tiny marks, may turn into an overwhelming and frustrating experience for them.

CONSIDERING STUDENTS' AGE, PHYSICAL CHARACTERISTICS, AND PRIOR EXPERIENCE

Students' age, strength and coordination, and prior experience with a material are major considerations for teachers when choosing media for drawing. For younger children, larger sized pencils and crayons can be easier for them to grasp and manipulate than smaller ones. While compressed charcoal, pastels, crayons, and pencils can be used regularly with young children, I use ink with dip pens and brushes with them only when I have helpers and/or a small class size. For both younger students and older students who have little prior experience with drawing materials, starting with limited media and gradually introducing new materials and surfaces to draw on is an effective way to ensure open experimentation with each. Older students especially appreciate using more sophisticated materials and this can be accomplished with the gradual introduction of special papers, additional colors of drawing materials, and special erasers and tools for blending (see Figure 2-30).

BALANCING EFFICIENCY WITH STUDENT AUTONOMY

Balancing efficient distribution and prepping of materials with kids' autonomous movement in the studio setting is another essential consideration for teachers. It's important for kids to feel like they can move about their workspace, to locate and get what they need to do their work and to share their results and see what their peers have accomplished. But too much movement can be distracting. Depending on the

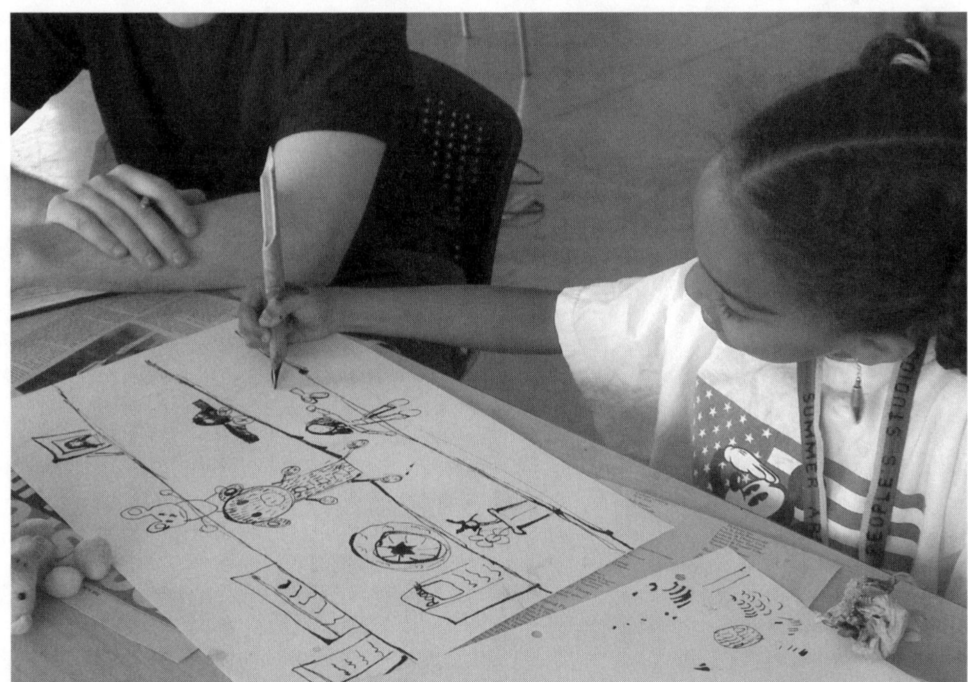

F 2-30: Ink drawing with bamboo pens

age and number of students in the class, it's helpful to have pencils sharpened, charcoal and pastels in containers, ink and washes prepared and poured in small cups, brushes, pens, erasers, and other tools set out in containers, and options for drawing surfaces laid out ahead of time. Depending on what you're working with for the class session, having students look at what is available and make individual selections about what they'd like to use that day encourages them to make thoughtful selections.

ANTICIPATING MESS AND PLANNING FOR CLEANUP

Protecting work surfaces, anticipating spills and accidents, and troubleshooting cleanup can contribute significantly to an experimental ambience in the classroom. Have kids wear smocks to protect their clothes when they work with charcoal, pastels, and liquid ink and washes, and cover their tables or desks with newspaper. Use containers with wide flat bottoms for water, with sides tall enough to support a leaning paintbrush or pen. Preplan how messy materials will be collected, stored, and washed, and how hands will be washed (buckets of soapy water and clean water for rinsing hands work well, or individual soapy wipes and wet paper towels, if you do not have room access to water).

REFLECTING ON AND ARTICULATING LEARNING

Display and discuss with students what was learned in media explorations—ask kids to point out in their work what they discovered and learned how to do with materials, and what these different marks and effects can be used to express or represent in a drawing. As much as more formal works are, these explorations are records of their learning. Displaying them with brief written explanations makes students' learning through experimentation in art visible to everyone.

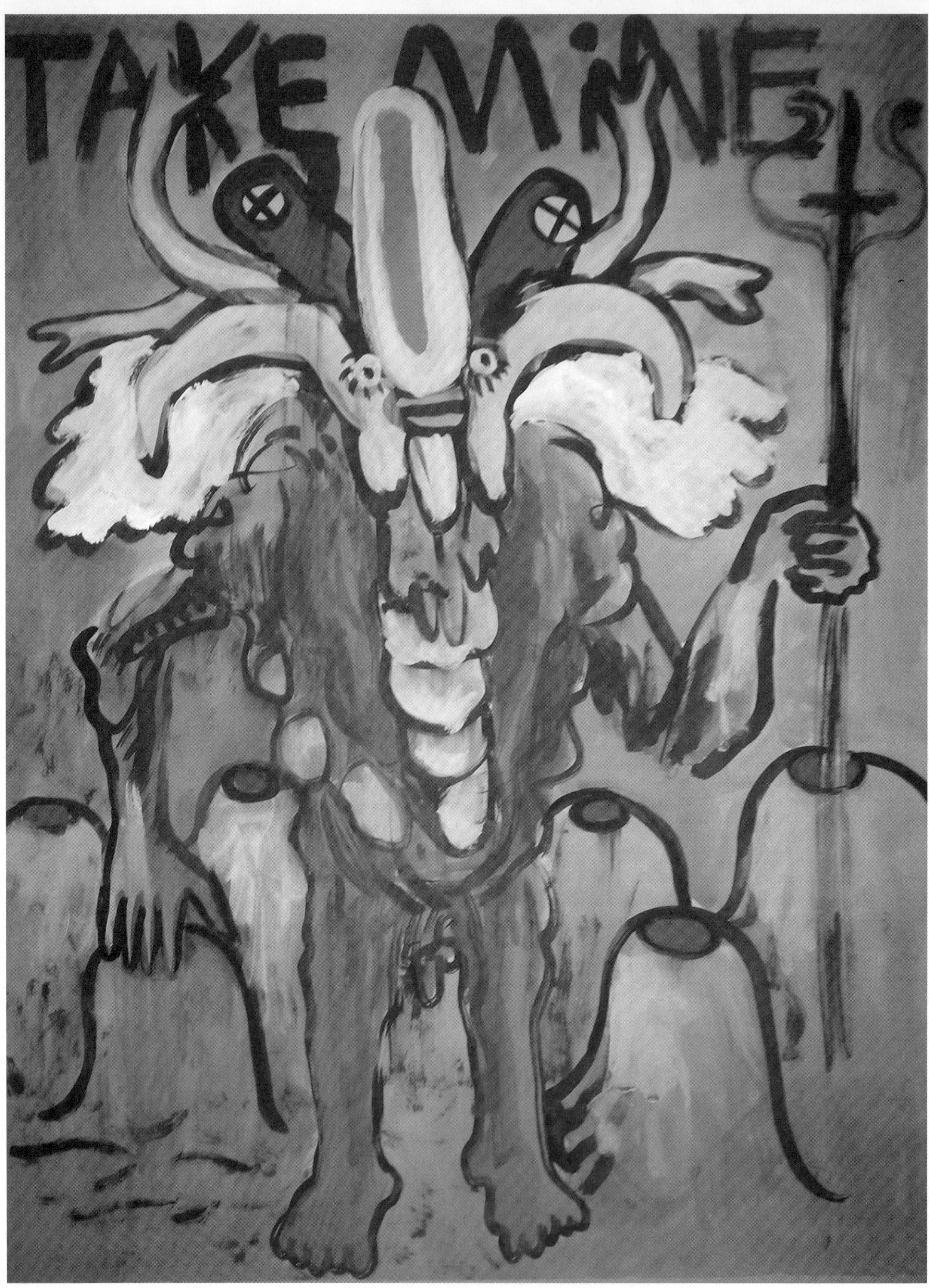

Ben Campbell, Take Mine, 2012

Working Wet

3

Tempera,
Watercolor,
Gouache,
Acrylic, and
Oil Paints

. . . I laid down the tone that I knew the painting was going to have. And I figured out then what was going to be white and what was going to be yellow, and how much color the painting could carry and still be the red studio. And it just evolved over the days. You see dead spots, and you enliven those. And then that makes that spot maybe look a little dead there, so you put some orange up there, and it all responds to what you've done.

—Susan Rothenberg, on the painting Red Studio (2002–2003)[1]

THE PROCESS OF ART MAKING for young people relies on independent decisions and judgments, aesthetic choices and edits, and other actions with materials—just as it does for adult artists. This thinking and practice about artwork "in the making" draws on insights developed through direct experience with the materials at hand, the qualities and characteristics of those materials in terms of what can be done with them, and the technical and expressive potential they afford. In the area of painting, experiential insights about materials center on paints and related materials, brushes and other mark making tools, and supports, or surfaces for painting.

What are the qualities of tempera, watercolor, gouache, acrylic, and oil paints? What kinds of brushes, tools, and supports can be used and to what visual and expressive ends? What colors can be discovered through mixing and blending and

---

[1] Art: 21 (2005e). Interview—Susan Rothenberg: The Studio. Retrieved July 19, 2013, from http://www.art21.org/texts/susan-rothenberg/interview-susan-rothenberg-the-studio.

how might those colors suggest meaning of different kinds? In this chapter, we investigate the characteristics of a variety of paints that are mixable with water, and, as in Chapter 2, explore each material through open-ended but systematic play. This play with a purpose leads to understanding how different kinds of paint, tools, and supports create visual effects that communicate ideas in an artwork. With a personal, experiential understanding of diverse painting processes and approaches, teachers can encourage in students the kind of experimentation and skill development, independent judgment, and aesthetic awareness that are at the heart of the art making experience.

Figuring out What Materials Can Do

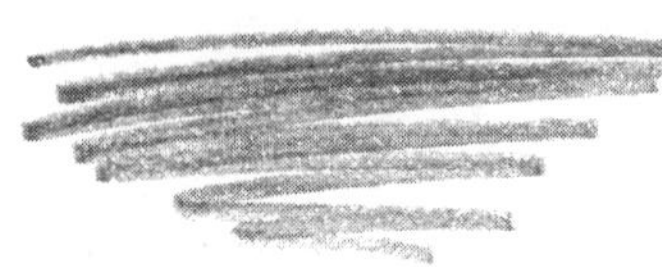

CHOOSING MATERIALS, SUPPORTS, AND PAINTING TOOLS

How might the creaminess of tempera paint and gouache—and their opaque, velvety, or glossy finish when dry—suggest meanings that are different from those conveyed by the flowing transparency of watercolor? What are some ways that paint can be used to create different marks and effects that in turn may communicate distinct ideas? Look carefully at the paintings in Figures 7 and 8 in the color insert and, as you did in Chapter 2, make a list of descriptive words that come to mind for each work. How do the artists' uses of oil paint and the marks, arrangements, and effects they create communicate these ideas? How have the artists taken paint, a material, and used it as a *medium* for communication?

Aside from the expressive potential of various paints and the technical approaches they encompass it's important for teachers to understand painting materials from both a safety and developmental, or age suitability, standpoint. Regarding safety issues, some pigments used in paints are organic and others are inorganic, or synthetic—and some organic pigments, such those made with cadmium, are toxic and not approved for use with children.[2] Throughout this chapter, the paint colors presented in the materials explorations sections are certified nontoxic and approved as safe for use with children. When choosing paint colors, you should always read the manufacturer's information carefully to determine their suitability for use with young people.

Among a range of painting materials that are approved for use with young people, what kind of paint is best for very young children? For middle school and high school students? What kinds of paper and other supports work well with different types of paint? For the studio explorations that follow, each material is presented separately with suggestions for systematic exploration and experimentation. Beginning with limited color and ending with a full range of color, explore the materials using the open-ended prompts in each section. As with the drawing materials in Chapter 2, use your studio journal to document the expressive effects that different materials, tools, and painting surfaces create, and the concepts,

---

[2] While Cadmium Red is made with cadmium, which is very toxic, Cadmium Red Hue is formulated to look like Cadmium Red but does not contain cadmium. Many paints with names containing the word "hue" are nontoxic and approved for use with children (check manufacturers' specifications).

skills, and ways of thinking that can be taught with them. Also note the practical applications of your discoveries for choosing and using these materials with kids of different ages. As with drawing materials—and as you'll see with other media as well—a good approach is to invite kids to experiment with a single painting material or limited materials at first, and encourage them to create the greatest range of effects possible. For more experienced students, more colors, a variety of brush and tool options, and other types of paper or other supports can be introduced to extend the possibilities. Be sure to explore all of these options in depth so that you can inventory for yourself the expressive potential of each combination.

Paper and Other Supports

To stand up to the application of wet materials, papers for painting are generally heavier than those used for drawing. They vary in their surface, color, and size, and all of these characteristics influence the visual and expressive effects that can be achieved. As with drawing, visual uniformity in students' works can be avoided by giving kids choices regarding size and type of paper, as appropriate.

Many of the considerations for drawing surfaces apply to the medium of painting. Student-grade and professional-grade papers differ according to their durability and permanence. Sheets of student-grade paper (at least 80 lb. to reduce buckling, heavier is better) are suitable for younger or less experienced kids and for general use by students of all ages (Strathmore, Bienfang, Canson, and other manufacturers offer a variety of student-grade papers specifically for painting). Cut assorted sizes of squares and long rectangles and have these available along with sheets from standard ream sizes. For very large individual paintings and for murals, paper from rolls (36″ or 48″ wide) can be stretched out and taped to a wall. As a class, brainstorm other surfaces that could be interesting—for opaque paints, brown paper grocery bags trimmed into sheets, panels cut from recycled boxes, and patterned papers are possibilities. When using acrylic and oil paints, canvas pre-stretched on wood frames or rigid boards come in a variety of sizes and can be added as surface choices, along with hardwood panels. As students become more experienced with a particular painting material, let them select the kind of surface they would like to work on, without making the number of choices overwhelming.

As with drawing, many artists go beyond traditional surfaces to seek out alternative supports for their work, such as repurposed paper, vintage paper ephemera, rigid boards, fabrics, and three-dimensional objects (see Figure 3-1). Aside from these options, students can use painting materials when making prints (see

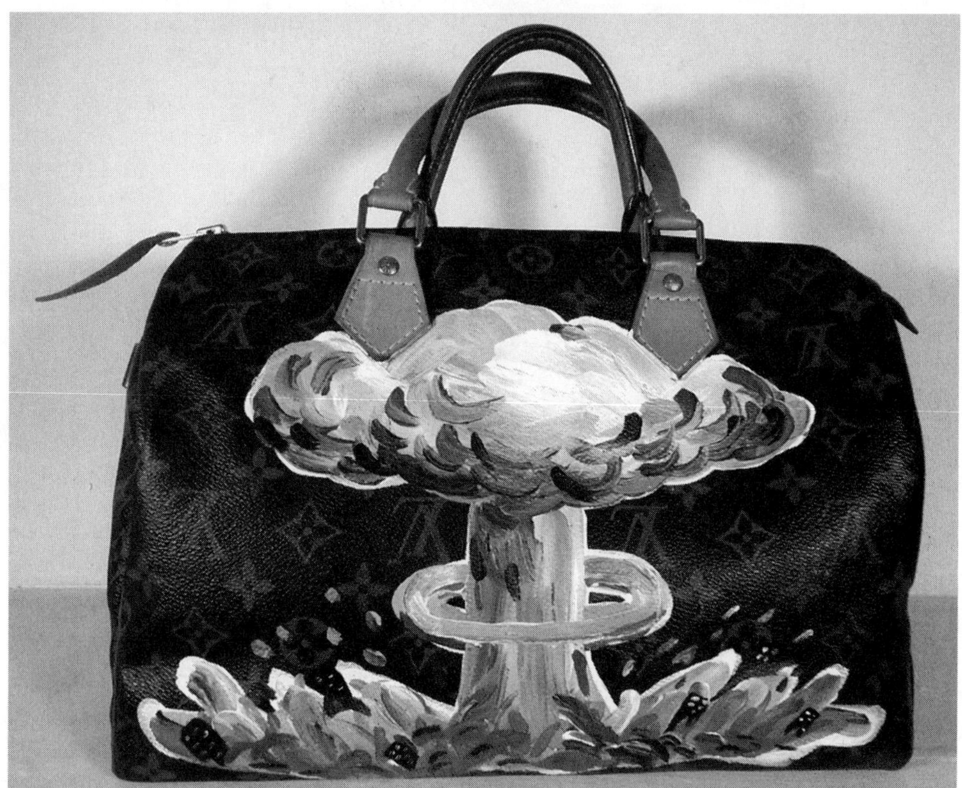

F 3-1
James Bradley, Black Friday, 2011, acrylic on handbag, 9″ × 12″ × 8″.

Chapter 4) and collages (see Chapter 5), and on the surfaces of three-dimensional objects they create (see Chapter 6).

Brushes

There are hundreds of different types of brushes for painting, and it can be challenging to identify those that will best serve specific painting situations. The consistency and physical qualities of various paints call for certain types of brushes—stiff bristles versus soft hairs, for example—while considerations like the area of painting surface to be covered and visual qualities of marks to be made influence selections about brush size and shape. Brushes with long handles allow more distance between students and their work, so kids have the option of standing while working and have a fuller view of their compositions as the work progresses. Shorter handled brushes are good for close detail work. Short, wide and flat, and fat and rounded handles are often good for very small hands to grasp with growing control. These can also be good for students whose physical characteristics make it difficult for them to hold thin-handled brushes.

In the materials explorations that follow this section, I suggest particular brushes for you to experiment with based on the type of paint featured (see Figure 3-2). As you try out different brushes, aside from noting how they work with various types of paint keep track of their suitability for kids of different ages and physical capabilities. When choosing brushes for the classroom, you should invest in the best brushes you can afford and not opt for the least expensive (these typically do not last very long).

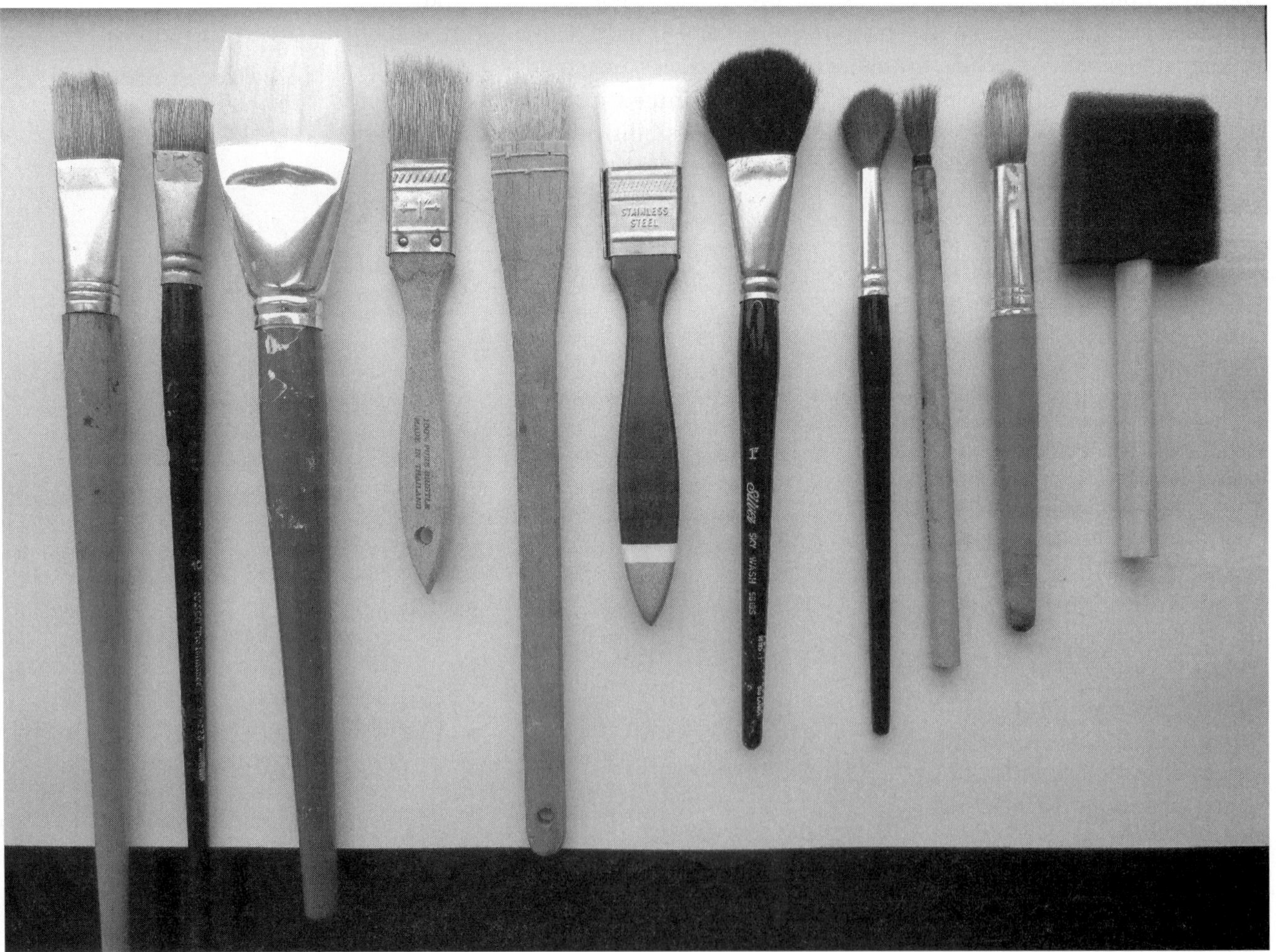

F 3-2: Common paintbrushes, from left: flat bristle, bright bristle, bright synthetic, chip bristle, flat hake, flat wash synthetic, wash hair, round hair, round sumi hair, round bristle, foam

Proper care of brushes is simply washing thoroughly with mild soap and water after use and, when dry, storing upright in a container with the handles down.

Common brush shapes include flat (flat ferrule[3], square brush end, medium or long hairs), bright (similar to flat but with shorter hairs), filbert (flat ferrule, oval brush end, medium or long hairs), round (round ferrule, conical brush shape), wash (flat ferrule, wider than flat brushes, with square or oval brush ends), and mop (rounded version of wash brush). The fibers used in brushes range from squirrel, ox, sable, and other soft hairs to stiffer boar and hog bristle to synthetic—the softness or stiffness of the fiber makes it work best with more fluid and thin or more creamy and thick paints. In addition to width measured in inches, brush manufacturers use a numbering system to specify size—from 20/0 (extremely small) to 30 (large). The size of the brush, type of fiber used, and quality of construction directly affect its cost.

Other Painting Tools

Like drawing, painting for many artists is in large part about mark making on a surface. While different types of brushes made of hair, bristle, or synthetic fibers offer a wide range of visual effects there are other painting tools that further expand the possibilities for mark making. Foam applicators, foam brushes, and foam rollers, sponges, bunched up paper towels, and crumpled stiff paper are examples of alternatives to traditional brushes. Artists also alter painting tools and common household objects and use them to apply paint to create new and interesting effects.

Giving students too many options with regards to painting tools tends to result in them not mastering any of the tools, as they move from one to the other in quick succession, attracted by the novelty of each. As teachers of art, one of our goals is that students develop skills and expertise with studio materials and tools. To this end, it's best to begin with limited options, such as one or two brushes, and gradually introduce new tools as you see that students are deepening their skills. The idea is to push a single tool in many directions, getting to understand and put to use its various capabilities, before considering a new tool.

Paint Holders/Palettes

Artists have myriad ways of dispensing paint and setting up for painting. When planning for painting in the classroom, it's important to consider each student's spot as an area of unobstructed action and provide easy access to paint, a spot for mixing colors, and water and a sponge or rag for blotting the brush after rinsing in between colors.

Wet paints are best presented in a way that keeps the colors separate from one another and allows for mixing on the painting surface or on a tray before applying to the painting surface. For tempera, plastic palettes shaped like muffin pans (or repurposed metal muffin pans) are a good size; alternatively, flat plastic containers with lids (for storing dispensed paints between use) can cut down on cleanup and waste. I set these on a repurposed baking sheet or tray of a similar size. For tube watercolors and gouache, white metal butcher trays or palettes with smaller wells work well for dispensing paint and mixing colors. For acrylic and water-mixable oil paints, disposable palettes made of sheets of treated paper cut down on cleanup in the classroom. Dried forms of tempera, gouache, and watercolor (large pans, pans, or half pans) come in their own tray.

---

[3] The ferrule is the part of the brush that fastens the hairs to the handle.

Water Containers

Students need access to containers of water so they can rinse their brushes before changing paint colors. Containers should be tall and wide enough, and made from plastic that is of sufficient thickness, to handle the weight of brush handles resting against the sides when the container is filled with water. Quart-sized, wide bottom containers made of translucent plastic work well so the color of the rinse water is visible—then the water can be changed when needed. Repurposed deli and restaurant food containers are ideal for most situations.

Drying Systems for Wet Artwork

Kids need to know what to do with their paintings when they are finished, and teachers should have a plan ready to go before the painting activity even begins. Depending on your classroom setup, class size, size of the art works, and budget, you can designate an out-of-the-way section of the floor, use available ledges or shelves, or invest in a drying rack with stacked wire shelves that flip up and down to store individual works safely. For paintings done with thicker paint, a clothesline and clothespins strung inside the room works well.

Managing Mess

Painting can be a messy activity, and that's part of its allure. It's essential to have in-process and end-of-class cleanup strategies in place that anticipate spills, smears, and hands that need washing. Students should wear some kind of protective covering while painting—I always have oversized shirts available, even for older kids, and I require that they be worn in most circumstances. Some teachers keep stain remover in the art room so that major spills on clothing can be treated immediately, with a note sent home with the student. Covering tables with recycled newspaper and having plenty of paper towels, rags, and cleaning sponges on hand will also help to minimize the disruptions and time involved in cleaning up—once dry, painted areas of table covers can be further recycled as collage materials (see Chapter 5).

Protective Sprays

Although not generally necessary and often not recommended because they may dull color vibrancy, spray fixatives can be used to seal materials that remain water reactive when dry (like tempera, watercolor, and gouache). Once again, they are not approved for use in the presence of children—always read and follow all directions and safety warnings carefully when using protective sprays.

Experimenting with Paint

As discussed in Chapter 2, presenting students with limited options to begin with—in painting this would be one or a just a few colors and one brush—and encouraging them to find many ways of working within those limitations forces them to be inventive and resourceful, practice flexible and divergent thinking, become fluent with ideas, and take risks through in-depth experimentation. They learn to think *in* paint as they push the selection of colors, brushes, and tools in a variety of ways to develop an inventory of marks, mixtures of color, and other effects they have learned to achieve. As with all materials explorations, we share our results and talk about how the marks, new colors, and effects students have created might suggest particular ideas in a painting. We then use these findings as we turn to creating works based on ideas and themes. When students are presented with too many colors and brushes at once, they are likely to forego sustained experimentation with color mixing and mark making, thus missing the learning that will allow them to create more accomplished and visually interesting paintings.

New papers and other supports can be added as options along with additional colors and brushes as students gain experience. As with drawing, offering choices for what to work with and on allows students to make thoughtful, informed choices instead of continually opting for materials that are novel or convenient and using them in a limited way. The painting materials themselves should flexibly afford divergent uses and applications—mixing, layering, thinning, and so forth—so paints, brushes, water, and other mark making tools, and a growing variety of surfaces on which to paint, are typically all that is needed. As you complete the activities that follow, sequenced for you to experiment one by one with a range of painting materials and supports, continue to keep notes as you work with each type of paint, tool, and surface. Remember that the goal of exploring with paint is to learn about the qualities and potential of different types, how separate colors can be combined to make new ones, what different brushes and tools can be used for, and how various surfaces influence the effects that can be achieved. We experiment as teachers not so that we can then direct students to mix a certain color or create a particular effect—but rather so that we can teach students the processes of exploring and discovering these things for themselves. Table 3-1 contains some ideas for focusing your work once you have explored in depth the different materials featured in this chapter.

TEMPERA

Paint

From the Latin *temperare*, meaning blending or mixing, tempera paint is a term that has several meanings, and because of this there is some confusion about the paint to which it refers. The oldest form of tempera—made with egg to suspend and bind the paint's ground pigment—predates oil paint as an artists' medium and was used widely by artists in the Middle Ages. Around the second third of the twentieth century in the United States, the term "tempera paint" began to be used synonymously with "poster paint"—a fast drying, water soluble, and inexpensive opaque paint popular with sign painters and graphic artists, as well as with teachers for use with children in schools. Tempera is known for its opacity, richness of color, and matte (not shiny) and flat (not textural) quality when dry. Because of its rich colors and ease of cleanup (soap and water), tempera is used widely in art classes for children and teens.

Today's tempera paints intended for young people's art making are composed of ground pigments and binders other than egg (forms of wood glue, for example). They are sold in ready-to-use (pourable) forms in varying viscosities and quantities, and as cakes in solid form and powders to be mixed with water before use. Some manufacturers advertise their tempera paint products as lightfast, but tempera is not considered a professional artists' medium because there are no scientifically based permanency ratings available that serve to establish its archival integrity. Ready-to-use tempera is sold by a number of companies, and some manufacturers offer different grades of the product—"premium" or "premier" lines often have a higher pigment concentration and/or thicker consistency than lesser grades or "student" lines.

Table 3-1 Ideas for Focusing Painting

- A painting based on a part of something—a cropped portion of another painting or an object, a part removed from or attached to a larger object, figure, etc.
- A painting that incorporates a tool or common object.
- A painting that shows people together or apart from one another.
- A painting that features a pet or other animal in its daily routine.
- A painting of an observed, remembered, or imagined outdoor scene.
- A painting that extends the image or ideas from a previously created drawing, collage, print, or sculpture.
- A painting of a place that uses color and other design elements to communicate a feeling about that place.
- A painting that shows people in action or motion—moving, bending, reaching, etc.
- A painting of life forms on a newly discovered planet.
- A painting of a scene or event from a different historical period.
- A painting that translates and/or builds upon the instrumentation, melody, and tempo of a piece of music.
- A painting that is based on building up areas of paint, or removing and erasing them.
- A painting that camouflages an attached object or collage element.
- A painting that frames an observed, remembered, or imagined view from a window or doorway.
- A painting that features a light source and its visual, spatial, and/or dramatic qualities and functions.
- A painting that depicts an object but supplies it with a human-like characteristic.
- A painting that responds to a poem, or an excerpt from a poem.
- A painting of yourself in a favorite or memorable scene from a book.

- A painting that suggests the feeling of a familiar room or part of a room.
- A painting that transforms a common object or piece of furniture.
- A painting that transforms a wall.
- A painting that commemorates an event.
- A painting that is about an action or movement—bolt, bounce, dart, flee, flick, hurl, ram, propel, rush, scamper, scramble, scurry, spin, streak, swerve, swoop, whisk, zoom, etc.
- A painting that presents a point of view about a pressing issue.
- A painting that plays with scale—substantially enlarging a tiny object or detail, or miniaturizing a massive one.
- A painting that shows a scene or subject from an unusual vantage point—looking down from above, looking up from below, close up, far away, through a keyhole, etc.
- A series of paintings that show an object or scene at different times of day or in different kinds of light.
- A series of paintings that depict the same subject or theme but use different color combinations to play with its meaning.

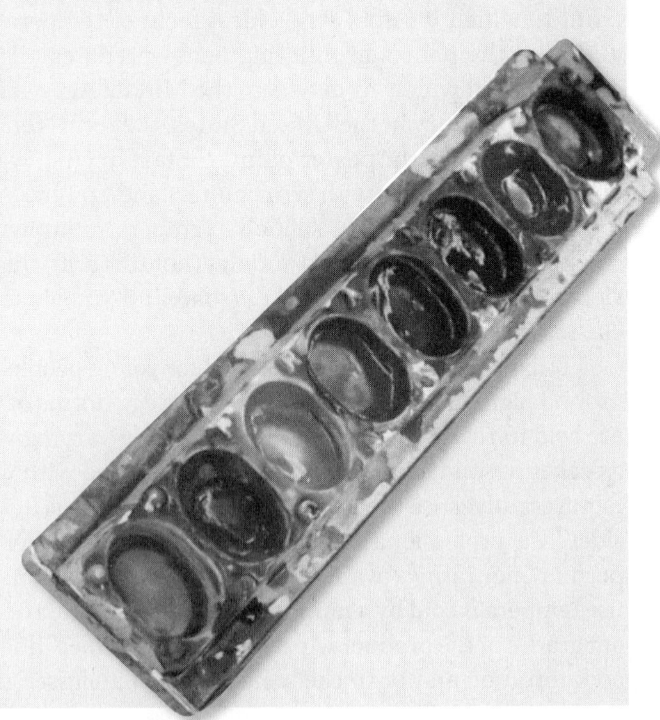

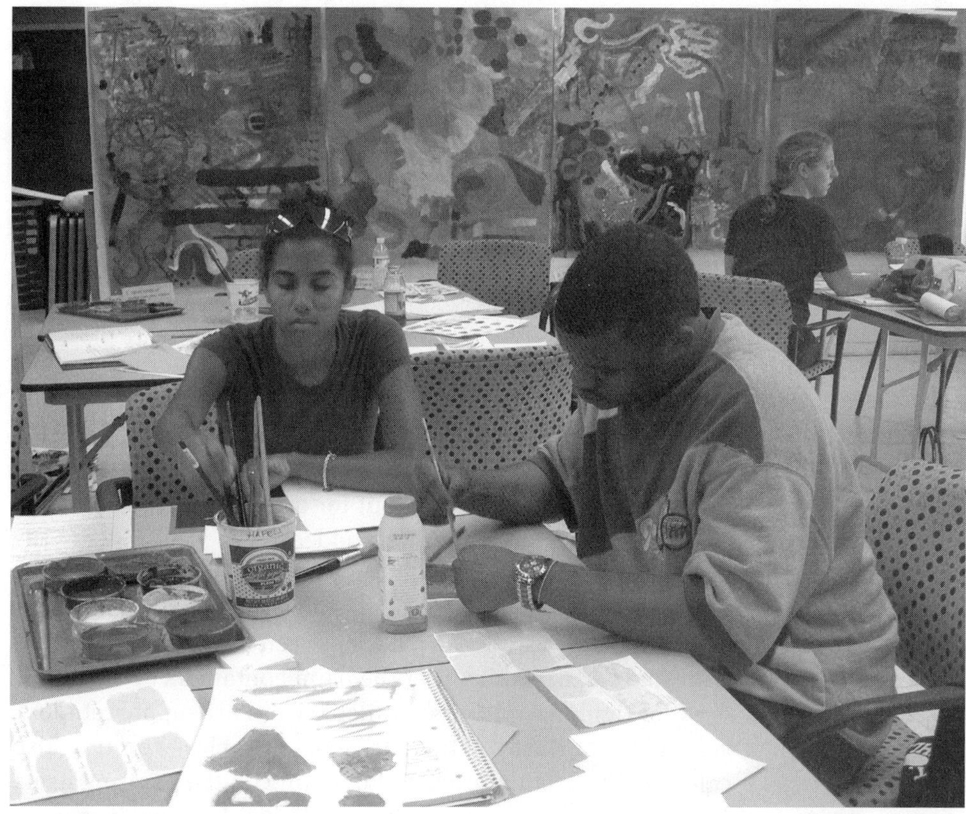

F 3-3: Testing different brands of paint

Choosing good tempera paint can be overwhelming. The options and considerations are many, and quality varies widely across different brands. Color richness and material consistency across colors, degree of coverage on the painting surface, shelf life, and cost are some important criteria to consider. Some teachers use only one brand while others mix and match across brands based on preferences for colors and color mixing capabilities. More expensive paints do not necessarily guarantee better quality according to the criteria above—in the exploration below I suggest several brands that are commonly used with kids of all ages.

Over the past several years, manufacturers have sustained an ever-expanding array of new tempera paint products—washable formulas, for example. In my experience the quality of pigment content, particularly, color richness and surface coverage, is lacking in the washable formulas. Buying a good quality of tempera paint and having kids wear oversized shirts to protect their clothing allows the teacher to not have to sacrifice a rich artistic experience for fear of clothing stains. Glitter paints, tempera paint "pens," and squeezable tubes with brushes attached—self-dispensing products—are other available options. Although these may be appropriate in certain situations, in general a basic range of paint colors, good quality brushes, and paper or other supports are all that is needed for ongoing painting experiences. Your best bet is to test out a few different brands of paint and choose the one that has the best coverage and consistently rich colors according to your budget (see Figure 3-3).

Brushes

Tempera is viscous, so the best brushes to use are those with stiff bristles. Bristle brushes are available in flat and round shapes in a range of diameters and widths, with long and short handles. While it's good for children to ultimately experiment with a wide variety of brushes, it's best to start with one or two, offering more later on to add complexity to the learning experience. For very young children a flat brush that is ¾″ wide is fine for beginning—you can add a ¼″ wide and wider flat brushes as well as round brushes as students become more experienced. For older beginners, experimentation with a few different brushes at one time prior to beginning a painting is helpful for them to understand what actions and visual effects are possible with each. The goal is to experiment with each new brush to see how many ways it can be used to create marks and effects of different kinds, and to ultimately be able to make thoughtful selections for different purposes (for example—large, flat brush for painting large areas, small brush for smaller areas and details, flats for square and rectangle shapes, rounds for lines of varying widths and for dots and other small shapes).

Trays and Palettes for Color Mixing

Teachers use a number of methods for dispensing tempera paint, including recycled egg cartons and small plastic cups. As mentioned previously, repurposed muffin tins or similarly sized plastic palettes work well, but for ongoing classroom use in which tempera is pulled out regularly, I prefer flat, lidded plastic containers—the kind I use are about 4″ wide and are sold wholesale for food storage (available online from plastic supply companies). The size accommodates brushes of varying widths and the tight fitting lids allow you to store the paint between uses, which substantially cuts down on waste and cleanup time. I set the paint containers up on repurposed baking trays or white rigid plastic trays (available from art supply retailers, such as Dick Blick) for easy transport to students' spots at tables—the tray also provides a space for color mixing as an alternative to mixing on the painting itself. If paper size and table space allow, students can have individual setups. If space is tight, they can share one painting tray among two to four students. The painting setup on the tray also accommodates a container of water and sponge or rag for blotting the brush, as noted previously (see Figure 3-4).

Papers

Papers for tempera painting are typically made from sulphite (processed from wood pulp), cotton (often called "rag"), or a combination of the two. Sulphite is considerably less expensive than cotton and is also less durable. Given its affordability, it is the paper of choice among many teachers. Sulphite comes in several

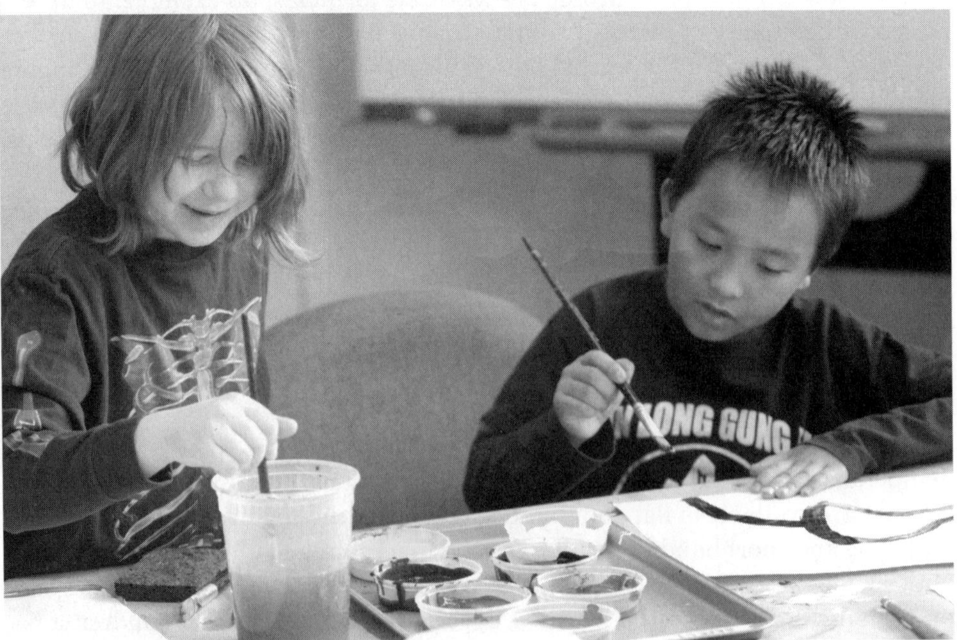

F 3-4: Tempera setup in the art class

weights—for tempera, you will need a heavier weight (at least 80 lb.) to stand up to wet paints and the surface action of brushes and other tools. For sizes, larger sheets such as 18" by 24" invite students to step outside the standard 8 1/12" × 11" page frame that characterizes most of their other school-day experiences. This large size can easily be cut in half to sheets of 12" × 18," in quarters to sheets of 9" × 12" for smaller projects, or into various square and rectangle sizes as well. Beyond white paper sheets, you can use heavyweight white or brown kraft paper on a roll (36" or 48" wide) cut into large sheets (and taped to the wall or spread out on the floor), colored construction paper, Yupo translucent synthetic paper, brown paper bags split open, irregular sizes of panels cut from plain or patterned cardboard boxes, and patterned sheets from newspaper, repurposed wrapping paper, and other sources.

Exploring Tempera

What kinds of effects can you create from a limited variety of colors, painting tools and surfaces? How might you design an exploratory experience for beginning students at different age levels? Keep working notes in your studio journal about your discoveries, along with practical insights about setting up for classroom experimentations with paint.

Materials:

Paints—red, magenta (cool red), blue, turquoise or cerulean, yellow, black, and white liquid tempera dispensed through one of the methods described above. If you have the time, it would be good to compare for yourself how various brands of liquid tempera differ with regards to creaminess, opacity, flow, color blending capabilities, and so forth. Some brands to try include Blick premium grade and student grade, Sax, Prang, and Crayola Premier. Also, try testing out a palette of solid tempera cakes (brands to try include Blick, Richeson, and Sax).

Brushes—flat bristle (assorted widths such as 3/4" and 1/4" long handled, 1 ½", 2" short handled), round bristle (assorted sizes)

Tray set up for holding paints, along with sponge, water, paper towels

Selection of various sizes of papers—several sheets of 80 lb. (or heavier) white sulphite paper, brown butcher paper in large, table-sized sheets or smaller sheets cut from brown paper bags, colored construction paper, heavier colored paper (Canson Mi-Teintes works well), card stock in various colors, heavy and medium weight printed or patterned papers, Yupo translucent synthetic paper

Getting Started:

1. The bright colors, smell, creaminess or fluidity, and sound and feel of a brush pushing paint around on paper can be highly stimulating parts of the painting experience. With one color of paint, one brush, and a sheet of white paper, use the brush in different ways while you focus on the materials themselves. What are the visual qualities of the paint and what actions does it invite? What does it smell like? Note how you pay attention and respond to these and other qualities of your paints, tools, and surfaces.
2. Experiment with different ways of mark making on separate sheets of white paper by responding to the prompts that follow. Rinse your brush in the water and blot it on the sponge as you change colors.

a. What kinds of marks can you make with each brush—its tip, front, edge? What happens when you move your arm/wrist/hand in different ways—sweeping, stroking, tapping, swirling, circling, scrubbing, looping, etc.?

b. What new colors can you make from the paints? Try using primary colors (reds, yellow, blues) to mix secondary colors (oranges, greens, purples). Also experiment with adding white in various amounts to any color to lighten it (this will create a range of tints) and adding black to the same color to darken it (this creates tones).

c. What happens when you use a lot of paint? What happens when you use hardly any?

d. What happens when you use a lot of water on your brush? What happens when you use just a little?

e. Can you make the paint look fast? Slow? Quiet? Angry?

   Make the paint look different from what's already on the paper and give your new look a name.

f. What are different ways of arranging marks you make with the brush? What happens when you put things close together? Far apart? What happens when you paint over parts of areas that have dried?

g. Using glue, attach several smaller sheets of different colored papers on a larger sheet. How does the same paint color look on different paper colors?

Note: When inviting students to engage in these explorations in the classroom, you can have them work independently or with a partner on individual sheets of paper (see Figure 3-5). Alternatively, have students explore the materials as a large group collaboration (see Figure 3-6). Cut seven large sheets of paper from a roll to

F 3-5: Experimenting with tempera paint. (below, left)

F 3-6: Collaborative group exploration with tempera. (below, right)

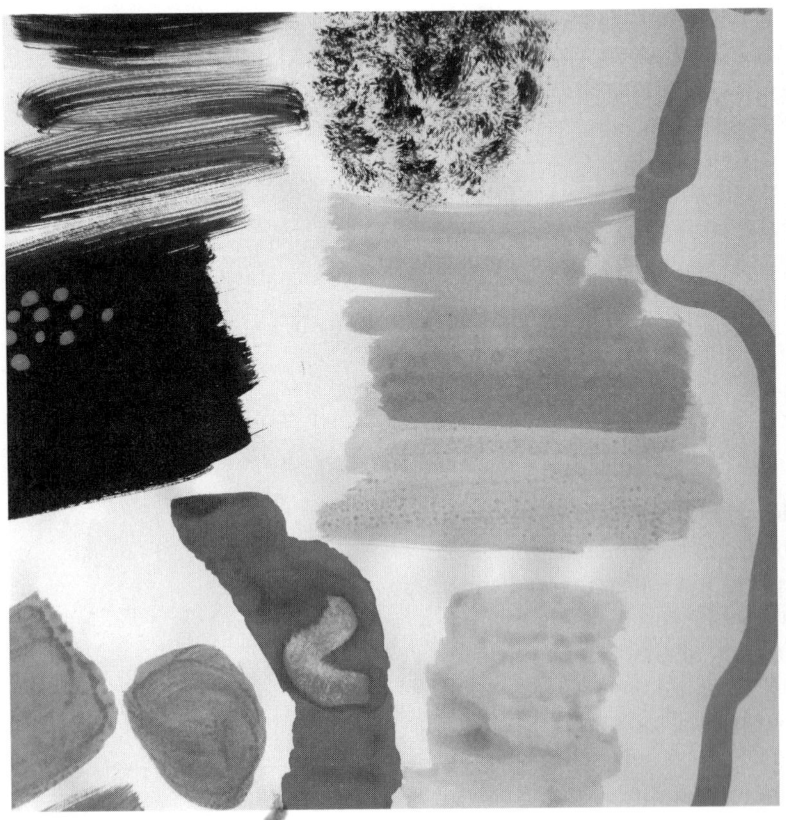

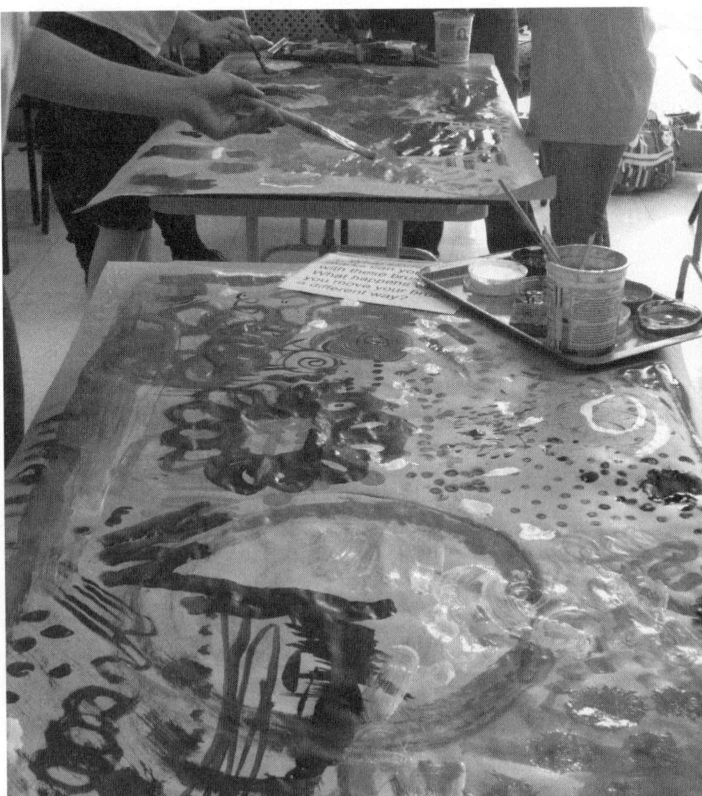

fit the table surface or to tack on walls around the room, and place one written prompt (from above) and one painting setup with extra brushes at each painting site. After introducing the seven prompts, break students into groups and assign each group a table or wall space to start. Explain that the groups will have about five minutes at each site to respond to that site's prompt before moving on to the next site. Keep time and announce site changes until all groups have had a chance to add to the exploration according to the prompt. Have students refresh the water containers at each site as needed.

3. Try all of the papers and other surfaces. How does what you paint on—the color, size, texture, and weight of the support—change what you're able to achieve? How do you respond differently to the look and feel of each painting support?

WATERCOLOR

Paint

Painting with pigment dispersed in water dates back to ancient times, and after the invention of paper it was practiced by artists throughout history and in many parts of the world. Hard cakes of color were introduced in the late 1700s in England—by the 1830s, cake watercolors were available in portable, metal boxes. In 1846, the paint manufacturer Winsor & Newton introduced moist watercolors in metal tubes. Watercolor paint is composed primarily of finely ground pigments and gum arabic, a water-soluble sap-based substance that is the most transparent of all paint binders.

While tempera and gouache are known for their opacity, watercolor's distinguishing quality is transparency. Tempera and gouache can be thinned with water when needed, but watercolor paints are specially formulated so they can withstand application as transparent layers of color. Some colors are more transparent than others, and manufacturers like Winsor & Newton label colors as transparent (T), semi-transparent (ST), semi-opaque (SO), or opaque (O). Different colors also vary in the way they granulate, or produce a mottled effect on the paper when dry, and in their lightfastness, or permanency—additional tube labeling codes reflect these characteristics. Both student grade and professional grade watercolor paints are available from a variety of manufacturers—among the differences between these types is the amount and quality of pigment used to produce the paint colors.

In watercolor painting, light areas are established primarily by allowing the paper to show through thin layers of applied color—this is basically a staining technique. In addition to the differences noted previously, some colors are more powerful stains than others, which means that they are more difficult to lift and blot out of the paper. Beyond the wide range of hues available, watercolor easily lends itself to creating a variety of effects with brushes of different sizes and shapes and with varying amounts of water. As with other materials, the various visual effects you create can suggest different ideas and meanings in your painting.

In addition to the color mixtures that can be achieved, differences in visual smoothness or texture of the paint on the paper, color strength and brilliance, degrees of transparency and opacity, and the paper texture itself make for a considerable range of possible effects. There are also various mediums that can be added to the paint—these can increase granulation of colors that usually produce a smooth finish (granulation medium); increase the flow of washes (ox gall liquid);

increase brilliance, gloss, and transparency (gum arabic); or produce a shimmering effect (iridescent medium). Products applied directly to the paper before painting can shield selected areas from the paint in early phases of the work (masking fluid) or make it easier to lift dried areas of color from the paper (lifting preparation). These additives are not necessary for most school-based watercolor painting activities. They can, however, add complexity to the experience for more advanced students who have developed considerable understanding of and skills with watercolor.

Note: The color choices available for watercolor, acrylic, and oil paints are vast—Winsor & Newton offers a spectrum of 96 colors in watercolor paints and 120 colors for oils—so deciding on which colors to buy can be challenging. Some artists work with a lot of colors and use them without much mixing and others choose a limited range and do a great deal of mixing. A good starting palette is one that includes both opaque and transparent colors and cooler and warmer hues in the reds, blues, and yellows families—a cool blue and a cool red (more magenta) will make a purple hue that is very different from that which comes from a cool blue and a warm red.

Throughout this chapter, I suggest sets of student grade paints for you to purchase because those are what you will be using with your students. While the consistency of the paints and names of colors may be different from professional grades, these sets contain basic colors that will allow you to mix a wide range of new colors. If you want to forego the sets and purchase single colors, the following list is a typical starting point for painting students working with watercolor, acrylic, and oil paints—while manufacturers vary slightly in terms of color specifications and appearances, I've labeled these as warm (W), cool (C), transparent (T), and opaque (O). Within the category of student grade paints, the colors on this list are typically certified nontoxic and carry the AP certification for use with students, but be sure to read the label of the particular paint manufacturer for verification.

> **Red:** Alizarin Crimson Hue or Permanent Alizarin Crimson (CT), Quinacridone Magenta (CT), Cadmium Red Hue (WO)
>
> **Orange:** Cadmium Orange Hue (WO), Burnt Sienna (WT)
>
> **Yellow:** Cadmium Yellow Hue (WO), Lemon Yellow or Hansa Yellow (CT), Naples Yellow Hue (WO)
>
> **Blue:** Cobalt Blue Hue (WT), Ultramarine Blue (WT), Phthalo Blue (CT), Cerulean Blue Hue (CO)
>
> **Green:** Phthalo Green (CT), Sap Green (O)
>
> **Purple:** Dioxazine Purple (CT)
>
> **White:** Titanium White (O)
>
> **Black:** Lamp Black (O)

Brushes

Diluted watercolor paint is thin and fluid, so the best brushes to use are those with soft hairs, which will hold the liquid. Like the stiff-bristled brushes, these are available in round and flat shapes, with long and short handles of varying diameters and widths. Larger brushes made of fine, soft, synthetic fibers and those with squirrel, camel, or badger hair work well for laying down color in large areas (called a "wash") while smaller flat and round brushes are good for straight-edged areas and details. Here, too, while it's good for young people to ultimately be able to experiment and become familiar with a wide variety of brushes, it's best to start with one or two so that they can focus on and master those first. Once students have gained some experience, a good range of brushes to have on hand would be two to three round brushes (small, medium, large) and two to three flats (1/4″ to 1″), along with a wider flat brush for washes. Mild soap and water are all that are needed for brush cleaning—olive oil soap not only cleans but also conditions the brush fibers.

Trays and Palettes for Color Mixing

Much of the color mixing in watercolor painting happens on the paper, either by painting one color over another while wet, or letting the first layer dry before adding another color on top. But it's also important to have a space for color mixing besides the paper. The open areas provided by white enamel butcher trays (found in art supply stores) work well, or you can use more economical plastic white palettes with divided wells for keeping colors separated from one another. You just need to make sure that the sizes of brushes students are working with will be accommodated by the size of the mixing areas in whichever approach you choose.

Paper

Watercolor painting typically involves a lot of water soaking into the paper, so the paper itself needs to be durable. Sulphite papers used for drawing and other class-room projects can be used, but they are less conducive to watercolor because they are too lightweight and the fibers tend to break down and visibly mix with the transparent paint. Student grade watercolor papers are made from a combination of cotton and sulphite, and artist grade watercolor papers are 100% cotton or linen fibers.

Watercolor papers come with surfaces that have a rough finish, medium finish (cold pressed), or smooth finish (hot pressed) and the different surfaces produce correspondingly different light effects in the finished painting. Heavyweight papers (over 260 lb.) can be used without any preparation but sheets of lightweight paper (72 lb. is the lightest) should be dampened or soaked and then attached with gummed tape or staples to dry on a rigid surface. This technique, called "stretching," prevents the paper from wrinkling and buckling during painting.

Watercolor paper is available in loose sheets, pads, and blocks of individual sheets that have adhesive around the edges—this provides the rigidity necessary and eliminates the need for stretching. Because watercolor painting is based in transparent layers of color, white or very light paper colors work best. Yupo translucent synthetic paper can also be used with watercolor paints—and the effects of transparent color on translucent paper can be very interesting. Yupo paper cannot be stretched and does not need to be soaked.

Note: To stretch watercolor paper, soak the paper in a tub of water or use a wet sponge to apply water to each side—heavier papers will need more wetting time than lighter weight papers. Lay the damp paper on a drawing board, sheet of gator board (available at art supply stores) or homasote (available at building supply stores). If using a drawing board, attach the paper to the board using four pieces of gummed paper tape, one along each side with the tape overlapping the paper ¼″. If using gator board or homasote, use a staple gun to attach the paper to the board ½″ in from the paper's edge, beginning in the center of each side and then stapling 1″ out from either side of the center along each side of the paper. When the paper is completely dry it is ready for painting—you can create the painting while the paper is attached to the board. When the painting is complete and the paper is dry, use a blade to cut inside the tape perimeter or remove the staples.

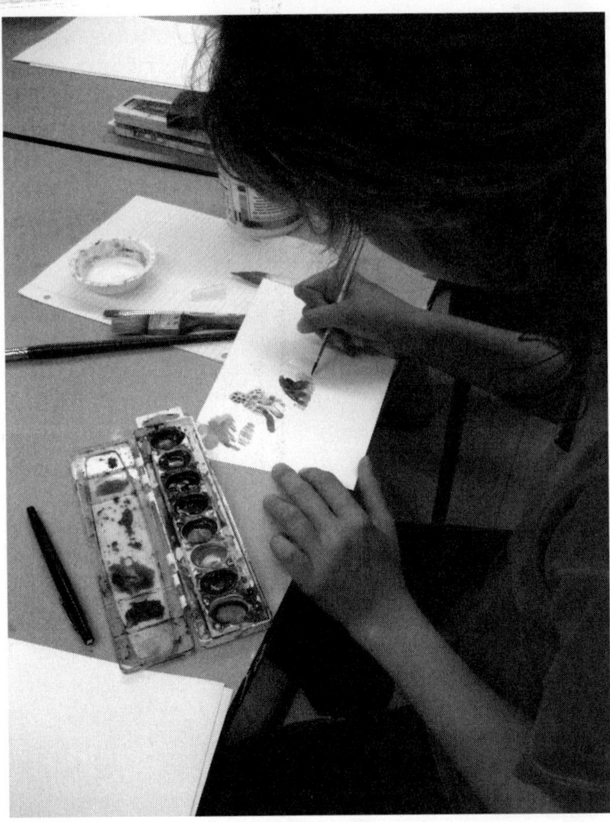

F 3-7: Exploring color layering with watercolor

Exploring Watercolor

Smooth, rough, dry, and wet papers, and dry and wet brushes—along with a range of paint colors—can be used to create a variety of effects. Use the prompts here to experiment with different types of watercolor paint, various brush sizes and shapes, and different color strengths and mixtures, water applications, and paper surfaces (see Figures 3-7 and 3-8). Keep detailed notes that will help you remember the colors, brushes, and papers you used to achieve different results, and note which types of paint seem to work best as you consider their use with young people of different ages.

Materials:

Paints—Try student-grade brands in both cake form (Prang and/or Crayola, 8-color set) and tube paints (Reeves, Grumbacher Academy, or Van Gogh 10- or 12-color set). Also try Stockmar liquid watercolor paints (available in jars). You can compare cake watercolors to tube and jar paints with regards to color saturation and vibrancy, dilution and flow, transparency and opacity, color blending capabilities, and so forth.

Brushes—flat synthetic fiber (assorted widths 1/4″ to 1″), round synthetic or soft hair fiber (small, medium, large), flat synthetic wash (1 ¾″ or 2″—Princeton and Loew-Cornell make inexpensive options)

Container of water (or two, one for rinsing brushes and one for diluting paint), metal butcher tray for mixing, small cups for mixing washes, palette with wells for individual mixtures

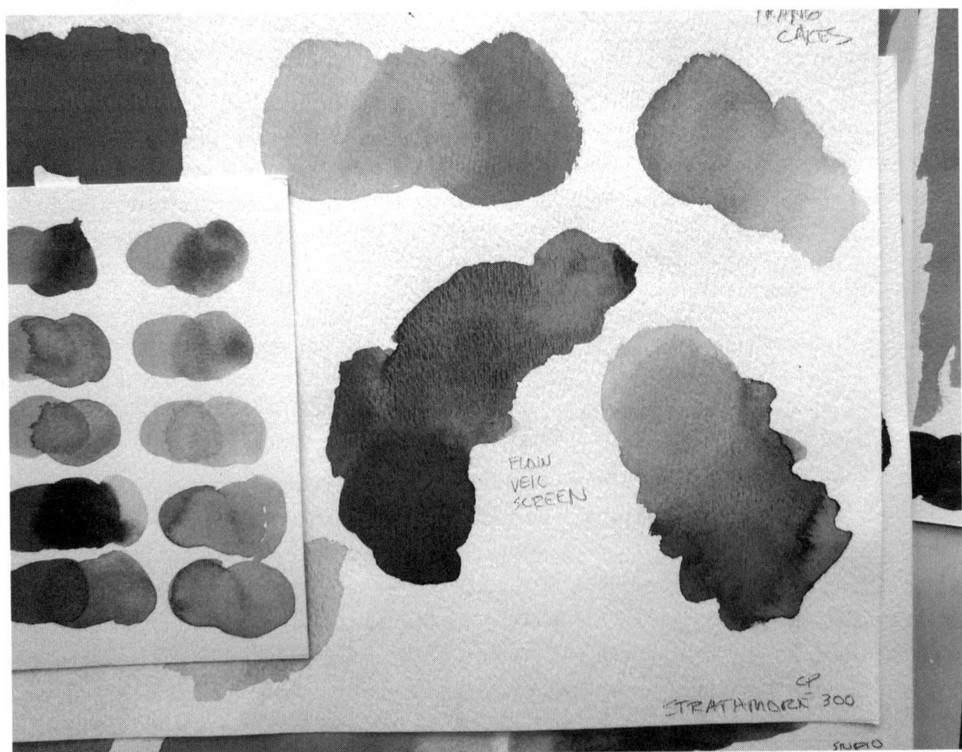

F 3-8: Paint test sheets and notes

Salt, plastic wrap, natural sponge, paper towels

Watercolor paper block—student-grade (Fabriano and Strathmore 300 Series
are good brands to try), small sheets of watercolor paper in various weights
and surfaces (hot pressed, cold pressed), Yupo translucent and opaque synthetic paper

Getting Started:

1. Using one color of paint and one or two brushes, mix water into the paint
to dilute. Squeeze paint from the tube or jar onto the palette or dilute pan
paint with water. Transfer to a well on the palette and dilute with a small
amount of water to make a strong mix. Using the brushes one at a time,
load each brush with paint and use it in different ways on a sheet of paper,
creating different types of lines and line widths and other marks. Vary the
amount of water used, adding more to increase transparency. What are
the visual qualities of the watercolor paint? What do you notice about how
it interacts with the paper? How are the synthetic and soft hair brushes
different from the bristle brushes used for tempera? How do the characteristics of watercolor compare to those of tempera? Note these and other
qualities of your painting materials.

2. Experiment with the different techniques that follow. Rinse your brushes
in the water as you change colors, and change the water frequently to keep
colors clear.

   a. Basic color mixing and diluting—use the cakes in pans and tube/jar
colors squeezed in small amounts on the palette (put a dab of each color
on the center part of the palette next to a well for mixing, keeping like
colors adjacent to one another). Working one by one with the colors, first
add water to get a strong mix then load your brush with diluted paint of
a single color and apply in a small area of the paper. Rinse the brush,
load with a second single color, and apply next to the first color. Keep the
outer edges of the two colors intact on the paper so that you can see the
colors you started with, and mix the colors together in the center where
they abut edges (see Figure 3-9). Systematically, in additional areas and

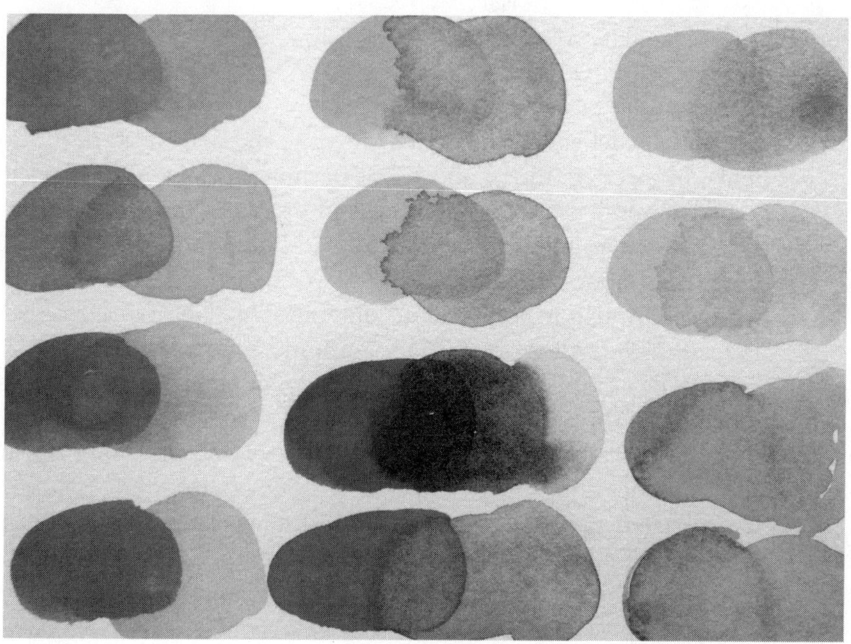

F 3-9: Color mixtures and
dilutions

on new sheets, mix reds with yellows, reds with blues, and yellows with blues. Try other combinations, keeping notes on the colors you are using (look for colors that blend well and those that don't, colors that are clear and transparent and those that show granulation and texture). Make another series of tests that explore dark-to-light changes in a single color, by adding water to achieve increasingly lighter colors on the paper (adding white to a color creates tints, adding black creates tones).

b. Advanced color mixing—You can also make a grid matrix that systematically documents your color mixtures and dilutions. Across the top and left side of a sheet of paper, paint 1″ by 1″ areas of unmixed color that move top to bottom from very concentrated to very light in each area. Organize the colors so that the warm hues (yellow, oranges, reds) are spread out on the top and the cool hues (blues, greens) are stacked in the side column. In the empty space of each square that corresponds to the top and side colors, paint small areas of different concentrations and dilutions of those two colors mixed together.

Note: Teachers often direct students to fold their paper in half repeatedly to divide it into a grid—this can create an uneven paper surface that is not conducive to painting with thin watercolors. If you have kids create grids by folding (an alternative is to use light pencil lines), folding at the crease in both directions (backwards and forwards) will create a more even surface.

c. Basic (flat) wash—Using a single color, dilute enough paint to cover a large area of the paper. Next, wet the area with clear water (it is helpful to lightly outline this area in pencil for reference). When the area is just damp (not wet), use a wide flat brush loaded with diluted paint to make a stroke from left to right at the top of the area. Quickly reload the brush with paint and make a second stroke from left to right, parallel and adjacent to the first, carefully touching the edges and drawing the paint from the first stroke down into the second one. Continue in this way with additional strokes until the entire area is covered, touching the top/bottom edges of each stroke and making the area look as even as possible.

Note: Inclining the paper surface very slightly will allow gravity to aid an even application.

d. Advanced washes—To make a graded wash (light to dark or dark to light), proceed as in (b) above but premix washes of light, medium, and dark intensities. To work from light to dark, begin at the top with the lightest wash and systematically add darker washes as you move down the paper. For dark to light, work in the reverse order. This process can also accommodate moving from one color to a second instead of light/dark transitions—premix the washes not from light to dark for a single color but from one color to the other, with varied mixtures of the two in between. You can also lay one wash on top of another (called a superimposed wash) by letting the paper dry in between applications.

e. Try different papers—Test out the different textures of hot pressed (smoother) and cold pressed (rougher) papers. Also experiment with the Yupo translucent and opaque synthetic paper.

   f. Make marks with a variety of brushes—Systematically use the round and flat brushes one at a time to explore mark making. Use each brush to make strokes pulled upward, strokes pulled downward, and strokes that radiate from a center area of color in various ways. With the flat brushes, make short, chunky marks of various lengths grouped together. Use the round brushes to make long and short marks grouped together (this is called scumbling). See what kind of lines you can make by twisting and dragging upward with different brushes, and try the same technique but moving downward. Try using very little paint on the brushes and explore this dry brush approach to create textures. Experiment further with mark making using your own invented techniques. Also explore different arrangements of marks—repeating, alternating, overlapping and layering, and so forth.

   g. Try variations of wet, damp, and dry paper—What happens when you adjoin a new color to a wet color area (wet-into-wet)? What happens when you wet the paper with clear water then gently dab on a bit of

Artist Profile: **ANNE PETTY**

Anne Petty works primarily in oil, a medium she finds to be "fairly forgiving most of the time." Of the difference between oil and watercolor (see Figure 9 in the color insert), she writes that:

watercolors allow me to loosen up and to give up some of my control. It forces me to plan out certain things from the very beginning and to remain flexible when things don't go according to plan. I appreciate how I am more aware of the space around the subject when I am using watercolors.

Petty also writes about the shifts in thinking and approach that come with moving from oils to watercolors:

My process has to change when I work with watercolors; something I welcome. The construction and process of the painting has to be different. While I begin with certain intentions for the piece, I love the unpredictable moments I am confronted with, perhaps where two shapes of color merge due to the wetness of the paint. I like the surprises watercolor can present if you choose to let it, and the challenge of figuring out how much I can say with how little information.

In describing her reasons for choosing to work with watercolor and her responses to the medium, Petty says:

I feel like I am more accountable for my decisions with watercolor. I've painted paintings on top of paintings on top of paintings with oils. You can't do that with watercolor. They force me to slow down and focus in the moment more.

If I try to control a painting too much, it can get stale and stiff. Sometimes I'll use more water than I think I should, just to give up some of that control, working with and reacting to the nature of the medium. These moments keep me engaged and can change the course of a painting in surprising ways. I make a mark, step away, and react. I paint for the process, not the product, so it's important to continue to push the materials around in hopes of discovering something new.

How does the artist present what she describes as "little information" to convincingly portray forms and figures from life? How does she apply and build up layers to achieve these effects?

highly concentrated pigment? What happens when you brush clear water onto color just painted?

h. Explore lifting and blotting—You can create interesting textures by sprinkling common table salt on wet areas of paint, and then brushing the salt off once the paint is fully dry. You can also lift wet color from the paper by blotting gently with a damp brush, cotton swab, piece of paper towel, or rag. For interesting textures try blotting wet areas with crumpled paper and plastic wrap and small natural sponges—try other materials for lifting and blotting as well.

i. Try superimposing—What happens when you paint a new color over an area that has dried? What new colors can you make this way?

3. With your watercolor test sheets spread out in front of you, study the different techniques you were able to achieve and consider what ideas and meanings the visual results of these techniques might suggest. Look for ideas that emerge from different colors, blends and mixtures, textures, and degrees of transparency and opacity. How might you use some of the marks and effects you created in a painting? How, moving from simple to complex, might you structure watercolor experiences for young people of different ages and levels of experience?

Note: As with the tempera explorations, when kids are experimenting with watercolor in the classroom you can have them work independently or with a partner on individual sheets of paper—or you can set up stations with different prompts for students to rotate through.

GOUACHE

Paint

Similar to watercolor in its composition, gouache is known as an opaque watercolor (see Figure 10 in the color insert). While some brands add chalk or other materials to achieve this opacity and surface coverage, others, such as Winsor & Newton, rely on high levels of pigmentation. Like watercolors, the consistency of the paint varies from color to color, with some more opaque than others and labeled to reflect this—Winsor & Newton labels its gouache colors as transparent (T) or opaque (O), but even the transparent colors are more opaque than watercolor. While gouache colors can be mixed, this process is sometimes tricky when working with colors that are themselves mixtures of several different pigments (muddiness can come from over mixture). For the cleanest and clearest mixtures, it's best to start with single pigment colors. In general, light colors often appear darker when they dry on the paper and dark colors look lighter, so it's good to paint areas completely as recreating mixtures to match dried areas of color is difficult.

As a technique, gouache painting can be traced to the fifteenth century in Italy (*guazzo*) and to the fourteenth century elsewhere in Europe. It has been used widely by painters, often in combination with watercolor, and by designers, illustrators, comic artists, and animators. Although both gouache and tempera are opaque, gouache is generally more expensive and is stiffer in material consistency—also, many gouache colors have high permanency/lightfastness ratings while this is not the case for tempera. Gouache comes in both tubes and cakes, and while you can introduce it to younger students I have found it's best used with more advanced students who have mastered tempera techniques and are looking to broaden their range of experience with more professional painting materials.

Brushes, Trays, Palettes for Color Mixing, and Paper

Brushes, trays, and palettes that are good for watercolor painting are also generally suitable for gouache. The same goes for papers, and since gouache is an opaque material that does not rely on the paper color for light areas in the painting, colors of the surfaces used can go beyond the whites that are suitable for watercolor.

Exploring Gouache

What kinds of effects can you create from a limited variety of colors, painting tools and surfaces? Document your discoveries in your studio journal, and note practical insights about setting up for classroom experimentations with this type of paint.

Materials:

Paints—Try student-grade brands in both cake form (Pelican 12-color set) and tube paints (Reeves or French School 10-, 12-, or 18-color set). As with the other paints you've worked with so far, you can compare cake to tube gouache paints with regards to color saturation and vibrancy, dilution and flow, opacity and transparency, and color blending capabilities.

Brushes—flat synthetic fiber (assorted widths 1/4″ to 1″), round synthetic, or soft hair fiber (small, medium, large)

Containers of water for rinsing brushes and diluting paint, metal butcher tray for mixing, small cups for mixing colors, palette with wells for individual mixtures

Assorted watercolor papers, heavier colored papers (Canson Mi-Teintes), Yupo translucent synthetic paper

Getting Started:

1. Using one color of paint, one brush, and a sheet of white paper, use the brush in different ways while you observe the visual qualities of the paint. How does it compare to watercolor and tempera? What actions does it invite? Note how you pay attention and respond to these and other qualities of your materials.

2. Experiment with different ways of mark making on separate sheets of white paper according to the prompts that follow. As with the other paints you've explored, rinse your brush in the water and blot it on the sponge as you change colors.

   a. What kinds of marks can you make with each part of the brush? What happens when you move your arm/wrist/hand in different ways?

   b. What new colors can you make from the paints? Try using primary colors to mix secondary colors, experiment with adding white in various amounts to individual colors to make a range of tints, and add black to the same colors to make a range of tones.

   c. What happens when you use varying amounts of paint on the brush?

   d. What happens when you use varying amounts of water?

   e. Can you make the paint look different ways to suggest different ideas?

Artist Profile: **LUCY FRADKIN**

Lucy Fradkin works in oil or gouache on paper or board (see Figure 11 in the color insert).

Her portraits reference ancient frescoes and mosaics that, according to the artist, "capture a timeless moment through a contemporary eye." Fradkin's work is "inspired by Indian and Persian miniatures, the vanishing art of hand-painted signage and the sacred and folk arts." She writes that: "Following in the tradition of genre painters, I place figures, often women, in domestic settings. The figures are quiet and inactive, which contributes to the solemn and mysterious atmosphere of the scene."

Fradkin writes about her studio process:

At times I incorporate collaged decorative elements from a variety of sources including old catalogs, field guides and vintage books into the work. Through meticulous cutting and pasting, I develop intricate designs and motifs which become a subtle aspect of the surface of the work. I use color and pattern to evoke emotion and tell stories of daily life where the viewer is drawn into an intimate world. My work is clearly inspired by the traditional, but the impact of personal history is evident in the quiet presentation of issues of gender and race.

What feelings or impressions do you sense from Fradkin's portrayal of her subject? How do the ways in which the artist uses paint and manipulates form play into your interpretation?

    f. How many ways can you arrange marks you make with the brush? What happens when you put things close together? Far apart? What happens when you paint over parts of areas that have dried? How else can you layer and arrange marks?

    g. Using a single paint color on a variety of paper colors, and note how the paint color appears to change according to its background paper color.

3. Try all of the papers and other surfaces. How does what you paint on—the color, size, texture, and weight of the support—change what you're able to achieve? How do you respond differently to the look and feel of each painting support?

4. With your gouache test sheets spread out in front of you, study the different techniques you were able to achieve and compare the visual qualities of the dried gouache paint to those of tempera and watercolor. How and when might you introduce gouache and integrate its use into students' painting experiences?

ACRYLIC

Paint

Acrylic paints intended for use by artists evolved from the manufacture of synthetic, acrylic resin-based industrial paints around the middle of the twentieth century. They differ from tempera, watercolor, and gouache in that once dry they are no longer water-soluble. They are also flexible when dry, which makes them suitable for painting on canvas and other fabrics as well as on a wide variety of other surfaces (see Figure 3-10). Acrylics are compatible with water so they do not

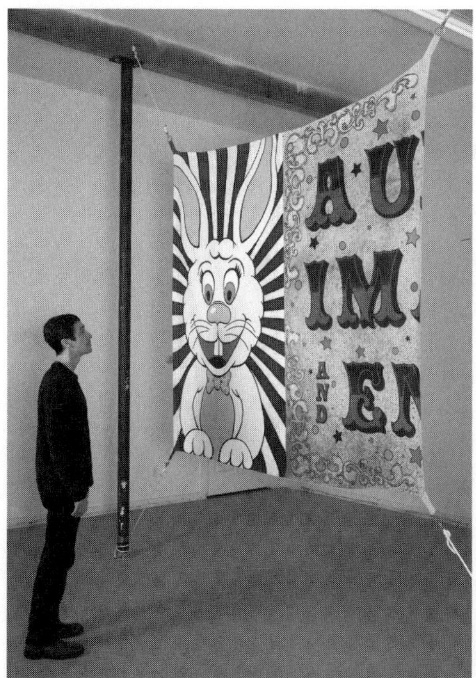
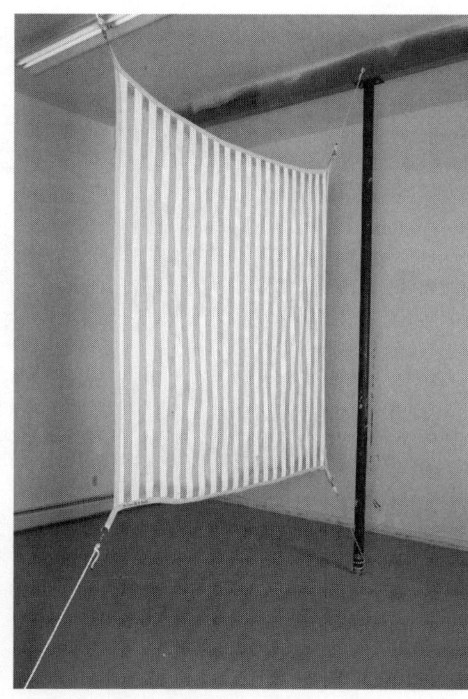

F 3-10
Seamus O'Brien, One Night Only, *2009, acrylic on canvas, 7' × 7'.*

require the solvents necessary for working with traditional oil paints. Also unlike traditional oil paints, which dry slowly and with variable drying times from color to color, the drying time for acrylics is short and uniform across colors. Given that the lightfastness/permanency ratings are comparable, artists may opt for acrylics or oils based on preferences for speed in drying time (although acrylics can be treated to slow drying time and oils treated to accelerate it), ability to lift and rework dried areas by applying solvents (this is not possible with acrylics), and perceived ease in painting with water-soluble acrylics versus traditional oils and solvents.

Like watercolors, acrylics vary from color to color in terms of lightfastness and permanency and like gouache, the way they appear when wet can be different from how they look when dry. Like gouache and watercolor, the consistency of the paint varies from color to color, with some more transparent or opaque than others and often labeled as such. There are also different forms of acrylics available—from thin, pourable solutions to thick, heavy-bodied formulas, as well as professional and student grades. The wide range of hues available is similar to that of watercolor and oils, and acrylics also can produce a variety of effects with different brushes, various other tools, and with different amounts of water and types of additives.

As with other types of paint, a range of effects can be achieved through various color mixtures, color strength and brilliance, degrees of transparency and opacity, and the support or surface on which the painting is done (see Figure 3-11 and Figure 12 in the color insert). There are also various mediums that can be added to the paint—these can increase flow on nonabsorbent surfaces (flow improver); create thin layers (glazing medium); increase transparency, viscosity, and depth (gloss gel); increase transparency and flow (gloss medium, matte medium); build up depth in layers (modeling paste); and increase drying time (slow drying medium). Many other mediums are available for altering the appearance of the paint, along with varnishes that are used to protect the finished painting from

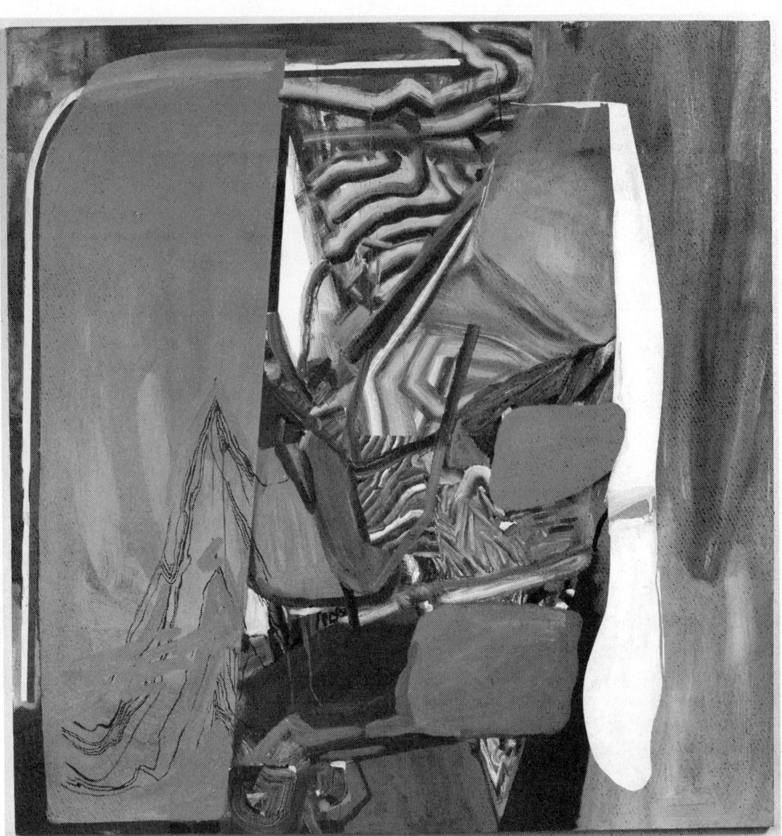

F 3-11
Matthew Choberka, I Wasn't Really Very Scared, 2012, acrylic on canvas, 90" × 84".

dirt, fading, and color shift. As with watercolor mediums, additives during the painting process are not necessary for most school-based activities but can add complexity to the experience for advanced students. Once finished and completely dry, acrylic paintings should be coated with acrylic solution varnish for protection.

Brushes and Other Tools

Both natural and synthetic fiber brushes are suitable for painting with acrylics—stiff bristles work well for thick paint and for creating textured areas and softer hairs are best for applications that use more fluid, thinned down paint. As with other paints, you will want to experiment with a selection of round and flat brushes in smaller and larger sizes and introduce these to students sequentially so that they learn in depth about the capabilities of each new option. It's important to remember that once acrylic paint dries it is no longer water-soluble. Brushes with dried paint are much more difficult to clean, so keep brushes wet while painting and clean them with mild soap when finished.

Beyond brushes, painters use many other tools to apply paint to their work—rollers, brayers, palette knives, scrapers, sponges, sticks, straight-edged pieces of cardboard, toothbrushes, eyedroppers, feathers, combs, rags, cheesecloth, string, and even brooms. Students enjoy identifying and experimenting with nontraditional painting tools and creating their own tools. This can be incorporated into ongoing painting experiences in the classroom.

Trays and Palettes for Color Mixing

Plastic or metal trays or palettes can be used for acrylics, as can ice cube trays and disposable/reusable plastic plates, but any paint that dries on the surface needs to be scraped off and this can be challenging to manage with students in the classroom. Disposable palettes—pads of plastic-treated paper available in a variety of sizes—work very well in the classroom. As an inexpensive alternative to disposable palette paper, freezer paper (in rolls, found in the grocery store) can be cut into smaller or larger sizes and taped to the work surface. Because acrylic paints dry quickly, it's a good idea to have a spray bottle filled with water to mist over the palette while you're working. Many artists also keep plastic wrap and sealable plastic containers handy for storing palettes filled with large quantities of paint, so that they don't dry out between work sessions.

Supports

Typical supports include canvas on wood stretchers, canvas panels and sheets (Fredrix and Blick make inexpensive options), wood panels, and heavyweight paper (Canson, Strathmore, and Hahnemühle make paper specially formulated for use with acrylics, and watercolor and printmaking papers can also be used). With students, anything to which acrylic paint will stick is suitable for use. As with drawing, artists work on many kinds of surfaces (including patterned fabric and three-dimensional objects) and these alternative supports often are integral to the meaning of the work. While it's not always necessary, many artists apply a coat of primer or gesso to canvas and other fabrics and surfaces before painting with acrylics—this seals porous surfaces and provides for better adherence of the paint. Gesso can also be used on the back of paper used for painting, to prevent warping during the process. You can also stretch the paper before beginning to paint, as discussed in the section on watercolor.

For students just beginning to paint with acrylics, panels cut from cardboard, foamcore, gator board, and mat board and backing board (used to frame art work) are good surfaces for learning the basics, with other supports such as canvas panels and pads and canvas on stretchers added later on.

Exploring Acrylics

As with watercolor and tempera, assorted brushes, tools, and supports—along with a range of paint colors—can be used for acrylic painting. Experiment with different brush sizes and shapes, color mixing approaches, painting techniques, and supports. Continue your working notes about materials and tools you use to achieve different results, and consider their use with young people of different ages.

Materials:

Paints—student-grade tube paints (Liquitex Basics or Reeves 12-color set)

Painting mediums—try a gloss medium or matte medium (for transparent effects) and modeling paste (for adding thickness)

Brushes—assorted synthetic and bristle brushes from previous painting explorations (brushes with natural soft hairs do not work as well with the thicker consistency of acrylics)

Containers of water for rinsing brushes and diluting paint, plastic palette or disposable palette sheets from options described previously, spray bottle filled with water

Palette knife for color mixing and selection of alternative painting tools drawn from the list on p. 92

Assorted papers from watercolor and gouache explorations, small panels cut from cardboard, foamcore, and/or gator board, canvas sheets or panels

Getting Started:

1. Begin your exploration with limited materials, as you did with the other paints, using one color and just one or two brushes. Squeeze paint from the tube onto the palette, dip your brush in water and blot out excess moisture, then load your brush and apply the paint in different ways in a small area of the paper. Add a little water to the paint on the palette, mix it into the paint with your brush, and try out the diluted paint on the paper. Working quickly, replenish the paint as necessary and using the brushes one at a time, create different types of lines and other marks on a sheet of paper. Vary the amount of water used, adding more to increase transparency. What are the visual qualities of the acrylic paint? What do you notice about how it interacts with the paper? How do the brushes behave with this type of paint? How do the characteristics of acrylic compare to those of the other paints you've used so far? Make notes about your observations.

2. As you experiment with the different techniques that follow, rinse your brushes and change the water frequently to keep colors clear. During your work session, keep your used brushes stored in a container filled with water to cover the fibers so that the paint doesn't dry and harden on the brush.

   a. Basic color mixing and diluting—put a dab of each color on the palette, keeping like colors adjacent to one another. Working quickly one by one with the colors, load your brush and apply in a small area of the paper. Rinse the brush, load with a second color, and apply next to the first color. As with the watercolor exploration, keep the outer edges of the two colors intact on the paper so that you can see the colors you started with, and mix the colors together in the center where they abut edges. You can also experiment with mixing color on the palette instead of on the paper (use a palette knife to mix the paints). In additional areas of the paper and on new test sheets, mix reds with yellows, reds with blues, and yellows with blues. Try other combinations, keeping notes on the colors you are using (look for colors that blend well and those that don't, colors that are more transparent and those that are more opaque). Make another series of tests that explore dark-to-light changes in a single color, by adding black to get darker tones and white to achieve increasingly lighter tints (notice how adding titanium white to more transparent colors increases their opacity).

   b. Advanced color mixing—Make a grid matrix similar to the one you made with watercolors. Across the top and left side of a sheet of paper, paint areas of unmixed color, organizing the colors so that the warm hues are spread out on the top and the cool hues are in the side column. In the empty space of each square that corresponds to the top and side colors, paint small areas of different concentrations and dilutions of those two colors mixed together—you can also add tints and tones to this chart.

   c. Washes—on damp paper, explore making flat, graded, and superimposed washes as you did in the watercolor exploration.

   d. Painting mediums—experiment with adding matte or gloss medium to the paint and see what kinds of transparency effects are possible, and add modeling paste to the paint to explore three-dimensional textures (impasto).

   e. Try different papers and supports—Test out the different papers, canvas panel, cardboard panels, and other surfaces you may wish to try.

f. Make marks with a variety of brushes and tools—As with the watercolor experiments, use the brushes one at a time to make strokes pulled upward and downward and strokes that radiate from a center area in different ways. Use the flat and round brushes to make long and short lines of different widths grouped together in various ways (scumbling). Use the tips of the brushes dabbed gently on the paper to create marks (stippling). See what kind of lines you can make by twisting and dragging upward and downward with different brushes. Try using just a little paint on the tips of your brushes to create textures (dry brush). Experiment with the alternative painting tools you have to work with, using your own invented techniques. As with the other painting explorations, try different arrangements of marks—repeating, alternating, overlapping and layering, and so forth.

g. Try variations of wet, damp, and dry paper—What happens when you paint a new color next to and touching a wet color area (wet-into-wet)? What happens when you brush clear water onto color just painted? How does the acrylic paint behave differently from the other paints you've worked with?

h. Try layering—What happens when you paint a new transparent color over a transparent area that has dried? What new colors can you make this way? What happens when you paint over a dried opaque area with an opaque color, and then scratch or scrape through the top layer to reveal the color below (scrafitto)? What happens when you build up dried layers of transparent colors mixed with gloss or matte medium (glazing)?

3. With your acrylic test sheets spread out in front of you, study the different techniques you were able to achieve. Look for ideas and themes suggested by different colors, blends and mixtures, textures, and degrees of transparency and opacity. How might you use some of the marks and effects you created in a painting? Moving from simple to more complex, how might you structure acrylic painting experiences for young people of different ages and levels of experience?

Artist Profile: **AMBER CARKY**

Amber Carky writes about her work (see Figure 13 in the color insert):

A painting for me is never complete; I merely let it reach a state of resolve and allow it then to be seen. They are a reflection of my relationship or experience with a certain space at the time in which I engage with it. Always am I observing, studying, painting, and then repainting the subject of my gaze.

These paintings exist as only a small portion of my continuing body of work. At large I paint the world surrounding me. I can be inspired or intrigued simply by daylight passing through a living room bay window and falling up in a cluttered indoor space, or can

find interest in the documentation of a young woman's lived-in space in an enormous panoramic image. I tend towards the same subjects over and over, and often times seek out the same place or image at different states of time or development. I paint the same house in sunlight, snow, rain, dawn, and twilight. With this I entertain my curiosity in the progression or change that occurs in our everyday lives and reflects our ever changing and developing society.

These places I chose for one reason: their familiarity. They are spaces I know well, have resided in, or have visited often. They are completed on site, alla prima, in whatever conditions are present.

WATER MIXABLE OIL

Paint

The history of paints made from pigments dispersed in drying vegetable oils dates to the Middle Ages, but oil paints were not widely used by artists for easel painting until the fifteenth century. Many artists today continue to use oil paint even given the widespread use of acrylic painting techniques, and their approaches to and purposes for using the medium vary widely (see Figures 3-12 and 3-13). For these artists, oil paint is the material that has been time-tested with regard to durability and permanence over long periods.

Traditional oil painting requires turpentine, mineral spirits, and other solvents, and the hazardous characteristics of some of these materials make them unsuitable for general art classroom use. In recent years, however, paint manufacturers have developed "water mixable" (also known as "water miscible") paints, which are nontoxic and safe for classroom use. Known as the alternative oil paint, water mixable oil paints contain a modified type of linseed oil or safflower oil that both binds the pigments and allows the paint to accept water. Although there are some differences in the way the paints behave while you work with them, water mixable oils act much like traditional oil paints—they are slow drying, so the paint can be reworked over a long period of time, and they are suitable for painting on canvas and other fabrics and on the same wide variety of other surfaces as acrylics and traditional oils. Like acrylics, water mixable oils do not require the hazardous solvents necessary for working with traditional oil paints. With lightfastness/permanency ratings comparable to traditional oils and to other types of paint, many artists who are concerned about the hazards of traditional oil paints are switching to water mixable oils.

Water mixable oils are available in a wide range of hues. These paints also vary from color to color in transparency/opacity and lightfastness and may look different wet compared to dry. Also similar to other paints, various mediums can be added—to increase flow, gloss, and transparency (water mixable linseed and safflower oils), reduce wet/dry color differences (thinner), build up thickness and texture (water mixable impasto medium), and increase drying time (water mixable fast drying medium). As with other painting mediums, additives during the painting process are not necessary for most school-based activities. Once finished and completely dry, all oil paintings should be coated with varnish for protection.

Brushes and Other Tools

Some manufacturers, such as Winsor & Newton, have developed special synthetic brushes for water mixable oil paints. This is because brushes typically used with traditional oils (brushes made from animal hair) may become too soft and limp when in contact with water—which makes controlling the paint difficult. However, it's worth it to experiment with a range of brushes to see what works best for particular effects and brands of paint. As with acrylic paints, you will want to include a selection of synthetic and natural bristle, round and flat brushes in smaller and larger sizes. You should keep brushes wet while painting with water mixable oils and clean them with mild soap when finished. The tools beyond brushes that apply to painting with acrylics are also suitable to painting with oils.

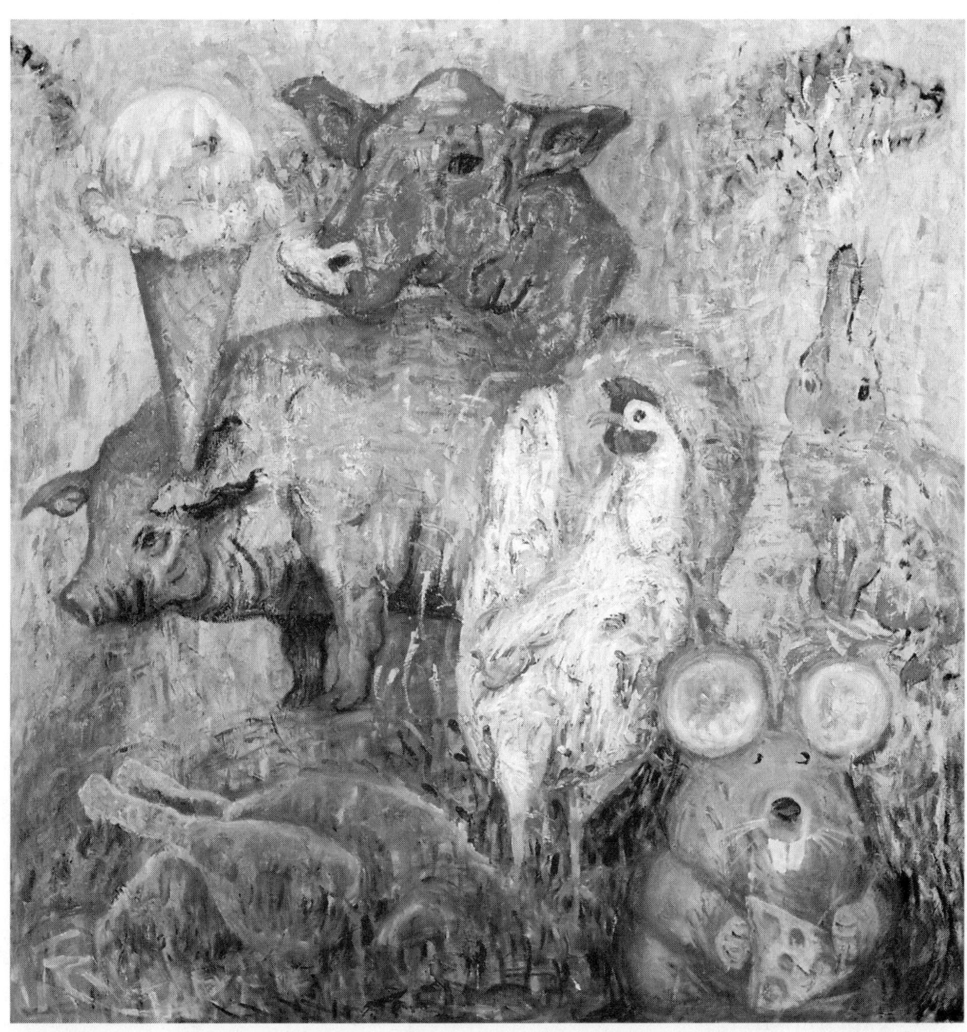

F 3-12
Robin Arnold, How Now, *2006, oil and wax on canvas, 64" × 60".*

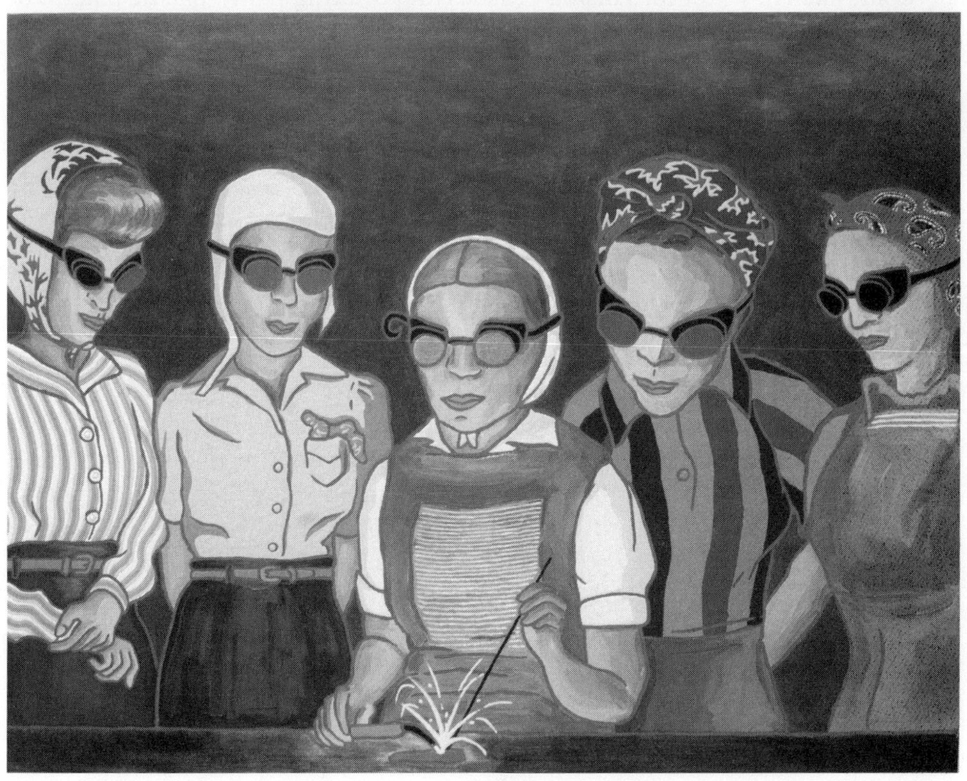

F 3-13
Nancy Mladenoff, The Ladies: Munitions Plant 5, 1940s, *2012, oil, oil enamel, and flashe on canvas, 24" × 30".*

Trays and Palettes for Color Mixing

As with acrylic paints, disposable palettes work very well in the classroom. Wood, acrylic, and other surfaces can also be used but will need to be wiped and cleaned after use. Disposable palettes simplify and substantially reduce time required for cleaning up at the end of class.

Supports

The supports that are suitable for acrylic painting are also good for oil. However, with all oil paints it is necessary to apply primer or gesso to canvas, other fabrics, papers, and other surfaces before painting. As with acrylic painting, for students, preprimed canvas panels and pads are a good introduction to oil painting supports and stretched canvas can be added to the mix for students with more experience.

Exploring Water Mixable Oils

Different types of brushes, tools, and supports can be used for painting with water mixable oils. As in your other paint explorations, keep working notes about materials and tools you use to achieve different results and their use with young people as you experiment using the prompts that follow.

Materials:

Paints—Student-grade tube paints (Reeves 12-color set)

Painting mediums—Nontoxic Weber Oil water mixable oil color mediums (set of four) include fast-dry medium, gel painting medium (extends paints), modified linseed oil (thins and improves flow), and UV varnish (provides protective coating)

Brushes—assorted synthetic and bristle brushes from previous painting explorations

Containers of water for rinsing brushes and diluting paint, plastic palette or disposable palette sheets from options described previously, spray bottle filled with water

Palette knife for color mixing and selection of alternative painting tools used for acrylic paints

Preprimed canvas sheets or panels

Getting Started:

1. Approach this initial investigation of water mixable oil paints in the same way as you did with acrylics. Begin with one color and just one or two brushes. Squeeze paint from the tube onto the palette, dip your brush in water and blot out excess moisture, then load your brush and apply the paint in different ways on a small area of the canvas. Add a little water to the paint on the palette, mix it into the paint with your brush, and try out the diluted paint. Working quickly, replenish the paint as necessary and using the brushes one at a time, create different types of lines and other marks. What are the visual qualities of the oil paint? What do you notice about how it interacts with the canvas? How do the brushes behave with this type of paint? How do the characteristics of oil compare to those of the other paints you've used so far? Make notes about your observations.

2. As you experiment with the different techniques that follow, rinse your brushes and change the water frequently to keep colors clear.

   a. Basic color mixing and diluting—Set up your palette with the paints organized as before. Experiment with mixing pairs of colors together on the canvas and try premixing with a palette knife on the palette, keeping notes on the colors you are using in terms of their blending qualities. Test out light-to-dark changes by mixing tints and tones of various colors.

   b. Advanced color mixing—Make a grid matrix similar to the one you made with other paints. Across the top and left side of a sheet of paper, paint areas of unmixed color, organizing the colors so that the warm hues are spread out on the top and the cool hues are in the side column. In the empty space of each square that corresponds to the top and side colors, paint small areas of different concentrations and dilutions of those two colors mixed together—you can also add tints and tones to this chart.

   c. Painting mediums—Experiment with adding some of the water mixable oil color mediums to the paint. Test out the fast-dry medium and compare the drying time of the same color with and without the fast-dry medium added. Use the gel painting medium and modified linseed oil to increase the transparency of the paint and add impasto medium or modeling paste to alter the body and texture. Use the UV varnish on finished paintings once they are completely dry.

   d. Make marks with a variety of brushes and tools—Use the brushes and other painting tools as before to explore different painting approaches. Vary the amount of paint you use, painting with a lot of thick paint in some areas and thinned out paint in others, and using the dry brush technique elsewhere on the surface. As with the other painting explorations, try different arrangements of marks—repeating, alternating, overlapping and layering, and so forth.

   e. Try layering—Working wet-on-wet, try layering new colors over already painted areas of the canvas, experimenting with both thicker and thinner paint consistencies. What happens when you build up layers of transparent colors mixed with gel medium or modified linseed oil? The dry time for water mixable oils is generally faster than for traditional oils, but oil-based paints are slow to dry compared to other paints. Once your paint tests are dry (this could take one to two days to more than a week), try painting over different areas. What happens when you paint over part of a dried opaque area with an opaque color? What happens when you build up dried layers of transparent colors mixed with gel medium or modified linseed oil?

3. With your oil paint test sheets spread out in front of you, study the different techniques you were able to achieve. Make notes about your responses to working with water mixable oils in comparison to the other paints you are now familiar with, and reflect on how, when, and in what contexts these paints would be suitable for use with students.

MIXING PAINTING AND OTHER MEDIA

As with mixing drawing materials, many artists work with different types of paint and other media simultaneously (see Figure 3-14). You've seen in your own work how the transparency of watercolor is different from the opaque chalkiness of tempera—these distinct qualities may suggest or lead to different ideas and

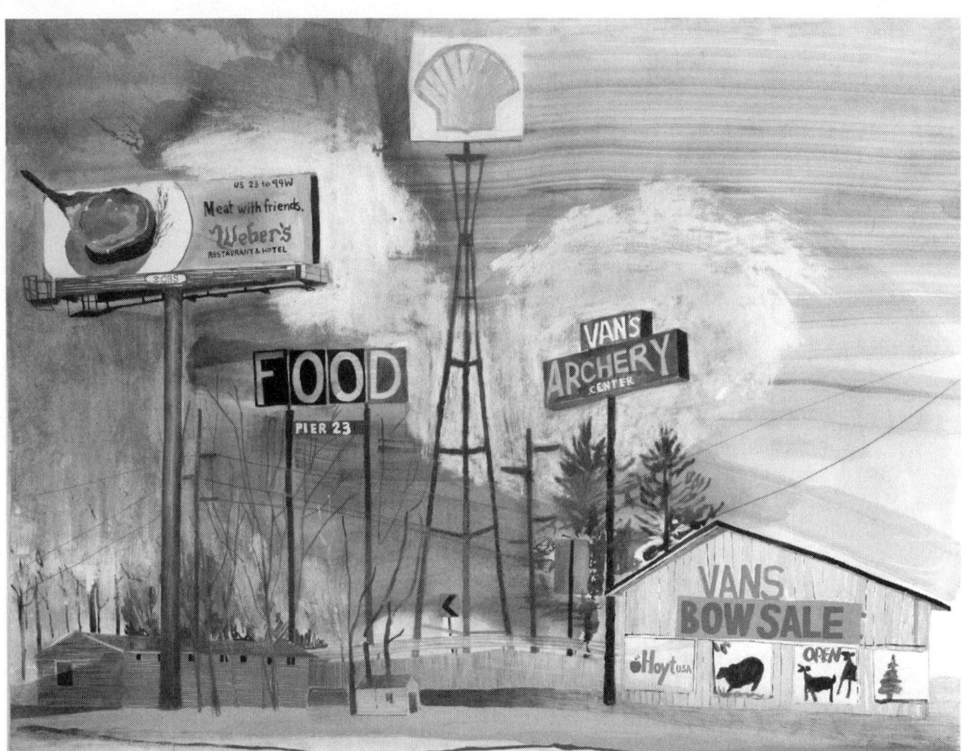

F 3-14
Karla Wozniak, Weber's, Ann Arbor, MI, 2008, mixed media on paper, 34" × 44.5".

representations that come together in a single artwork. After students have had a chance to work with and master individual paint types, I invite them to experiment with multiple painting and drawing materials. As discussed previously, through experimentation with materials certain themes may begin to emerge for the student, themes that can be carried forward in the artwork as it progresses. At other times, we brainstorm thematic ideas first and then students individually select materials whose qualities and capabilities lend themselves to the details of the artwork.

Exploring Mixed Media with Paints and Other Materials

From all of the materials you've worked with so far, select different groupings to combine on different surfaces. How might watercolor and gouache or watercolor and acrylic be used together? How might crayons be used with watercolor and oil pastels with tempera, gouache, acrylics, and water mixable oils? How might pencils, colored pencils, and ink pens be used with watercolor? As in your other explorations, note in your studio journal discoveries about new effects and expressive ideas made possible by mixing media.

Materials:

A selection of tempera, watercolor, gouache, acrylic, and water mixable oil paints and mediums
Brushes—assorted synthetic, bristle, and soft hair brushes
Selection of alternative painting tools drawn from the list on p. 92
Containers of water
Palettes, containers, and trays for dispensing paints
Assorted papers and other supports
Graphite pencils and colored pencils
Oil pastels
Water-soluble pastels
Ink pens

Getting Started:

1. Select combinations of materials and work with them in different ways (see Figure 3-14). Try painting watercolor over unworked areas of crayon drawing, and use oil pastel over dried tempera, watercolor, gouache, or acrylic, and with oil paints. Explore the how pencils and water-soluble pastels work with watercolor. Find other interesting combinations of material families.
2. Try these media combinations on a variety papers and surfaces. How does the kind of support contribute to the visual results?

STUDIO REFLECTION: PAINTS

Spread out your painting experiments and note the variety of techniques you used and the range of visual effects you were able to achieve. Think about how the different marks and effects you've created could be used to suggest specific ideas, feelings, moods, states, or qualities in a painting (see Figures 3-15a and 3-15b).

Reflecting on your written observations and looking at your test pages, what painting materials and surfaces do you find most interesting? Most expressive? Most fun to work with? Most challenging? Most disappointing? Most surprising? Why?

How do the working processes for each type of paint and the materials themselves compare to one another? Do you prefer some over others? What are the characteristics of the material and process that draw you to them? Compare your responses to what the artists below have to say about their choices and use of materials.

F 3-15a: Paint and mixed media test sheets. (below, left)

F 3-15b: Paint and mixed media test sheets. (below, right)

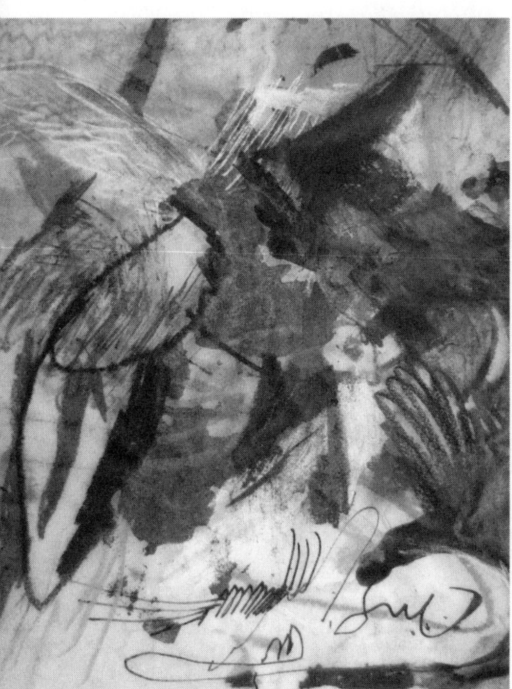

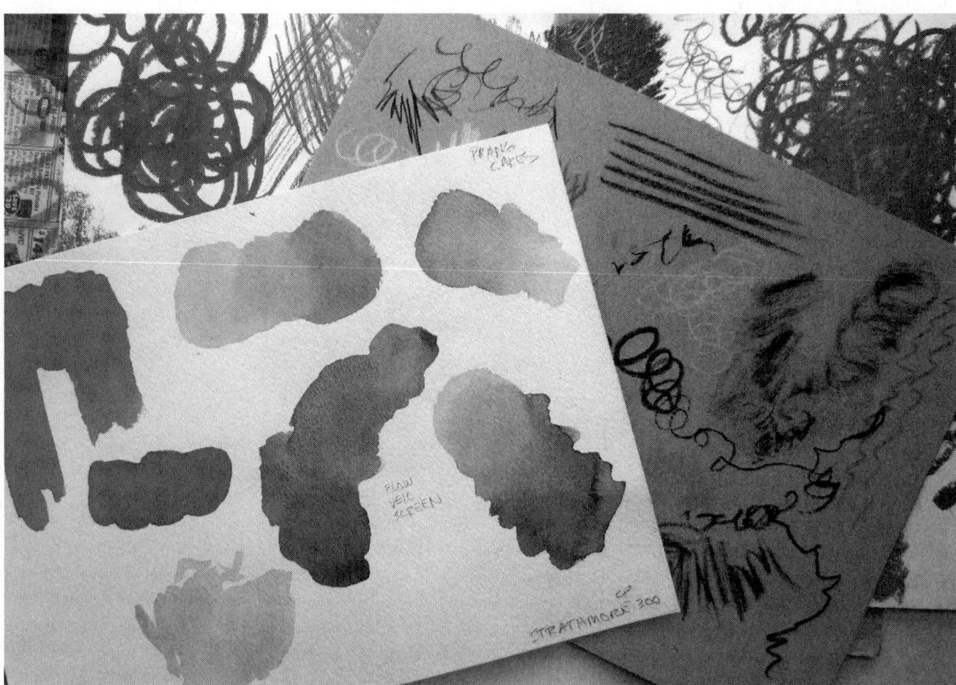

More Artists on Media

Artist Profile: **ROBIN ARNOLD**

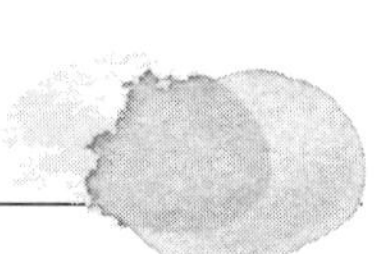

In Robin Arnold's paintings content and imagery are layered in motifs that both reveal and conceal human concerns (see Figure 3-12 and Figure 14 in the color insert). She writes:

Content and imagery are layered in my work; human concerns underlie visible motifs. I use oil paint for the superior richness, depth and transparency of its color. It dries slowly, allowing blending and revision, and it can be successfully used for heavy or thin applications. Each painting is something of a negotiation: I don't make rigid plans in advance, so I can embrace discoveries as I work. I layer images to build content, create new forms, and obscure elements that aren't working well. I turn the canvas occasionally while painting to consider other possible resolutions.

In Compost, *my creative process—turning the canvas and layering imagery—echoes how garden compost is made. Flipping elements upside down suggests a state of transition. Sketchy rendering and transparent glazes evoke cycles of decay / rebirth in the garden. A central golden flower serves as the compost bin's core of heat.*

In the painting How Now, *oil paint is mixed with a cold wax medium to create thick textures of foods and animal skins. Layered images here invite viewers to separate fact from fiction in human / animal relationships.*

Artist Profile: **SEAMUS O'BRIEN**

Seamus O'Brien's paintings play with ideas of artifice and façade, and the exuberance of childhood amusements (see Figure 3-10 and Figure 15 in the color insert). He writes about his work:

My artwork objectifies the lifelike facades and childlike ambiance reflected in popular amusement institutions and explores the way our culture attains a sense of happiness through the delusional remolding of reality. Theatrical elements are naturalistically integrated and combined with children's toys to create a suspension of space and time. My work experience in businesses that specialize in the cultivation of staged "realities" has left me with a mixed sense of apprehension and affection. These facades, in some respects, are my reality.

O'Brien says of his work with materials:

I believe that the content of one's artwork will dictate how the work will be created, i.e., the process. But in the case of the painted banners the medium itself has a recognizable historical association. In order to create the work I had to be aware of the parameters that are created by this association so that I could successfully integrate the content into the material.

My parents were circus performers and for over twenty years my family toured across North America performing under the big top. The first sewn canvases that I used for this series were given to me as a birthday gift from my older brother who runs his own circus school in Columbus, Ohio. The canvases were purchased at a local hardware store and sewn to include the seams (in some cases located right down the middle of the canvas) and any product imperfections into the work. Being that they were a gift, the size, material, and look of the banners is solely attributed to my brother's artistic tastes. This too created parameters for the work, but I find that those restrictions can sometimes help in the creative process.

For two years I kept the canvases in a box in my studio because I wasn't quite sure what to do with them. Then one evening as I was working with another artist in New York, the imagery for the series came to me, and at that point all the details just fell into place. Because of my professional background in the theater, responding to the materials felt like second *nature to me and I could work with or around any imperfections in the canvas. The fact that someone close to me had sewn the banners only added a level of "reality" to the painting . . . or maybe honesty, which is something I strive for in my artwork despite the theatricality of my references.*

Artist Profile: **BEN CAMPBELL**

Ben Campbell paints exuberantly luscious characters in fantastical surroundings, caught up in narratives drawn from another time and place (see Figure 3-16 and Figure 10 in the color insert). He says about his use of materials:

I work primarily with ink, watercolor and gouache to create drawings and paintings.

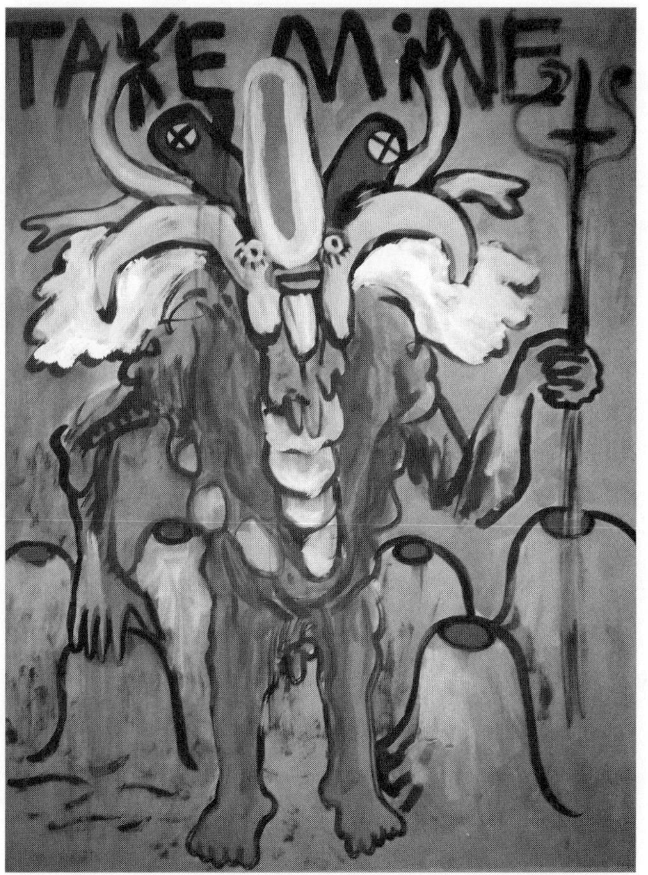

These materials are attractive because of the variety of processes they allow—the duality between their immediate intensity of pigment and value and their potential for subtlety and ephemera. They facilitate my working process, which is grounded in using rapid, automatic drawing to create a vocabulary of images that I incorporate into a personal cosmology expressed in large paintings. In my large works, the material duality of the water based paint and ink is used for variety of mark making— from large visceral gestures to minute repetition. As in the ancient tradition of ink painting, the water based mediums create a dialogue with my automatic process—the hand reacting to the often uncontrollable whim of the pigment in water. Layers of paint can be applied and then scrubbed and washed away, leaving remnants of earlier stages, a timeline of sedimentary pigment below the surface, further indicating the automatic and unconscious nature of creation.

F 3-16
Ben Campbell, Take Mine, 2012, gouache, ink, and watercolor on paper, 22" × 30".

Artist Profile: **KARLA WOZNIAK**

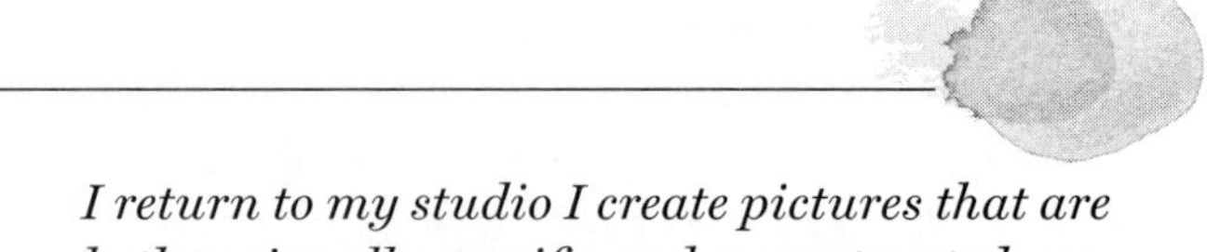

Karla Wozniak's paintings, inspired by road trips across the United States, depict suburban sprawl, automotive culture and commercial landscape, and the gradual turnover of natural environments to the illuminated insistence of signs and street life (see Figure 3-14 and Figure 16 in the color insert).

She writes about her work:

My recent artworks are medium-scale oil paintings and works on paper. I make paintings of the American landscape in transition. I am fascinated by urban development, neglect and how places change over time. I think we can learn a lot about our culture from the appearance and organization of our cities, suburbs and countryside. And particularly now, with the current economic situation, our landscape continues to mutate.

My paintings are inspired by places that I visit and document around the country. When

I return to my studio I create pictures that are both regionally specific and a constructed, authored view. My handling of materials is rigid in some places, open and improvisational in others. Texture and physicality is very important in my work, and my paint ranges from thin and transparent to impasto. Often surfaces seem washed or abraded away. Fracturing and synthesis are both apparent in my compositions and certain aspects of the pictures are rendered, while others dissolve into abstraction. This fracturing of space and shifting of focus parallels how we actually look at landscapes—from changing viewpoints over a period of time, often framed by a car window.

What kinds of ideas do these paintings suggest about their subjects? How does Wozniak's handling of paint and use of transparency and opacity contribute to your interpretation?

Artist Profile: **ELIZABETH GILFILEN**

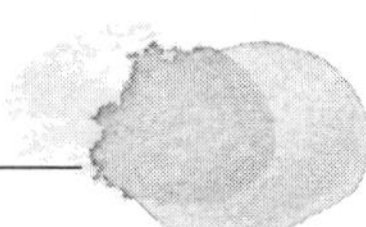

Elizabeth Gilfilen's paintings are conversations between the qualities of materials and the visual structures they ultimately form (Figure 3-17 and Figure 7 in the color insert). Her paintings and works on paper begin with drawing marks in paint.

My paintings and works on paper begin with drawing. Like a conversation, fluid marks evolve, colliding as a thought or hunch becomes form. I am interested in delineating the moment when the fleeting actions of thought rest, assuming a unique structure.

Gilfilen writes about her working process as a flexible and constantly changing space of action and location:

Through improvisation, I instigate a conversation between fluid material and the depiction of internalized structure. I am interested in the threshold where the personal impulse to create collides with more collective understandings of form. Slippages between the act of making and locating image allows me access to a provocative, unfixed space that is continuously re-defined.

As you look at the work, what ideas come to mind based on the use of paint and the marks that compose the image? How does Gilfilen's structuring of marks suggest the process of creating the painting? What kinds of actions might you associate with this work? What makes you say this?

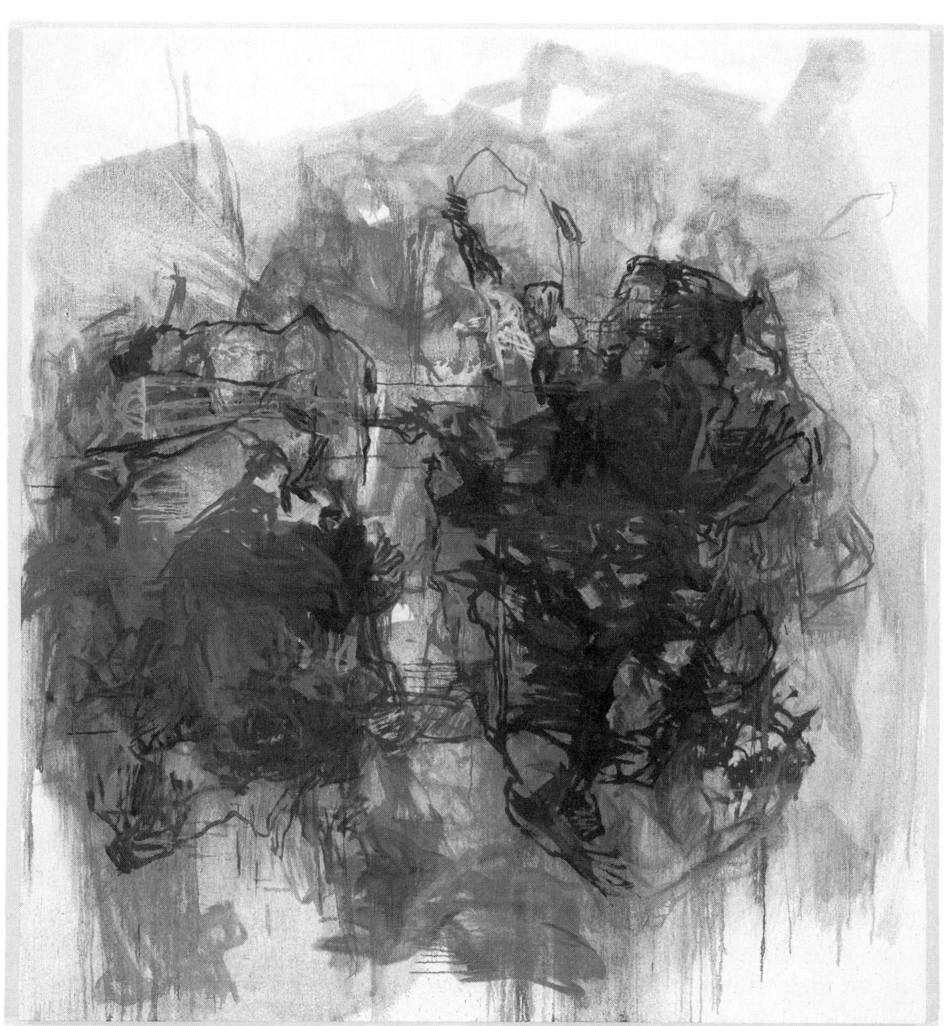

F 3-17
Elizabeth Gilfilen, Hive Mind,
2011, oil on canvas, 72" × 65".

Thoughts about Painting as a Studio Practice

What is a painting? Given that today, photographs can be manipulated with the "painting tools" of a piece of computer software and the resulting image printed out on canvas, and considering that some artists do not use paint at all but create painterly works that actively engage the formal issues and concerns of the genre, this question defies easy answers. What types of goals and intentions for painting and approaches to the process of painting can you find in the artists' comments throughout this chapter?

Like drawing, painting is an open concept in contemporary art with boundaries that seem to defy exact positioning. Artists explore paint materials and painting concepts to play with not only a wide range of formal and thematic ideas and questions but also the sensory and expressive qualities of materials and the effects that can be gotten from experimental and open-ended work with them. For young people, painting functions in similarly divergent ways. At times kids

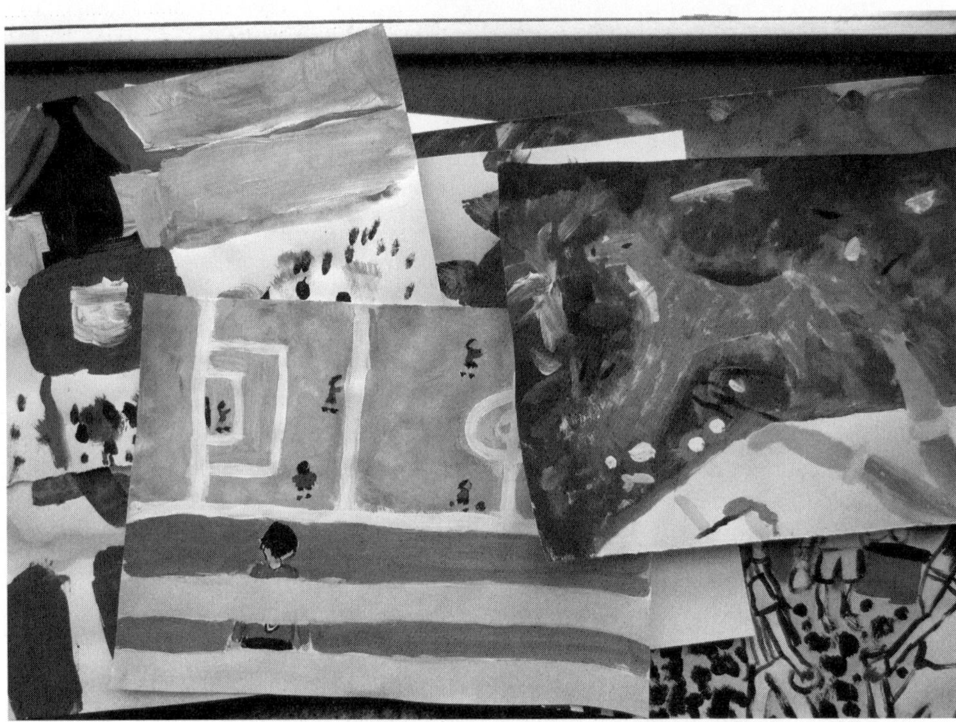

F 3-18: Children's tempera paintings

are eager to experiment and endlessly fascinated by painting materials and their ability to create colors and textures and other effects (see Figure 3-18). At other times, they become focused on portraying things from "real life" in a convincing way. As with drawing, while sometimes only the essentials that serve to communicate an idea, story, or feeling are necessary to a child's work, at other times a focus on detail becomes a goal in itself for the painting.

One of the misconceptions students and teachers sometimes have about paint—and, by extension, painting—is that they are merely a means to "color in" the outlines of a drawing. From the perspectives of the artists profiled in this chapter, there are many other actions, roles, and intentions that painting entails. As with drawing, what happens with materials as a painting takes shape—how the artist responds to what's happening on the painting's surface and thinks in and responds to materials as potentially "meaning something"—can push ideas and the painting itself in new directions, beyond the constraints of any previously drawn boundary lines. The quote by painter Susan Rothenberg that began this chapter is an example of this kind of "flexible purposing." And through your own exploration of different paints and painting techniques you've seen how this fluidity of direction can be essential in coming to understand a material and the possible paths one can take in working with it.

While identifying concepts and skills to teach, choosing approaches, and designing painting lessons for kids of different ages will come later in Chapter 7, begin to think now about some of the differences between drawing materials and processes and painting materials and processes, and how you might use them separately and together in lessons you would like to design. Consider how you might invite kids to paint from observation, imagination, and narratives of their own experiences and research and note your ideas for later development. We turn now to practical considerations for presenting to kids the kinds of materials for painting featured in this chapter.

Setting up for Working with Painting Materials

ESTABLISHING A CLIMATE OF EXPERIMENTAL INQUIRY

In painting, establishing a climate of experimental inquiry leads to students discovering their own ways of working with paints and tools, then sharing these different approaches with the class so that everyone can benefit. As with drawing media, I often invite individual students to lead the painting demonstrations—I ask the class to think of different things we could do with various paints, colors, brushes, and surfaces. I invite volunteers to demonstrate divergent approaches to creating marks and effects, and we imagine how those could be used in a painting. When students are expected to come up with a wide range of approaches to working with paint they have to push the materials in new directions—by experimenting and taking risks. This constant exploration with painting materials and with ideas sets the tone for ongoing experimental inquiry.

MATCHING TIME ALLOTTED AND PROCESSES OF WORKING WITH MEDIA

Exploring different types of paint and documenting and sharing the results requires intense focus, as does using different techniques in a painting—so allowing for enough time when working with painting media is an important consideration when structuring lessons. Coordinating the sizes of brushes and tools with the areas of painting surfaces to be filled, according to the time students have to work, is critical in painting. As with drawing, working on a large surface using a brush or tool that makes tiny marks—and being rushed to do so—can turn into an overwhelming and frustrating experience.

CONSIDERING STUDENTS' AGE, PHYSICAL CHARACTERISTICS, AND PRIOR EXPERIENCE

Students' age, strength and coordination, and prior experience with painting are major considerations when choosing materials. As mentioned previously, wider brush handles are easier for younger children to grasp than narrow ones, and larger brush heads and mark making tools allow for faster coverage of painting surfaces. While different paints are safe for use with all ages, some, such as tempera, are better suited for young children and older beginners because they are easier to control and manipulate, which aids students' mastery and skill development. For both younger students and older students who have little prior experience with painting, starting with limited colors, tools, and surfaces and gradually introducing new options ensures ongoing experimentation. For older students who are ready for additional challenge and new options, moving from tempera to watercolor, gouache, acrylic, and water mixable oils—along with the gradual introduction of special papers, boards, and canvas—provides a good scaffold for continued exploration and discovery.

BALANCING EFFICIENCY WITH STUDENT AUTONOMY

As much as is practically possible depending on space configuration and number of students, kids should be able to move about their workspace to locate and get what they need to do their work, and to share their results and see what their peers have accomplished. It's helpful to have paints prepared in containers or set up so that students can dispense the materials for themselves, brushes and other tools set out in containers, and options for painting surfaces laid out ahead of time. Having students look at what is available and choose what they'd like to use that day encourages them to develop artistic autonomy.

ANTICIPATING MESS AND PLANNING FOR CLEANUP

F 3-19: Documenting what was learned through media exploration.

Protecting work surfaces with newspaper, having kids wear smocks, anticipating spills and accidents, and planning for cleanup will help to promote experimentation and focused work in painting. As mentioned previously, water containers with wide flat bottoms and with sides tall enough to support a leaning paintbrush are essential. Communicate to kids how paints and palettes, water, brushes, and

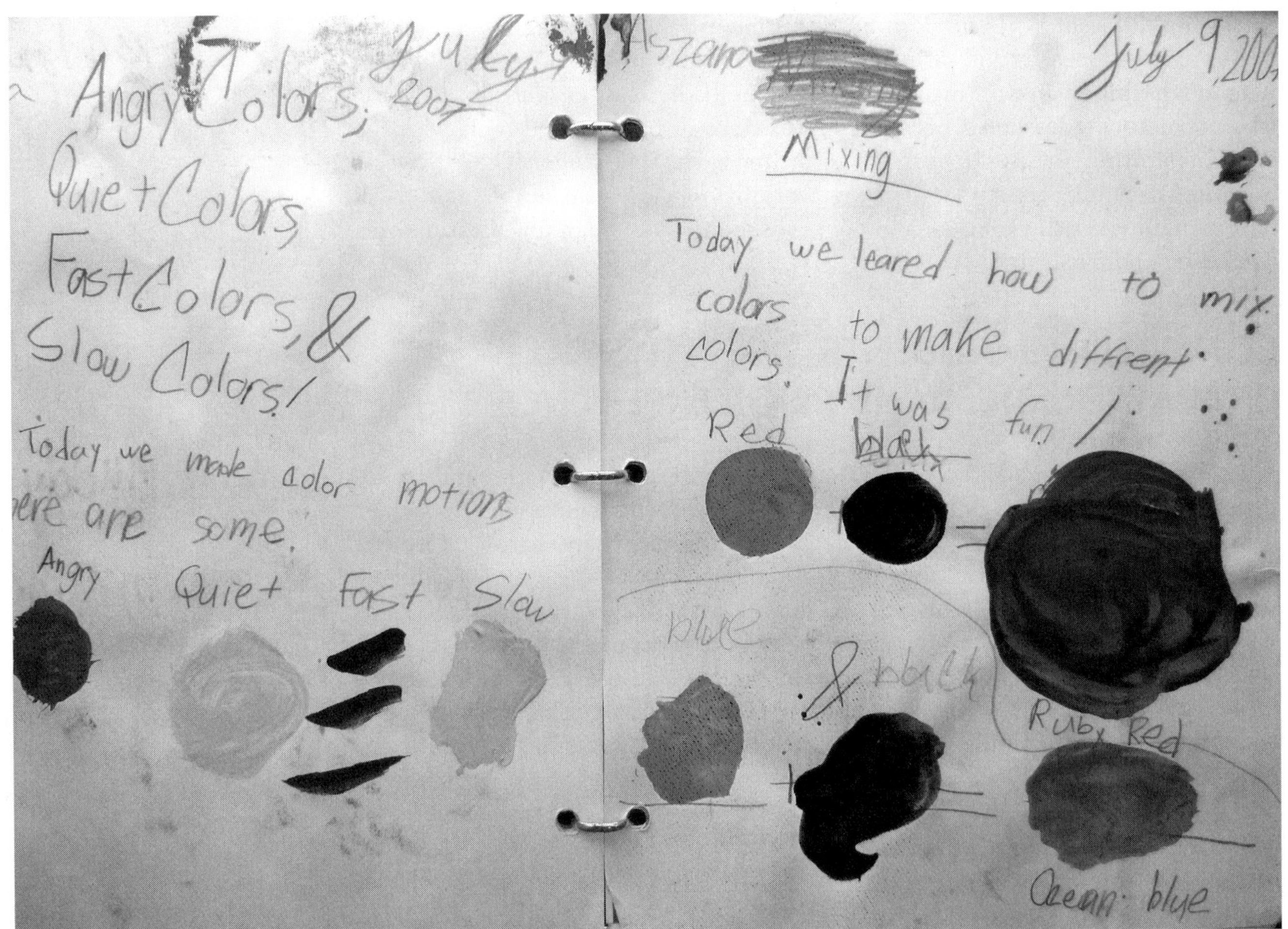

tools will be collected, stored and cleaned, where wet work will be taken to dry, and how they will wash their hands at the end of class.

REFLECTING ON AND ARTICULATING LEARNING

At the end of the painting session, display and discuss with students what was learned. Ask them to show what they learned how to do with paints, colors, and tools through experimentation (see Figure 3-19), and ask them to talk about their finished works in terms of both narratives and meanings they may be interested in sharing and what they discovered and learned how to do. Brief written explanations about the goal of the painting experience and what was learned in individual paintings creates an archive of skills, concepts, and ways of thinking in paint that can be used as a resource in subsequent lessons and communicated to the school community.

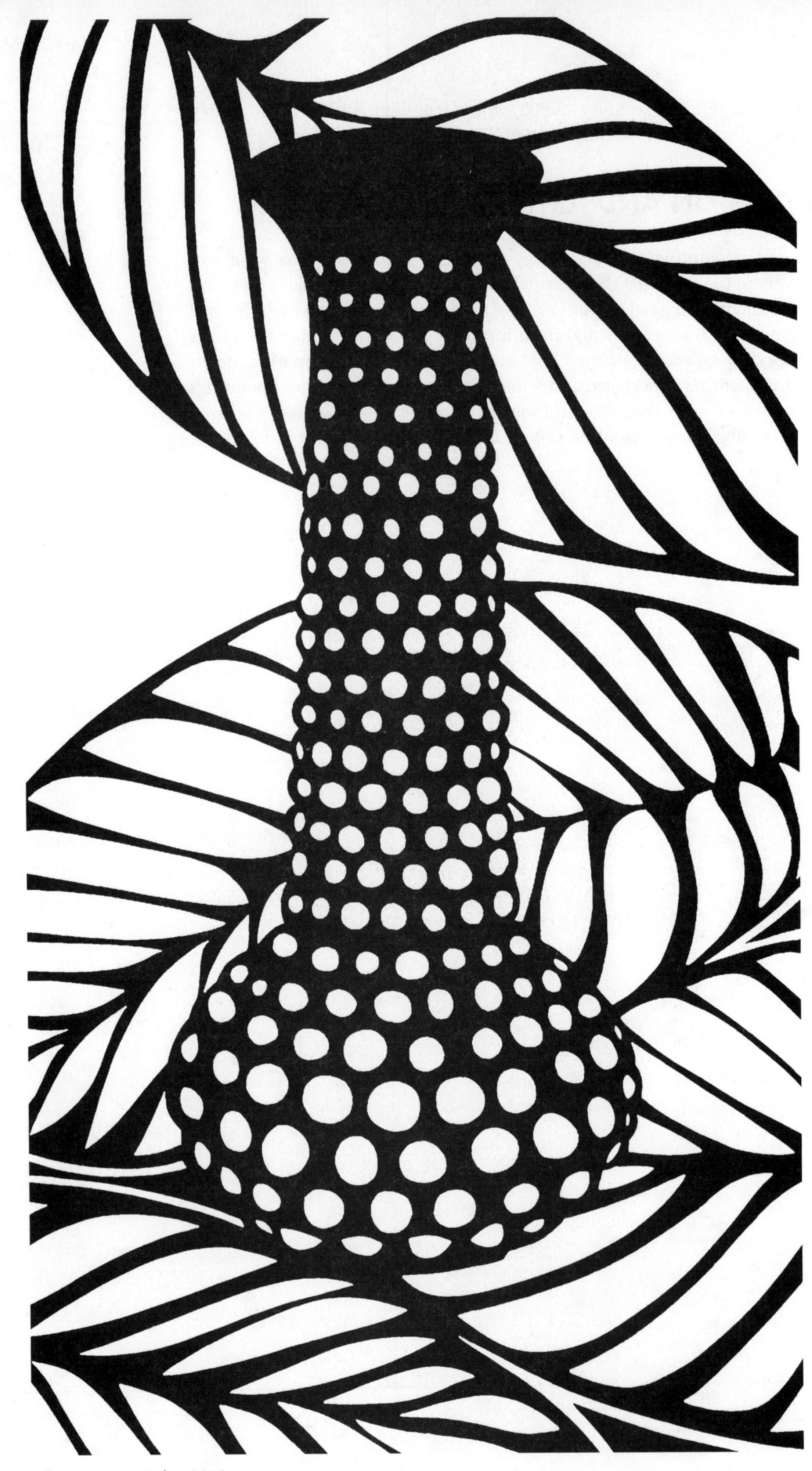

Allison Reimus, Relic, 2010

4

Printmaking

Working in Multiples

The thing that interests me the most about making prints is how it slows down my hand. Each time I return to the print, I am re-educated in the ways of patience. The process of creation becomes methodical in a way that's different than drawing. I trade the immediacy for reflection. When making prints, time operates differently for me. I use the print lab as a testing ground, a site to investigate the possibilities. I see the time with the print as a pilgrimage to gain new truths to then take back to painting. But it's not all taking and no giving though. The print wants something in return.

—Trenton Doyle Hancock[1]

It's been a little tricky because I'm suddenly going into two dimensions after working in three. You have to ask yourself, what is this about? Is this about making pictures of ideas that you want to do or is it about really the idea of trying to make a drawing that has its own reality? That's the challenge.

—Martin Puryear[2]

---

[1] From the essay "Tunnel" by Trenton Doyle Hancock. Retrieved August 7, 2013, from http://www.ipcny.org/files/NP11_Summer%20brochure%20draft.pdf.
[2] Art: 21 (2002). SHORT (video from the series "Exclusive")—*Martin Puryear: Printmaking.* Retrieved July 19, 2013, from http://www.art21.org/videos/short-martin-puryear-printmaking.

PUT SIMPLY, PRINTMAKING INVOLVES the creation of an image by impression of a matrix (the source of the image to be printed) on a surface. The use of a printing plate, block, stone, or stencil allows for multiple productions of a single or similar image. In art, a print is not considered to be a copy made from an original (as a photographic reproduction of a drawing or painting would be, or a copy made from an original in a photocopier)—it is an original work of art based on an image designed from the outset to be produced, not reproduced, using one of several printmaking methods. While prints are frequently produced as numbered editions, or sets in which the images look identical or nearly so, some prints are meant to stand as singular images and are not intended to be considered as multiples.

The origins of printmaking can be traced from prehistoric human hands printed and used as stencils on cave walls, and from diverse cultural and communication practices throughout the ancient world. In China, for example, carvers incised classic texts and other cultural artifacts into stone slabs. Then, thin paper was laid over the surface and pressed into the carved areas, and inked. When the paper was removed from the stone, areas pressed in the crevices (and protected from the ink) remained light, providing a light-on-dark image. Repeated many times, this pulling of prints from the stone provided a means of widely distributing historical information, poetry, scholastic texts, calligraphy, and images of artworks, similar to the ways in which books later functioned. As printmaking practices, along with the production of paper, spread throughout Asia, the Middle East, and Europe, new technologies developed and different methods emerged.

Printmaking techniques are categorized by the part of the printing matrix that holds the ink to be transferred to the print. In relief printing, the image is printed from the raised part of a printing block or plate, which is inked with a roller—the recessed areas of the block do not receive ink, allowing the paper or other support to show through in the corresponding areas of the print. Relief printing surfaces are carved from wood—and from linoleum, rubber, and Styrofoam commonly used in school settings—or built up from the surface in a type of relief collage to make collagraphs (discussed later in this chapter). Intaglio techniques, which also involve an uneven surface on the printing plate, work in the opposite way—here, the ink is applied to the entire surface and pressed into the crevices, then wiped away only from the top level. In printing, the plate is put through a press with a dampened sheet of paper on top and the ink is transferred from the crevices to the paper. Engraving and drypoint (carving and scratching into the plate with tools), mezzotint (roughening the plate with tools), and etching and aquatint (which use acid to remove areas of the plate) are all methods of intaglio printmaking. Planographic techniques, which include lithography and monotypes, use printing surfaces that are neither raised nor lowered and screen printing, in which the ink is forced through a thin mesh material that is blocked in some areas to create the design, are two other approaches.

This chapter focuses on relief prints, screen prints, monotypes, and mixed media prints, all approaches to printmaking that can be done with students of different ages and levels of experience, and without a printing press. What actions and ways of thinking are practiced and encouraged when working with various printing processes and with multiples? How are these different from those that characterize drawing and painting practices? What tools and materials are used in printmaking? Which approaches would be best for young people of different ages? Document your findings as you experiment with the printmaking activities presented later in this chapter.

Figuring out What Materials Can Do

PRINTING SURFACES AND SUPPLIES

Relief, silkscreen, collagraph, monotype, and mixed media techniques each call for different approaches and materials for preparing the printing matrix—which, along with other variables, can lead to distinctive visual characteristics in the finished prints. Collectively, these techniques can produce effects that range from clean edged and controlled to loose and painterly, from opaque to transparent, and from a smooth look with flat areas of color to textured and atmospheric effects that give an illusion of space and three-dimensionality. Look closely at the prints in Figures 4-1 and 4-2, and note the qualities of each. In what ways are they different? What characteristics do they share?

Inks

The type of ink used and the way in which it is applied to the printing matrix can greatly affect the visual qualities of the print. While some printmaking approaches, such as monotypes, can be done with paints, most call for specially formulated printing inks. These inks differ in base materials according to technique (some are oil based and others are water based) and

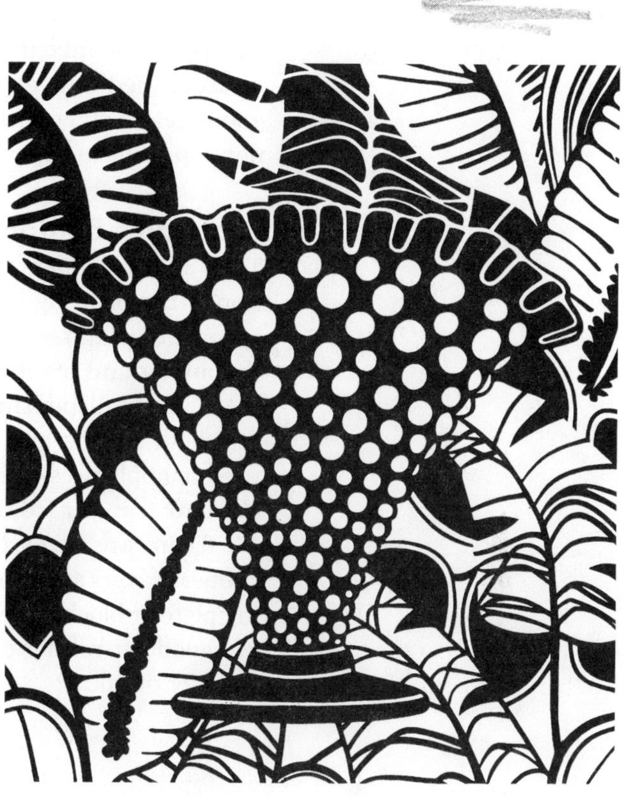

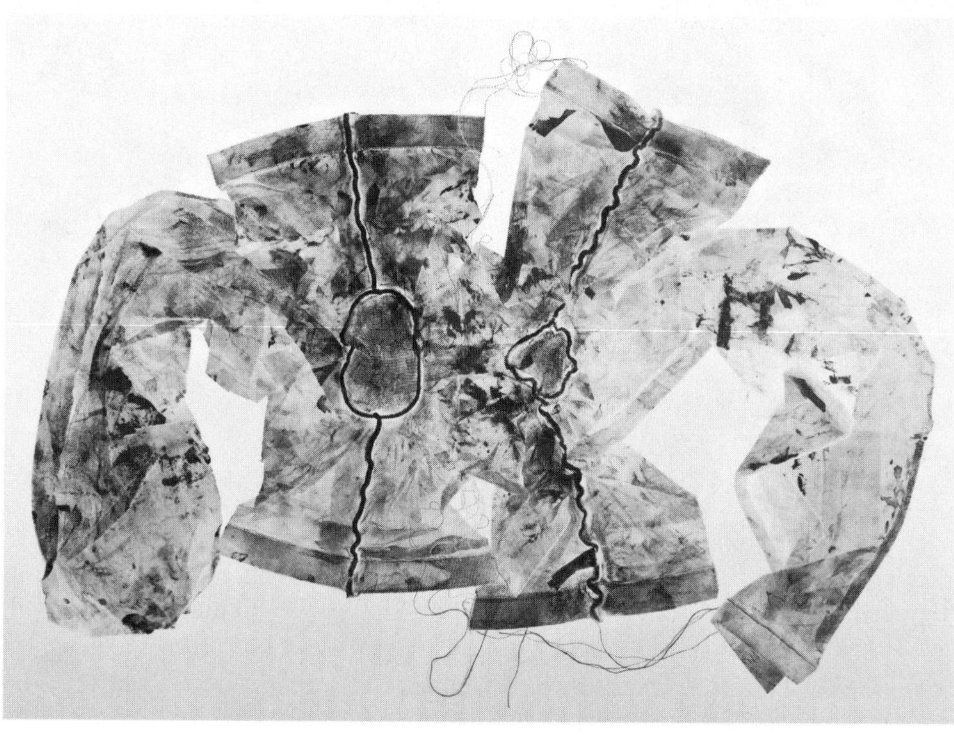

F 4-1
Allison Reimus, Relic #3, 2011, linoleum block, 8" × 9.5". (above)

F 4-2
Julia Elsas, Untitled, 2011, monoprint, 22" × 30". (left)

viscosity (some are stiff and dense while others are more creamy). Like paints, printing inks can be mixed with extenders that promote transparent effects in the finished work.

For relief printing with students, water-based block printing inks work best because they are easy to clean up (Speedball and Blick brands both come in a variety of colors and are sold in tubes and jars). Block printing inks are pigment based and somewhat like the consistency of acrylic paint, but stiffer and stickier. Colors can be mixed, extender medium can be used for transparent effects, and retarder medium can be added to slow drying time. As with other media, it's a good idea to start with one color and gradually expand the selection as students develop skills in the process.

Tools and Equipment

Tools and equipment for printmaking vary by approach, especially in the preparation of the printing matrix (see the sections that follow for descriptions of items specific to each technique). Equipment commonly used in many approaches for the inking and printing part of the process includes sheets of Plexiglas or other material for dispensing ink and brayers—rubber cylinder rollers with handles—that hold the ink and transfer it to the matrix (see Figure 4-3). Brayers are also used to apply pressure to the back of paper laid onto an inked matrix surface, for even ink transfer from matrix to paper.

There are many brayers available and each type functions differently. Soft rubber brayers are excellent for transferring ink from the inking plate to the printing plate or block. Hard rubber brayers can also be used for inking, and both types are good for rolling on the back of paper placed on the printing plate for even transfer of ink.

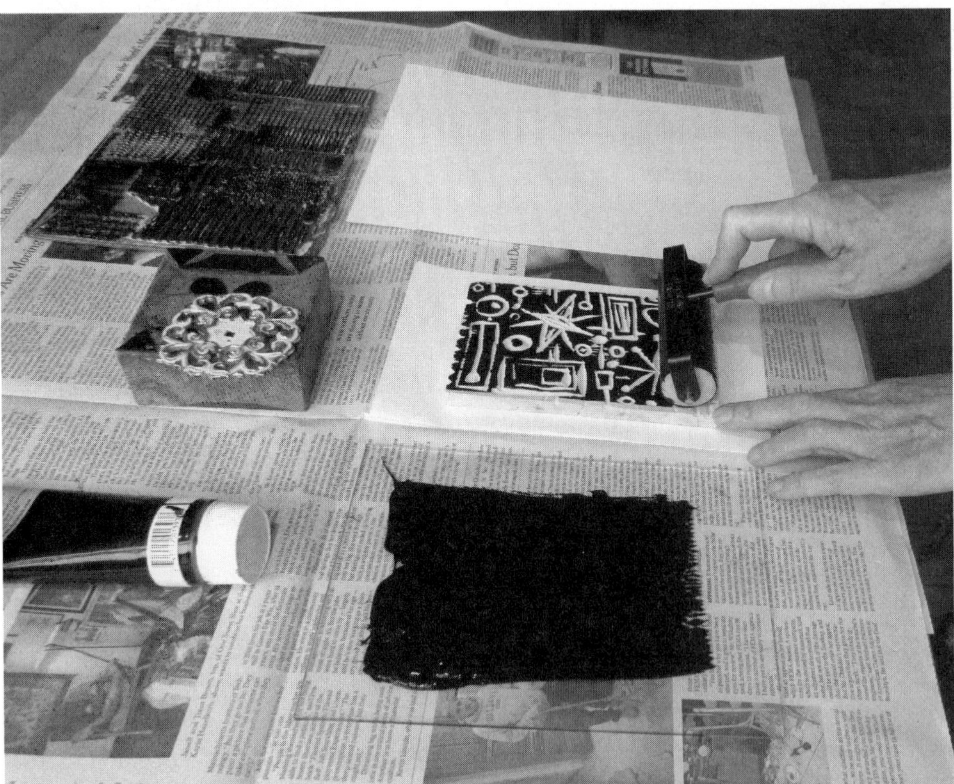

F 4-3: Inking trays and brayers

Papers and Other Surfaces for Printing

Printmaking can be done on many types of paper—heavy, lightweight, smooth, textured, solid, patterned, neutral, and colored, among other alternatives. Artists typically use archival, 100 percent cotton papers specially formulated for press-based printmaking—in other words, durable when soaked in water and run through a press, and able to absorb ink when damp or dry. Popular choices include Arches, Canson, Fabriano, Rives, and Stonhenge, among others (these papers are also excellent for painting and drawing). There are also less expensive blended-fiber papers available—these are typically made from cotton mixed with other fibers or from alpha cellulose. Printmakers also use papers made of kozo (paper mulberry tree native to eastern Asia), hemp, manila, gampi (a Japanese shrub), and mulberry, imported from Japan, Thailand, and India. Canvas (later stretched on a support frame or left unstretched), other fabrics, T-shirts and other types of clothing, tote bags and other accessories, walls, and three-dimensional surfaces are additional alternatives for surfaces.

Beyond professional-grade printmaking papers, many other kinds of paper can be used with students—construction paper, fadeless paper, newsprint, patterned paper, metallic paper, transparent and translucent surfaces all are options for exploration. Because the paper does not need to be soaked for techniques that don't require a press, it can be lighter weight and less durable. You can also use a variety of fabrics—natural fibers and synthetic materials and smooth, textured, matte, and satin surfaces. The fabric should be prewashed and dried if you plan to wash it after printing. You can also print on the surfaces of objects, or on walls. Before printing, walls and objects to be printed on should be washed and dried and any glossy surfaces should be lightly sanded.

The type of surface you print on, along with both the printing matrix and the techniques used to apply ink and press the print, all contribute significantly to the look of the finished print. As with ink choices, starting with limited options and gradually adding more as students gain experience will encourage them to explore and develop skills in focused, in-depth ways.

Experimenting with Printmaking

As with other media, presenting techniques or groups of related techniques one by one allows students to explore and learn about each one in depth, and to gradually develop the skills and dispositions that constitute thinking and practice in the medium. As you complete the printmaking activities that follow, note not only the qualities and technical possibilities for each printmaking approach but also the expressive effects that different techniques and actions promote and the concepts, skills, and ways of thinking that can be taught with them. Also, as with other media, note the practical applications of your discoveries for choosing and using these different approaches with students of various ages.

STAMPING

Stamping is one of the simplest forms of printmaking. It can be done using any surface that can be dipped in or coated with ink or paint and pressed onto another surface (see Figure 4-4). Found objects, food items that can stand up to wetness

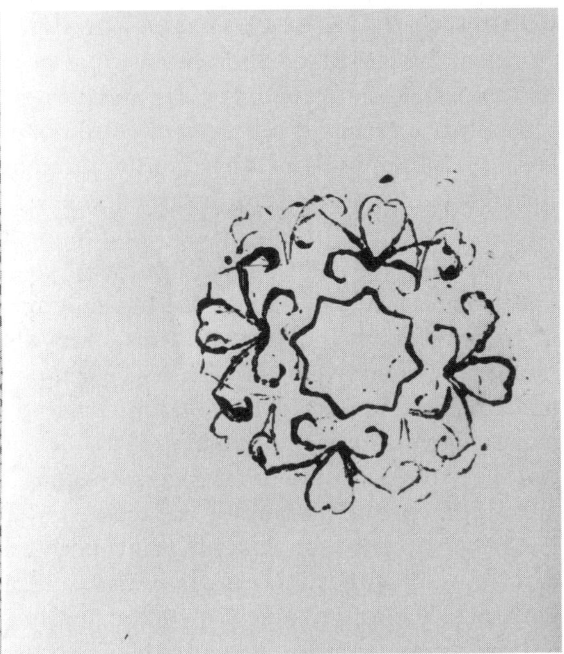

F **4-4:** Stamping with objects

and pressure, corks, thread spools, drinking glass and cup rims, jar tops, carved alphabet blocks and other flat-surfaced toys are all excellent for exploring the stamping technique. As with collage, you can begin your search for stamping materials at home and broaden your hunt to include materials exchanges, second hand stores and flea markets, and the outdoors. The list in Table 4-1 contains ideas for a beginning collection of objects.

Exploring Stamping

What are different ways of stamping? How do the materials and tools used here interact with one another? How is printing with paint different from printing with ink? What are some new approaches that emerge as you explore the materials and techniques that follow?

Materials:

Potato (halved), large pepper (halved and seeded), large mushroom (halved lengthwise), other vegetables for printing
Assortment of found objects for printing
Wood blocks, small enough to grasp easily
Self-adhesive printing plate (vinyl or Styrofoam)[3]
Corrugated cardboard or foam core
Glue
Scissors
Tempera paints, assorted colors including black and white
Water-based block printing ink in tubes, in a few assorted colors including black and white

---

[3] Available at art supply stores—Speedball and Blick are good options for brands.

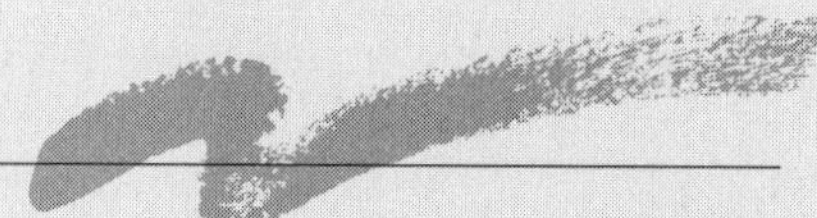

Table 4-1 Objects for Stamping

corks	fruits and vegetables
bottle tops	box lids
jar lids	golf balls
wood blocks	berry containers
bubble wrap	sticks
hair combs	pine cones
toothbrushes	bundle of rope
corrugated cardboard	clothes pin
shoe soles	sponges
thread spools	cookie cutters
toilet paper tubes	scrunched paper and foil
popsicle sticks	game pieces
cotton swabs	small plastic toys
kitchen utensils	

Trays (metal, Styrofoam, plastic) for paint
Small Plexiglas sheets (about 7″ × 10″) or Styrofoam trays for inks
Rubber brayers
Paintbrushes
Assorted papers—colors, neutrals, metallic, tissue, patterns, lettered texts
Assorted smooth-faced fabrics—colors, patterns
A three-dimensional object to print on (something you'd like to transform)
Newspaper for covering work surface

Getting Started:

1. For each object you print, take a moment to consider the following questions. What does the object look and feel like? What are its social or cultural associations? How do you think it will look when printed? How might you use it to create an interesting image on its own, or in combination with other things?

2. Experiment with different ways of stamping in response to the suggestions that follow, and invent your own approaches as well.

   a. Vegetables—Keeping colors separate, pour tempera paint onto trays just enough to coat object surfaces that will be printed, and lay out a piece of white paper. Blot the cut surface of the potato with paper towel to dry if needed and, holding the cut side down, press the flat surface into one color of tempera paint, then press on paper. Try this a few more times, varying the pressure each time you print. Try it a few more times, varying the amount of paint. How do using more and less pressure and more and less paint change the visual qualities of the print? Using another sheet of paper, try printing in different directions (by moving your arm or rotating paper), repeating the shape to form patterns and overlapping and layering prints to build up dense areas—continuing to use different amounts of ink and pressure. Using just the potato and one color of paint on white paper, how many different visual effects can you create?

On a sheet of colored paper, still using the potato, try different colors of paint, experimenting with the printing techniques. Try using the paintbrush to apply the paints to the potato in different ways. Explore a variety of paint and paper colors. Then, print the other vegetables in the same way. Finally, wash and dry the potato and carve into the printing surface with the knife—you can make a series of paired, angled linear cuts that meet at the bottom to form a V and remove the strips inside to create cut-out channels, draw a simple shape and cut away the outside areas, or take a different approach. Experiment with adding this new printing tool to the mix, varying stamps, paint and paper options, and printing techniques. What prints and printing effects are the most interesting to you? Why?

b. Objects—Gather the objects you would like to print and proceed as above, varying paint application, printing pressure, compositional arrangements, and colors of paint and papers. Wash off the paint and dry the objects. Which things are the most surprising in terms of the images that can be created? Which objects when used together create the most interesting compositions?

Note: You can attach small, hard-to-grasp objects to the end of wine corks or to small wooden blocks to facilitate printing. Use hot glue to attach the parts together.

c. Make your own stamp—Using the self-adhesive printing plate and scissors, cut shapes to form a design or other image, peel off the backing from the shapes, and press pieces onto a wood block (remember that the image will print in reverse). You can also cut shapes from corrugated cardboard or foam core and glue to a block or cork.

To print the stamp, squeeze or spoon a line of ink, about the width of the brayer, across the inking tray an inch from the top. Press the brayer into the ink and roll it down and back up on the tray a few times to coat the brayer evenly (the ink may make a snapping sound on the brayer). Roll the brayer over the printing surface of the stamp and print the stamp on white paper, exploring different arrangements, patterns, and layering techniques. Clean and dry the stamp, brayer, and inking tray, and then experiment with the other colors of ink and paper. Also try stamping on fabric. How do the prints made with ink compare to those made with paints? What kinds of effects are possible with each material?

Take the object you are going to print on and decide whether you'd like to use the stamp you just made or create another one to transform the object. How will you use stamping to change, accentuate, or reconsider the object's appearance, function, and identity? What relationship can be made between the object and the image printed with the stamp on the object's surface?

CARVED BLOCKS AND PLATES

Carved wood blocks for printing were produced in China in the eighth century and in Europe in the fourteenth century—they were used to illustrate books, print designs on fabrics, and depict religious, cultural, and historical themes and narratives. Albrecht Dürer in Germany (late fifteenth and early sixteenth centuries), Katsushika Hokusai in Japan (eighteenth and nineteenth centuries), Paul Gauguin in France (late nineteenth century), and Expressionists Edvard Munch (late nineteenth and early twentieth centuries) and Ernst Ludwig Kirchner (early twentieth century), among other artists, popularized the technique.

Young children and beginners can learn woodcut-style relief printing using Styrofoam printing plates (Scratch-Foam made by Scratch-Art and Sax Foam printing plates are both good options). These plates are drawn into directly with pencils or sticks and printed using block printing inks. For older and more experienced students, synthetic rubber blocks (Soft-Kut and Blick E-Z Cut) and battleship gray linoleum (Blick Golden-Cut or Easy-to-Cut) sheets can be used along with special linoleum cutters, which come in a variety of tip shapes for making different kinds of cuts (Speedball and Blick both make sets that include a handle and assortment of interchangeable metal tips). A metal, wood, or masonite bench hook (metal and wood bench hooks are available from art supply stores), keeps the plate from moving while being carved—these are highly recommended for safe cutting (see Figure 4-5). The bench hook is placed on the table so that one edge hooks against the edge of the table—the printing block is placed on the bench hook with one side against the top edge so that you don't have to hold the block while you're cutting into it. As the plate or block is being cut, the top edge of the bench hook prevents the cutting tip from uncontrolled movement beyond the work area, safeguarding against potential injury. If you use a metal bench hook, it can double as an inking tray.

F 4-5: Cutting rubber block with linoleum cutter and bench hook

Note: To make a wooden bench hook, use a 9″ × 12″ piece of 1/4″ plywood or 1/8″ masonite and two approximately l″ × 2″ wood strips that are 9″ long each. With the board oriented vertically, nail one strip to the front of the board at the top and one strip to the underside along the bottom edge.

Exploring Carved Blocks and Plates

How can Styrofoam, rubber, and linoleum be cut to produce relief designs and images for printing? What are the differences between these materials as you prepare them for printing and in the finished prints? How do different types of paper and colors of ink contribute to the visual and expressive qualities of a print?

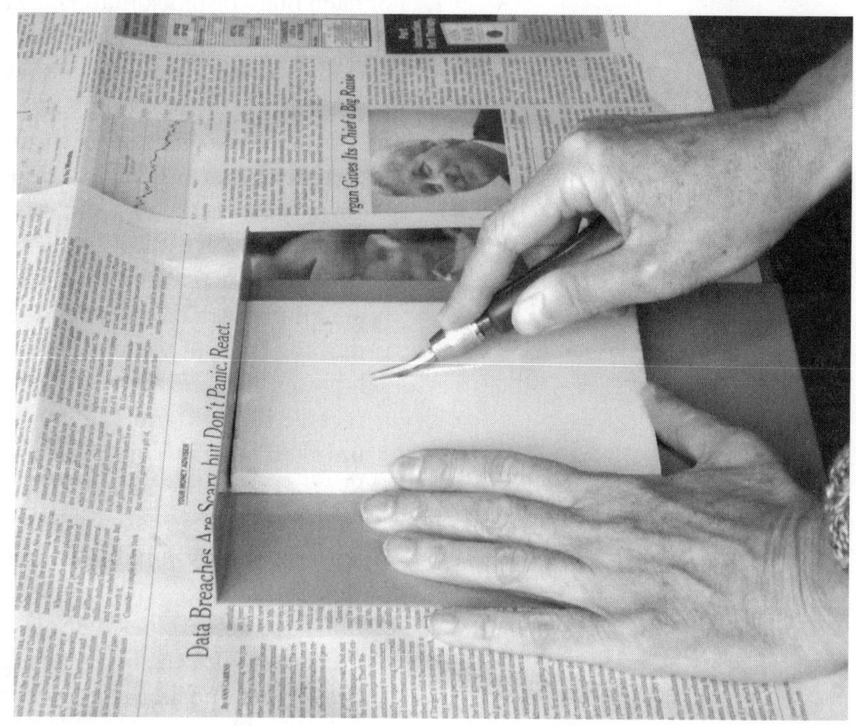

What are some ways of inking and printing the plates that lead to more varied effects? (See Figure 4-6.)

Materials:

2–3 Styrofoam printing sheets (standard 9″ × 12″ sheet cut into 4 ½″ × 6″ quarters)
2–3 synthetic rubber printing blocks (same general size as above)
2–3 battleship or alternative linoleum printing blocks (same size as above)
Linoleum cutters with handle, assorted sizes of V and U shapes
Pencil
Black permanent marker
Ruler
Water-based block printing ink in assorted colors including primaries and black and white
Rubber brayers (4″ wide)
Small trays or Plexiglas sheets for rolling out inks (wider than the brayers)
Large spoon
Assorted thin papers and other surfaces to print, in various sizes of rectangles and squares larger than your printing blocks and plates—colors and neutrals (construction paper, fadeless, tissue), metallic, patterns, lettered texts and images, acetate, vellum
Assorted smooth-faced fabrics—solids, patterns
Newspaper for covering work surface
Paper towels
Bench hook

Getting Started:

1. For each plate or block material, consider the surface and the characteristics of the material and their possibilities for mark making to create designs and images (remember that the carved image on the plate will be reversed when printed on paper). As you move to the inking and printing process, note the qualities of the ink and how it interacts with the printing plates and blocks and with various papers and other surfaces.

   a. Styrofoam test plate—On a test plate, use a pencil to incise lines into the surface. Press forcefully enough so that you can feel the cuts when you run your hand over the surface, but don't press so hard that the pencil point makes a hole in the bottom of the plate. Experiment with making lines of various types and lengths, straight and curved, overlapping, layered, and so forth. Remember that the raised areas will receive the ink and the lower areas will not (these areas will be the uninked paper color in the final print).

   b. Synthetic rubber block test plate—Unscrew the head of the linoleum cutter handle to loosen it, insert the curved end of one of the V-shaped cutters, and tighten the head to secure. Place the bench hook level on the table surface with the bottom wall against the table edge, and position the rubber block against the front raised wall. Hold the handle of the cutter with the blade facing away from you, and with the bottom of the V cutter positioned downwards. With your non-cutting hand away from the block or placed on the block behind the cutter, carefully and slowly make linear incisions in the surface of the block, moving from the bottom to the top of it, away from you. Try making different kinds of line cuts, and turn the block to make lines in different directions. Experiment with straight lines and curved lines. When you have a good feel for how the tool works, try the other blades and note the differences in how they remove the rubber and the width of lines they create. Try outlining a shape with a small V cutter and removing the center of the shape with a U cutter.

c. Linoleum test plate—If the linoleum is stiff or cold, heat the top slightly with a hair dryer or place near a heater to make it more pliable (do not overheat). Use the cutting methods for the rubber block on the linoleum, experimenting with the different cutting tips to make a variety of lines and carved out areas on the plate.

d. Printing test plates—With one color of ink on white paper, print the test blocks to see how the three materials work as printing matrices. Apply a strip of ink to the inking tray, roll the brayer to get an even coat of ink on it, and roll the ink onto the first block (you may need to apply two coats—be sure the ink does not flow into the incised areas). Carefully pick up the inked block, center it overhead and face down on the printing paper, and press the block on the paper. Holding the block and paper together so that neither shift, carefully flip the block and place on the table with the paper on top, back facing up. To apply even pressure and transfer the ink effectively, rub the entire back of the paper with the heel of your hand or the back of a large spoon, or apply pressure across the surface by rolling over with a clean brayer. Carefully lift the paper from the block by peeling away from one of the corners, and set the print aside to dry. Study the finished prints to see what adjustments you may need to make in terms of cutting (depth of incised

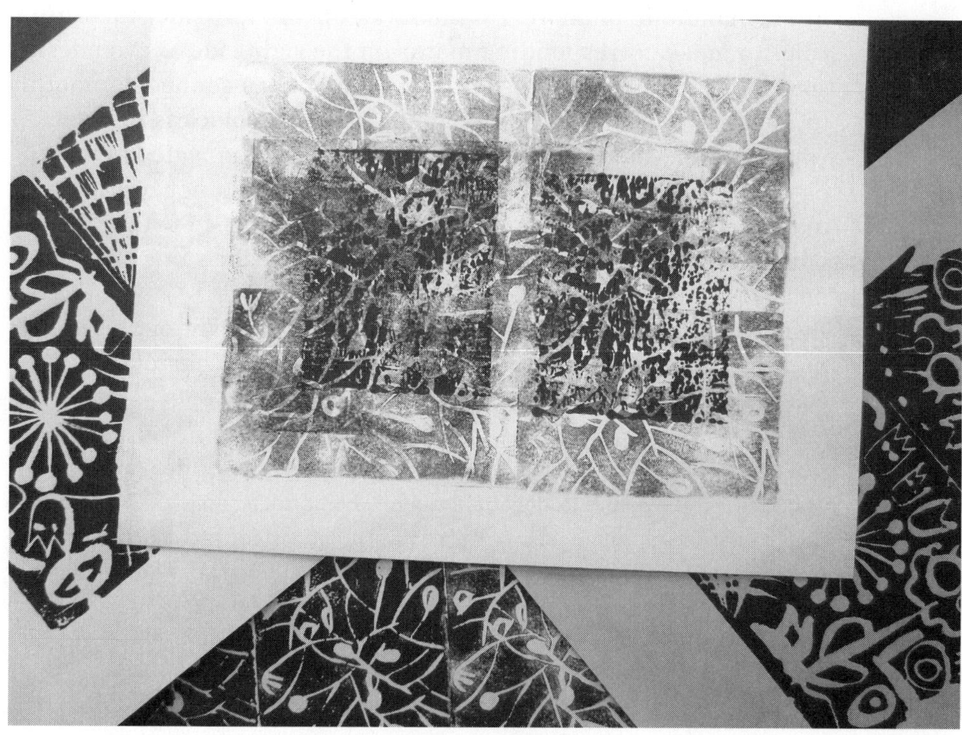

F 4-6: Block prints

areas), amount of ink, and pressure on the paper during the printing process. What areas show interesting effects? How did you create them? What areas show bold application of ink? What did you do to get this result?

Note: Drying times for inks are variable according to temperature and humidity. To protect and preserve your tools and equipment, be sure to wash and thoroughly remove ink from printing blocks, brayers, inking trays, brushes, and any other tools before the ink begins to dry on them—once dry, the ink is extremely difficult to remove.

e. Planned design or image—Now that you understand the process and its potential, choose one or more new blocks to develop into a design or image (see Table 4-3 for subject and theme ideas). You can cut the block freehand or first draw an image on the surface as a guide. What colors of ink and what papers will you use for these new prints? Before you begin the printing process, see the final printing section that follows for alternative, experimental inking approaches.

Note: You can also transfer an image on paper to the block by placing the paper image side up on the block and sliding a piece of carbon paper (carbon side down) between the back of the image paper and the block. Drawing over the lines in the image will transfer it to the block. To reverse the image so that it prints as it appears on the paper, use tracing paper to trace the image then flip the tracing over and darken the lines on the reverse side. Lay the reversed image on the carbon paper and draw over the lines again to complete the transfer.

f. Connected repeating pattern—Choose a block and draw an image or design that begins and ends at the same points on the side edges. First, make one or more guide marks on the left side, then use a ruler to make corresponding marks on the right side. As you design your block, be sure that the left side of the image connects smoothly to the right side, at the guide points, when the block is printed. As you print the block repeatedly to create the connected repeating pattern, line it up so that the edges touch but do not overlap. You may find it helpful to make a grid on the printing surface to help with this placement—the grid units should be the same size as the printing block.

g. Print an edition—Choose one block and print an edition, a series of multiples made from the same block printed in one color of ink on one color of paper.

Note: An edition is either limited, where the number of prints is determined at the outset and no more will be produced, or open, with no set limitation. For artists, the practice of limiting the number of prints in an edition stems from a desire to increase the market value of their work (a smaller print run potentially leads to higher demand and higher prices). Edition size is also limited by the durability of the plate, which wears down with multiple printings.

Prints in an edition are signed and numbered by the artist using a system that identifies both the number assigned to the particular print and the total number in the edition (8/50 means that the edition consists of 50 multiples). Other markings include A/P, to designate artist's proofs that are kept by the artist, separate from the regularly numbered prints. Additional markings may indicate trial proofs leading up to the final version as the plate and inking are in development and a printer's proof that designates the final version of the print, the basis or standard for all that follow in the edition.

While printing editions should not dominate kids' experiences with the medium, it is a great way for them to build a collection of each other's work (through group print exchanges) and showcase their work in the community (through exhibitions and sales). The versatility of the medium lends itself to teaching about art and design production and entrepreneurship—prints can take the form of notecards, bookmarks, notebook covers, and T-shirts and other clothing items. Prints done on fabric can be further developed into stuffed toys, wall hangings, mobile phone and eyeglass cases, wallets, and carrier bags, among other things—students themselves will have many good ideas for things that would be great to produce with printmaking techniques.

h. Reduction prints—Choose a rubber or linoleum block to develop as a reduction print, in which a single block is used to make a multicolor print through successive phases of cutting and inking. You can prepare the block through freehand cutting or by transferring an image to use as a guide. If you are working with a transferred image, decide which ink colors you'll be using and how they will be assigned to the different parts of the image (in the printing you'll work from light to dark). Make the first set of cuts—these will end up in the print as the bare paper color and the first ink color application will become the initial background color of the image.

Print the block on your choice of papers. Because you will be making additional cuts in the block in each successive phase, all sheets of paper in the edition need to be printed from the beginning of the process. Next, wash and dry the block and make the second round of cuts—any areas that are removed from the block this time will show up in the print as the first ink color you used. Ink the plate with the second color and place the block on top of the first printed image, being careful to line up the edges for accurate registration. Continue cutting and printing color by color on all of the papers until the edition is done.

i. Printing: Alternative approaches—Take one of your plates and experiment with other ways of printing it, beyond what you've done so far. First, explore printing the plate multiple times on the same sheet of paper, with the edges of the inked areas touching each time you add to the print. On another sheet of paper, experiment with overlapping and layering prints of the same plate, rotating the plate in a different direction as you print. Also try printing multiple blocks on the same sheet of paper. Within all of this, vary the colors and amount of ink you use, the paper you print on, and the amount of pressure you use to maximize your range of effects.

You can also experiment with different ways of inking the plate. Try a split fountain technique, in which two colors of ink are squeezed onto the inking plate so that the line of ink across the top is half one color and half the other, with the two colors joined in the middle.

Artist Profile: **ALLISON REIMUS**

Allison Reimus works in painting and printmaking to explore decorative elements of domestic interiors (see Figure 4-7). She writes:

I have always been fascinated by ornamentation and its purpose within the domestic interior. Some people consider function and usability to be the most important features of household objects, while others rely heavily on decoration for decoration's sake. For the latter, does the purely decorative then become a necessity, making it functional, or is it strictly a psychological frivolity and how do we distinguish one from the other? My work references the domestic interior, the human psyche and the act of painting through the manifestation of such questions; not meant as a definitive answer, but a mere attempt to try and understand how painting, as act and object with intellectual and cultural purposes, fits into the scheme. Through formal and spatial considerations, I hope to simultaneously question the notions of painting as decorative object and also as an idea, capable of transforming a surface into something other than what can be defined by its physical properties.

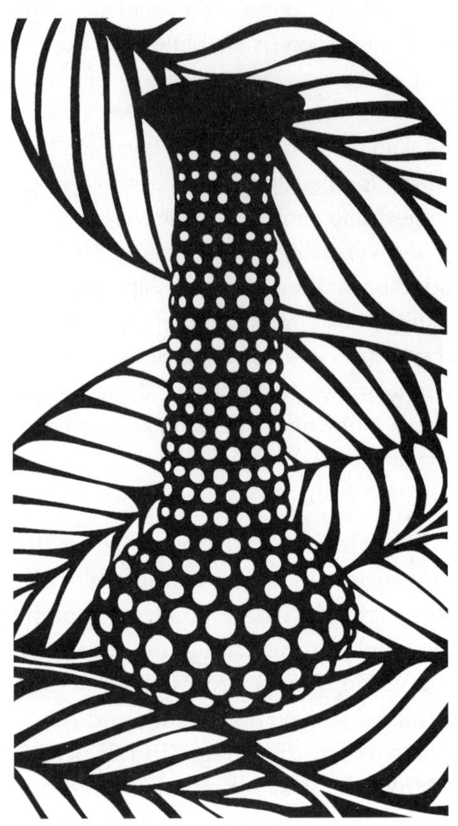

F 4-7
Allison Reimus, Relic, 2010, linoleum block, 6" × 12".

When you roll out the ink to coat the brayer, the colors will mix in the middle to make three colors. Carefully center the brayer over the block before pressing onto it, and roll up and down to transfer the ink. It is also possible to add multiple colors of ink to the block by using narrow brayers, each with a different color of ink. And you can use a paintbrush or cotton swab to add small amounts of a color over or next to another color previously rolled on with a brayer. This technique is similar to *à la poupée* ("with the doll")—the name refers to the doll-shaped wad of fabric, or *poupée*, used to dab on the ink in intaglio printing.

2. Try printing the plates and inks on a wide variety of papers and on the plastic and vellum sheets. What different effects are you able to achieve? Which prints are particularly interesting to you? Why?

COLLAGRAPHS

Collagraphs were made in the nineteenth century and became popular among artists with the rise of collage in the early twentieth century. Similar to collage,

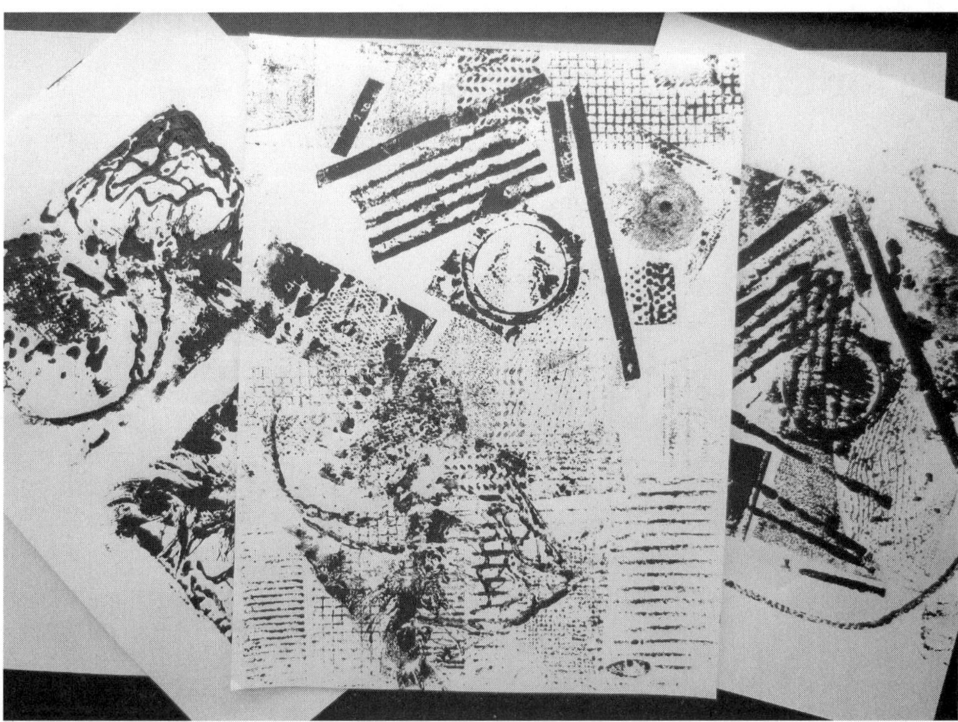

F 4-8: Collagraph prints

a collagraph printing plate is built up from elements that are glued down to a base. Plates can be made of smooth, flat cardboard shapes and from materials that provide interesting textures, such as corrugated cardboard (with the top paper layer peeled away), burlap, mesh screen, string and yarn, dried glue, sponges, bubble wrap, sandpaper, crumpled paper, buttons, foam packing material, drinking straws, sticks, leaves, grass, and other repurposed materials. The hunt for and transformation and arrangement of compositional elements are key to the design and construction of the printing plate.

Collagraph printing is often considered a relief printing technique, in which only the top surfaces receive and hold the ink to be transferred. But it also can function as an intaglio technique in which the entire plate is inked and the raised areas wiped clean to allow the lower areas to transfer ink to the paper. Some artists use a combination of both approaches. Along with monotype printing, described later in this chapter, collagraph techniques are among the most open and versatile of printmaking approaches and are well suited for a high level of experimentation and innovation in the art class (see Figure 4-8).

Exploring Collagraph Prints

What are different ways to construct collagraph printing plates? How do the visual and tactile qualities of various materials translate to a printed surface? What kinds of effects can be produced from different ways of arranging and juxtaposing plate elements and from various approaches to inking and printing the collagraph plate?

Materials:

Selection of materials for constructing plates (see Table 4-2 for suggestions)
Rigid cardboard or flat wood bases

Table 4-2 Materials for Collagraph Plates

matboard	leaves
corrugated cardboard	string
flat jar lids	twine
flat plastic bottle caps	yarn
strapping tape	sponge
bubble wrap	scrunched foil
hair combs	feathers
toilet paper tubes	drinking straws
popsicle sticks	steel wool
cotton swabs	sandpaper
kitchen utensils	buttons
sticks	mesh screen
grass, straw, raffia	burlap

White PVA glue, tacky glue
Scissors
Water-based block printing ink in assorted colors including primaries and
  black and white
Rubber brayers
Paintbrushes
Container of water
Small trays or Plexiglas sheets for rolling out inks (wider than the brayers)
Large spoon
Assorted thin papers and other surfaces to print, in various sizes of rectangles
  and squares larger than your printing blocks and plates—colors and neu-
  trals (construction paper, fadeless, tissue), metallic, patterns, lettered texts
  and images, acetate, vellum
Assorted fabrics to print—solids, patterns
Newspaper for covering work surface
Paper towels

Getting Started:

1. What are the possibilities for printed images of each of the materials? What
   are different ways of arranging elements on the base board? During the
   inking and printing process, keep notes about the collage elements you use
   on your plates and the qualities of the printed images that come from them.
   a. Smooth board plate—Cut pieces of smooth-faced cardboard in a range
       of shapes and sizes. Play with possible arrangements of these ele-
       ments to form an image or design and glue the pieces to a base using
       white glue.

   b. Texture plate—Gather the materials that have a texture you can feel and experiment with different ways of altering and arranging them in a composition. Glue the pieces to the base using white glue and tacky glue (for objects that are more difficult to attach).

   c. Linear plate—Try making a plate that focuses on linear elements that are layered in different ways. You can drizzle glue in straight lines and arcs and glue down string, yarn, twine, and other linear materials.

   d. Found objects—Play with different ways of juxtaposing bits and pieces from all of your materials, including those you used on other plates and other items such as buttons, foil, leaves and other natural materials—attach these to the base.

Note: While not required, you may find it useful to coat your collagraph plates with acrylic gel medium to seal them before inking and printing. This will prevent the ink from absorbing into the surfaces of the collage elements used on the plate. If you do not use a coat of gel medium, the plate will become sealed when the first application of ink for printing has dried.

   e. Printing—When the glue on the plates is thoroughly dry, print each one using one color of ink and one color of paper. Roll a generous coat of ink over the plate—you may need several coats, depending on the absorbency of the materials. Use your hand, a brayer, or a spoon to apply firm pressure to transfer the ink to the paper. You can also put the plate on the floor and gently stand on it, but put a protective sheet of paper over the printing paper if you use this method.

     You may need to let your plates dry before changing ink colors, depending on what colors you use. As with the carved block prints, try printing the plate multiple times on the same sheet of paper, experimenting with placement, overlapping, and layering. Print multiple plates on the same sheet of paper, varying inks, paper, and methods. Explore split fountain and *à la poupée* techniques as well.

2. Print the plates on a wide variety of papers and on the plastic and vellum sheets. You can also lay thin paper over a dry collagraph plate and make a rubbing of it with a soft pencil, pastel, or crayon. Similarly, you can run an inked brayer across thin paper placed on the dry plate to pick up the raised plate's textures from underneath. From all of your collagraph tests, what different effects are you able to achieve? Which prints are particularly interesting to you? Why?

STENCILS AND SILKSCREEN

Stencil printing can be traced to ancient China as early as AD 500 and, later, Japan and other regions where it was used to create designs and images on paper, fabric, clothing, and decorative items. As these printing processes became more refined, intricately cut stencils were attached to silk fabric stretched over a wood frame—here, the ink was applied to the fabric screen and forced through it. Areas around the stencils allowed the ink to reach the printing surface, creating the design.

    In the seventeenth century, direct stenciling (also called *pochoir*) was used in European countries to print textiles, wallpapers, and other decorative materials.

In the late nineteenth century, new screenprinting technologies further developed these decorative arts and introduced a new use for the stenciling technique—the production of advertising signs and posters.

In the 1930s, artists in Europe and the United States began to explore screen printing as an artistic medium and during this time the term serigraphy was adopted to distinguish fine art screen printing from commercial uses of the technique. There was much experimentation with screen printing by US artists participating in Depression-era arts programs funded by the federal government, and in the 1940s, artists such as William H. Johnson produced silkscreen prints. But it was not until two decades later, in the Pop Art movement of the 1960s, that screen printing became widespread among artists. While Andy Warhol is credited with initiating the broad adoption of screen printing, many artists have worked with the technique, including Robert Rauschenberg, Ed Ruscha, James Rosenquist, Bridget Riley, Gerhard Richter, Richard Hamilton, Kiki Smith, and Shahzia Sikander.

In a stencil print, the contrast between what is inked and what is blocked from being inked creates the image on the printing surface—stencils are used as masks to prevent the coloring medium from reaching some areas of the printed image while allowing it to reach other areas (see Figures 4-9 and 4-10). In a standard or positive stencil image, the cut out, open area inside the outer contour of the image allows ink or paint to reach the printing surface while the area outside the contour is blocked. In a reverse or negative stencil image, the inner area is blocked by the stencil and the outer area surrounding the stencil image receives the ink or paint.[4]

Stencils used without a screen can be made from paper, cardboard, plastic, polyester film (commonly called Mylar), wax coated or plastic coated stencil paper, freezer paper, or tape, among other materials. For stencil printing on fabric, walls, and wood, self-adhesive contact paper works well because it is tacky enough to stick to the printing surface but easily removable at the end of the process.

Stencils used as part of a screen printing process are considered direct (prepared right on the screen) or indirect (prepared away from the screen and later attached to it). Materials used for direct stencils include oil pastels, masking tape or screen tape, screen drawing fluid, and screen filler (Speedball makes screen

F 4-9

Mike Elko, Tin Can Telephone (left), 2005, two-sided screen print on painted wood box, with rope, hardware, 20" × 12" × 3". (below, left)

F 4-10

Mike Elko, Tin Can Telephone (right), 2005, two-sided screen print on painted wood box, with rope, hardware, 20" × 12" × 3". (below, right)

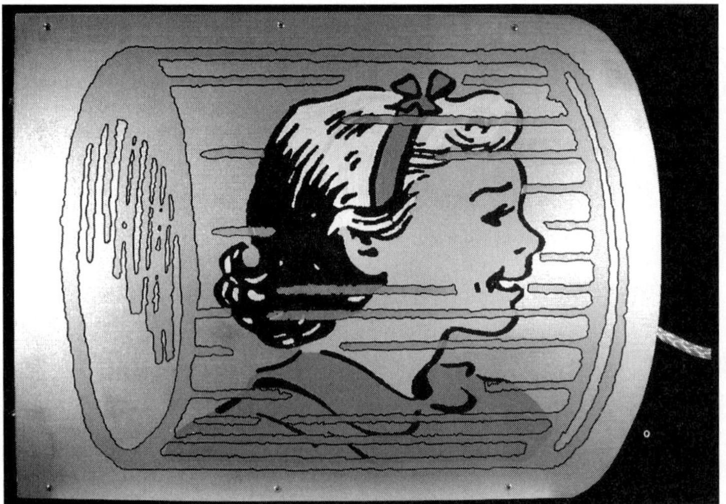

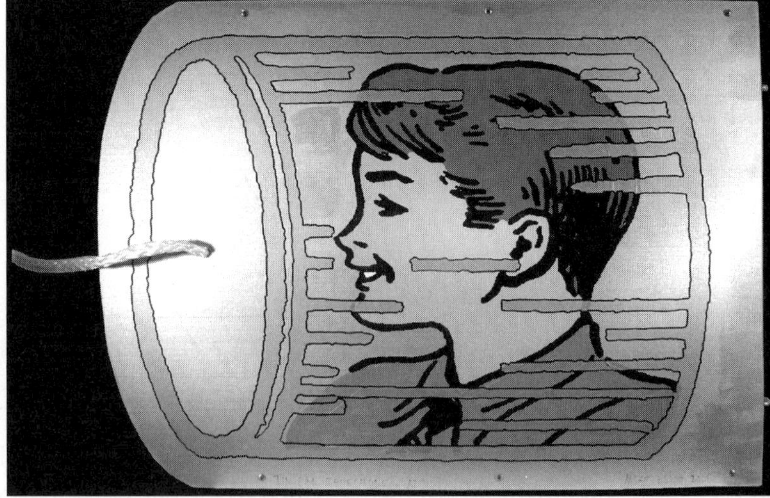

---

[4] Negative prints made with human hands as stencils are present in Paleolithic cave paintings, dating to 30,000 BC.

drawing fluid and screen filler). Screen filler is a liquid formula that is applied with a brush or squeegee directly to the areas of the screen that will be blocked from printing—it is used with screen drawing fluid, which is painted on the parts of the screen that will print (the screen is rinsed to remove the drawing fluid, allowing the ink to pass through during printing). For indirect stencils, a good option is to use lightweight photocopy paper cut with the stencil image—in printing, this is placed between the screen and the surface to be printed on.

Note: Screen stencils can also be prepared using a light-sensitive photo emulsion, which is applied to the entire screen, and an opaque stencil that blocks the light from reaching the treated screen during exposure. When the screen is exposed to light, the emulsion thickens and fills the holes of the mesh screen in the areas unblocked by the stencil. After exposure, the screen is rinsed and the treated areas blocked by the stencil are dissolved in water and removed from the screen. One advantage of this technique is that you can use computer generated/accessed images as stencils—inkjet prints on acetate can work well as stencils for photo silkscreen. Because it is more durable than a paper stencil, you can also produce more prints with photo emulsion stencils, and this is the case for the drawing fluid and screen filler method as well.

In screen printing, the ink is applied to a thin, mesh material that is blocked in some areas. As the ink is forced through the screen with a squeegee, it passes through the unblocked areas of the screen to the printing surface but is prevented from doing so in the blocked areas. This variation of blockage and open passage of the ink creates the design or image.

Beyond stencil materials, screen printing requires the screen itself, which is made from a mesh material stretched across a wood or metal frame, ink formulated for screen printing, and a squeegee. While you can construct your own screens, premade options are widely available (Blick, Gold-Up, and Ryonet are good to try). Mesh materials are typically no longer silk but polyester—monofilament mesh is designed for printing on paper and multifilament mesh is for printing on fabric with textile inks. The fineness of the mesh weave, indicated by a number—number of threads per inch for monofilament mesh and a number of Xs for multifilament—is lower for coarser weaves (more ink passes through) and higher for finer weaves (more detail is possible). Aside from the type and fineness of the mesh, you will need to consider the workspace available and screen sizes that can be accommodated within it.

Squeegees for printing are wood handles fitted with polyurethane blades for spreading the ink and forcing it through the screen. Blades range from soft to hard and this variation affects the flexibility of the blade. The bottom edge may be finished in different ways (blade cut) as well, allowing for various inking situations. The squeegee should be at least an inch wider on each side than the image you are printing, and should fit comfortably in the screen, with room to maneuver on either side. A squeegee with a blade that has a straight cut on the bottom and medium hardness/softness (typically measured by durometer) will work well for basic printing needs.

Water-based inks for stencil and screen printing are available for different printing surfaces—some inks are formulated for printing on paper while others are for printing on fabric (both Speedball and Blick manufacture each type). For stencil printing without a screen on fabric, acrylic paints can be used (Createx medium body acrylics work on both paper and fabric, and can also be used with a screen). Many manufacturers also offer mediums that can be added to the inks—retarder slows the drying time and increases the window of work time for printing (water based inks and paints begin to dry in about 15 minutes), and transparent base thins out the ink and creates transparent effects. Other tools and supplies that are useful for stencil and screen printing include cutting tools for stencils, a stencil brush (cylindrical head with evenly cut tip), tape for sealing screens, plastic containers with lids for storing inks, rubber gloves, spatulas, and plastic scrub brushes for cleaning screens.

Like other printmaking techniques, stencil and screen printing can be done on a variety of surfaces, including paper, canvas, fabric, glass, and metal. The texture or tooth of the surface will affect the crispness of the image—smooth surfaces will result in a more even and consistent application of ink than rough surfaces. When printing on textiles, check the specifications of the ink to make sure that it is formulated for the fiber content of the particular fabric you are working with and for the mesh of the screen. If the fabric is to be washed after printing, make sure to wash and dry it prior to printing. Most will also require heat setting with a household iron.

Exploring Stencil and Silkscreen Prints

Experiment with stencil and screen printing by trying out the techniques that follow. How might you use these approaches to make prints based on different open-ended themes or topics? What different uses can you think of for items that are printed using stencils and silkscreen printing? How might you use these techniques with young people of different ages?

Materials:

Freezer paper
Soft lead pencil
Household iron
Scissors
X-Acto knife and self-healing cutting mat
Preassembled printing screen with medium weight mesh (120 if monofilament, 12×× if multifilament)
Photocopy paper for screen stencils
Screen drawing fluid
Screen filler
Paint brushes
Masking tape—2″ wide
Water-based screen printing ink in assorted colors (make sure to include fabric printing ink)
Acrylic paints for stencil printing
Retarders to slow drying time (optional, if you need to extend printing time beyond about 15 minutes)
Transparent base (optional)
Paper plate or paint palette
Stencil brush
Spatulas
Plastic scraper
Squeegee sized appropriately for applying ink to screen (see p. 210 for specifications)
Squeegee (or a rectangle of mat board) sized exactly to fit the width of the inside frame of the screen
Assorted papers and other surfaces to print, in various sizes
Assorted fabrics to print

An item made from cloth to print on—T-shirt, apron, tote bag, or other functional item (something you'd like to transform)
Newspaper for covering work surface
Soft plastic scrub brush, toothbrush, and sponge for cleaning screen
Paper towels
Rags

Getting Started:

1. How do different types of stencils and screen printing approaches vary in terms of the kinds of images they create? Test out the methods that follow, and print on a range of papers and on fabric. Choose one of the approaches to use on a functional item made from fabric. Keep notes about the techniques you use and the qualities of the printed images that come from them.

  a. Standard/positive stencil print—Using a sheet of freezer paper shiny side down, draw a design to be cut out and removed (the open areas are the parts that will print). In this type of stencil, all open parts of the design need to be joined—you can accomplish this by leaving small pieces of the stencil uncut, to act as tabs or bridges that connect the edges of the different open areas to one another. Cut the stencil using an X-Acto knife and self-healing cutting mat and discard all cut pieces, leaving the open areas. To attach the stencil to the printing surface, place it shiny side down on the paper or fabric and press with an iron set on medium to medium-high heat (an ironed-on stencil can be pulled off and repositioned and ironed again).

  Effective printing with a stencil brush involves several thin, lightly applied layers of paint or ink as opposed to one heavily loaded coat. To print, pour a dollop of ink or paint about the size of the stencil brush bottom onto a paper plate or other paint palette and fold a paper towel in half twice to use as a blotter. Load the brush by dipping it in the paint several times and tap it repeatedly on the paper towel to blot the excess. Use a straight up-and-down stippling technique to apply the ink over the stencil and fill in the open areas (don't use a side-to-side painting motion, as this could cause the ink or paint to get under the stencil edges). Clean the brush and let the color dry on the printing surface, then repeat the process until the desired saturation of color is reached. When the final coat is completely dry, carefully peel off the stencil.

  b. Reverse/negative paper stencil print—Use the approach above to create and print reverse/negative stencils, but this time keep the freezer paper cutouts to apply as stencils to the paper or fabric printing surface.

Note: For both of the stencil techniques above, you can print out high contrast, black-and-white images to use as stencils. Just lay the printed image face side up on the freezer paper, secure the edges with tape, and remove the dark areas of the image, cutting through both paper layers at once.

  c. Paper stencil screen print—Using photocopier paper or paper of similar weight, in a size that is at least 2″ smaller on all sides than the screen frame, cut the stencil design (the design can be standard or reverse but needs to be contained within the larger stencil sheet). To prepare the screen for printing, it needs to be taped to prevent ink leakage.

Note: In a sink that can accommodate the screen, use water and detergent with a sponge or soft scrub brush to thoroughly clean both sides of the mesh. Hold the screen up to the light to check for any areas still blocked by ink, and continue cleaning until all areas are clear. Thoroughly clean the squeegee as well, and dry both the screen and squeegee with a rag, then set aside to air dry completely before using them again.

Place it mesh side down on a work surface and press strips of masking tape evenly into the edges and along the frame and mesh on the top, bottom, and sides (one inch of the tape width should be on the frame and the remaining inch should be on the mesh). On the reverse side of the frame, press a strip of tape along each of the four sides over the groove where the mesh is attached to the frame. With the frame mesh side up, place the paper stencil on top with the edges near or covering the tape edges of the screen. Use tape to cover any exposed outer areas of the screen between the screen and the stencil and tape the paper stencil to the screen, overlapping the tape on the stencil by at least ½″ on all sides (this prevents leakage). Check to make sure that no other areas of the screen surrounding the stencil design need to be covered, and use tape to cover any of these areas as needed.

To prepare for printing, set up a table or floor surface that is larger than the screen with areas on either side for placing tools and the wet screen between printings—setting the corners of the screen on four overturned cups will keep it from transferring ink to the work surface, and designating an area for the wet squeegee and other tools will also minimize mess during the printing process. In the center printing area lay out newsprint to protect the work surface and place test sheets of paper or fabric to be printed on top (printing a few test sheets will prime the screen). Although not required, it is helpful to have some cushioning under the printing paper—a towel or thin blanket works well for this purpose.

Lay the screen stencil side down on the paper or fabric, lining up the stencil image so that it fits on the printing surface (you can make registration marks on the printing surface to line up each corner to center the image). Spoon out a line of ink across the mesh near the tape edge at the top of the screen. Holding the screen in place with one hand and the squeegee in the other hand at a 45 degree angle, drag the squeegee down the surface of the mesh, toward you, as you apply pressure to force the ink through the mesh. Turn the squeegee and using the same side of it drag the ink in the opposite direction, away from you, again applying pressure to force the ink through the screen. Do this several times up and down the mesh surface. As a final step, to flood the screen and prevent it from drying out between prints, pull the squeegee across the screen one more time, but without applying pressure. Place the squeegee off to the side, and lift the screen off of the paper, taking care to not slide it on the printing surface (sideways movement will smudge the print). Place the screen to the side, elevated from the surface of the work area, and move the printed paper or fabric to a clear, clean spot to dry. You can continue to print with the screen by repeating the steps above—you will need to stop printing, remove and discard the stencil, and clean the screen thoroughly as soon as the ink begins to dry (ink is very difficult to remove once it has dried in the mesh).

    d. Drawing fluid and screen block print—To prepare the screen for this technique, decide whether you will be making a standard/positive stencil, in which case the image you paint on with a brush is what prints in ink on the printing surface, or a reverse/negative stencil in which the background of what is painted on the screen is the print area that receives the ink. To make a standard stencil, you will use drawing fluid to paint the image on the screen, and screen filler to block out the remaining areas not included in the painted design. In a reverse stencil, you will not use drawing fluid at all—you'll use screen filler to paint the image on the screen and the surrounding areas will be left clear for the ink to pass through, thus creating the reverse image.

To create the stencil, you can either work from a drawing or other artwork or prepared image or paint the stencil freehand directly on the mesh. To use a prepared image, set the screen mesh side down on a work surface protected with newsprint, and place the stencil artwork image side down on the mesh, centering it in the frame. Tape the paper to the screen with masking tape, and flip the screen over so the mesh side is facing up. Trace the image onto the screen with a soft lead pencil, using the artwork taped to the reverse side of the mesh as a guide. When the tracing is complete, remove the artwork from the reverse side and set aside.

If you are making a standard/positive stencil, you'll need to use a paintbrush to apply drawing fluid (shake well before using) to the screen, still mesh side up, following the lines and shapes drawn in pencil. Remember that where you paint with drawing fluid will be open to allow ink to pass through to the printing surface. Let the drawing fluid dry completely on the screen. Next, using several tablespoons of screen filler (shake and stir well to mix) spread out in a thick line across the width of the screen at the top edge, and a squeegee or cardboard substitute, spread the screen filler evenly in a thin coat down the entire screen area. The screen filler needs to be completely dry before you can rinse the screen and dissolve the drawing fluid to open up the printing areas. In a sink sized to accommodate the screen, wash both sides with cold water and use a spray attachment if available or soft brush to dissolve the drawing fluid from the areas to which it was applied. Check to be sure that there are no blockages in the mesh in the printable part of the stencil. Dry the screen with a rag and allow to air dry completely. After taping the screen, mesh side down (as you did previously with the paper stencil), the screen is ready for printing (follow steps in previous section).

To make a reverse/negative stencil, follow the steps above for tracing the stencil image on the screen and removing the taped artwork. Instead of using drawing fluid to paint in the lines and shapes of the image, use screen filler with a brush sized appropriately for the areas of the stencil design. The screen filler needs to be thick enough to block the mesh so that ink does not pass through—hold the screen up to the light to check. Once the screen filler is completely dry, tape the screen to prepare it for printing—you will also want to use tape as a border to set off the outer edges of the print area from the paper or fabric printing surface. When the taping is complete, print the screen following the steps in the previous section.

Note: To make a freehand drawing or design without the aid of artwork used as a template, follow the steps above to apply drawing fluid and screen filler for a standard/positive stencil or just screen filler for a negative stencil. Use hot water and detergent to remove the dried screen filler after printing, or save the stenciled screen for future printing.

2. Try printing the stencils and screens on a wide variety of surfaces, including an item made from fabric (use a sheet of paper between layers of thin fabric as necessary to prevent ink seepage). Experiment with using more than one stencil in a single print (let the layers dry between multiple applications of ink). If you wish, test out the transparent base to see what kinds of color effects are possible. Which prints are particularly interesting to you? Why?

MONOTYPES

A monotype is like a printed painting—ink or paint is applied to a flat, smooth surface, such as a Plexiglas sheet, and the image is then printed on paper (see Figures 4-11 and 4-12). As the name implies, monotypes are single image prints and are not produced in an edition. Although the ink that remains on the plate after the first printing can be reworked and added to, subsequent images will not be the same.

Monotypes were made in Italy as early as 1640 by Giovanni Benedetto Castiglione, a printmaker who worked around the same time as Rembrandt van Rijn. Rembrandt experimented with a form of monotypes by inking his intaglio plates and not removing all of the ink from the areas normally rubbed clean. Artists in the nineteenth and twentieth centuries such as Edgar Degas, Paul Gauguin, Henri Matisse, Pablo Picasso, Maurice Pendergrast, Jasper Johns, and Sam Francis expanded the range of approaches to monotype printing by introducing new materials, like watercolor, into the process.

There are different approaches to preparing the plate for a monotype—you can use brayers and paintbrushes to build up an image (additive approach) or cover the plate with ink or paint and use rags, brushes, and other tools to selectively remove areas of color media (subtractive approach). Monotypes can be done

F 4-11
Mary Hafeli, Untitled, from Cries that are Wings series, 2006, monoprint, 12.5" × 12.5". (below, left)

F 4-12
Mary Hafeli, Untitled, from Cries that are Wings series, 2006, monoprint, 12.5" × 12.5". (below, right)

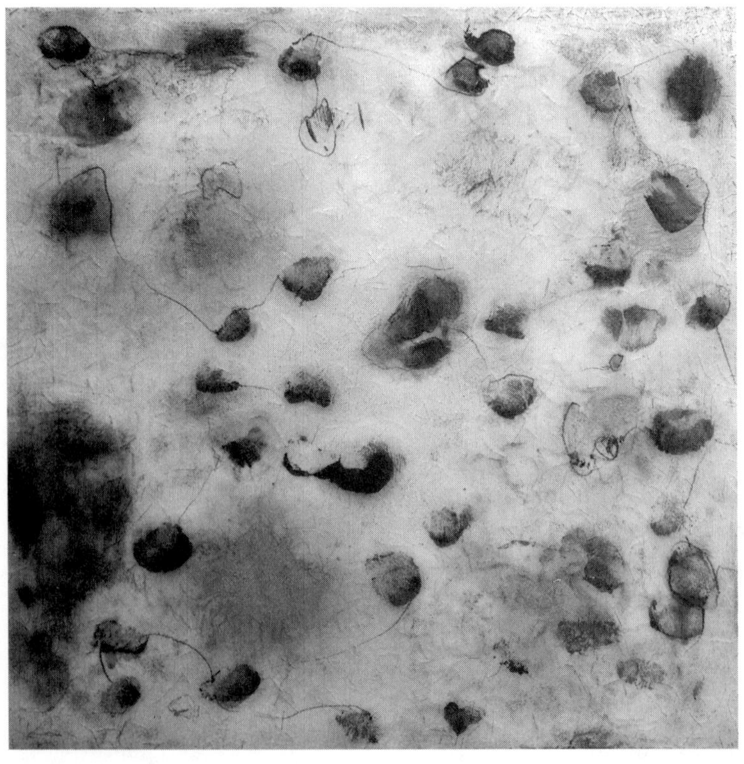

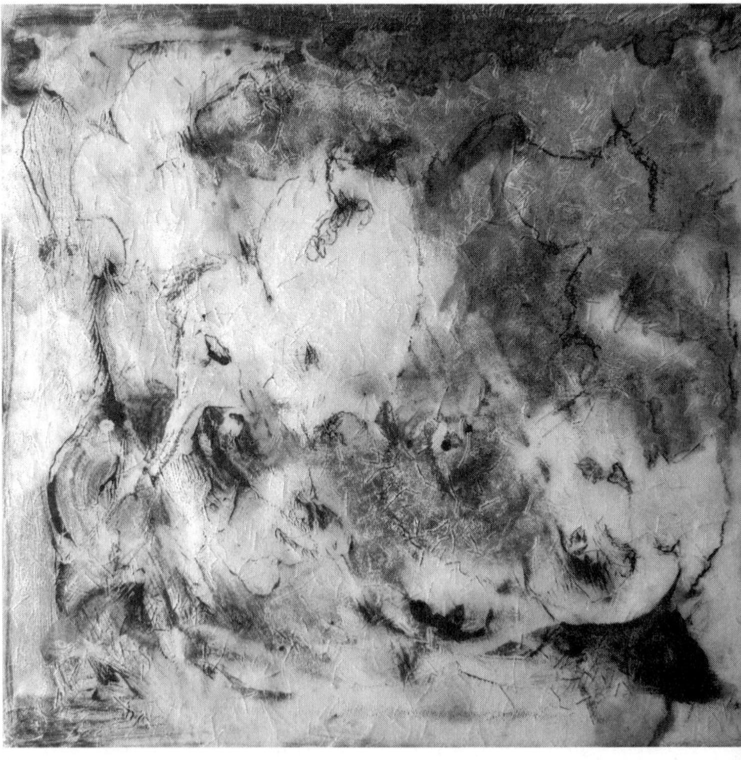

with printing inks used in other approaches (block printing, silk screen, intaglio), acrylic paints, oil paints, watercolors, gouache, and water-soluble pastels and pencils. There are also water-based materials that are specially formulated for monotype printing, such as Aku Kolor inks and Createx Monotype Colors. Corresponding extenders, for creating transparent glaze colors, and retarders, for slowing the drying time and increasing the time for preparing and printing the plate, can be added to paints and inks used for monotypes.

Exploring Monotype Prints

How can printing inks and acrylic paints be used to create single image prints? What kinds of thinking and action does the monotype process invite and support? How do the visual effects that can be achieved through monotypes differ from those of other approaches to printmaking?

Materials:

A selection of paints and inks drawn from acrylic, watercolor, gouache, block printing ink, monotype ink (optional)
Water-soluble pastels and pencils
Plexiglas printing plates
Low tack painter's masking tape
Rubber brayers
Small trays or Plexiglas sheets for rolling out inks (wider than the brayers)
Large spoon
Paint brushes
Container of water
Spray bottle filled with water
Assorted papers and other surfaces to print, in various sizes of rectangles and squares larger than your printing blocks and plates—watercolor paper, colors and neutrals (construction paper, fadeless, tissue), metallic, patterns, lettered texts and images, acetate, vellum
Assorted smooth-faced fabrics—solids, patterns
Newspaper for covering work surface
Paper towels
Rags

Getting Started:

1. What are the possibilities for printed images of each of the materials? During the inking and printing process, keep notes about the different materials you used on your plates and the qualities of the printed images that come from them.

   a. Additive plate—With the spray bottle, lightly dampen a piece of smooth faced (hot press) watercolor paper slightly larger than your printing plate. Working quickly (so the plate does not dry) and using a brayer and/or paint brushes, apply acrylic paint, block printing ink, or watercolor and gouache directly to the plate, experimenting with making solid and textured areas and covering the plate. Print the plate on the paper, using the heel of your hand and a clean brayer to apply firm pressure for the ink transfer. Recoloring the plate as you go, and working on both dampened and dry papers, create a few more monoprints using paints or inks. How do the various printing materials and wet and dry papers produce different results?

b. Subtractive plate—Use a brayer to apply block printing ink or use brushes to apply acrylic paint to a clean plate. Working quickly, selectively remove areas of color with rags or paper towels and a brush (try wet, damp, and dry brush applications), exploring different techniques. Use a pointed tool or stick to scratch out a linear design or image, or to create textured areas. Print the plate on a white or light colored sheet of paper. What kinds of effects are possible with this technique?

c. Stencil plate—Lay down strips or cut shapes of masking tape on the plate and apply ink or paint to cover the plate surface. Peel off the tape stencils and either print as is or add new colors to the areas on the plate left bare by the stencils, leaving the edges crisp or blending and adding additional color layers. You can also apply tape stencils or lay cut paper stencils on the printing paper before printing the plate.

d. Single transfer plate—Prepare a line drawing on thin white paper the size of your printing plate. On the back side of the paper, trace the lines of the drawing so that you have a reverse image. Cover the plate with a variety of colors, using printing ink or acrylic paint. Lay the printing paper over the plate and top this with the drawing, reverse side facing up. Use a pointed tool to firmly trace over the lines of the drawing, and apply additional pressure by rubbing with your hand in selected areas to transfer ink from other areas of the plate to the paper.

e. Multiple approach/mixed media plate—Use a combination of two or more approaches on the same plate. Include additive, subtractive, stencil, and/or transfer techniques and incorporate water soluble pastels and pencils, working wet or dry, on the plate (sand the plate before beginning and dampen the paper before printing).

2. Trying out all of the paints and inks you have available, print the plates on a wide variety of papers and on the plastic and vellum sheets. What kinds of effects are you able to achieve? What ideas are suggested through the different methods? Which monotypes are particularly interesting to you? Why?

MIXING PRINTMAKING AND OTHER MEDIA

Many artists who work with printmaking incorporate multiple printing techniques as well as hand drawing and painting techniques and collage materials—adding collage elements to the printing plate is called *chine-collé* (see Figure 4-13 and Figure 17 in the color insert). As with other media, when working with students it is important not to present them with too many materials and processes at once. When students have thoroughly explored and become skilled in using different printmaking approaches, expanding media is a good way to increase complexity and deepen ongoing creative exploration.

Exploring Mixed Media with Printmaking

How might drawing, painting, and collage materials be incorporated into the printmaking process? Document in your studio journal new insights and understandings about visual effects and expressive ideas made possible by combining printmaking with other media.

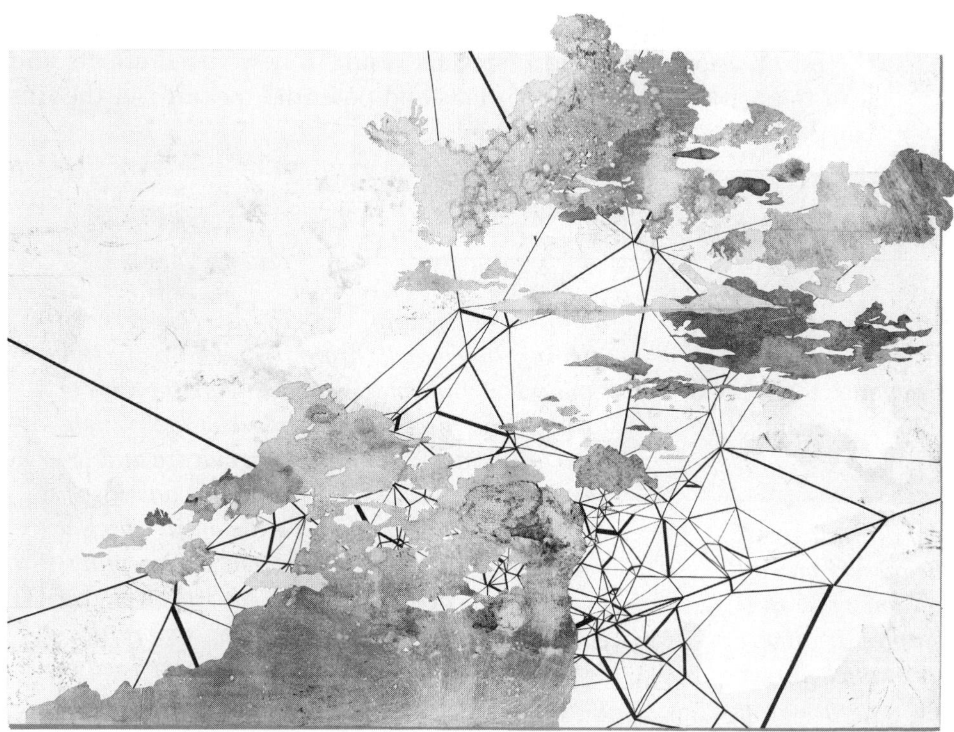

F 4-13
Val Britton, Trajectory I, *2010,
monoprint, collage, graphite,
and ink on paper, 31.25" × 43".*

Materials:

A selection of objects for stamping
Previously prepared plates, blocks, stencils, and screens for block printing,
 collagraph printing, and stencil and screen printing, and clean printing
 plate for monotype printing
Inks and paints for printing
Tools and equipment for printing—brayers, ink trays, squeegee
A selection of collage elements and attaching materials
Tempera, watercolor, gouache, and/or acrylic paints and mediums
Paintbrushes
Containers of water
Palettes, containers, and trays for dispensing paints
Graphite pencils and colored pencils
Oil pastels and soft pastels
Water-soluble pastels
Ink pens
An assortment of base papers and/or boards for mixed media prints

Getting Started:

1. Select printing techniques to combine and later identify some drawing
 and painting materials to add to the mix. Try making a print that layers
 stamping or block printing with stencil printing. Explore ways of combining graphite or colored pencil rubbings with collagraph prints. How might
 watercolor be incorporated into a monotype after it has dried? How can
 collage elements enhance block, collagraph, stencil and silk screen, and
 monotype printing approaches?

2. Try different media combinations in a variety of applications and on a
 range of printing surfaces. How does combining these materials

change the process of creating and composing in printmaking? How do the mixed approaches and materials result in new visual effects and lead to an expanded range of ideas and potential meaning in the finished works?

Artist Profile: JOHN PAUL MCCAUGHEY

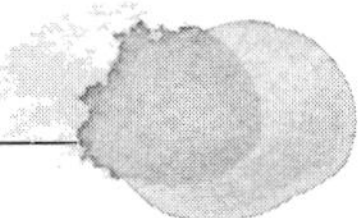

John Paul McCaughey's *The Sleep of Existing Conditions Produces Monsters* was constructed from three panels of found printed advertisements torn down from a bulletin board in Richmond, Virginia (see Figure 4-14). According to the artist:

> *. . . the colors are reminiscent of an industrial work-site, dirty and faded. The piece comes off the wall by about six inches in some areas and is riddled with sharp rusty staples. It almost feels like a chunk of something much larger and can be seen as an artifact due to the age of the advertisements.*

McCaughey writes:

> *The act of finding becomes important in this piece. By tearing through the layers of information, I am beginning to reveal its history. I am also staying true to the process of how these posters are placed and discarded; removal is almost always through tearing down. Nobody ever removes the staples. If just looking at it through the lens of process, this piece is not* really breaking any new ground. However, by turning the panels around and limiting the amount of information (text) that the viewer can see, the piece becomes more of a commentary on the debris of American culture and the sheer mass of useless paper and less about specific advertisements and the region in which it was removed from. The advent of computer-based social networking has caused us to rely less on twentieth century means of communication, such as snail mail. We no longer need to post flyers on event bulletin boards when there are such things as Facebook, Myspace and Twitter.* The Sleep of Existing Conditions Produces Monsters *now exists as a reminder of how beautiful the deterioration of our society and environment can be.*

How does McCaughey's selection and reconstruction of found printed materials function as a printed image? What impressions do you get as you look closely at this piece? What ideas and feelings do the materials suggest? Why do you think this is?

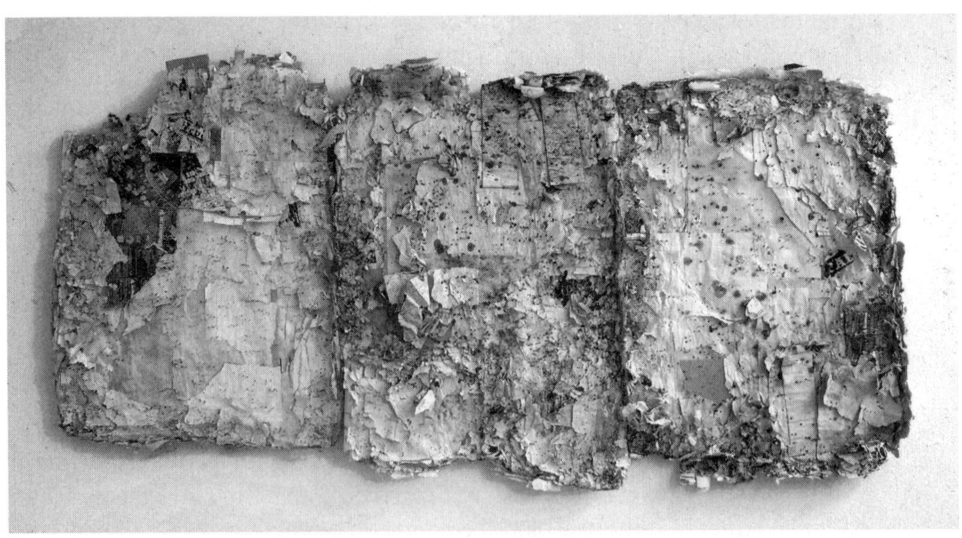

F 4-14
John Paul McCaughey, The Sleep of Existing Conditions Produces Monsters, 2011, manipulated advertisements and staples, 30" × 60".

MORE IDEAS FOR PRINTMAKING

As with other media and techniques, students are eager to make prints about experiences they've had and topics that interest them. They also enjoy exploring new ideas and themes in their work—ideas that are related to the art techniques themselves or to ideas that other artists focus on in their work. Table 4-3 contains ideas for open-ended prompts that can focus the printmaking experience—these ideas can also be combined with the materials-focused explorations throughout this chapter. While some focusing ideas may be technique driven, or highlight a concept having to do with a formal or compositional concern, students should always be given opportunities to develop expressive ideas in determining what it is they want their work to be "about," beyond formal and technical issues.

STUDIO REFLECTION: PRINTMAKING

Spread out all of your printmaking experiments and study the range of visual effects that you created through the various techniques you used. Think about how the visual effects from different approaches could be used to suggest particular ideas, feelings, moods, states, or qualities in a print.

Reflecting on your written observations and looking at your test prints, which images are most expressive? Most interesting? Most unusual? How do the working processes for each printmaking approach compare to one another? Do you prefer some over others? What are the characteristics of the material and process that draw you to them? Compare your responses to what the artists below have to say about their choices and use of approaches and materials.

Table 4-3 Ideas for Focusing Printmaking

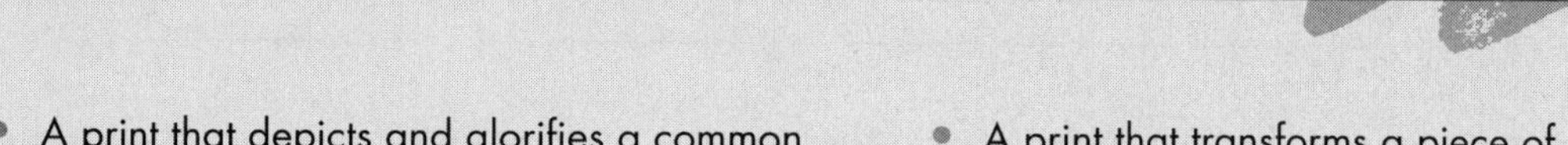

- A print that depicts and glorifies a common object.
- A print that extends the image or ideas from a previously created drawing, painting, collage, or sculpture.
- A print with a pattern that suggests a musical beat or rhythm.
- A print that moves in and out of focus.
- A print that transforms a piece of clothing or an accessory.
- A print that transforms a book or notebook cover.
- A print that transforms a piece of furniture.
- A print that transforms a wall.
- A print that commemorates an event.
- A print that makes possible written communication—stationery, invitation, etc.
- A print that presents a point of view about a pressing issue.
- A print that is used as a wrapping or container for something else.
- A group of prints that use the same printing plate, block, or stencil but look as different as possible from one another.

More Artists on Media

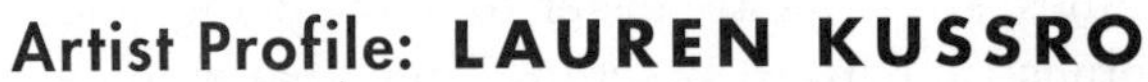

Artist Profile: **LAUREN KUSSRO**

Lauren Kussro's work is inspired by colors, shapes, and patterns found in the natural world (see Figure 18 in the color insert). According to Kussro, the printed constructions "utilize references to roots, flowers, coral, barnacles, cells and fungi" but "are rarely realistic copies of specific objects from nature." She says: "Observing and researching these objects and their components gives me insight and ideas about how to build my own structures in an aesthetically pleasing way. The sculptural forms then emerge from a sort of parallel universe."

What feeling or sense do you get from this work? What do you think the artist is intent on communicating about her subject? What is she focused on portraying? How do the materials and forms of the work contribute to your interpretations? Kussro writes:

I am drawn to the process of developing a body of individual pieces that make up a collective whole. Large groups of smaller pieces joined together by distance or by a physical connection contain a different kind of significance and presence than an individual piece. This relates to the human arena as well; as individuals we are unique and intrinsically different from our neighbor, but community is something we were designed for, and ultimately need in order to survive—spiritually, emotionally and physically. Our relational interactions with others are probably the most important and rewarding things we will invest in during our lives. The importance of community is therefore a concept I am interested in and am currently exploring by building my own colonies of forms.

Achieving a visual balance with an emphasis on layers of detail is always a goal when I am in the process of creating work. Sensory richness is important, so I use combinations of various materials, including paper, wood, paint, ink, thread, resin, and wax. All the different print processes and sculptural materials that I utilize are important, and the more facets and details I put into the pieces, the more there is for the viewer to explore and discover. In my current work, I aim to create environments that place the viewer in an arena where beauty is seen as relevant and acceptable, and can evoke emotions such as joy, hope, curiosity, contentment, yearning and delight.

Artist Profile: **ANNE GANT**

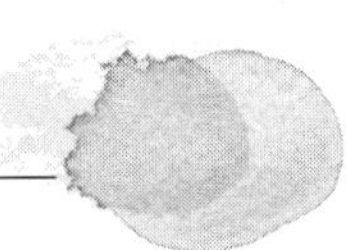

Anne Gant, who is trained as a glassblower, uses hot glass to make drawings and prints in a process known as pyrography (see Figure 19 in the color insert). She writes about her work with materials:

First, I sculpt hot glass into shapes and lines. Then, while the glass is still scorching hot from the glory hole, I press the glass forms into wet sheets of high quality rag paper. Instantly, the glass begins to burn and smoke the paper. In this dramatic process, the glass becomes cracked, scarred and destroyed. All that remains is its mark on the paper.

For Gant, the visual effects of the work "have a richness, translucency and liquidity that is an echo of the original glass form." The process also references other aspects of glass and its physicality and history, as seen in the artist's description of a recent body of work based on her study of Italian ruins:

By using piles and stacks of traditional Roman glass forms, I once again connect these prints to their glass craft origins. The amphora-style forms I am using reference unearthed antiquities. That feeling of ancient, dirt-covered pieces speaks not only to the ideas of preciousness of the original object, but also extends the meaning of the print when it is completed: the final prints are brown, crusty, and damaged, like an excavated shard. These burn prints are poignant, because they exist simultaneously as aesthetic objects in their own right, and yet also speak of the object that was lost.

Artist Profile: **JILL PARISI**

Like Lauren Kussro, Jill Parisi's work is influenced by her study of and response to the natural world (see Figure 20 in the color insert). And like Anne Gant, her methods include the use of pyrographic techniques for some of her work. She writes:

My artistic focus is the creation of invented botanical and zoological species. Using this premise, I explore the innate possibilities that printmaking, handmade paper, and drawing offer for the expression of an appreciation of humanity and sensitivity for the environment. The individual elements that comprise my work begin as two dimensional prints and drawings. Precise hand cutting, hand coloring and pyrographic techniques are employed; then I transform these elements sculpturally, or interpret them digitally as designs for translation into glass or other media.

Sometimes the pieces that I create are used as components for large installations that react to viewer proximity, fluttering in response to the air currents within an interior space, the outdoors, or the movements of passers by. Mirroring an ecosystem, these imaginary worlds also demonstrate the richness and beauty that diversity affords communities, and the importance of each individual within their surroundings.

Artist Profile: **TAMAR COHEN**

Tamar Cohen's work incorporates collage and silkscreen, and an interest in printed papers and books from the mid-twentieth century (see Figure 4-15 and Figure 21 in the color insert). She uses simple printing processes to focus and obscure the images and text content found in these papers, creating layered dialogues between foreground and background. She writes:

Two life-long passions that drive my work are my love of polka dots and my ongoing enthusiasm for vintage paper ephemera and books.

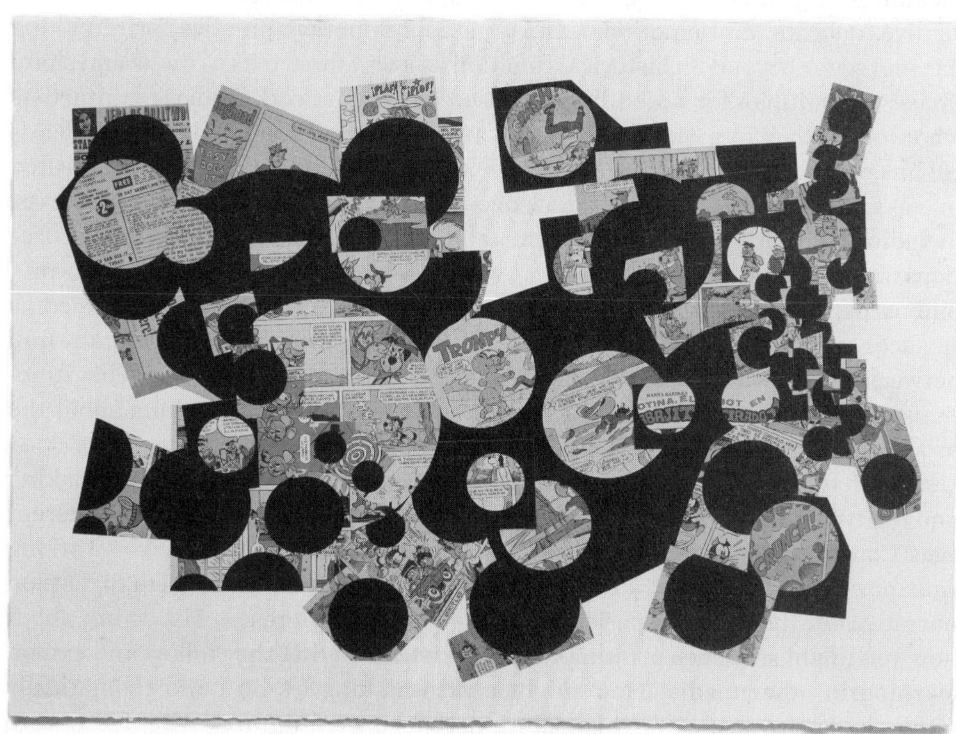

F 4-15
Tamar Cohen, Trompy, 2011, silkscreen on newspaper collage, 30" × 22.5".

(Continued)

Artist Profile (*Continued*)

I use collage and silkscreen to combine and juxtapose the two, creating a dynamic visual world of layered contrasts. This palette of visual obsessions inspires me in many ways, as I explore the relationship between high and low, order and chaos, the abstracted and the everyday. I also strive to push and challenge the boundaries of conventional printmaking: I paint with paper.

Dots are my figure, my landscape and my frame. Artists from Lichtenstein to Polke to Hirst have used the dot in their own work, whether as a sly allusion to the CMYK dots that comprise all printed images or in reference to its elemental and eternal shape. They serve to focus, reveal, subsume and re-contextualize my abstracted paper narratives. The root of my narrative choices begins with a love of paper and its physical tactile nature. I am drawn to paper and books produced in the 1950s and

'60s: a time when printing techniques were basic and information was conveyed in a more simple and unsophisticated way. I also use a printing process that has not changed in decades. I find this all refreshing in today's high-tech virtual world.

The choices I make are influenced by a range of criteria, including content, style, color, scale and sometimes simply intuition. I begin with a visually dense background collage, then use the dots and a layering of ink to alternately highlight and conceal the visual content. This creates a dialogue between the foreground and background by fostering a complex and ambiguous sense of space. Though I strive to make my own order out of the chaos, it is my hope that each viewer navigates his or her own path of discovery. Like the varied uneven edges of my work, interpretation is best when not limited by four corners.

Thoughts about Printmaking as a Studio Practice

Printmaking as an art form still encompasses evolving technical processes and the production of print editions—and, like artworks in all media, the images and meanings in printed works can be nuanced, humorous, confronting, layered, inventive, delicate, and emotional. But as a contemporary practice, printmaking has moved far beyond its historical function as a way for artists to make and share images in multiples for wider dissemination of their artwork. Today, many artists who work with printmaking techniques are unconcerned with editions of identical images and with the traditional contexts of printed works. They are interested in using printing methods to produce one-of-a-kind artworks in diverse contexts, including wall papers and stencils in installations, guerilla graphics in public locations (see Bansky's street work at http://www.banksy.co.uk/outdoors/index1.html), billboards, animated films, and found materials repurposed and reimagined as surfaces for printed images (see Figure 4-16). Prints are a vital and vibrant link between the museum and the marketplace, the elite and the everyday. What functions, goals, and intentions for printmaking and what other thoughts about the process can you find in the artists' comments throughout this chapter?

Begin to think about some of the distinguishing characteristics of printmaking and how you might use its techniques in your own lessons for students of different ages. Consider how you might invite kids to create printed images based on working from observation and imagination, and how you could encourage them to develop narratives of their own experiences in the prints they create. Also think about how you might sequence printmaking experiences so that they follow and extend learning in other media. How might a printmaking lesson build thematically upon a lesson featuring drawing, painting, collage, or sculpture? What follows are practical considerations for presenting to kids the techniques for printmaking featured in this chapter.

Setting up for Working with Printmaking Materials

ESTABLISHING A CLIMATE OF EXPERIMENTAL INQUIRY

A climate of experimental inquiry in printmaking invites students to experiment with established techniques for creating printing plates and stencils and for printing on various surfaces. But they also are encouraged to move beyond established processes to invent their own approaches. As with all other media, students often lead our printmaking demonstrations—I ask them to suggest alternative ways of preparing printing plates, imagine new methods for inking and printing, and think of different surfaces that would be interesting to print on. We also brainstorm topics the class would like to explore as content and themes for our work. This exploration with printmaking techniques and expressive ideas, and the trial and error that naturally occurs in the process of trying things out, sustains the climate of ongoing experimental inquiry.

MATCHING TIME ALLOTTED AND PROCESSES OF WORKING WITH MEDIA

Printmaking involves preparing plates, blocks, stencils, and screens to be printed and exploring and experimenting with various inking and printing procedures. Because of this two-step process, the techniques often take more time than direct

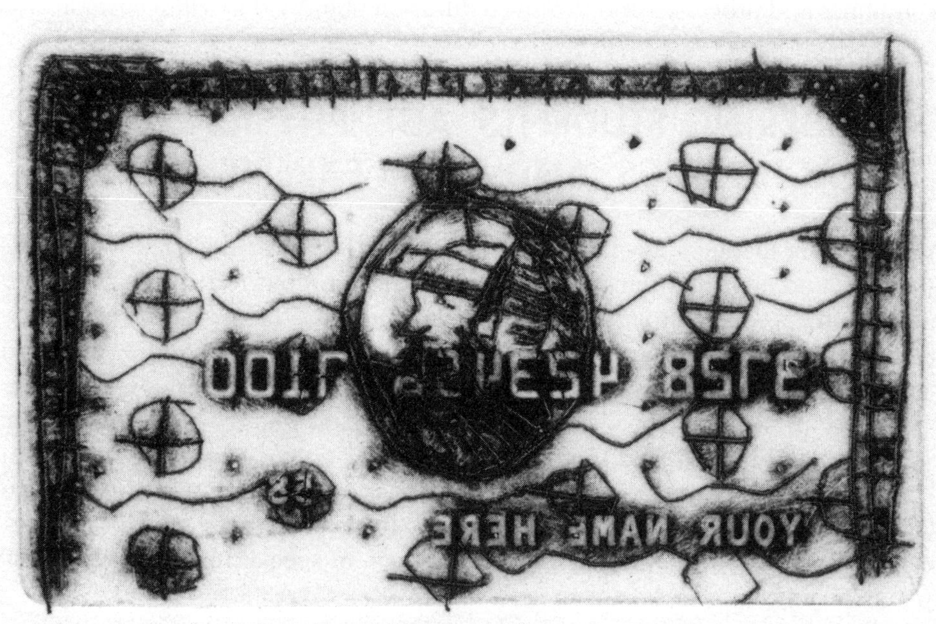

F 4-16

Ken Gray, American Roman, 2009, drypoint on credit card, 2" × 3.25".

F 4-17: Printmaking setup

studio approaches such as drawing, printmaking, and collage. In printmaking it is helpful to chunk lesson content into distinct phases (introduction and initial idea generation, research and media exploration, plate/block/stencil preparation, and inking and printing) to accommodate both students' optimal learning of the techniques and processes and the given duration of individual class periods.

CONSIDERING STUDENTS' AGE, PHYSICAL CHARACTERISTICS, AND PRIOR EXPERIENCE

As with other media, students' prior experience with printmaking and their age, strength, and coordination are important considerations when selecting techniques and approaches to use with particular classes. While all of the techniques in this chapter are appropriate for older students and many are fine for all students, the more complex ones (such as reduction prints) are better suited for those with some prior experience, and the techniques that require block cutting and carving should be matched to students' strength and coordination. For all students, starting the printing with limited colors and surfaces and gradually introducing new options ensures ongoing experimentation. For students who are ready for increased challenge, the gradual introduction of special inks and papers will sustain ongoing exploration.

BALANCING EFFICIENCY WITH STUDENT AUTONOMY

To encourage students to make thoughtful choices as they design and construct printing plates and, later, choose colors of inks and paints and types of printing surfaces, it is helpful to have materials and tools laid out by kind/type in clearly labeled containers. As with paints, it is also helpful to have printing materials set up so that students can dispense and collect the materials themselves. As much as possible, have students consider available materials and choose what they would like to use that day—this approach reinforces their development of independent artistic judgment. In the printing phase of the lesson, design the workflow so that students work in pairs sharing inking trays. This allows for both collaborative assistance with one another's printing projects and a reduction in the tools and equipment needed in individual workspaces.

ANTICIPATING MESS AND PLANNING FOR CLEANUP

As with painting media, protecting work surfaces with newspaper, having kids wear smocks, anticipating spills and accidents, and planning carefully for cleanup will help to encourage undistracted work and experimentation in printmaking (see Figure 4-17). Communicating about how plate preparation tools and materials will be collected and stored, how brayers, inking trays, and other tools will be cleaned, where wet prints will be placed to dry, and how students will wash their hands will also go a long way to ensuring that students' creative work time is maximized.

REFLECTING ON AND ARTICULATING LEARNING

At the end of the each phase of the printmaking experience and while the work is in progress, ask students to discuss what they are discovering and learning how to do as they gain experience with the techniques, and invite them to reflect on the themes and ideas in their artwork. As with other media, brief written explanations about the goal of the printmaking experience and what was learned in individual approaches creates an archive of skills, concepts, and ways of thinking that can be used as a resource in the art class and communicated to the community when included in exhibitions of students' work.

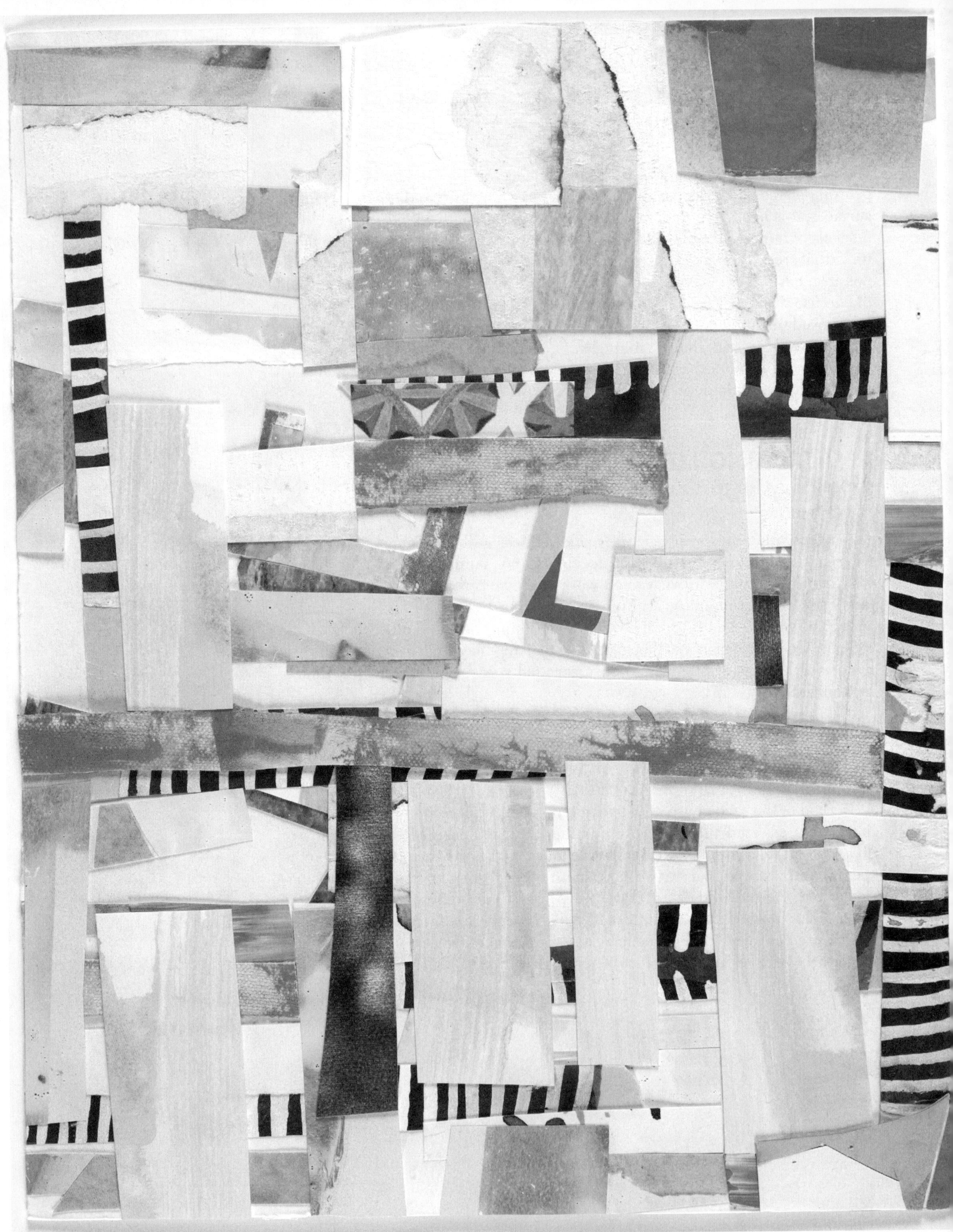

Barbara Campbell Thomas, Blocks on Blocks, 2012

Collecting, Altering, Layering, and Attaching

I see these objects that have this patina to them, that have this obvious history. It's loved and hated and loved again, and ultimately discarded. There are so many stories to be told within these objects.

—**Trenton Doyle Hancock**[1]

The waste of the world becomes my art.

—**Kurt Schwitters, inscribed on the reverse of his collage *Für Bieleny* (1935)**

COLLAGE (from the French *coller*, to stick or glue) is an art form that, in the most basic sense, involves attaching things to a surface. As a creative practice it stems from a variety of historical sources—including Japanese calligraphers who

---

[1] Art: 21 (2003). Trenton Doyle Hancock interview—It came from the studio floor. Retrieved July 10, 2013, from http://www.art21.org/texts/trenton-doyle-hancock/interview-trenton-doyle-hancock-it-came-from-studio-floor.

decorated their writing surfaces with bits of paper and fabric (twelfth century), medieval artists who attached gemstones and other precious materials to religious images (thirteenth to fifteenth centuries), shamans and spiritual leaders who used natural and symbolic materials to construct ritualistic objects, and nineteenth-century hobbyists who used a variety of memorabilia, paper, and fabric materials, along with human and animal hair, to make elaborately constructed mementos, family heirlooms, and valentines.

In the early twentieth century in Paris, Georges Braque and Pablo Picasso glued pieces of newspaper, wallpaper, and other printed materials directly onto the surfaces of their paintings, challenging that art form's primary function at the time—to create an illusion of reality. Incorporating these kinds of cast-off, everyday materials into painting also defied prevailing cultural attitudes regarding the "fine" aspect of fine arts, for newspaper and other common, discarded, and repurposed materials held no artistic value. The practice of collage as an art medium spread rapidly among other avant-garde artists in Europe. Cubists and Futurists adopted its approaches along with Dadaists, whose pairing of incongruent objects meant to mock and shock through the nonsensical, and Surrealists, whose composite constructions referenced Freud's unconscious mind, then a topic of study in the emerging field of psychology. Since that time, collage has become a major part of artists' studio practices—among many artists who are known for their collage work are Hannah Hoch, Kurt Schwitters, Max Ernst, Henri Matisse, Joseph Cornell, Anne Ryan, Romare Bearden, Lee Krasner, Robert Rauschenberg, Robert Heinecken, Betye and Alison Saar, Jess Collins, Eric Carle, Terry Gilliam, Martha Rosler, Ellen Gallagher, Lorna Simpson, Mark Bradford, Kara Walker, Wangechi Mutu, and Arturo Herrera. Because of its break with materials and ideas associated with traditional art forms like painting, in the minds of many artists and critics collage revolutionized modern art. As critic Peter Schjeldahl wrote on the influence of drawing on collage: "To argue that collage extended drawing gets the truth backward; collage subsumed drawing."[2] Collage's substantial impact on people and the ways in which they make things includes folk artists and scrapbook enthusiasts and goes beyond the immediate art world. Collage concepts and methods can be seen as a major influence on advertising, music videos, web design, social media interaction, and other cultural products and practices.

This chapter focuses on collecting suitable materials, altering materials in different ways, and arranging, juxtaposing, and attaching materials to construct various types of collage. Because it allows for constant reconsideration of alternative compositional possibilities—through easy and fluid repositioning of pieces and parts in the process before finalizing and gluing down—collage lends itself to a freeing sense of experimentation and play. For many artists and for young people, this is a major part of its attractiveness as an art form. What does collage entail? What ways of thinking and what kinds of actions come into play during the process of working in collage? What kinds of materials are good to use and what are different ways of working with them? Note your responses to these questions, along with other considerations for teaching, as you explore the collage process for yourself through the studio activities presented later in this chapter.

---

[2] P. Schjeldahl. (2010). Between the lines: What has become of drawing? *New Yorker*, November 29, 2010. Retrieved July 10, 2013, from http://www.newyorker.com/arts/critics/artworld/2010/11/29/101129craw_artworld_schjeldahl.

Figuring out What Materials Can Do

COLLECTING MATERIALS

A major aspect of collage, and one that is sometimes overlooked in the art classroom, is the incredibly diverse array of materials and objects that can be used. Robert Rauschenberg (1959) said that "a pair of socks is no less suitable to make a painting with than wood, nails, turpentine, oil, and fabric"[3]—this attitude certainly applies to the constant mixing of media that characterizes the process of making a collage. Collecting interesting materials is an ongoing activity for artists and for those who teach collage, but it is just as important for young people, as artists themselves, to hunt for and make decisions about materials they would like to incorporate into their work. As Trenton Doyle Hancock observes in the quote that introduced this chapter, materials, such as things that are discarded by others and "found" by artists, carry with them histories and associations that ultimately make their way into the interpreted meaning of the finished artwork. All materials, and the alterations that artists make to them, are suggestive of ideas and concepts based on their surfaces, forms, textures, degree of transparency and opacity, color, and other visual characteristics. Materials also connect us, through association and reference, to social and cultural worlds and places. As we have seen in previous chapters, artists recognize the potential for the inherent qualities of materials to mean something in their work, and deliberately select and play with different media throughout the studio process with this understanding in mind.

What ideas might a scrap of newspaper, as a collage material, express? How might these meanings differ from those of, say, feathers? Or twigs? Or a thin piece of plastic cut from a red and white circle patterned Target bag? Even without actually seeing these objects in front of us, we can begin to imagine how different types of materials come to us front-loaded with potential meanings. Add to this the endless possibilities for altering these materials—picture an edge cut cleanly with a scissors or blade and an edge that's raggedly torn—and the number of potential meanings grows considerably. For Figures 5-1 and 5-2, examine each collage closely and note the types of materials used, the ways in which materials have been altered and arranged, and images, ideas, and impressions that result from the process. What descriptive words come to mind as you consider each piece? How do the artists' uses of particular materials and technical approaches, and the arrangements of the collage elements in the overall composition, suggest these ideas?

Once you start considering your everyday world as a source for collage elements, you can begin to amass a collection of supplies. Materials do not have to be archival to qualify for use—over time ephemeral materials will fade or yellow and disintegrate and natural materials will take on new appearances. These visible changes can suggest meanings (time, age, past) that add interest to the work. For artist Ellen Gallagher, this is part of the attraction and fascination of the medium and its primary material, paper: "No matter how I may try to build it into forms, or arc it out, or cut it, it will darken and yellow, which I like. It has its own relationship to time."[4]

---

[3] Excerpt from artist statement, *Sixteen Americans* (Dorothy Miller, editor).
[4] Art: 21 (2005a). Ellen Gallagher interview—eXelento and DeLuxe. Retrieved July 14, 2013, from http://www.art21.org/texts/ellen-gallagher/interview-ellen-gallagher-exelento-and-deluxe.

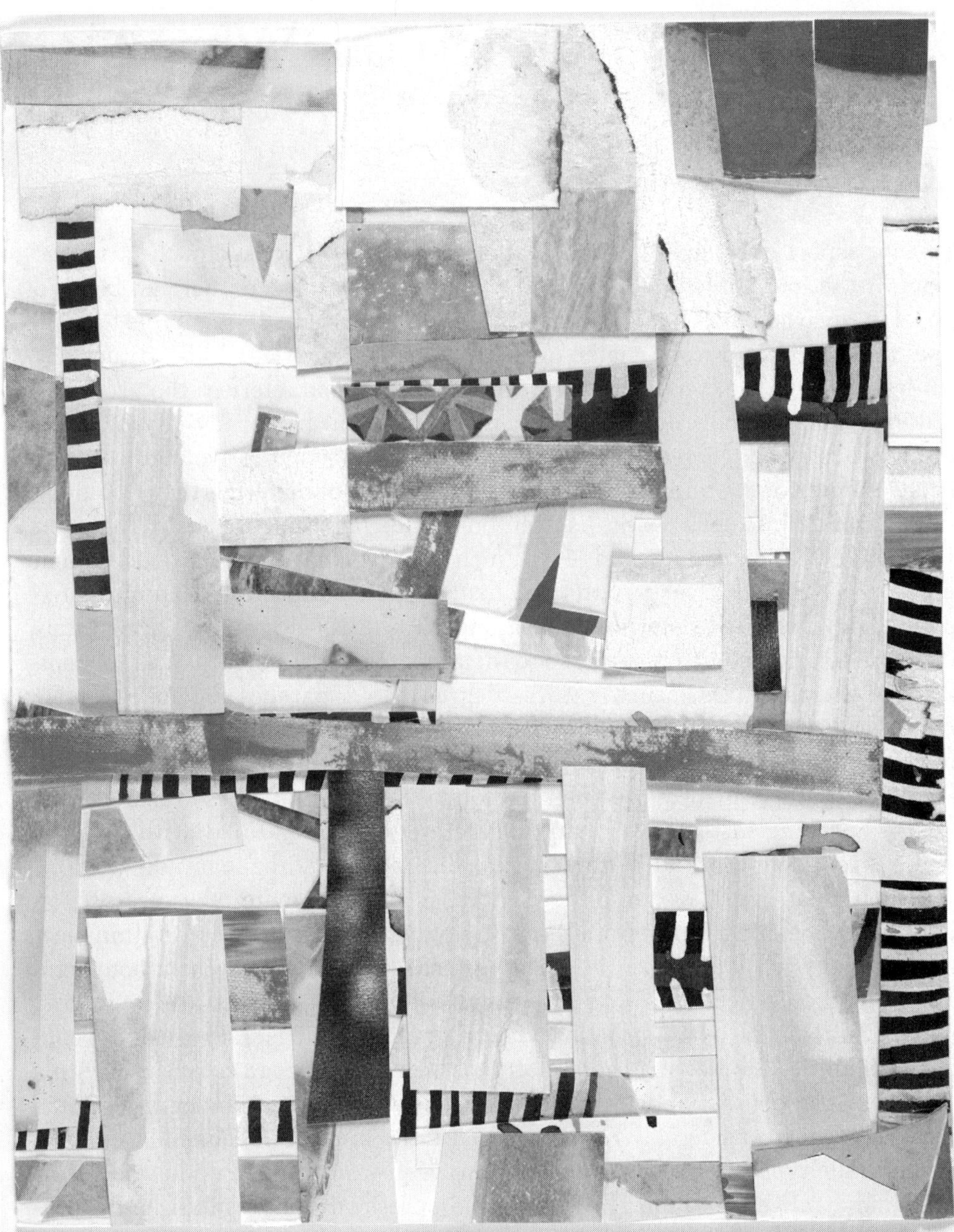

F 5-1
*Barbara Campbell Thomas,
Blocks on Blocks, 2012,
acrylic, ink, and collage on
paper, 11" × 8.5".*

When considering the expressive potential of various collage materials, it is helpful to consider visual qualities and characteristics, and concepts that can focus the collage making experience for first and ongoing experiences in the medium. In the studio, some artists store their materials randomly, while others prefer to organize collage elements in separate containers by type. In the art class with students, it's a good idea to sort materials and objects somewhat by type, even though each item often carries several distinguishing characteristics (younger kids, in particular, love to participate in the sorting process). Typical categories include (1) *visual and/or tactile* (by touch) textures (smooth, rough, furry, bumpy), (2) *individual colors or color families*, no matter what the material (reds, blues, yellows, or warms and cools, and blacks, whites, and grays), (3) *transparent, translucent, shiny, and metallic* (clear cellophane, plastics, foils), (4) *natural* (sticks and bark, dried grass fibers/flowers/leaves, rocks, seed pods), (5) *printed*

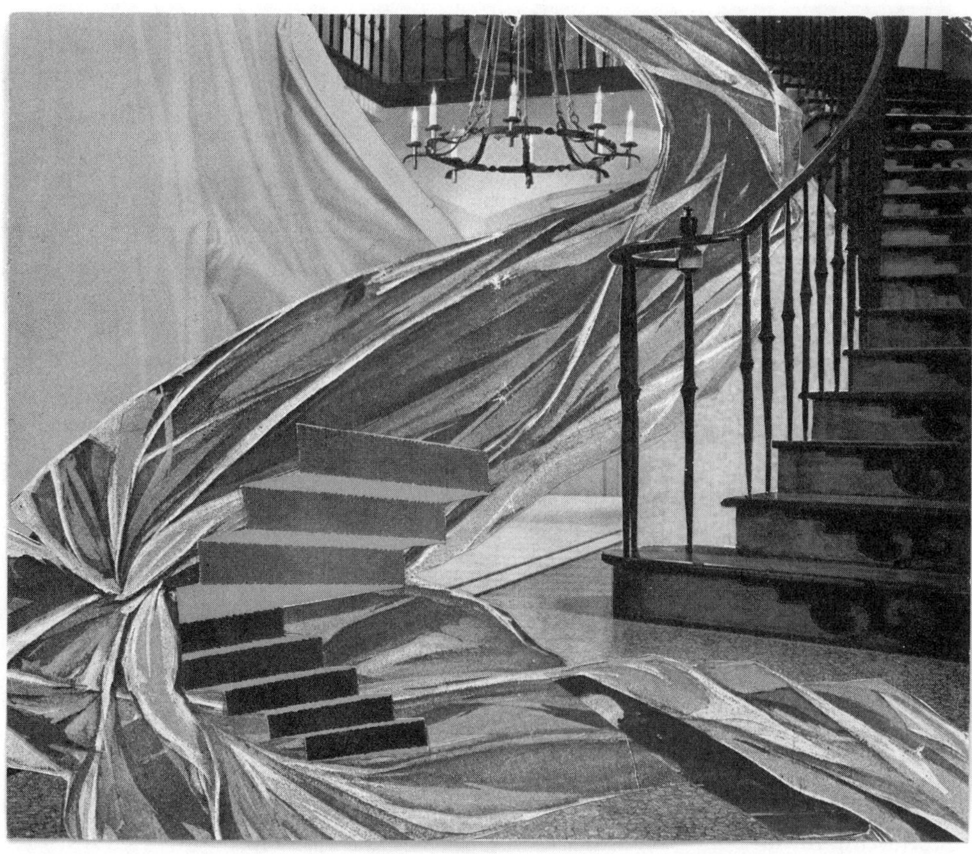

F 5-2
Sophie Aston, Better Homes
and Gardens #15, *2011,
collaged paper, 12.5" × 9.25".*

type and notation (lettering and numbers, advertisements, book pages, sheet music, sewing patterns, architectural drawings, maps, graphs and charts, diagrams, ruled and graph paper, ledger sheets, handwritten letters, notes, and lists), (6) *photographs and illustrations* (personal photographs, pictures and images on pages from magazines, newspapers, encyclopedias and books, comics, postcards, greeting cards, user's manuals for appliances, tools, and equipment), (7) *patterns* (gift wrap, scrapbook sheets, wallpaper samples, fabric), (8) *linear* (thread, yarn, twine, monofilament, wire), (9) *veiled* (mesh screen, netting, lace, and other open-weave materials), and (10) *small objects made from a variety of materials* (buttons, beads, plastic and metal tops from beverage containers, wood shapes, small toys and toy parts, discarded jewelry, hardware items). You can use papers and plastics of all kinds—packing materials, shopping bags, labels from cans and bottles, food and beverage stained paper towels from the kitchen and stained rags and paper towels from the art class, packaging from food, household, and studio items, stained and painted on table covers from previous art classes, and, of course art papers (colored drawing, construction, and tissue papers) and handmade papers, along with completed drawing, painting, and printmaking artworks and media explorations that are ready for recycling and repurposing. These materials are just the beginning of what can be assembled for use in collage (see Figure 5-3).

You can begin your search for materials at home. Check your trash and recyclables (emptied coffee filters and tea bags, shopping bags, wrapping paper, newspaper, catalogues, magazines, cellophane and tissue paper, foil, cereal boxes and the plastic liners inside), round up photographs and old letters (these can be photocopied), and gather fabric and any old sewing patterns you may have available along with thread, yarn, string, and twine. Branching out, look for materials in

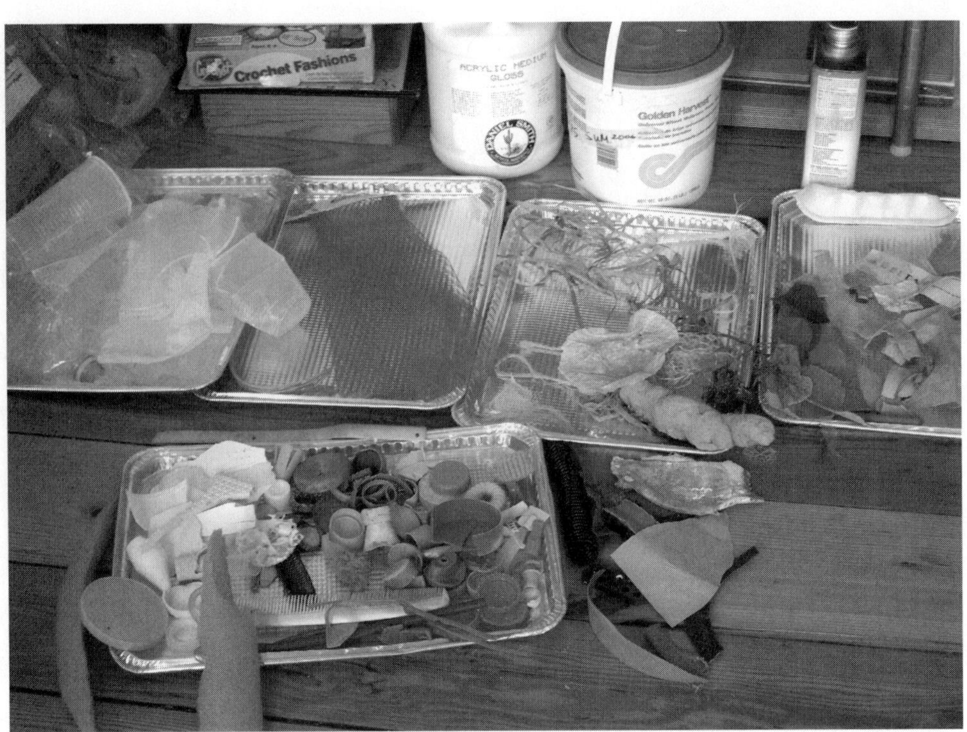

F 5-3: Assorted collage materials

the other immediate environments that encompass daily or routine activities. Following initial collage making experiences, I take younger students on collage walks and have my older students do this as homework—we find interesting discarded things on neighborhood and city streets and collect all sorts of natural materials from parks. Second hand stores, flea markets, materials exchanges, and library book sales are additional sources for great collage materials. Online image sources such as Creative Commons (http://creativecommons.org), Public Domain Pictures (www.publicdomainpictures.net/top-images.php), Reusable Art (www.reusableart.com), and Library of Congress Flickr Photostream (www.flickr.com/photos/library_of_congress) offer copyright-free image options (be sure to check the website for any restrictions).

While collage is about noticing the aesthetic and semiotic qualities in potential materials and hunting for and finding intriguing things to use, it also may involve preparing special materials using a variety of painting, drawing, dying, and printing techniques. Table 5-1 is a starter list of approaches for preparing collage elements (for other options, you and your students can revisit many of the techniques from your explorations of materials featured throughout this book). In the classroom, collage materials preparation activities can be set up as work stations to take place during one or two class periods (depending on the number of activities featured) prior to the design and assembly of the collage. Students rotate through several stations and prepare some of their own materials, and these can be used later, along with found materials and those provided by the teacher, in the collage composition process.

Other Collage Materials

While some collages are constructed exclusively with paper and other items attached to a surface, with no additional embellishment, others incorporate drawing, painting, and printmaking techniques as the assembly of the piece progresses and as finishing touches. Depending on the focus of the collage construction experience,

Table 5-1   Creating Surfaces for Collage Materials

- Lay a watercolor or ink wash and let dry. Layer random or repeated stamped prints using various objects (hard surfaces, bubble wrap, sponge, crumpled paper and foil) dipped in tempera, gouache, or acrylic. (Note: Watercolor, tempera, and gouache may bleed when attached during the collage assembly process.)
- Fold white and brown paper towels and newsprint into squares, rectangles, and accordion pleats—dip in two or three diluted dye (Jacquard Silk Colors are nontoxic), ink, or water paint colors. You can also use coffee and tea. Try scrunching the papers and dip dying as well.
- Fill a small spray bottle with diluted ink. Spray on newspaper or other printed paper, tissue paper, or plain paper. Use unadorned or add additional layers through printing, painting, or drawing.
- Use a pencil sharpener or small blade to collect shavings from wax crayons. Sprinkle shavings on a piece of waxed paper and cover with another sheet of waxed paper. Press with a warm iron to melt the crayon (use a piece of paper between the top waxed paper surface and iron).
- Apply a thick area of paint to a paper surface. Use a paint scraper (or piece of rigid cardboard) to remove some of the paint, creating interesting textures as you go, and let dry. Use as is or add additional layers, varying the directions of your movements. Try this on an assortment of papers.
- Mix acrylic paints with acrylic pouring medium (Liquitex works well) and pool various colors in connecting layers on a piece of plastic wrap. When dry, remove paint layer from the plastic.
- Photocopy or scan and print interesting images, texts, and flat objects on plain and colored paper, transparency film, and translucent vellum (formulated for your copier or printer).

you may want to make use of such materials as graphite, charcoal, Conté crayons, dry and oil pastels, colored pencils, pens, inks, watercolors, tempera/gouache, and acrylics.

Boards and Other Supports

Heavy papers and art boards are commonly used as surface backings for collage (Crescent makes a good option for collage boards), along with wood and canvas panels. But, as with other media, artists go beyond traditional surfaces to seek out alternative supports—boxes, wooden or metal furniture, common household, office, decorative, and hardware objects, walls, bound and extracted pages in re-cycled books, even shoes and other wearable items can serve as the base for collage.

Adhesives and Other Attaching Materials

Many types of adhesives can be used for collage, including polyvinyl acetate (PVA) glues. When working with kids you'll need to use a non-toxic brand, like Elmer's—common PVA-based glues are usually not archival, so you trade longevity of the artwork's stability for safety in the art class. You can also use wheat paste or rice paste (Dick Blick sells nontoxic versions of both), art paste (made by Elmer's), gel medium or Mod Podge (available in a variety of formulas and in both archival and nonarchival forms), and glue sticks. Heavy bodied craft glues (commonly called

Tacky Glue) work well for attaching nonporous objects and heavier boards. In addition to glues and pastes, collage elements can be attached by sewing (hand or machine), stapling (using standard and embellished staples), paper fasteners, pins, rivets and grommets, paper clips and binder clamps, and tape (clear, masking, colored). As with the selection, alteration, and arrangement of collage materials, the attachment methods can contribute additional visual layers to the overall work and these in turn may influence the meaning of the piece. For example, puncturing materials and stitching collage elements together with shimmering and richly colored embroidery floss can suggest ideas that are quite different from those that come from gluing, stapling, or taping. Collage artists understand these nuances and capitalize on them as they compose their work.

Tools and Equipment

Scissors, X-Acto blades and protective cutting surfaces (self-healing cutting mats are available at office, craft, and art supply stores), small containers for dispensing glues and pastes, brushes for spreading adhesives (available at hardware and art supply stores), and a brayer for rolling over glued parts (or a plastic scraper or small piece of rigid cardboard) to smooth edges are additional tools for collage. While scissors are suitable for a wide range of applications, X-Acto knives offer more elaborate paper cutting and alteration options for older and more experienced students.

Note: There are several issues that come into play when considering students' use of X-Acto knives—school, district, or institutional policy (some schools/districts consider any kind of knife to be a weapon and therefore do not allow the use of these tools in the classroom under any circumstances), students' age and maturity level, and the ratio of students to supervising adults in the classroom. Teachers must be thoroughly trained in safe cutting procedures and demonstrate proper practices—the same, of course, goes for students. Knife blades, along with all other hazardous materials, should be locked up when not in use.

Experimenting with Collage

In my work with students, scaffolding the collage making process involves them choosing from a selection of materials and supports those with which they would like to work, open-ended explorations for inventing myriad ways of altering and transforming materials, activities that focus on the arranging aspect of composing the collage, and explorations that encourage divergent approaches to attaching materials to the collage support. Isolating these considerations as students are starting out with the medium allows them to gradually build an inventory of skills and understandings, as well as dispositions, that support experimental inquiry in collage. I then expand the parameters of the project to involve expansive thinking and experimental activity in all aspects of the process at once. As with all materials explorations, we share our results and talk about how the materials, actions taken to transform them, and different arrangement and attachment methods can contribute certain ideas and suggest meanings in their work—and we refer back to these findings in subsequent collage lessons.

As you complete the activities that follow, document your thoughts about not only the qualities and technical possibilities for each material but also the expressive effects that different materials and actions promote and the concepts, skills,

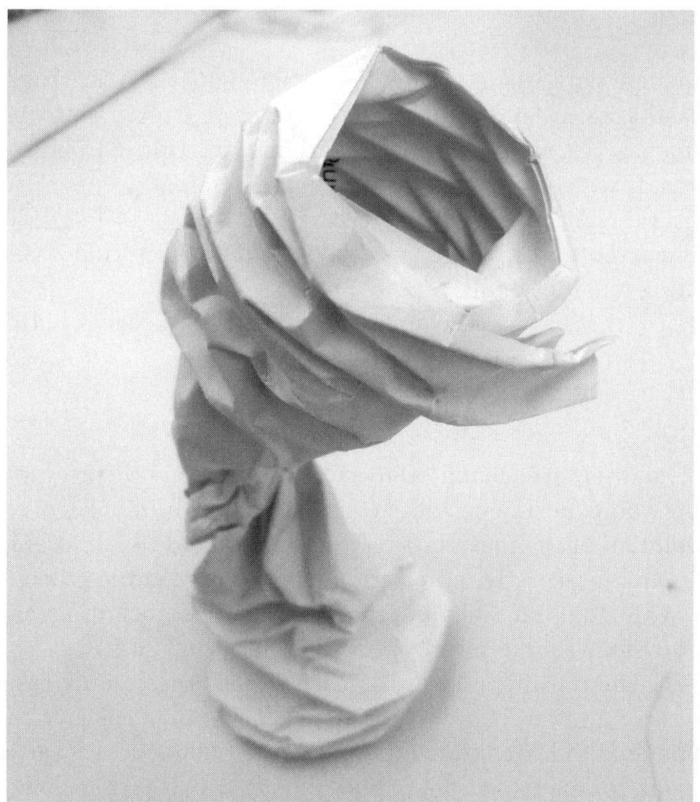

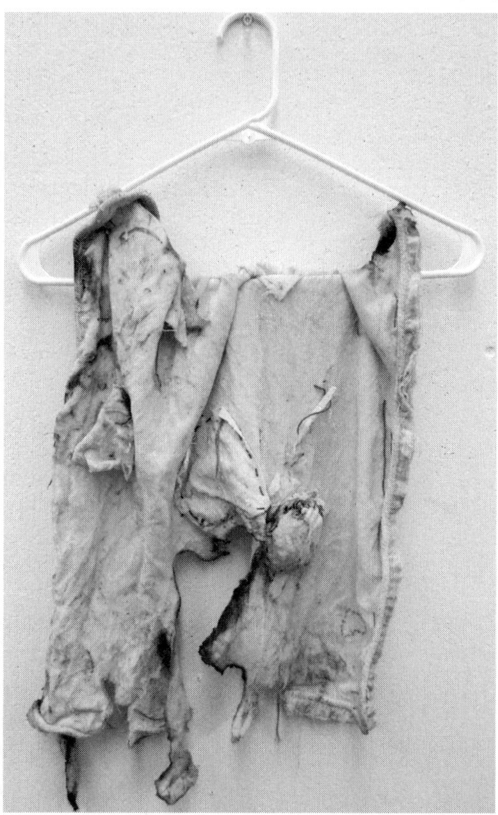

and ways of thinking that can be taught with them. Also, as with other media, note the practical applications of your discoveries for choosing and using these materials with children and teens.

F 5-4: Paper exploration. (above, left)

F 5-5
Cecilia Oh and Lowell Wynn, Untitled, 2013, deconstructed and collaged pillow cover, 18" × 35" × 2". (above, right)

CHANGING MATERIALS

While some things will be used with no or little alteration—for example, cutting or tearing off a particular size or shape of a material or extracting printed areas of image or type from a larger piece—many artists who work in collage extensively transform paper, fabric, and other elements to the point that these everyday materials may become unrecognizable (see Figures 5-4 and 5-5). As discussed previously, these actions on materials contribute their own meanings to the ways in which the finished piece is interpreted and understood. While some techniques are constructive in that they physically add to the material, others are destructive as they involve taking away from, or breaking down, the material. The explorations that follow are designed for you to experiment with a variety of materials transformation techniques—you will use the collage elements you create here later in the chapter as you arrange materials in a series of assembled works.

Exploring Changing Materials

What are different ways to transform common materials for use in collage? Try out the techniques that follow, many of which were developed or co-opted from nonart technologies by European artists in the first third of the twentieth century. Beyond these techniques, what are some new approaches that emerge as you experiment?

Materials:

Paper (solid colors and patterns in various weights and opacities), corrugated cardboard, plastic, fabrics in various colors, patterns, and textures, text and images from magazines, photocopies, photographs, and transparencies
A selection of yarn, thread, string, twine, and ribbon
A selection of natural plant materials
Scissors, hole punch, toothpick, skewer, or other pointed object, ruler, X-Acto blade and cutting mat (optional)
Objects with surfaces that have tactile textures, or reliefs (bark, coins, buttons)

Getting Started:

1. What are the qualities of each material you have to work with, prior to any alteration? As you experiment with transforming each one, keep notes about the evolution of the material's characteristics and the different expressive ideas and interpretive associations that emerge in the process.
2. Experiment with different ways of altering materials according to the suggestions that follow, and invent your own approaches as well.
   a. Tearing—The many different ways of tearing (*déchirage*, from *déchirer*, "to tear") paper and cardboard materials fascinated early collage artists, and torn materials have continued to figure prominently in the process.[5] Try different approaches: ripping fast and straight, tearing slowly to create straight, curved, and jagged edges, tearing in a spiral, holding down a ruler over the paper and tearing against the edge, and so forth. What are some other ways to tear the paper? What shapes can you make? What kinds of edges can you create?

   Note: Depending on the type of paper fiber and the way the fibers are arranged, different papers tear in particular ways. Some papers tear differently vertically as opposed to horizontally. Try tearing a piece of newsprint top to bottom, then turn the paper 90 degrees and tear again. What do you notice?

   b. Cutting—Try different ways of cutting (*découpage*) your flat materials with scissors, making straight and curved cuts, jagged and scalloped cuts, spirals, and so forth. Fold the material in half and cut out an area of both layers that includes a part of the fold, and try this again after folding the paper multiple times. Experiment with making repeating, parallel cuts from the edge to the center of the material to create fringe and other effects. For pictorial images, beyond cutting around the contours of things to use as they appear, use images as filler for other, unrelated objects—a flower shape cut from a scientific diagram, for example.

   If you wish, experiment with the X-Acto knife to see what kinds of effects other cutting techniques may produce—be sure that the hand positioning the material on the surface below is not in the cutting path of the blade, and replace blades frequently so that you are always cutting with a sharp one (visit the manufacturer's website, http://www.xacto.com/faq.aspx, for more information about use and care of these cutting tools).

---

[5] *The Tearingness of Collaging*, a collage done by Robert Motherwell in 1957, is an example of both the visual effects and prominence of this technique.

Note: Cutting with the blade or scissors at an angle so the top of the blade is angled out from the material makes for smooth joints in the finished work.

   c. Transferring surface images through rubbing—Max Ernst, beginning in 1925, incorporated *frottage* (from *frotter,* "to rub") into his collages and the method spread among other artists. This technique involves placing paper or fabric over objects with relief surfaces, and "rubbing" back and forth with a pencil, piece of graphite, crayon, or other dry drawing material until the image on the object's surface emerges on the paper. Explore making rubbings from textured surfaces of objects you have available—coins, buttons, mesh screen, wood and bark, leaves, brick, grouted floor tiles, outer soles of athletic shoes and snow boots—find other surfaces for rubbings as well. Also experiment with layering one rubbing over another on the same piece of paper or cloth.

   d. Scraping and peeling—An outgrowth of frottage, *grattage,* or scraping through top layers to reveal the characteristics of what's below, was popularized by Ernst as well using canvas wet with paint placed over three dimensional objects. With a palette knife, spatula, or another scraping tool, the artist applies pressure while scraping the paint from the canvas, revealing the edges and textures of the objects placed below it. Other approaches to grattage involve covering a layer of paint that has dried on the support with another layer of paint, then scraping and scratching through the first layer to reveal the second one (similar to the *scraffito* technique in ceramics—see Chapter 6).

     Artists also use the technique of grattage to scrape, dig, and peel away the top layer of paper or cardboard, incising lines and textures into the surface and revealing the interior of the material. Using the pointed objects you have available from the list of materials, experiment with scraping and scratching through the top surfaces of some of your paper and cardboard materials. Experiment with peeling back top layers of thicker paper and board materials. What effects does this produce?

   e. Twisting, folding, creasing, rolling, crumpling—Experiment with changing the look and form of paper and other stiff materials by folding, crumpling, scrunching, wadding, rolling, and twisting. What kinds of transformations can you make? Also undo some of these actions by unfolding, untwisting, uncrumpling, and so forth to reveal the textures created by these actions.

   f. Unraveling—Explore deconstructing woven fabrics and spun and twisted linear fibers by unraveling, fraying, and distressing the materials. How do these actions change the expressive nature of the materials?

   g. Wrapping, bundling, knotting, inserting—Use pieces of linear and flat materials together to experiment with tangling, knotting, wrapping, and other actions that build three-dimensionality, change the physical presence of the material, or connect one thing to another. Try folding clear and translucent materials to make holders for other things, so that the inside layer is fully or partially visible.

   h. Punching, piercing—Use pointed tools to poke through paper and open weave materials in different ways, and use a paper punch to further explore this process of taking away material from collage elements.

3. Try the techniques on a wide range of materials. What kinds of actions do particular materials lend themselves to? Which approaches result in the most interesting changes to the material?

Artist Profile: **DONNA RUFF**

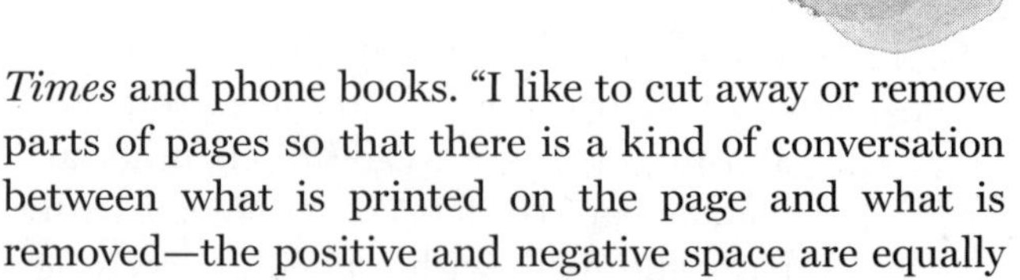

Donna Ruff uses a variety of actions, tools and materials to deconstruct and otherwise dramatically transform paper of many kinds (see Figure 5-6 and Figure 22 in the color insert). "I'm attracted to paper's fragility and pristine beauty," she writes, "yet my work involves scarring, incising, burning, and puncturing its surface. These processes are simultaneously destructive and constructive, providing an image that confounds reductive comprehension as drawings." Her sources and inspirations range from sacred texts to *The New York Times* and phone books. "I like to cut away or remove parts of pages so that there is a kind of conversation between what is printed on the page and what is removed—the positive and negative space are equally important. I'm always aware of allowing glimpses of what is left behind."[6] According to the artist:

Different bodies of work develop differently, but for the most part I work with self-imposed systems, which might be based on geometry, on

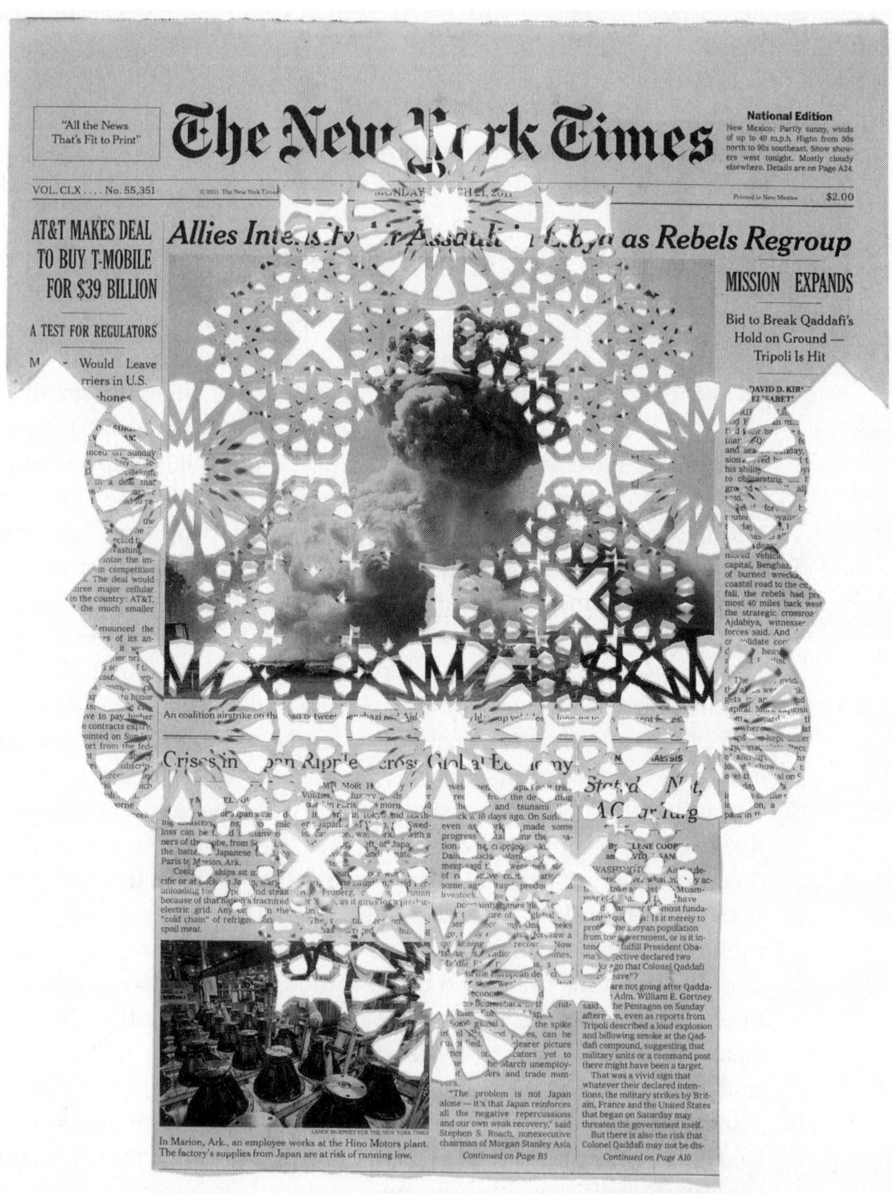

F 5-6

Donna Ruff, 3.21.11, 2011, cut newspaper, 16" × 11.5".

---

[6] H. Seckoff. (2013). Donna Ruff's Cut Newspapers Reconstruct Our Ways of Seeing and Reading, *Huffington Post*, November 13, 2012. Retrieved January 20, 2014, from http://www.huffingtonpost.com/2012/11/13/donna-ruffs-cut-newspaper_n_2118138.html.

page design, on floor plans, or on grids. I do this for several reasons, one of which is that it gives me a place to start, and if I have a few hours in the studio I can immediately jump in to what I had been working on. In between start and finish are many decisions. Sometimes a mistake is made, or a piece is cut or burned too much. Most of the time I work slowly enough so I don't have to fix something, but even if I make an error or something doesn't work I often find a way to incorporate the mistake into the piece.

COMPOSING AND ARRANGING

As with approaches to altering materials, methods for arranging things together on the collage support vary widely (see Figures 5-7 and 5-8). Collage elements can be overlapped, kept separate, piled, entwined, or woven. They can abut edges, repeat to form a pattern, stand out or fade into the background. They can touch the side, top and bottom edges of the support, extend past its edges, stick out from the surface, or hang in suspension. All of these compositional devices stand to influence interpretation of the finished work. In the activities that follow, work quickly and fluidly as you explore arranging elements and composing in collage. Use white PVA glue poured into a small container, a glue brush, and a brayer or small piece of rigid cardboard (for smoothing) to attach your pieces to a support.

Exploring Composing and Arranging

What are some ways of placing and arranging elements in collage? Use the techniques that follow to explore different approaches and go beyond these to invent your own methods.

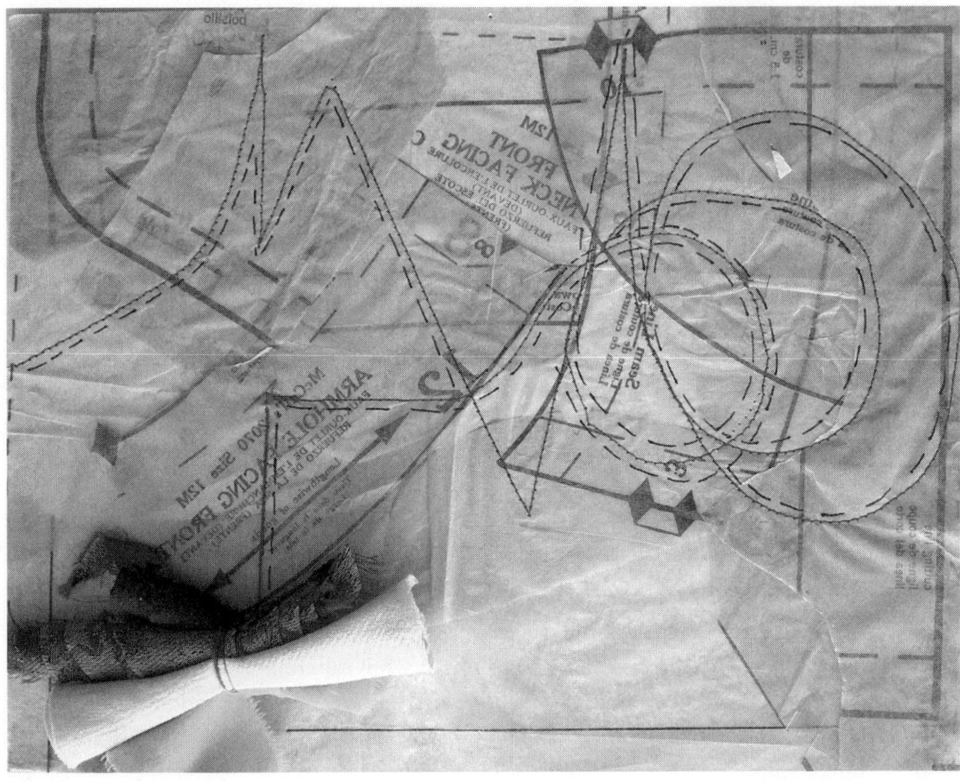

F 5-7
Stephanie Moon, Untitled, mixed media, 2009, 9" × 10".

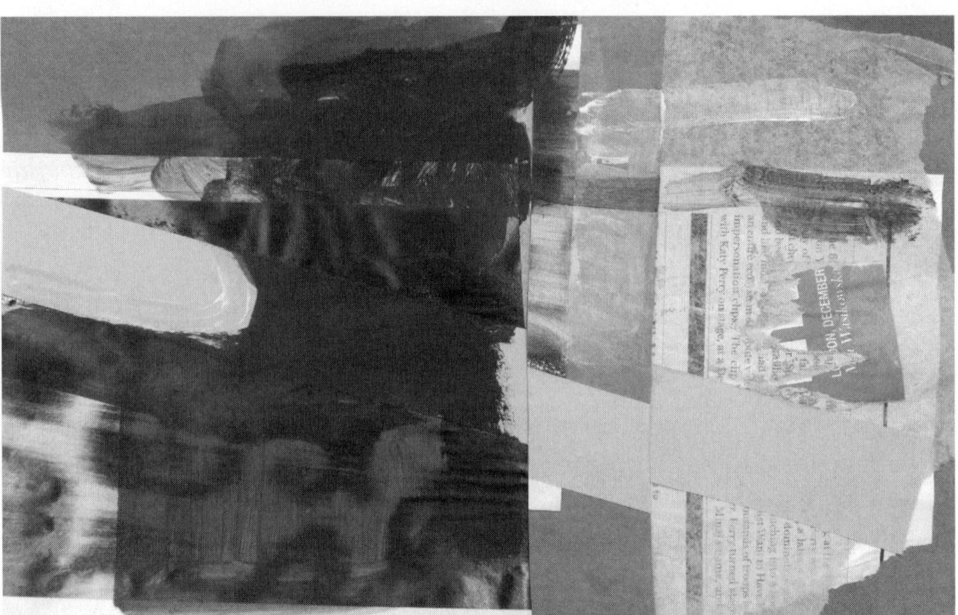

F 5-8
Kate Esbenshade, Untitled,
mixed media, 2013, 6" × 9".

Materials:

Your materials transformations and the materials and tools from the previous
  section
Small sheets of paper and board to use as supports
White PVA glue (Elmer's), small container for dispensing, glue brush, brayer,
  plastic scraper or stiff card (as needed, use these to apply even rolling or
  scraping pressure to materials after gluing)

Getting Started:

1. Collage is about juxtaposing similar and dissonant elements together in a
   composition that invents its own logic/order or creates ambiguity just by
   the proximity of one element to another, and this sense of playing with
   meaning is what makes the medium so intriguing. The suggestions that
   follow are intended for you to focus more on arranging collage elements
   and less on altering them in any elaborate way. As you work on the collage
   activities in this section, try out different ways of arranging materials—
   close to/far way, overlapping/layering/piling, poking through, at various
   distances from the edges of the support, and on or extending beyond the
   outer area or surface plane of the support. Start with the results of your
   explorations from the previous section and add materials as needed.
   a. Shapes—Assemble a small pile of cut paper squares, circles, rectan-
      gles, and triangles. Make a series of three collages, each incorporating
      the same elements. Make the collages look as different as possible from
      one another.

   Note: I often do this as a warm-up activity with older beginners or those who have
   not done collage in a while; I use a simplified version with young children (one collage, not three). We first brainstorm about what different shapes can be used for
   then students experiment and come up with their own designs and representational
   images. Besides serving multiple purposes in creating designs, shapes inspire representational ideas—rectangles can be torsos, cars, houses; round shapes can be

wheels, oranges, soccer balls, ponds; medium shapes can be heads, windows, doors, tree trunks; narrow strips can be hair, noodles, plant stems, etc. These conversations are usually all that is necessary for students to focus their ideas and begin.

    b. Color relationships—Collage is a wonderful way to explore color relationships—monochrome, black-on-black, white-on-white, primary and secondary, complementary, and analogous.[7] Make a series of collages, each limited to a particular color palette, again focusing on different ways of arranging materials together on the support surface.

    c. Textures—Gather materials that together offer a variety of textures—smooth, bumpy, rough, fluffy, ribbed, and so on and focus on various ways of placing these before finalizing and gluing.

    d. Lines—With a selection of linear elements from your materials, explore keeping similar things together, juxtaposing dissimilar things, nesting, interweaving, looping, and other ways of arranging.

    e. Printed images—From your collection of illustrations, photographs, and other images, make a series of collages that use primarily pictorial elements. As you experiment, focus on scale (play with both compatible and incompatible sizes of things) and reassembly (cut images into parts and reassemble the fragments, both related and unrelated, into new and unusual configurations). Make some joints and shared edges subtle or imperceptible, and others abrupt and obvious. How do these different approaches impact the look and expressive meaning of the work?

    f. Type and numbers—Gather printed materials that feature letters and numbers, cut or tear so that you are not using entire words, and experiment with various arrangements.

    g. Repetition—Make a collage that uses at least one repeating element.

    h. Light and space—Try different ways of layering transparent and translucent materials over various collage elements. What new effects come from this?

    i. Three dimensional—gather materials that have surface relief or depth, fold a small area of flat materials so that glue may be applied, and compose a collage in which the elements extend from the surface. As in other collages, consider various arrangements before gluing the final composition.

2. Make sure to try the arranging activities with an assortment of materials. What kinds of configurations do particular materials lend themselves to? Which approaches result in the most interesting compositions?

ATTACHING

Since the ways collage elements are attached can be exploited as visual components that add their own meaning to the piece, it's worth exploring these methods and the different ideas they can suggest. Once attached, materials may also be detached, peeled away, and partially removed to reveal underlying layers

---

[7] Traditionally speaking, complementary color pairs that contain a primary color are the primary, say red, and the secondary color that is the mixture of the remaining two primaries (yellow + blue = green). Primary-secondary complementary colors are red-green, blue-orange, yellow-purple; you can locate these and other complementary colors directly opposite one another on a color wheel. Analogous colors are those that are in the same area—for example, blues ranging from green blues to purple blues, oranges ranging from yellow oranges to red oranges.

Artist Profile: **SOPHIE ASTON**

Sophie Aston's collages incorporate painted elements and magazine images in scenes meant to promote a sense of "subtle disquiet" (see Figure 5-2 and Figure 23 in the color insert). She writes:

In recent collages I have spliced painted elements into rearranged interiors culled from vintage Better Homes and Gardens *magazines. The abstract gestures of Expressionism are suggested within pristine spaces—Maverick furniture, incongruous curtains, and curtains of paint, in turn occupy and deny the picture-space. Perspective is made unstable and objects repeat themselves with a meta insistence. I feel that each room plays host to an unknowable source of disquiet.*

According to Aston, while at a residency in Vermont she "became fascinated by the New England homes (as a European in America for the first time the wooden buildings were exotic to me)." In subverting "idealised domestic interiors . . . by the insistent duplication of elements of décor," shifting interpretations of the work defy fixed meaning. Aston writes, "'meaning' always slips away, what remains, and is reflected back to us, is simply the fact of our seeking."

What ideas come to mind when you study these works? What makes you say this? What has the artist done in the work to suggest these ideas?

---

of materials, providing both a history of the collage's material layers and visual documentation of some of the actions that were taken to make it (see Figures 5-9 and 5-10). As you build your inventory of approaches, keep notes on the expressive potential of each to use later in ongoing collage work.

Exploring Attaching

What are different ways of attaching elements in collage? Use the techniques here to explore different methods and experiment further to discover your own.

Materials:

Materials transformations and the materials and tools from previous sections
Small sheets of paper and board to use as supports
White glue, Tacky Glue, Mod Podge or gel medium, a small amount of wheat paste, rice paste and/or Art Paste mixed with water according to directions, small containers for dispensing glue, glue brushes, brayer, plastic scraper or stiff card
Large needle and assorted threads, string, and so forth
Stapler, assorted staples, paper fasteners, binder clamps
Adhesive tapes—clear, colored, and so forth

Getting Started:

1. For the attachment activities that follow, continue to use the results of your explorations and add materials as needed, as you arrange materials in a series of collages. You also may want to cut up some of the collages completed in the previous section and use those fragments as you compose new arrangements. Use the list of prompts in Table 5-2 to focus your work—or depart from those suggestions and proceed with other ideas for selecting and arranging materials.

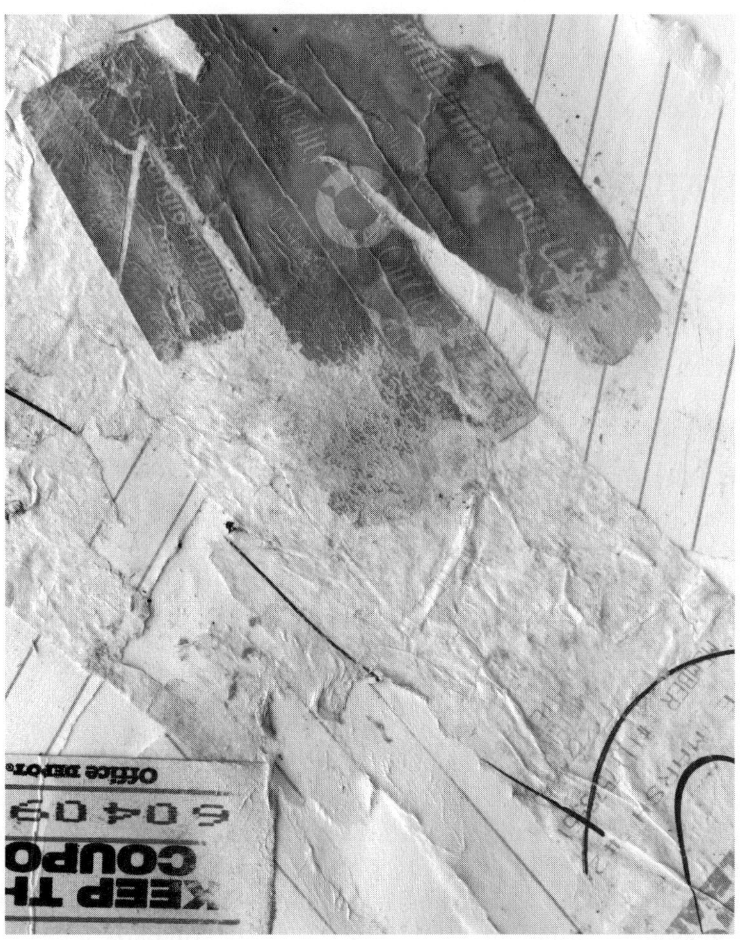

F 5-9: Peeled collage layers

F 5-10: Peeled collage layers

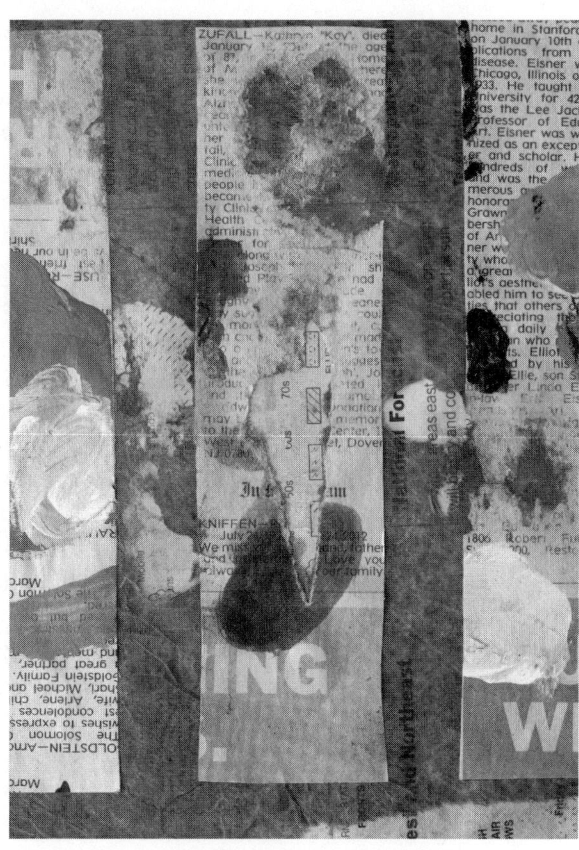

a. Glue—Try out all of the glues and pastes. White glue can be used as is or thinned with water and both used underneath and layered on top of porous materials. Experiment with each adhesive, noting how they work during application and how they appear when dry. Explore *décollage*, or the tearing and peeling away of paper elements once dry. What kinds of effects can be created by partially removing layers?

b. Tape—Make a series of collages that feature tape as both a prominent design element and an attaching method with paper and plastic materials. Try clear tape with transparent and translucent elements and colored tape with black and white printed text and images. Experiment further with other combinations.

c. Pierce and clamp—Use a selection of thread elements to explore sewing as attachment and embellishment, and try stapling, paper fasteners, and binder and paper clips.

d. Extend and suspend—Experiment with ways to make some elements extend out from the front surface of the support, or hang in suspension.

2. Try attaching a wide range of materials. What approaches do particular materials lend themselves to?

ALTERNATIVE SUPPORTS

Like the rest of the materials in a collage, supports—as base forms on which things are applied and layered—can both supply their own visual qualities and suggest expressive ideas (see Figure 5-11). Just about anything with a smooth surface can be used as a collage base, and the hunt for alternatives can be combined with your on-going collection of materials.

Exploring Alternative Supports

Beyond paper, board, and other traditional collage bases, how can objects serve as interesting supports? Use the techniques here to explore different options and experiment further to discover your own.

Materials:

A selection of paper and fabric materials
One or two objects from the following (look for items with smooth surfaces): rigid cardboard boxes, a small furniture item (such as a stool or end table), common household, office, decorative, and hardware objects (picture frame, vase, toy, etc.), recycled hardcover books, shoes
White glue, Tacky Glue, Mod Podge or gel medium, small containers for dispensing glue, glue brushes, brayer, plastic scraper or stiff card

Getting Started:

1. Play with ideas—Consider the objects you have available and the ideas and meanings people typically attribute to them. How do you want the collage elements to interact with these associations? Do you want to further traditional connotations by adding collage elements that reinforce them? Or do you want to disrupt this kind of connectedness by introducing collage elements that are incongruent with traditional interpretations and that present the object and its interpretation in a new light?
   a. Choose materials—Select the colors, textures, images, and/or type-based materials that you want to work with (thinner materials work best). Be sure to gather enough to cover the surface of the object.
   b. Alter materials—Make alterations as needed to prepare for arranging and attaching.
   c. Experiment with different arrangements—You can use tape on the backs of collage elements to play around with different compositions then photograph the finalized arrangement as a reference for attaching. Or you can begin immediately with the gluing process, repositioning elements as you go (this method risks damaging collage elements that become fragile with the application of wet glue, so you need to be careful and work quickly).
   d. Attach collage elements—Use Mod Podge, gel medium, white glue mixed with water (up to 50% dilution), or another solution (depending

on the objects to be joined) as an adhesive. Brush a coat of adhesive onto an area of the object's surface or onto the material itself, apply collage elements and smooth them out, and let dry. Apply another adhesive layer and second layer of collage elements if needed, and smooth that out. Seal the top collage layer with adhesive if needed.

2. Try a different object and another selection of materials. What approaches do particular materials and objects lend themselves to?

MIXING COLLAGE AND OTHER MEDIA

As mentioned previously, some collages are constructed with paper and other items, with no additional embellishment, while others make use of drawing, painting, and printmaking techniques as the piece is assembled and completed. Many artists regularly incorporate graphite, charcoal, Conté crayon, dry and oil pastels, colored pencils, pens, inks, watercolors, tempera/gouache, and acrylics during the assembly process (see Figures 5-12 and 5-13). While it's important for students to also have an opportunity to do this, it is equally important not to overwhelm them with too many materials at once, before they are ready. They should be able to achieve increasing detail with cut paper, for example, and not need to rely on an easier solution to creating small details, such as pencil or marker. The best approach is to observe closely to see when students have thoroughly explored and become skilled in using different kinds of collage materials and approaches before expanding the options.

Exploring Mixed Media with Collage and Other Materials

How might painting and drawing materials be incorporated into the composition of a collage? As in your other explorations note in your studio journal discoveries about new effects and expressive ideas made possible by mixing media.

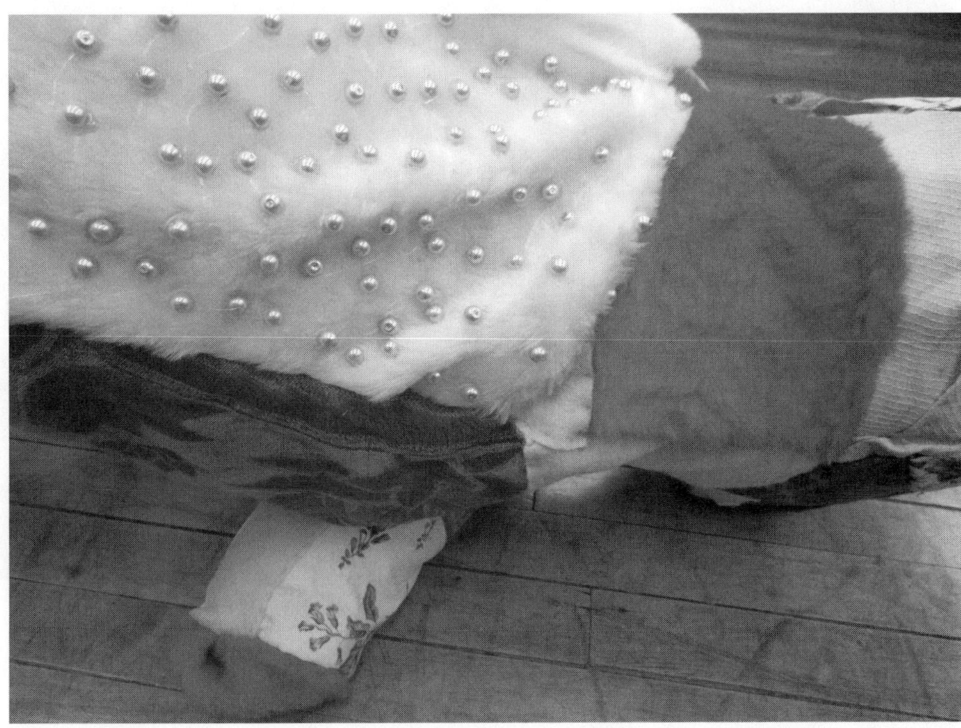

F 5-11
Haydee Naula, Untitled (detail), 2013, fabric collage on inflatable cow, 24" × 18" × 12".

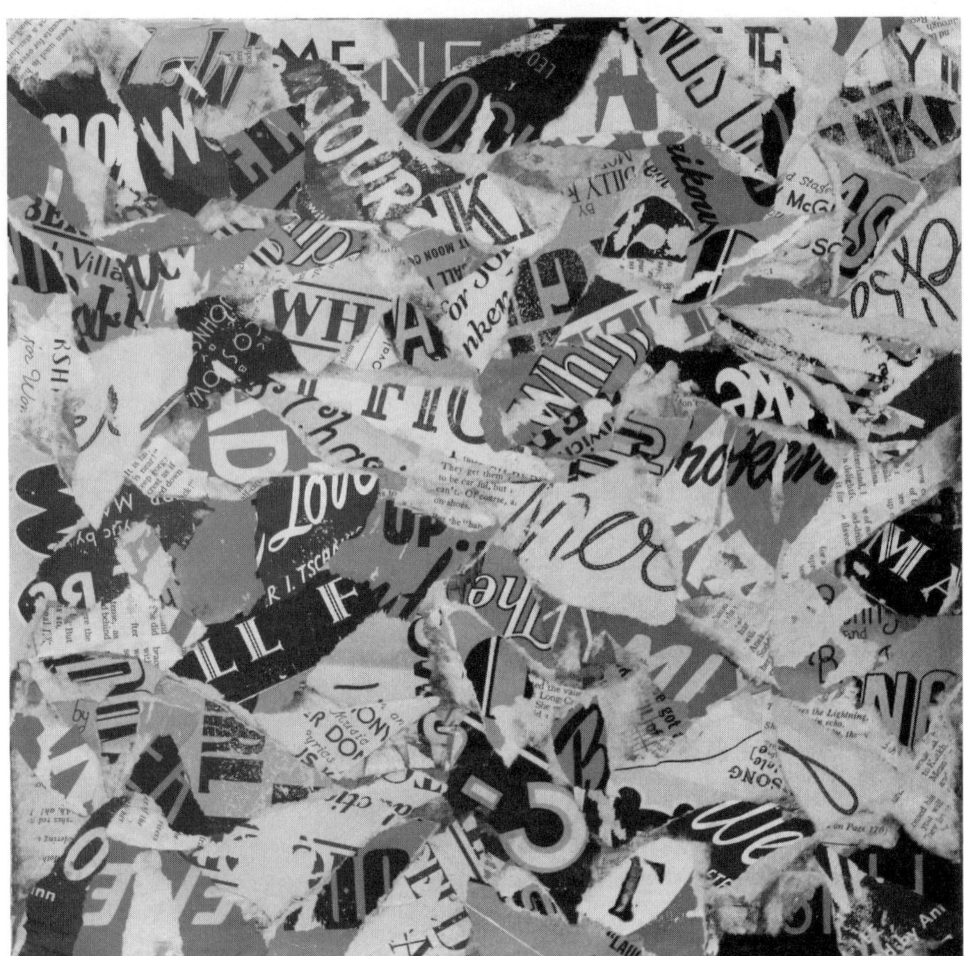

F 5-12
Susan Reedy, Lasso, 2012, vintage magazines and sheet music, acrylic on canvas, 12" × 12".

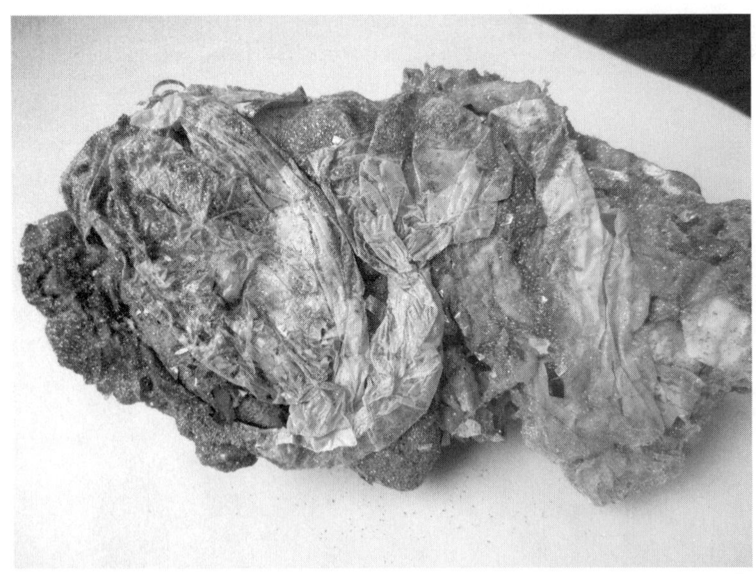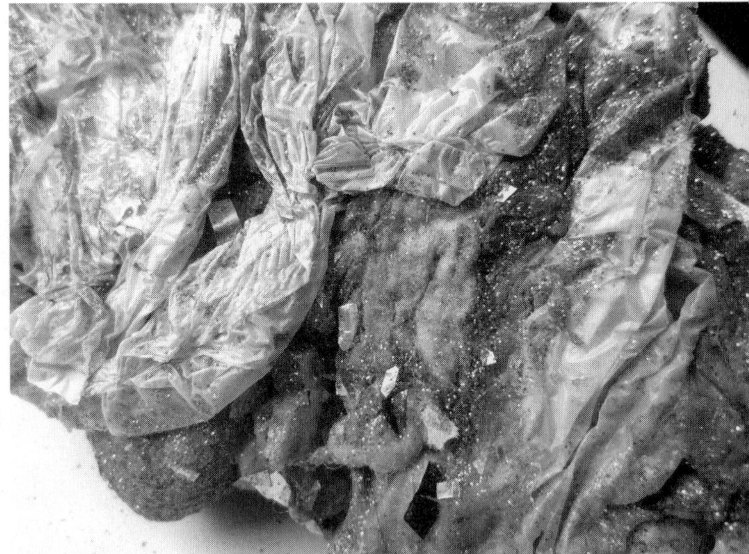

F 5-13
Kate Esbenshade, Untitled, 2013, mixed media, 7" × 4" × 5".

Materials:

A selection of collage elements, supports, and attaching materials
Tempera, watercolor, gouache, and/or acrylic paints and mediums
Paintbrushes
Containers of water
Palettes, containers, and trays for dispensing paints
Graphite pencils and colored pencils
Oil pastels
Water-soluble pastels
Ink pens

Getting Started:

1. Select collage and drawing/painting materials to explore in different combinations. Try using watercolor with colored tissue and other translucent papers and with black and white texts, experiment with acrylic on color printed backgrounds and on fabrics and other nonpaper materials. Explore how pencils and water-soluble pastels work on different surfaces.
2. Try different media combinations in a variety of applications. How does adding these materials change the process of creating in collage? How do the materials support new visual interest and meaning?

MORE IDEAS FOR COLLAGE

With a growing understanding of materials and their visual effects and meanings, students are eager to explore different topics and subjects they find interesting—themes from their personal experience and from the world around them. Table 5-2

Table 5-2   Thematic Ideas for Collage

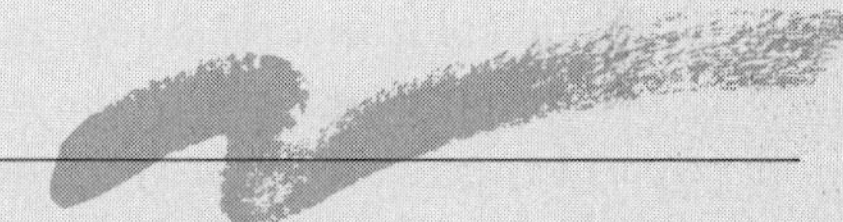

- A collage about a person or animal you know well.
- A collage based on experiences of a place.
- A collage that commemorates a significant personal event.
- A collage that explores a significant social/cultural/historical event.
- A collage that suggests movement from an action—leap, crawl, pounce, drift, spin, crash, etc.
- A collage that features people in a daily activity.
- A collage that conveys a feeling.
- A collage that suggests a sound or piece of music.
- A collage in response to a lyrical poem.
- A collage that suggests a smell.
- A collage based on observing an object or group of objects.
- A collage that suggests a memory.
- A collage that represents a bodily or mental state—disbelief, sleep, chill, boredom, glow, awakening, etc.
- A collage that is ironic, humorous, or puzzling.
- A collage that presents a position on an issue of concern (social, cultural, environmental, global).
- A collage that represents past, present, and future.
- A collage about hopes and dreams.
- A collage that holds a secret message.

contains some focusing ideas that I use regularly with students—we brainstorm different approaches to representing ideas related to these themes and various ways collage materials can be used. These themes can also be combined with the materials-focused explorations throughout this chapter.

STUDIO REFLECTION: COLLAGE

Spread out your collage experiments and note the variety of techniques you used and the range of visual effects you were able to achieve. Think about how the different marks and effects you've created could be used to suggest specific ideas, feelings, moods, states, or qualities in a collage.

Reflecting on your written observations and looking at your test pages, which collage materials and surfaces do you find most interesting? Most expressive? Most fun to work with? Most challenging? Most disappointing? Most surprising? Why?

How do the working processes for each type of material compare to one another? Do you prefer some in relation to others? What are the characteristics of the material and process that draw you to them? Compare your responses to what the artists below have to say about their choices and use of materials.

More Artists on Media

Artist Profile: **BARBARA CAMPBELL THOMAS**

Barbara Campbell Thomas combines collage with acrylic paint and ink on paper (see Figure 5-1 and Figure 24 in the color insert). She is interested in creating "an imagined visual representation of the collision between experienced reality, remembered reality and embellished reality."

Campbell Thomas has written that her work

revels in high-keyed color, the juxtaposition of shape and pattern, and the literal inclusion of bits of daily ephemera—colored cardboard from a cracker box, tin-foil or a child's worn T-shirt. These nearly chaotic, adamantly physical images are a means of locating some kind of ecstatic, exuberant, ever unfolding space analogous to our dense existence.

What kinds of ideas come to mind when you look at these works? How do the selection, alteration, and arrangement of collage elements contribute to your interpretations?

The notion of building an image piece by piece, shape by shape—one shape pushed up next to another—is a potent visual and conceptual idea for me. Underlying the idea is the possibility that such building relationships could, in theory, continue on forever . . . bit by bit, piece by piece, slowly, slowly. Simple relationships that become complex by virtue of infinite accumulation are the base off of which I jump these days.

Artist Profile: **SUSAN REEDY**

Like Barbara Campbell Thomas, Susan Reedy includes ephemeral materials and references ideas of memory and time in her work (see Figure 5-12 and Figure 25 in the color insert). She writes:

My work investigates themes of language, memory, and preservation of ephemeral materials that are in danger of becoming extinct in our digital age. The work is created with vintage papers that have been discarded and partially destroyed: sheet music, dictionaries, fragments of billboards and prayer books.

The work is inspired by the inherent beauty of these vintage materials and by the textural qualities sometimes seen on outdoor surfaces— walls, signs, etc.—that are in a state of flux due to the ravages of time, the elements, and neglect. In the work the text and imagery of the source material becomes altered during the creative process so that new and unexpected combinations of form and context emerge. The art work reflects the poetic beauty of the imperfect state of

the source material and utilizes its inherent sensuous nature.

Reedy's approach merges built-up layers with scraping away—adding and subtracting, constructing and deconstructing. What qualities and impressions are suggested by her use of vintage materials and the ways in which she alters and juxtaposes collage elements in her work?

The creative process involves alternating layers of paint and paper that are built up, stripped away then partially rebuilt, often in many successive layers. This additive and subtractive process results in an expressive surface that is rich in paint, altered imagery, and text. The technique used to transform the images—the scraping, tearing and painting over—both destroys and preserves these vintage materials using contemporary thinking about surface quality and composition.

Artist Profile: **BARBARA KENDRICK**

Barbara Kendrick's work is about "taking the familiar and making it strange" (see Figure 26 in the color insert). She grafts parts of seemingly unrelated images that reference natural and manufactured worlds, creating "unexpected juxtapositions" and narratives that make unlikely sense. She describes her process as one of composing as she goes along. "I improvise with found materials, creating mistakes that might lead to surprising outcomes. It's like choosing to get lost in a foreign city because that leads to the most interesting part of the trip." According to Kendrick,

The fluidity of collage offers opportunities for visual puns and analogies and gives me surprising ways to think about illusion, deception

and representation. I am interested in boundaries that unravel, the edge between being and becoming, the point at which a thing is precise and slips away. I like taking the familiar and making it strange.

In the collages I combine the natural with the manmade, splicing and grafting together representations of "animal, vegetable and mineral." I like the way collage is a hybrid with an inherent instability and slipperiness. Our complicated relationship with nature stimulates the way I choose to use contradiction in my work. Assembling collage material from my large inventory of images leads to unexpected juxtapositions—the "necessary accident." I take these unlikely connections and craft them into convincing fictions.

Artist Profile: **ANDREW POLK**

Andrew Polk's series "Life after Death" incorporates images from the Civil War, the Filipino War, World War I, World War II, the Korean War, and the Vietnam War (see Figure 5-14). According to Polk, "the works attempt to construct prologues to the lives of the depicted dead and to acknowledge the interweaving of lives around the world and through the generations." He writes, "Each life is interwoven with those from before and after. We are who we are, and what we are, because of the events that precede us."

Polk uses photographic images and digital strategies in these collages but also works by hand with painting and drawing materials, moving back and forth between the two studio approaches. Each collage in the series contains three elements: a documentary photograph from the US National Archives, its official identification (including a description, date of the work, and the name of the photographer), and a handwritten narrative fiction. Polk writes that the "image is stained, painted, folded, and torn; digitally collaged; and then handworked with paints, charcoal particles, and other materials." Its "various marks, tears, stains, and splatters" add distinct layers of visual detail and effect, augmenting the narrative fictions of the works.

What kinds of stories does Polk's use of images, text, and drawing and painting materials suggest? How does he weave together the different visual, material, and textual elements of his work in narratives that incorporate both the present and past—"those who came before us"?

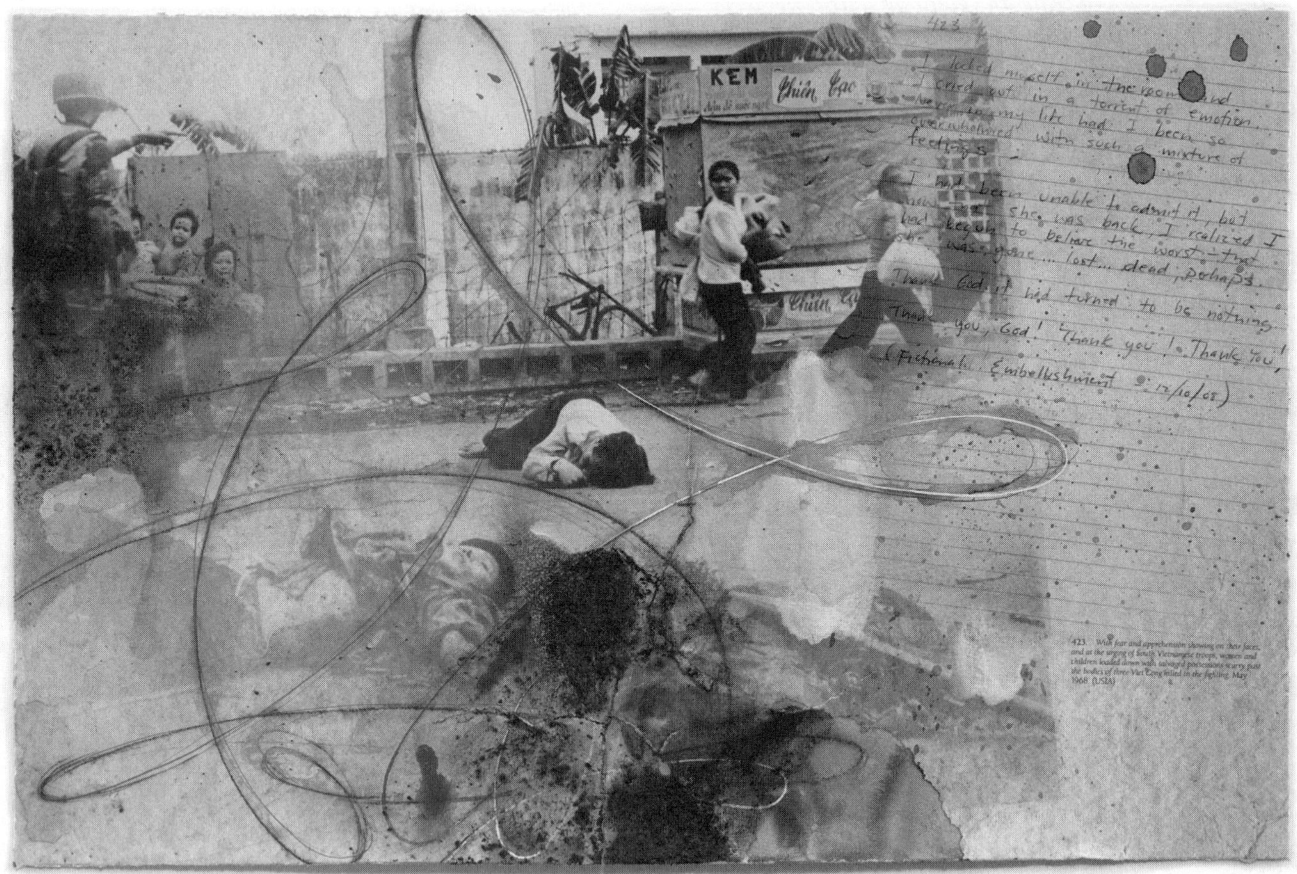

F 5-14

Andrew Polk, Fear and Apprehension, *2009, mixed media and inkjet on paper, 12" × 18".*

Thoughts about Collage as a Studio Practice

Since its integration into the studio methods of artists over the last century, collage has served as a generative forum for experimentation and boundary pushing. There are no strictures for composing in collage—no set materials one must use, no fixed collection of technical approaches for altering, arranging, and attaching elements together. As with other art forms but perhaps most pointedly in collage, artists explore the physical and expressive qualities of materials. They seek and arrive at intriguing matches between the qualities that set one material apart from another, and the distinctive meanings individual materials and their combinations and placements can evoke (see Figures 5-15 and 5-16).

Children and teens approach collage in a variety of ways as well. As with drawing and painting, young people may at times wish to make collages that focus solely on color, shape, texture, or other design concepts and their relationships. At other times, they will be interested in using collage approaches to create narrative works that incorporate people, animals, objects, and settings in some sort of story, or topical theme.

Alternating collage experiences with drawing/painting and three-dimensional work can provide students with alternative ways of learning how to construct images of people, animals, and other subjects they are interested in depicting in their work. For example, when students are eager to draw and paint detailed human bodies with arms, legs, and torsos that bend and angle in different positions (throwing a ball, running, sitting cross-legged), it can be helpful to first build those figures out of paper shapes—different sized rectangles that can serve as parts of arms, legs,

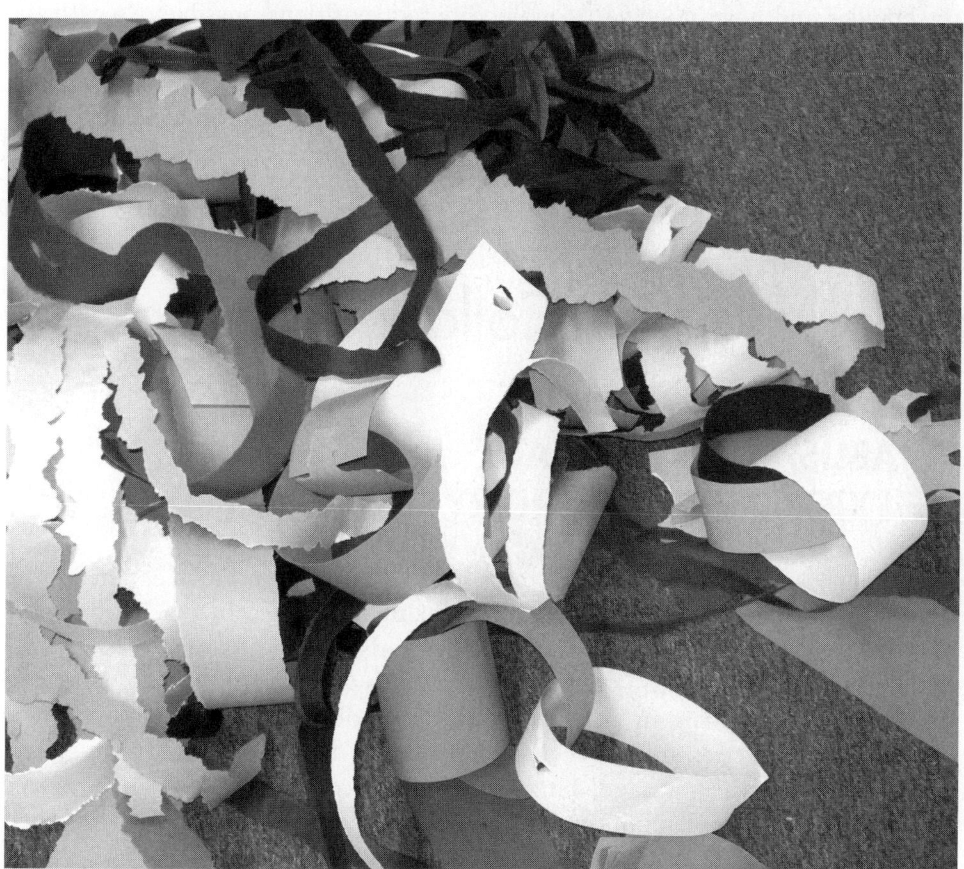

F 5-15: Manipulating and placing materials in a collage in process

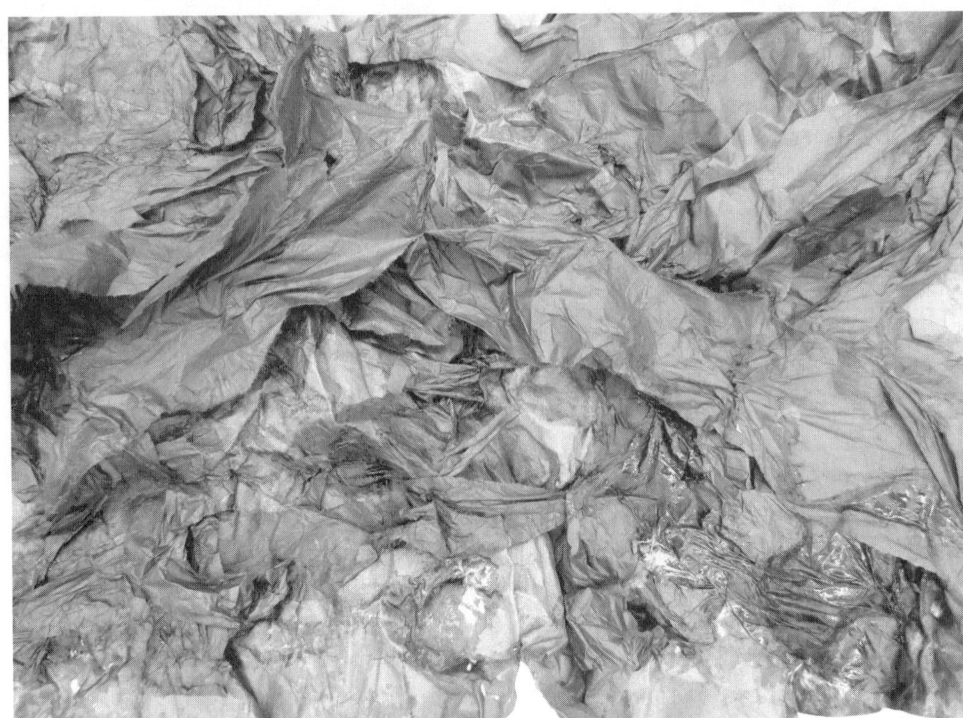

F 5-16: Alteration and placement of materials in a finished collage

torsos, and so forth. Physically moving and placing the paper body parts helps students to envision, when they then go to draw or paint, how arms bend at the elbow or shoulder and how other joints make different positions possible. As with the other media we've explored so far, think about some of the differences between working in collage and working in drawing, painting, and printmaking, and how you might use these studio approaches separately and together in lessons for your students. In the final sections, we consider practical issues for presenting to kids the kinds of collage experiences featured in this chapter.

Setting up for Working with Collage Materials

ESTABLISHING A CLIMATE OF EXPERIMENTAL INQUIRY

As emphasized throughout this chapter, establishing a climate of experimental inquiry in collage leads to students discovering and inventing their own ways of transforming and composing with materials. In brainstorming with my students, I ask them to think of all the different ways that we can transform the materials we are using in the lesson, and how different materials and their distinctive properties might be used to suggest ideas, feelings, states, and moods in a design or image. I then ask them to imagine as many ways as possible that collage elements can be placed on the base surface—near together,

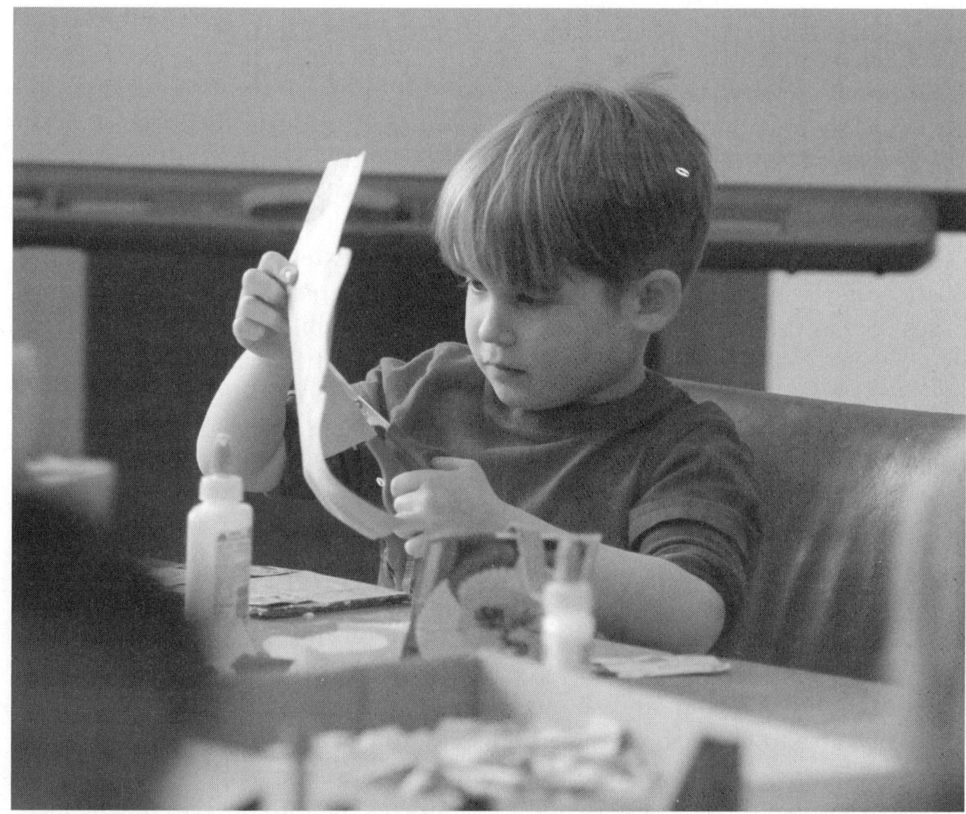

F 5-17: Collage in the art class

far apart, touching at the corners or edges, overlapping and layering, stacking and piling up from the surface, extending beyond the outer perimeter of the base, and so forth. This constant exploration with changing and arranging materials and with ideas that emerge in the process sets the tone for ongoing experimental inquiry (see Figure 5-17).

MATCHING TIME ALLOTTED AND PROCESSES OF WORKING WITH MEDIA

Altering materials, trying out different placements of things, and attaching collage elements in compositions takes time. You can structure your lessons to focus on different parts of the collage process one at a time. For example, for a focus on arrangement and composition, you can give younger children a variety of precut shapes in different colors and keep the alteration of collage materials to a minimum. For a focus on changing and transforming materials, have the students explore a wide variety of altering techniques in one class period and compose and attach the pieces in a following session, or work with smaller bases if needed so that there is not so much space to fill. As much as possible, students should be given some choice regarding sizes and shapes of bases, types and colors of materials, and actions that can be taken in constructing the piece, as well as what the work will be about and how it will look.

CONSIDERING STUDENTS' AGE, PHYSICAL CHARACTERISTICS, AND PRIOR EXPERIENCE

For younger and older students who are new to collage, starting with limited materials and gradually introducing new options and conceptual prompts encourages continued interest and experimentation. For older and more experienced students, collage experiences can be deepened and extended through the introduction of new kinds of papers and fabrics, found materials, and nontraditional bases such as three-dimensional objects. Very young children will need targeted experiences in which they can explore and practice cutting with scissors and attaching collage pieces with glue. As mentioned earlier, dispensing glue in small containers and having students use brushes to apply it is a good strategy for focusing their learning about how much glue is necessary in the collage process.

BALANCING EFFICIENCY WITH STUDENT AUTONOMY

As with all other media, and as much as is manageable given class sizes, kids should be able to move about their workspace to locate and get what they need. Once again, giving students the opportunity to consider what is available and choose what they'd like to use that day encourages them to develop independent artistic judgment.

ANTICIPATING MESS AND PLANNING FOR CLEANUP

Because collage can involve a wide variety of materials that most teachers like to keep organized, it's helpful to have papers, fabrics, and other materials sorted and labeled in containers and set up so that students can select particular materials for themselves (and return unused materials to their designated place at the end of the class period). It's also helpful to protect work surfaces, have kids wear smocks if necessary, and plan carefully for cleanup. Communicate to students how scraps will be returned or thrown away, unused materials put back in their containers, and glue containers and brushes collected, cleaned, and stored. Also, have a designated place where collage works will be stored at the end of class.

REFLECTING ON AND ARTICULATING LEARNING

Discuss with students what was learned and expressed through collage at the end of the session—invite them to talk about their finished works (and those of their peers) in terms of the many ways materials were altered and arranged together in

different kinds of compositions (see Figure 5-18). Ask them to interpret expressive meanings in the works and analyze the ways in which those meanings were made possible by the artist's selection of and actions with materials. Brief written explanations about the goal of the collage experience and what was learned and expressed in individual students' works creates a record of skills, concepts, and ways of thinking in collage that can be used as a resource in subsequent lessons and in exhibition of the works.

F 5-18: Collage wall with prompts

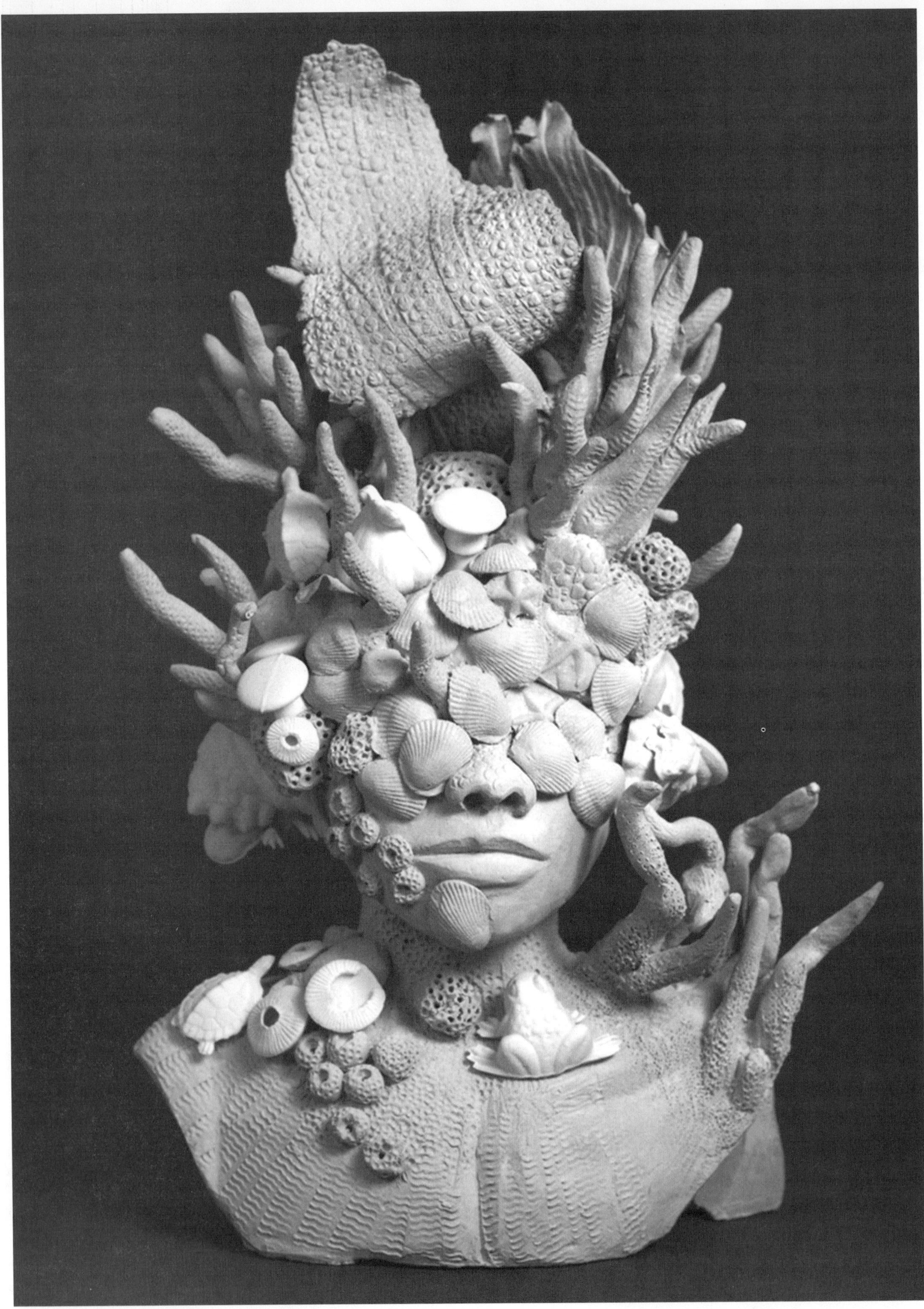

Morel Doucet, Bloom, 2013

Forming and Building

When I first came to New York, I had no money, obviously (no one had any money). And I had the Year of Aluminum Foil. I did the Year of Little Tiny Wire Structures. And then I would get a router or a tool, and it was the Year of the Router, the Year of the Jigsaw. It's as if, with every new material, there's actually a whole new image that comes about, from that color, from that material. I like that. So now, I've got all of these materials and all of these tools. There is a real range of how I would use steel, how I would use plasters and polyesters, different kinds of paints, from dyes to oils. I will use every variation and just about every surface and every material that I can imagine. I'm sure there are billions out there that I haven't done.

—Judy Pfaff[1]

[1] *Art: 21* (2002). Interview—Judy Pfaff: *Buckets of Rain*. Retrieved August 9, 2013, from http://www.art21.org/texts/judy-pfaff/interview-judy-pfaff-buckets-of-rain.

WHILE SCULPTURE TODAY CAN INCORPORATE just about any "material"—sugar (both liquefied and cubed), ice, sound, light, garbage bags, chocolate, insects, tea bags, human hair and nail clippings, dirt, living organisms, egg shells, melted toys, and scotch tape—prehistoric sculpture was made from such materials as stone, clay, bone, ivory, and wood. And while definitions of sculpture are no longer restricted to concepts of three-dimensionality (today light, video, and sound installations are often found in exhibitions of sculpture), up until the mid-twentieth century sculpture was considered to be objects and forms that had volume—height, width, and depth—as opposed to paintings, drawings, and prints, which were two-dimensional and flat. Early sculptors in different parts of the world made reliefs, small figurines, vases, sarcophagi, amulets, and large statues using chisels, mallets, and adzes for stone, wood, and ivory carving, clay for molding and modeling and, later, bronze for casting. Ancient sculptural works were intended for display in private homes, public buildings, gardens, and religious buildings, and for placement in tombs. They were produced and excavated in sites that collectively make up an extensive geographical reach, spanning such locations as Mesopotamia, Egypt, Greece, Rome, Turkey, Serbia, Spain, Germany, Russia, China, Japan, India, Celtic regions across Europe, and Pre-Columbian regions across the Americas.

In Europe, Romanesque and Gothic sculpture in the eleventh through fourteenth centuries was tied in large part to the architectural structure and ornamentation of churches and cathedrals. In the periods following—Renaissance sculpture in the fifteenth and sixteenth centuries, Baroque, Rococo, and Neoclassical sculpture in the seventeenth to mid-nineteenth century—sculptors were commissioned not only by religious leaders but also by wealthy arts patrons and political leaders who were interested in amassing palace art collections and publicly commemorating both themselves and culturally noteworthy events. In the twentieth century, sculptural forms and themes generally reflected the art movements that were at the time influencing other art genres, such as painting. Similarly, in Asian, Islamic, African, and Latin American regions during the same period, religious, political, and decorative themes infused the production of sculptural works.

Like other areas of art and their histories, the commemorative, votive, didactic, and ornamental aspects of sculpture shifted as a focus on figural works based in realism gave way to a growing emphasis on abstraction and other considerations in the early and middle parts of the twentieth century. With this change in focus and purpose came new materials and technical approaches such as welding, assemblage, incorporating nontraditional materials and found objects, and building with industrially prefabricated units. Artists also appropriated fabrication techniques, such as papier-mâché,[2] from such practices as doll and puppet making and stage design. Today, sculpture incorporates such an expanded range of materials and diversity of forms—three-dimensional objects, performance, large scale installations, environmental works, video, site specific works, and sound constructions—that the term is widely considered to have lost any set boundaries by which it is consistently defined.

---

[2] As a practice of combining paper or fiber materials with an adhesive in layering on or forming objects, papier-mâché has a long history. Egyptian death masks and coffins produced in ancient times, doll heads beginning in the sixteenth century, architectural and industrial forms during the eighteenth and nineteenth centuries, and ceremonial masks and decorative art forms produced in countries throughout the world are among many examples of the widespread use of the technique.

This chapter focuses on constructing forms with paper, board, wire, pliable mesh screen, foil, papier-mâché, found materials, plaster, and clay—all approaches to construction that can be done without a great deal of equipment and with students of different ages. What ways of thinking and practice are taught and encouraged when building? How are these different from those that characterize approaches that are mostly two-dimensional? What tools and materials can be used in forming and building? Which techniques are best for young people of different levels of experience? Keep notes on your findings as you experiment with the construction activities presented later in this chapter.

Figuring out What Materials Can Do

COLLECTING MATERIALS

As with other art forms, the techniques used in making three-dimensional works are typically considered additive, where separate parts are combined to make the form, or subtractive, where a solid mass of material is reduced and altered by removing portions from the whole. And like other media, materials used for forming and building possess distinctive physical properties, sensory characteristics, and sociocultural connotations. The techniques and final forms of three-dimensional works—freestanding, relief, draped, suspended, stationary, projected, kinetic, performative—also suggest interpretive content.[3] Collectively, materials, the techniques and processes used to work with them, and the finished constructions can suggest multiple ideas and meanings. Look closely at the works in Figure 6-1 and Figure 27 in the color insert, and note the materials and techniques used to make them. What are the different ways in which materials have been used? How have materials been formed into objects? How do the surfaces of the artworks compare to one another? In what ways are the forms and functions of the two works different? What characteristics, if any, do the two pieces share? What ideas come to mind for each piece? Why do you think this is?

F 6-1
Mihaela Savu, Mighty Aphrodite, 2012, aluminum, tulle, 5′ × 5′ × 4′.

---

[3] As I write this, *Harvest Dome 2.0*—a 24′ diameter sphere, constructed from 450 discarded, storm-snapped umbrella frames and 128 plastic soda bottles— is being carried by canoes down the Harlem River and up the East River in New York City to be installed in a nature park in upper Manhattan. This public art project, a project of Amanda Schacter and Alexander Levi of SLO Architecture, is meant to serve as "a revelation of the city's accumulated, waterborne debris" (http://www.kickstarter.com/projects/481224446/harvest-dome-20). It was funded in March 2012 with a $7,500 Kickstarter campaign (the fundraising goal was exceeded as a result of contributions from 77 backers).

Paper and Board

Cardboard and stiff papers are ideal materials for introducing building and forming to students because they are easily manipulated, altered, and separated into pieces that can then be reassembled in sculptural forms. Similar to experimental approaches to altering and arranging collage materials in a mostly flat composition, working with board and paper can focus on exploring divergent ways to change the materials and alternative ways of arranging and attaching them together in three-dimensional structures. When working with cardboard, students can use flat sheets that they alter and attach to build a structure, or boxes and other containers that can also be transformed and attached together in a built construction.

In three-dimensional work with paper and board, papier-mâché is a simple and easily adaptable layering of paper and glue that can be used over a cardboard base or armature to make a wide variety of forms and objects. Papier-mâché layers can also be applied over other kinds of bases and armatures (wire, mesh, scrunched or wadded up paper or foil, blown up balloons) or applied on the inner or outer surface of a mold, to be removed when the wet material is dry. An alternative type of papier-mâché material can be cast in a mold—when dry, the solid, dense form can be further altered with hand tools. Paper, cardboard, and papier-mâché constructions are left as is—so that the original surfaces of the building materials are an integral part of the composition and its meaning—or embellished with paint and other materials according to the function of the object and expressive intentions of the artist.

Wire, Mesh Screen, and Aluminum Foil

Wire is a versatile sculpture material on its own and it can also be used with other materials in mixed media constructions. Different thicknesses, or gauges (for gauges, the smaller the number, the thicker the wire), are good for particular purposes—thicker wire can be used to form all parts of the structure and thinner wire can be used for building on the upper parts and sides of the construction and for joining parts. Sturdy wire can also be formed into an armature for papier-mâché or clay sculptures. Wire materials include pliable, aluminum sculpture wire, pipe cleaners, twist ties, and other easily bendable types that are great for young children, coat hangers, vinyl coated electrical, construction, and craft wire, thin, paper coated and bare wire used for floral arranging, and fine gauge wire used for beading and jewelry. Finished works can be left unpainted to show the original materials or added to with acrylic paint.

Fun Wire, Twisteez, and Artistic Wire are craft materials available in a range of colors, gauges, and lengths from art and craft supply stores. Traditional sculpture wire—soft, thick, and easily bendable aluminum armature and other wires (Blick makes an economical option for armature wire)—are also available in a variety of gauges and lengths. Florist and jewelry wires are available at craft and art supply stores, and twist ties—coated in colored and metallic plastic, and paper—come in different lengths and in spools, and are available at online shipping suppliers like Uline. Like the search for collage elements and assemblage materials (discussed below), there are plenty of sources for assorted wire materials beyond traditional suppliers, including local materials exchanges, dry cleaners, and recycling centers. For tools, pliers, wire cutters, and scissors (good for very fine wires) are all that is necessary.

Aluminum foil and pliable mesh screen (Amaco Wireform Mesh offers several options) are good materials for immediate and direct molding and shaping. Lighter and heavier weight screening is available in different mesh sizes and can be used on its own, over an armature as the skin of a construction, or as the armature itself for clay, plaster, and papier-mâché forms. Aluminum foil can be scrunched, twisted, and wadded into solid forms—these, too, can stand on their own without embellishment. Solid forms fashioned from aluminum foil can also serve as armatures for the application of other materials.

Wood and Natural Materials

Wood and natural materials are also well suited for three-dimensional works. Scrap wood is available in a variety of sizes and shapes from home improvement suppliers and lumber yards, and can be combined with other wood items like tongue depressors, popsicle sticks, coffee stirrers, skewers, toothpicks, balsa wood rods, and dowels. Beyond using glue to attach parts together, more experienced students can learn different ways of joining materials through the use of simple hand tools, allowing them to design and create kinetic and interactive constructions in addition to stationary sculptural works.

Other natural materials—such as small tree branches, twigs, grasses, pine cones, flowers, rocks, and dirt—can be used for making three-dimensional constructions. These works are typically made and displayed indoors or conceived as outdoor, site-specific sculptures that are planned from the start to be displayed in a particular location.

Found Objects

An array of interesting materials and objects can be collected for use in assembling three-dimensional works, a studio process historically referred to as *assemblage*. As with collage and other media, artists purposefully select, alter, arrange, and attach elements in three-dimensional constructions with the understanding that the objects and materials themselves as well as their juxtaposition and the ways they are attached actively contribute to the meaning of the work.

All kinds of found objects are suitable for three-dimensional construction (see Figure 6-2). And, similar to gathering collage materials, there are many

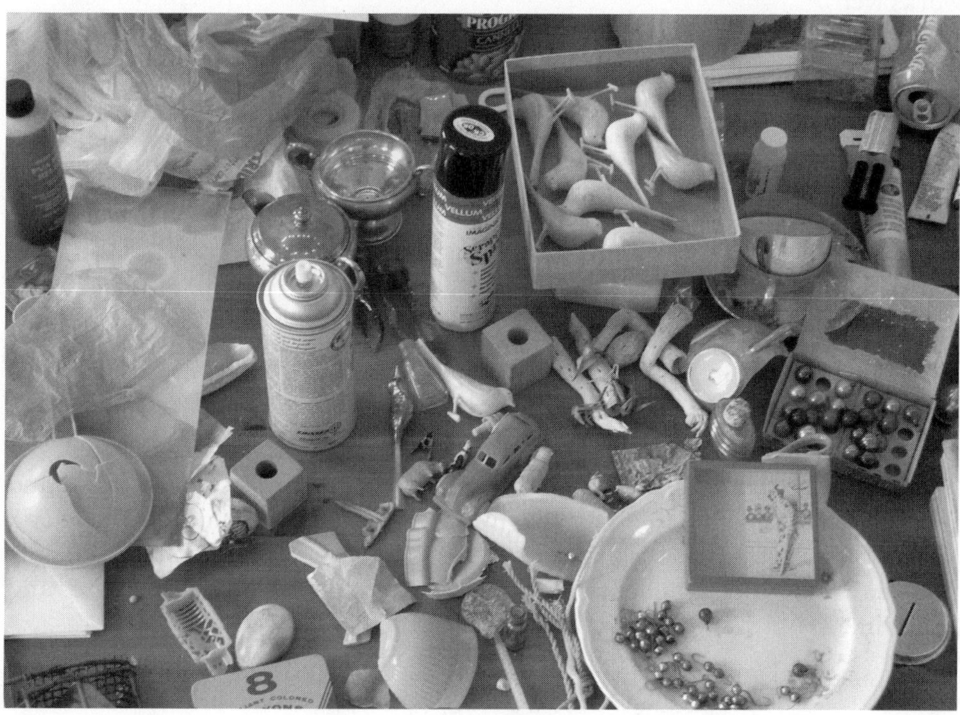

F 6-2: Assorted found construction materials

sources for amassing an interesting collection of items that can be repurposed as components for sculptural works—including recycling bins, materials exchanges, second hand stores, and flea markets. I often put out a request to students' parents and caregivers to save certain types of objects and materials and ask students to maintain a personal collection of interesting things they would like to incorporate in their sculptural work. They bring these items to class when the time comes for creating found object sculptures in class.

Adhesives and Other Materials for Assembling Parts

While some materials, like paper and board, can be combined and joined using glue, students should be given lots of opportunities to experiment with and discover attaching methods that don't require adhesives. Cutting slits in pieces to be joined and then fitting the pieces together, creating pegs to fit through corresponding cutouts in cardboard (see www.bloxes.com for ideas), and twisting strips of the material into linear elements that can then be threaded through holes in the pieces to be joined—these are just some of the possibilities, and students will be eager to invent and share their own solutions.

Many of the adhesives used in collage are also suitable for building with paper and board, including white PVA glues like Elmer's. For other materials, manufacturers also feature specially formulated, non-toxic glues for wood (like Elmer's Carpenter's Wood Glue and Carpenter's Wood Glue Max), china and glass (Elmer's China 1 Glass Cement), and stone, metal, and other assorted materials (Elmer's ProBond Advanced). Heavy bodied tacky glues and clear adhesive dots (Zots) are also good for heavier and hard to-hold objects. While its use by young students requires close adult supervision, a low temperature hot glue gun with nontoxic glue sticks can also be used in the art room. As with other specialized tools and equipment, you will need to both gauge your students' readiness for working with glue guns and be sure that there is constant supervision in the area of the room where they are being operated (setting up a station and getting a volunteer assistant to supervise it works well).

Depending on the type, materials used in three-dimensional construction can also be attached with nails, screws, string or twine, wire, needle and thread, staples, paper fasteners, pins, rivets and grommets, paper clips, binder clamps, and tape. It is important to think carefully about the attachment methods that you offer as options so that students are presented with ever growing challenges. For example, you may not want to offer tape if students are relying on it too much as an easy solution—and instead lead them, through "creative constraints," to develop skills with tools and with other approaches to joining materials. As with the selection, alteration, and arrangement of collage materials, the attachment methods can contribute additional visual layers to the overall work.

Glues and pastes for papier-mâché include non-toxic wheat paste and rice paste (both available from Dick Blick), art paste (made by Elmer's), gel medium, and Mod Podge. While you can make your own paste from flour and water, specially formulated pastes have the advantage of smooth mixing and application. Pastes made from natural grains like wheat and rice will last only a few days in liquid form before beginning to mold, while synthetic pastes and glues, like art paste, can be kept for long periods in between projects.

Clay

Clay's history as both an artistic medium and functional material can be traced to ancient times and many parts of the world. It was used to make, among other things, vessels for storage, cups and other dishware for beverages and food, and bricks and tiles for constructing and adorning palaces and public buildings.

Ceramic clays, when molded and formed into objects and dried, are usually fired or baked in a kiln or other container that is heated to a high temperature. The firing promotes a chemical reaction in the material and makes it hard and rigid when cool. While some types of clay require the application of glaze and additional firing to seal the clay and make it watertight, others may be left unglazed or glazed for coloring and other decorative purposes.

There are many types of ceramic clay. Low-fire clays, commonly dug from the ground and containing a high amount of iron, are often fired in a pit or container filled with combustible organic materials that fuel the fire. The smoke produced in the process—along with metal oxides and other materials (leaves, steel wool) pressed directly on the piece—create decorative markings on the clay surface. Terra cotta clays, which are orange in color due to their high iron content, and earthenware (see Figure 6-3)—both clays that are used for a variety of purposes— are fired at higher temperatures than low-fire clay. Stoneware, durable clay often used for dinner wear, is fired at higher temperatures still. Porcelain, kaolin-based clay used for fine china, was developed more than 2,000 years ago in China. Porcelain is fired at very high temperatures and in the process becomes completely vitrified, resulting in a translucent, glass-like, white body when cool.

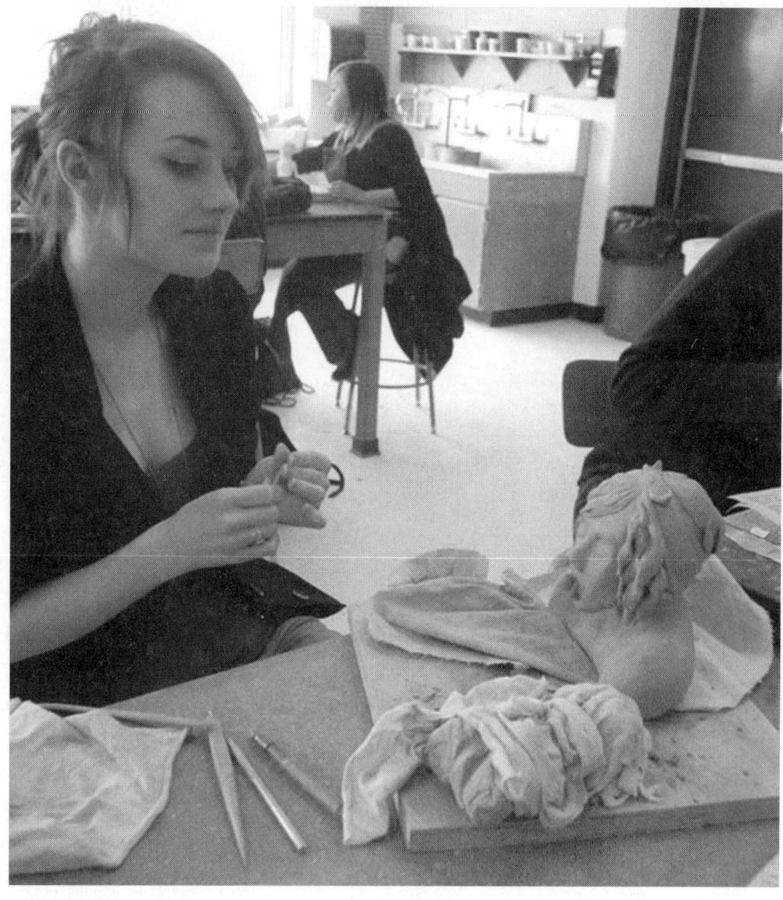

F 6-3: Clay in the art class

Beyond these common types of clay are other ceramic materials. Paper clay contains shredded paper pulp that reinforces the clay while it is being worked. This makes possible thin walled forms and other delicate applications—during firing, the reinforcing paper burns away, leaving only the clay. Egyptian paste is self-glazing clay developed in Egypt around 500 BC—fired at low temperatures, it was and still is used to make beads and jewelry. Brick clay, which is durable, coarse, and often high in iron and reddish in color; aggregate clay, which contains additives like grog, minerals, and crushed glass for texture; and colored clay, which incorporates stains or oxides in the clay body are other types available. All of these are water-based, and contain clay minerals and other raw materials.

Other Forming Materials

There are also modeling and forming materials composed of substances besides clay minerals, including polymer clay, air-dry or self-hardening clay, cellulose-based compound, plasticine, salt dough, and plaster. Polymer clay (Fimo, Sculpey) comes in a range of colors and hardens when heated at low oven temperatures, while self-hardening clays (Crayola, Amaco Marblex, Stonex, and Mexican Pottery, Sculpture House Claystone, Sheffield) do not require heating. Few of the polymer or self-hardening clays feel like ceramic clay as you work with them and for the most part they are not waterproof when dry. If a kiln is available, it's worth the time investment in firing to use a soft, pliant ceramic clay body because students can easily manipulate it. It also offers many options for surface treatments.

Nonceramic modeling clays are either oil/wax-based or water-based and do not dry or harden to a rigid solid. Plastalina (made by Van Aken) is a firm, plasticine clay that contains oil and wax and comes in many vibrant colors. Used widely for professional and student animation projects, among other things, older students can also use it to create nonpermanent, personally crafted still life objects for observational drawing and painting. More pliable oil-based and wax-based modeling clays (Crayola, Sculpey EZ Shape), suitable for younger students, also come in a variety of colors. Water-based modeling doughs, like Crayola Dough and Creativity Street Modeling Dough, are more pliable still. Within a single brand/formula, different colors of modeling clays can be twisted, rolled, and manipulated in other ways to create semi-blended effects, and mixed completely to create entirely new colors.

Plaster, another nonceramic material, is a gypsum-based cement powder that when mixed with water undergoes a chemical reaction involving heat. As the material cools and dries, it hardens to a rigid form that can be sanded, painted, and sealed. Plaster can be cast, modeled, and used to make molds. It comes in both powder form and embedded in gauze (Plast'r Craft, Blick Plaster Cloth, Activa Rigid Wrap)—strips or sheets of the material are dipped in water then typically wrapped around a base or armature. Finally, Sculptamold, made by Amaco, is a cellulose-based modeling compound that is mixed with water and applied over a base. When dry it can be sanded, smoothed, sawed, nailed, finished with paint, and sealed with acrylic matte or gloss medium.

Tools and Equipment

Students, including very young children, are eager to learn how to use some of the same tools and equipment that artists commonly use for three-dimensional work. Choosing tools that are appropriate for kids is not difficult—with supervision, they can easily learn how to use manual hand drills with crank handles (Fiskars is a good option), pliers, wire cutters, stubby screwdrivers, a bench vise, saws (for sticks, small items), hammers with lightweight heads (you can mark the handle with tape for guided hand placement), sanding blocks, clamps, levels, and lightweight tape measures (students should always wear safety glasses when using hand tools). Montessori Services (montessoriservices.com) is a great source for child-appropriate tools. Other useful tools include plastic knives, fishing line or a wire for working with and cutting through moist clay, a rolling pin, forks, and textured objects for pressing into the clay surface to make textures and designs, and scissors. It's also good to have staplers and a staple gun handy, to attach works done in wire and other materials to cardboard and wood bases.

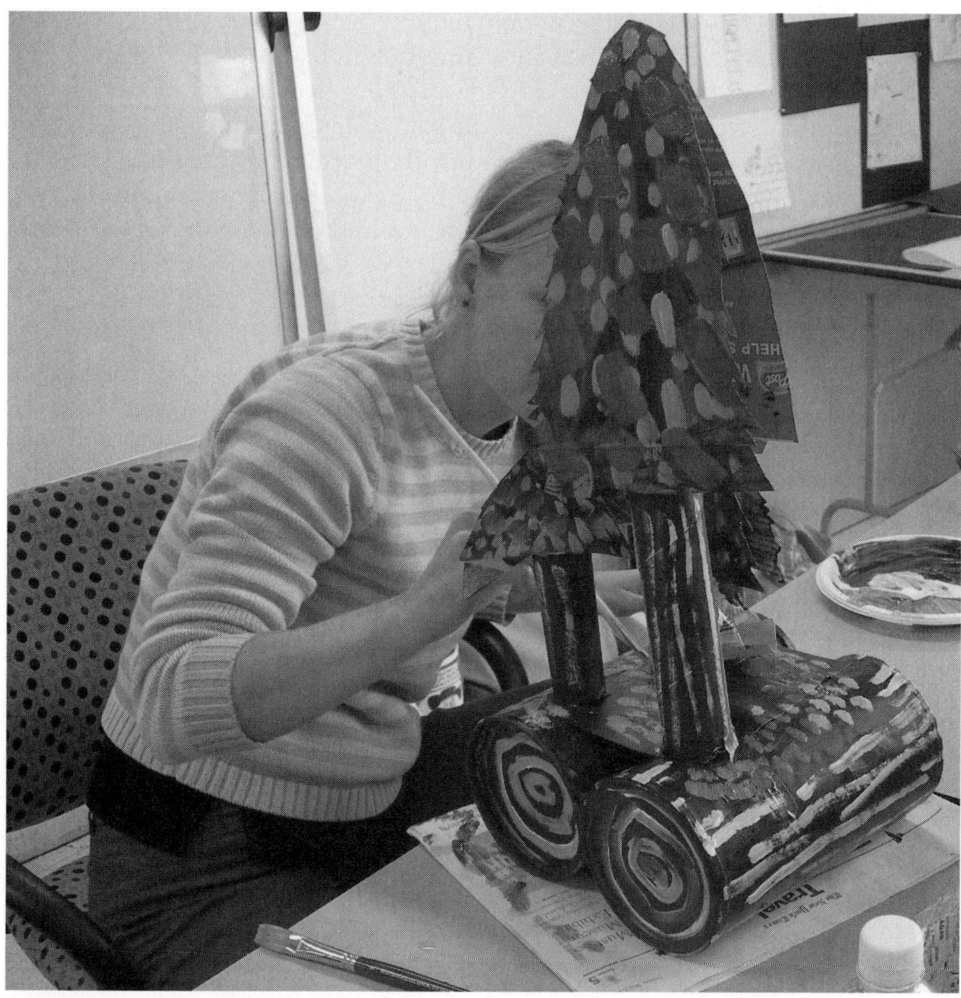

F 6-4: Painting cardboard construction

Paint and Other Embellishments

The consideration of different options for surface treatments should be a major part of making three-dimensional work. Depending on the sculptural material itself, pencils, pastels, tempera, watercolor, acrylic paints, and shoe polish (nontoxic brands include DuPre General Store) can all be used to embellish sculptural forms (see Figure 6-4). For objects made of ceramic clay, colored glazes (containing silica that turns glass-like when fired) and colored slips (clay and other materials mixed with water) are painted on the surface before firing.

Experimenting with Building and Forming

Explore building as you work with paper, board, wire, papier-mâché, clay, and the other materials featured in the activities that follow. As with collage, experiment with various ways of changing and altering materials, and arranging and attaching parts together in a three-dimensional form.

For all of the materials investigations in this chapter, document your emerging insights about the ways in which three-dimensional construction is different from working flat. Throughout your explorations, you'll discover that in addition to all of the considerations that are in play while working two-dimensionally, you need to consider mass and weight of materials, balance, stability, motion, and other concepts. One of the most important differences between working flat and working "in the round" is that you now need to consider not just the front of the artwork but the back, sides, and all spaces in between, making sure that there is visual interest all the way around. Be sure to rotate small pieces frequently as you work, and periodically walk around larger pieces that may be hard to move.

As part of your process, reflect on and document the ways of thinking promoted by each building approach, based on the qualities, technical possibilities, and expressive effects that are possible with different materials and techniques. Also consider the teaching implications of your discoveries for choosing and using these materials and techniques with students of different ages. Note the concepts and skills you will need to focus on as a teacher when students make sculptural works in your art class.

Note: For all of the materials investigations that follow, you can make works that are about simply the materials themselves and how they interact with one another or you can construct pieces that are also in response to a particular theme of your choosing. Table 6-1 contains a list of suggestions for working thematically.

PAPER AND CARDBOARD

Building with paper and board is one of the simplest approaches to working in three dimensions. Construction paper, card stock, tag board, railroad board, poster board, corrugated cardboard, and scraps of mat board are all excellent for exploring ways of altering and attaching materials.

Exploring Paper and Cardboard

How can flat paper and board be transformed to create a three-dimensional form? What are different ways of working with these materials to create separate building elements? How can boxes and tubes be used in building forms? How many ways can you invent to join pieces together to create a structure that stands? And how might the addition of paint change the combination of building elements even further?

Materials:

Assorted sizes, shapes, and colors of construction paper, card stock, and/or poster board
Assorted sizes and shapes of corrugated cardboard and mat board
Assorted cardboard boxes and tubes
Scissors
White glue and tacky glue
Masking tape
Tempera paints, assorted colors including black and white
Trays (metal, plastic) for paint palettes
Paintbrushes and water containers
Paper towels
Newspaper for covering work surface

Table 6-1

Thematic Ideas for Three-Dimensional Construction

- A sculpture that serves as a shelter or residence.
- A sculpture that adorns a body part.
- A sculpture that transports people from one place to another.
- A sculpture that envelopes or enrobes and transforms a person or group.
- A sculpture that jiggles, dangles, and makes sounds.
- A sculpture based on a fond memory or experience.
- A sculpture done in response to very close observation of something.
- A sculpture that contrasts two ideas in relation to one another—open-closed, heavy-light, near-far, stable-precarious, etc.
- A sculpture that suggests characteristics and activities of a particular person or animal.
- A sculpture that dramatically transforms a common object and gives it new meaning.
- A sculpture that is about gesture and/or movement.
- A sculpture that holds and serves a special or particular food.
- A sculpture that reimagines a sound or piece of music.
- A sculpture that is a creature—creepy, fierce, magical, etc.
- A sculpture that bends, twists, and loops.
- A sculpture that is imbued with human traits.
- A sculpture based on observing an object or group of objects.

- A sculpture that drapes or leans.
- A sculpture created for and in response to a specific place.
- A sculpture that creates rhythm by repeating one or more element.
- A sculpture that glorifies or monumentalizes a common object.
- A sculpture that incorporates light and shadows as part of the work's composition.
- A sculpture that represents a feeling or bodily/mental state—disbelief, sleep, chill, boredom, glow, awakening, edgy, serene, woozy, flustered, bubbly, etc.
- A sculpture that is about the feeling of things.
- A sculpture that could get lost among things found in a certain place—an urban street, a forest, field, or garden, a grocery store, etc.
- A sculpture that performs a useful, unnecessary, or ridiculous task.
- A sculpture that presents a position on an issue of concern (social, cultural, environmental, global).
- A sculpture that presents a paradox.
- A sculpture that focuses on empty spaces or voids.
- A sculpture that pokes fun at something.
- A sculpture that's an action toy.
- A sculpture that asks or answers a question.
- A sculpture that takes over the walls, floor, and/or ceiling of a corner or room.
- A sculpture based on one of your own artworks that was done in a different medium.

Getting Started:

1. Try out different ways of changing single sheets of paper—folding, tearing and twisting, scrunching, etc.—to make a few three-dimensional forms that rise up from the table surface and stand upright. What do you have to consider as you make something that stands without tipping over?

   Next, using both paper and different kinds of cardboard, create squares, strips, and other shapes by cutting and tearing. Make an assortment of pieces with different qualities—sharp-edged, soft and fuzzy, angular, rough, etc. How might you use some of these elements to make a standing structure? Will you use torn pieces, cut shapes, or a combination? How do pieces with torn edges suggest meanings that are different from those with cleanly cut edges? Which pieces will you use at the lower, middle, and top areas of the construction? How will you reinforce the bottom to make it sturdy enough to hold the collective weight of the pieces above?

Using glue, attach the elements to make a structure that stands on its own and as you work, try out different ways of joining the pieces. Experiment with folding edges to create flat areas for applying the glue. Also try making shallow cuts along an edge and perpendicular to it, and folding the cut parts, alternating back and forth so that the tabs spread out from opposite sides (right and left) of the fold. Apply glue to the bottom of the tab "feet" and join the piece to another element of the construction. How is the process of constructing a standing structure from multiple parts different from forming and shaping from a single material?

2. Experiment with different ways of changing materials and placing, combining, and attaching construction elements as you respond to the following prompts.

a. Build a structure as tall or wide as it can go—Cut or tear a piece of lightweight board (11″ × 14″ or smaller) into pieces that you would like

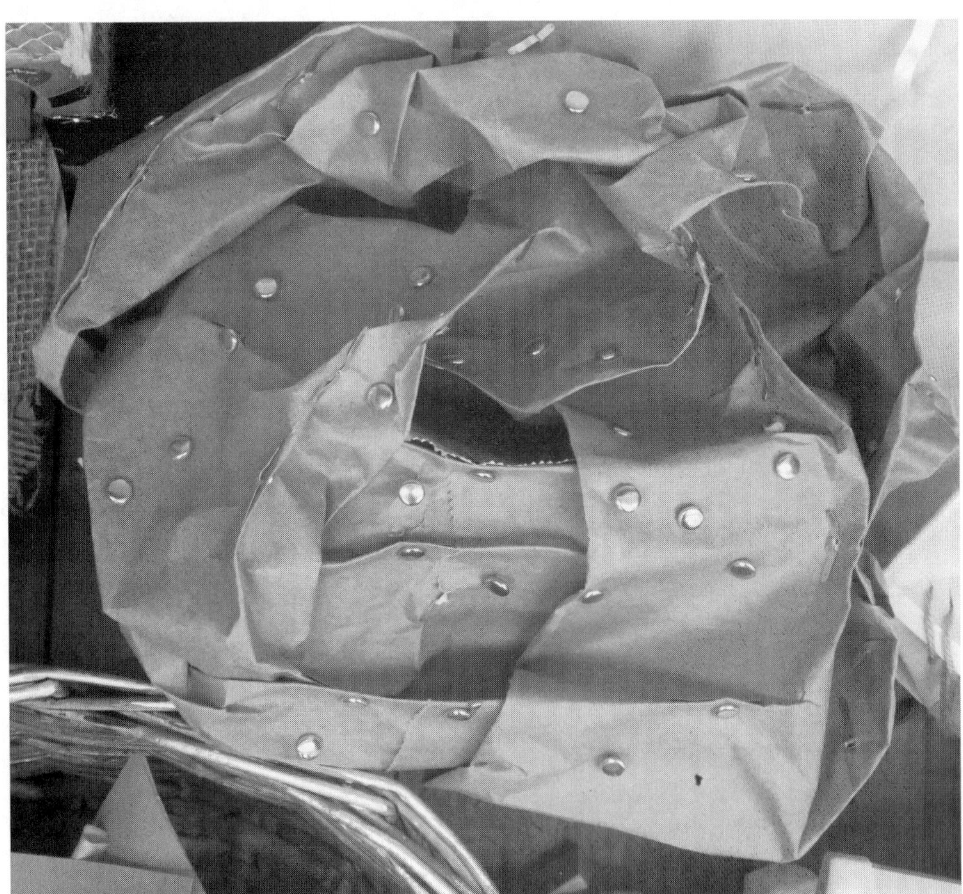

F 6-5
Kate Esbenshade, Untitled, 2013, mixed media, 12″ × 13″ × 5″.

to use for building. Using various gluing methods explored previously, attach the pieces to make the tallest structure possible, with the bottom set on the table. If you wish, make another construction, this time with a single base and parts that span out as wide as possible (the parts should not touch the table). What different issues and considerations come into play as you build up and out?

b. Build a structure without using glue—Using various sizes and shapes of lighter and heavier materials, explore different ways of attaching pieces to make a standing structure (see Figure 6-5). What can you do to the materials to join them together? What can you do with scissors? With tearing? With piercing and puncturing?

c. Transform a single sheet of board—Experiment with changing the look and form of a piece of corrugated cardboard or other heavy board by peeling, scoring and folding, slicing, fringing, scratching, tearing, fraying, crumpling, creasing, scrunching, wadding, rolling, and twisting. What kinds of expressive transformations can you make as you build three-dimensionality, change the physical presence of the material, and connect one thing to another?

d. Build a structure with boxes and tubes—Consider different ways of altering corrugated and other cardboard boxes and tubes (from paper towels, wrapping paper, toilet tissue). How can these forms be combined into a standing structure?

e. Transform the surface—Choose one or more of your constructions and add color with tempera paint. First, consider the sculpture's form and materials and think about what ideas they might suggest. Do you want to use paint to reinforce those ideas, and if so, how might you use color, opacity/transparency, and particular painting techniques to do that? Or do you want to introduce some new or contrasting ideas into the piece? What colors and paint effects might accomplish that?

WIRE, MESH SCREEN, AND FOIL

Working with wire in a three-dimensional way is often referred to as form of "drawing in space." This term is loosely used to describe approaches to drawing that are considered nontraditional or alternative because while they may feature elements of drawing, like line, they do not involve a flat surface as a support. Alexander Calder, whose wire sculptures are commonly associated with three-dimensional drawing, is among those who pioneered the technique in the late 1920s in Paris. His often quoted remark, "I think best in wire,"[4] is an excellent reminder to art teachers that student artists also gravitate toward particular ways of working. That is why it is so important to offer not only diverse materials and technical approaches but also a variety of ways to envision and create two- and three-dimensional images and forms (see Figure 6-6).

---

[4] Cited in: "Conversation with Bernice Rose," in D. Marchesseau (1989), *The Intimate World of Alexander Calder*, p. 122.

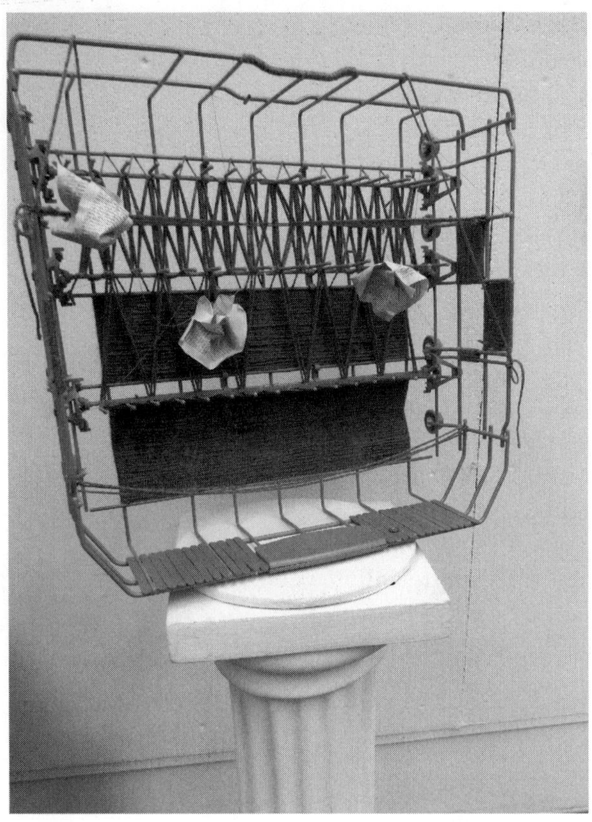

Zoe Davis, Untitled, mixed media, 2013, 28" × 25" × 6".

Exploring Wire, Mesh Screen, and Foil

What are some ways that different types of wire can be used to create three-dimensional constructions? How can wire mesh and aluminum foil be manipulated to create a variety of forms? What are the differences between these materials as you work with them?

Materials:

Aluminum armature wire
Wire coat hangers
Vinyl coated craft wire in various colors, gauges, and
  lengths
Florist wire
Fine gauge beading wire
Pipe cleaners and twist ties
Wireform metal mesh
Alumnium foil
Wood scraps and mat board for bases
Pliers
Wire cutter
Stapler and staple gun

Getting Started:

1. Work in experimental ways with each type of wire, and consider the qualities and possibilities for bending, arcing and looping, angling, winding and wrapping, and attaching. Similarly, investigate the range of actions and manipulations that can transform wire mesh—molding over a rigid form, pinching or crimping, twisting, pulling apart to expand, gathering, pleating—and a similar range for aluminum foil. Note the distinctive forming characteristics of each material as well as its potential for suggesting representational and expressive ideas, such as volume, mass, strength, delicateness, gesture and action, stability, lightness, heaviness, and so on.

   a. Drawing in space—Using armature wire and other wires, make a standing construction that creates an "outline" sense of solid form. In your mind's eye, pretend you are transporting lines wrapped around and travelling through a three-dimensional object to the space in front of you, and construct that form with wire. Where will you use the heaviest gauge wire? Where will you use the finer wire? How will you attach wires together? How can you use the wire expressively, as you would a pencil or pen, emphasizing and building up certain areas and leaving other areas more open in contrast?

   b. Suspended wire construction—Make a wire construction that is suspended from the ceiling. Think about how a central structure could support the attachment or hanging of additional parts, and construct the individual pieces from various wires of your choice. As you attach the pieces together, consider the idea of weights/

counterweights as you work to achieve the balance you desire in the piece. Remember to rotate or walk around the piece as you work, so that you can view it from different angles and make adjustments as necessary.

   c. Screen forms—Manipulate sheets and pieces of wireform mesh in a variety of ways to create a series of related objects of different sizes. Try out different arrangements of these forms, walking around the work to view it from multiple angles. How is the mesh different from the wire in terms of working process and visual effects that can be achieved?

   d. Foil forms—Create a series of related objects or figures by working with foil in different ways. Make the bottom of each of your pieces touch the tabletop in at least two places.

   e. Combining materials—Considering the different qualities of wire, mesh, and foil and the various effects they make possible, make a standing construction that combines at least two of these materials, and that incorporates different parts that move. You may want to use a wood or cardboard base (you can staple the bottom of your sculpture to the base).

2. What materials did you especially like working with? Why? Which materials were most challenging? Most surprising? How can you imagine using these materials with students of different ages?

PAPIER-MÂCHÉ AND PLASTER

Papier-mâché and plaster can each be used alone or with various types of armatures for reinforcement and stability. They can also be used in molds to create all kinds of three-dimensional forms. These qualities, along with the many options available for surface treatments and embellishment, make them extremely versatile media.

Exploring Papier-mâché and Plaster

What possibilities for forming and building are offered by papier-mâché and plaster? What are the properties of each material, and how do these characteristics lend themselves to different technical approaches and to particular expressive ideas and meanings?

Materials:

Armature materials—wire, balloons, plastic bottles, heavyweight cardboard pieces, boxes
Plastic forms for molds, such as bowls, plates, cups
Liquid dish detergent
Object for transformation
Newspaper
Thread, embroidery floss, and thin string
White glue
Wheat, rice paste, or art paste—dry (to mix with water)

Flexible plastic buckets and shallow tubs
Plaster of Paris—dry (to mix with water)
Plaster cloth on a roll or in strips
Armature wire
Base for wire armature
Pieces of fabric and small cloth/fiber items of different shapes and textures
(gloves, doilies, burlap, canvas sneakers, shoelaces, yarn, ball of string/
twine) that would be interesting as plaster-coated forms)
Light-colored decorative sand (available at craft stores)
Soft modeling dough (like Playdough)
Small, flexible aluminum tart or pie pans, or shallow plastic container for
plaster casting
A variety of small firm objects to use as impressions for mold making (shells,
toys, household and hardware item with simple shapes, things from
outdoors)
A variety of small objects to use in plaster cast mosaic (buttons, discarded
game pieces, wire and mesh scraps, collected found objects)
Soft toothbrush or nailbrush
Particle mask
Safety glasses
Rubber latex gloves
Colored tissue paper and other thin, absorbent decorative tissues and papers
Masking tape
Scissors
Tempera, watercolor, and acrylic paints, assorted colors including black and
white
Trays (metal, plastic) for paint palettes and for placing wet forms
Paintbrushes and water containers
Newspaper for covering work surface
Paper towels

Getting Started:

1. Tear newspaper into half and quarter sheets, strips, and small shapes
for working with papier-mâché. Mix up some wheat paste, rice paste,
or art paste according to the package directions. The consistency should
be a little thinner than yogurt, and pourable. Pour the liquid paste into
a shallow container that is large enough for you to be able to dip your
paper pieces fully in the paste. You will also need a paintbrush to experiment with applying the paste selectively and trays for placing your wet
forms.
    a. Paper-and-paste forms—Considering your materials and their prop-
erties, what different forms can you create with just paper and liquid
paste? Experiment with different techniques—first, use the brush to
apply paste liberally to one side of a piece of newspaper so that it
soaks through, then change the form of the paper by experimenting
with draping it and shaping to make a standing form. Try dipping
other paper pieces in the paste (you may need to remove some of
the paste with your fingers, using them like a squeegee) and see what
additional forms you can create. Next, experiment with paste-soaked

paper pieces and sheets and other actions such as crumpling, wadding, twisting, coiling, and knotting. Place these on a tray and set aside to dry.

b. Papier-mâché over cardboard, boxes, and plastic bottles and containers—Create a construction using cardboard, boxes, and/or plastic containers that are altered to fit together as parts. Use masking tape to attach the parts, then apply paste-soaked newspaper strips and shapes in an even layer over the entire form. Smooth out the wet paper as much as possible with your hands, then apply another layer of paste-soaked paper. Continue smoothing and apply a third layer, smoothing the surface when you are done. Set this form aside to dry.

c. Papier-mâché over other armatures—You can layer papier-mâché over other armatures such as wadded up newspaper reinforced and held together with masking tape, wadded aluminum foil, inflated balloons, a wire armature, and objects that you are interested in transforming with an applied paper surface. You can also use flexible plastic objects—such as cups, bowls of various sizes, plates, and platters—as molds (see Figure 6-7). After you have applied several layers of paper and paste to the inside or outside of the mold, let the piece dry thoroughly then remove it from the plastic object. You can apply additional layers of paper and paste over the dried form if you want it to be stronger and more rigid. Dried forms can be left whole or cut with scissors into smaller pieces. You can also add small embellishments made from the paper and paste mixture—rolled and twisted pieces of different lengths, balls/beads, coiled forms, and so forth.

Other materials can be used with a glue and water mixture over a balloon armature. For example, you can make open-work forms from thread, embroidery floss, and/or string dipped in diluted glue and wound in different directions around the balloon form. Once the fiber material is dry and hardened, pop the balloon, peel it away from the inside of the form, and remove it through one of the open spaces.

d. Plaster wrap forms—Begin your work in plaster by assembling a roll of plaster cloth cut into small pieces (around 1″) and larger sizes, a bowl of warm water, a flexible plastic or rubber form to use as a mold for draping, liquid dish detergent, a wire armature attached to a base for stability if needed, and a thin tube, like a drinking straw or coffee stirrer (the use of safety glasses and gloves is recommended when using all types of plaster, including plaster cloth). From one of the larger pieces cut three or four identical shapes. Lay the first one down flat, dip the second one in water and lay on top of the first, smoothing the top surface, and repeat with the remaining shapes. You can let the shape dry flat or, when it is almost cured, lay it over a three-dimensional form to dry.

Experiment next with draped forms—dip a larger piece of plaster cloth in water and smooth the plaster in the cloth, then shape and drape the sheet to make a form that stands. Experiment with working wet and with allowing the plaster to begin setting a bit and become stiffer, as you see what kinds of forms you can create (add additional layers for strength). Try draping a piece of moistened plaster cloth over a nonporous mold form coated lightly with dish soap.

Also try wrapping small pieces of moistened plaster cloth over the wire armature, smoothing the plaster next to and between pieces to join them evenly, or leaving them more textured and rough. You can create other interesting effects by letting the plaster cloth layers begin to set and dry and then pulling them apart and scrunching one or both to create volume and allow light and airiness into the material.

You can use plaster cloth to create beads and small items for jewelry making. Cut the plaster cloth into shapes for rolling (for beads) or folding, and once the basic form is established brush the shaped plaster cloth with water. You will need to have the piece supported before wetting (beads can be strung on a straw or coffee stirrer that is suspended between two points while you wet them and work on them).

Note: Plaster cloth begins to set quickly, so you only have to hold or stabilize it in place for a few minutes. After the initial form is cured, you can add additional layers to strengthen it.

e. Plaster dip forms—Mix plaster and water according to package directions (always wear a particle mask when working with dry plaster powder). Use a flexible plastic bucket or other container (large enough to accommodate dipping of items) and prepare no more than the amount you think you'll be using for 30 minutes. Thin to the consistency of pancake batter. One at a time, dip fabric pieces to coat in plaster. Immediately begin experimenting with placing and draping the coated piece on a tray to shape into an interesting upright form. Continue dipping and shaping other pieces of fabric—try laying a wet piece over a nonporous object to capture its form (lightly coat the object with dish soap first). Dip other items as well (textured items like lace and doilies are interesting options, and clothing items are also possible), deciding how to shape them as you set them in place to dry. Set these objects aside.

f. Plaster cast forms—Use the remaining prepared plaster (mix more if needed) to experiment with plaster casting. Beyond pouring plaster into non-porous molds in basic and generic shapes, you can make molds of objects that have interesting qualities or hold special meaning. First pour or scoop a layer of decorative, fine sand in a small, shallow flexible container, dampen the sand thoroughly with water and smooth the top surface (there should be about an inch of sand). Next, press one or more objects into the damp sand and carefully remove them. Pour in prepared plaster to fill the cavity left by the impressions, filling either just to the edges of the impressions or to cover the entire top surface up to the edges of the container (for a plaque effect). When the plaster is thoroughly dry and hard (surface should be cool to the touch), remove the plaster form(s) and use a soft brush to gently remove the sand from the plaster

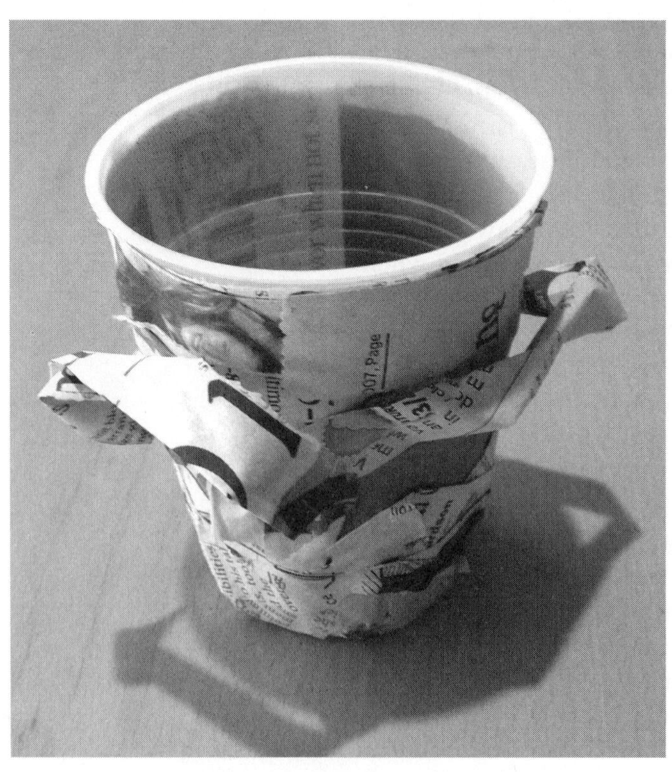

F 6-7: Papier-mâché using plastic cup as mold

surfaces. When plaster is completely set you may also rinse in water to remove sand residue. Plaster casts can be displayed on a wall (as the plaster sets you can create holes at the top for hanging), or used as tiles on an indoor wall area or on the ground in an indoor or outdoor installation.

You can also make plaster casts with modeling dough used in place of sand. Place a flattened slab of dough in the container (make sure it is thick enough to hold the mold impressions), press in objects to create the mold for the plaster, carefully remove the objects, and pour in the plaster as with sand casting.

Finally, you can use prepared plaster to make a mosaic piece. Pour plaster into a small, shallow container so that it comes to about ½″ from the bottom and wait for it to just begin setting (don't wait too long, the plaster should be soft enough to surround objects). Add mosaic items to the top surface much as you would if you were working with collage elements, making thoughtful decisions about placement and juxtaposition. It is also possible to carefully press objects into the soft plaster surface and immediately remove them—this will leave a textural impression of the items' edges and surface details.

Note: For more control when pouring plaster into molds, you can first pour it in a freezer bag, seal the bag and cut the tip of a bottom corner, then squeeze the plaster through the hole in the bag and into the mold.

Sand and modeling dough casting allow for making multiple casts (you will probably need to press the object in the recessed area again each time you make a new cast). When working with students to select objects for mold impressions, be sure to encourage careful hunting for interesting shapes and textures, and encourage students to bring in objects that have some kind of meaning for them. Similarly, when making mosaics, encourage students to be thoughtful about their choices of materials and the ways in which they are arranging the mosaic elements together.

In terms of safety and materials management, you need to be aware that because of the heat involved in the chemical reaction that occurs, and because the material sets to a solid form, no hands or body parts should be directly cast in a container filled with plaster (plaster-soaked fabric or gauze is fine for creating body parts). Let excess plaster dry in its mixing container, then remove the solid form and throw it away (never pour plaster in the sink or down the drain).

For advanced approaches to mold making that are suitable for older and more experienced students, such as two-part plaster molds, see the resource books at the end of this chapter.

g. Surface treatments—Lay out all of your papier-mâché and plaster constructions and choose at least one of each that you would like to develop further with color and other embellishment. Select paints to use based on the type of effects you are interested in creating—for example, bold and opaque colors, textures and layers, subtle or transparent effects. Experiment with various ways of applying the paint to see what kinds of effects are possible on the papier-mâché and plaster surfaces. Also try the colored tissue paper with papier-mâché paste on a papier-mâché surface. What kinds of effects are you able to achieve? How do the paints behave differently on each material?

2. What materials and techniques did you respond to most? Why do you think that is? Which materials and approaches were the most challenging? Most surprising? How might you use these materials with students of different ages?

WOOD AND NATURAL MATERIALS

Wood blocks and shapes are excellent for use with young people because their weight offers sufficient challenge as students learn about issues of balance and force. Because the pieces can be attached with glue or hardware fasteners like screws and nails, students can be inventive in both composing and joining parts together. In this way, they become skilled with a variety of hand tools, which they are typically eager and excited to use. Using wood blocks and shapes for construction yourself is a great way to learn how to use the simple hand tools your students will be using and to become familiar with the different ways of attaching parts that you will want your students to discover and master.

Natural materials are also well suited for three-dimensional work because they can be altered, combined, shaped and formed, and attached in myriad ways (see Figures 6-8 and 6-9). As with collecting materials for collage, students enjoy and should be encouraged to spend time gathering natural materials they would like to work with three dimensionally.

Exploring Wood and Natural Materials

Explore wood blocks and natural materials in a series of constructions based on the suggestions that follow. How might you use these approaches to make constructions based on one or more of the themes in Table 6-1? How might you use these techniques with young people of different ages?

Artist Profile: **TODD BALDWIN**

Todd Baldwin uses found and fabricated objects in assemblages that incorporate materials often associated with construction (see Figure 28 in the color insert). According to Baldwin, the work "takes a critical look at value, juxtaposition and the conflict between permanence and impermanence, and is driven by my fascination with the inner workings of museums." Through the use of such materials as steel, sheetrock, and in the work shown here, cardboard, Baldwin's work "lifts the humble qualities of familiar stuff to create delicate instances."

He writes:

As a preparator for a major academic institution, I am accountable for the safe handling and movement of all art objects. I am routinely involved in many facets of the museum's operation, from exhibition design and fabrication to the curatorial process and conservation. These activities inform my own art making practice.

Specifically, I collage garbage from the museum with other found and handmade objects, paying considerable attention to detail, arrangement and color, and re-purpose otherwise "useless" materials in new and engaging ways.

How does Baldwin's selection, alteration, and juxtaposition of such "useless" materials as cast-off cardboard and steel give them new purpose and meaning?

Note: Many of the construction activities in this chapter can be made more complex (as students gain experience) by the introduction of interactive movement. Students can explore different ways of creating constructions with moving parts and/or that engage the viewer in directly interacting with the work in some way.

Materials:

Assorted soft, scrap wood pieces for building
A selection from the following wood items—tongue depressors, popsicle sticks, coffee stirrers, skewers, toothpicks, balsa wood rods, and dowels
A selection from the following outdoor items—sticks and small branches, seed pods, pine cones, rocks, leaves, bark, flowers, long grasses
White glue, tacky glue, and wood glue
Scissors
Manual hand drill with crank handle
Drill bits
Hammer and nails
Screwdriver
Clamps
Small pruning saw (for sticks, small items)
Sanding block
Level
Staple gun
Safety glasses
Masking tape
Thin wire (like florist's wire)
Bench vise, if available
Paper towels

Getting Started:

1. What new issues come into play when building constructions with wood pieces and natural materials? What are different ways of attaching pieces using hand tools and hardware fasteners? In what ways can natural materials be altered, arranged and juxtaposed, and attached together to make a standing structure?

   a. Building with wood blocks, scraps, and glue—Make a small upright construction using woods blocks and scraps, and test out the three different kinds of glue (read the directions for each glue and let the glued ends set as directed before attaching).

   b. Building with wood blocks, scraps, and hand tools—Build a second structure using only hand tools and hardware fasteners, and make this construction look as different as possible from the first.

Note: When you introduce hammers to young students for the first time it's a good idea to model how to hold the nail with your thumb and index finger, tapping the nail lightly at first. As a demonstration, you can start the nail and have a student volunteer hammer the nail all the way in (mark the hammer handle with tape for proper hand placement). Big nails with wide heads are good because they are easy to grasp, while thinner nails can be set upright between the teeth of a comb to keep them in place. Hold or clamp the end of the comb until the nail is hammered in.

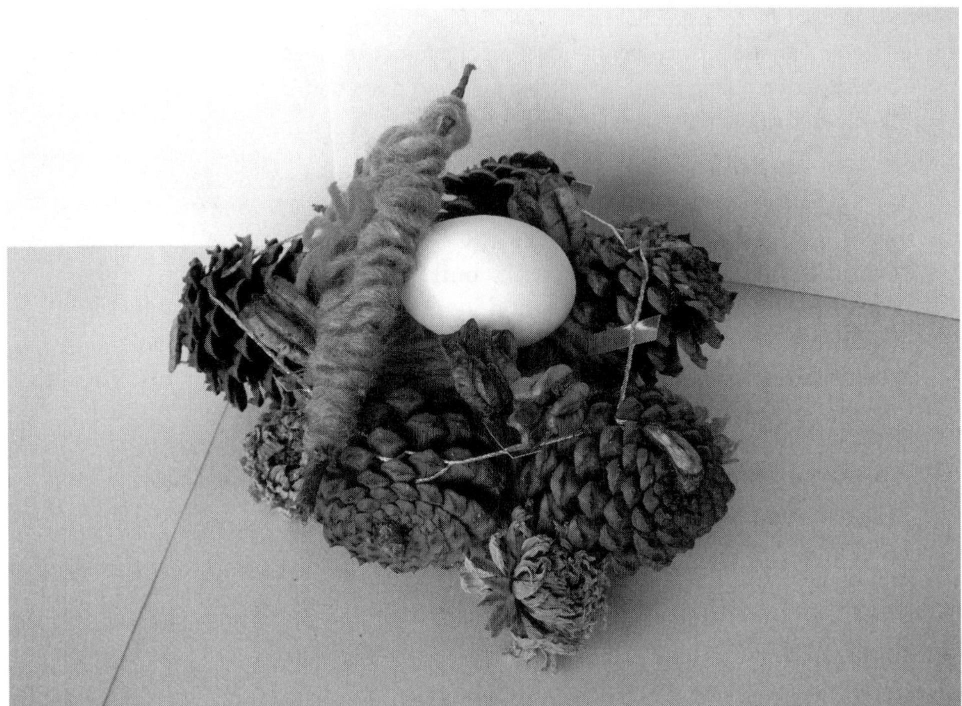

F 6-8: Constructing with natural materials

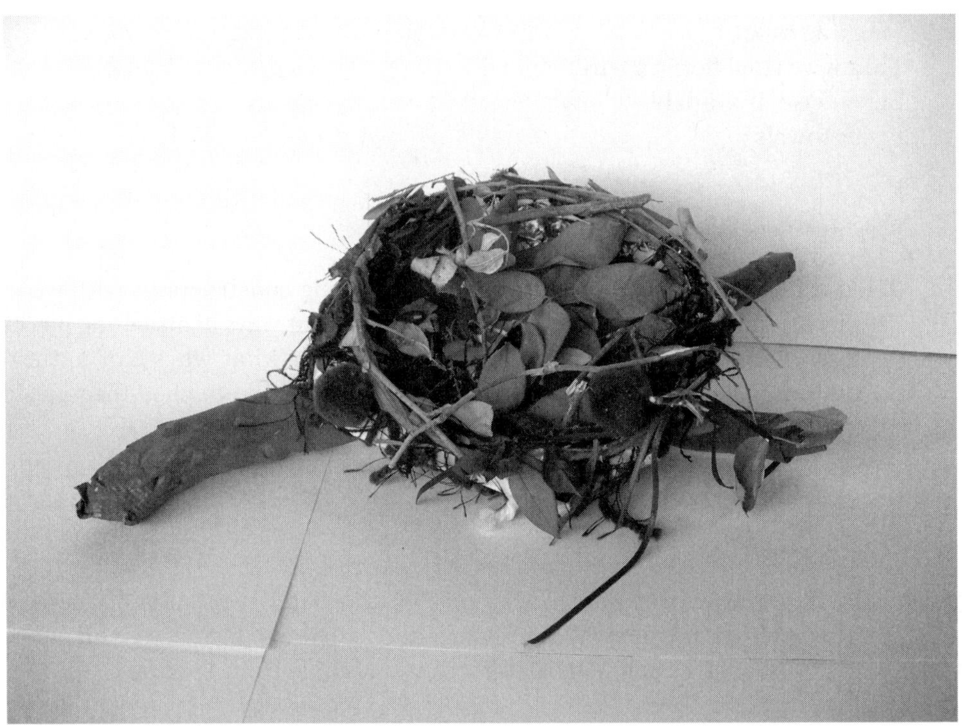

F 6-9: Constructing with natural materials

Model the use of each tool in the same way. With the manual drill you can mark the drilling spots and demonstrate how the drill works. With some practice, students can use these tools with ease provided the wood is soft enough. A vise or clamp is useful for preventing the wood from moving during drilling.

    c. Constructing with natural materials—Lay out the items gathered from outdoors and consider each one from the standpoint of alteration possibilities, combination with other materials, and attaching methods. Which materials seem to make sense together? Which bring an element of contrast or contradiction to the others? What are some different ways you can change the materials? How might you attach them together, either by using glue or by limiting yourself to just the materials themselves? What kinds of forms do the materials and attaching possibilities lend themselves to?

    d. Site-specific outdoor construction—Find a location outdoors for which you would like to create a site-specific work (be sure to secure any permissions that may be necessary). Gather materials that are at and around the area, and think about how you might alter and attach them together in interesting ways to create a construction that communicates something about the place. (If you have never used a saw before, practice using it to cut small branches that cannot be snipped with scissors.) Just as important, consider the surfaces (bottom, top, and sides) of the containing area in which the construction will be built. How will the immediate site be integrated into your overall construction of the work? Complete the piece and document both the work and your experience of making it.

2. In what ways is working outdoors, with natural materials, and in response to a particular site different from the other work we've done so far? What are some considerations for doing this kind of construction with students of different ages? How might you organize and plan for the use of hand tools in your future work with students? How might you organize an area and opportunities for working with tools in your art class?

FOUND OBJECTS

From the French term *objet trouvé*, found object sculpture includes assemblage works composed at least in part of items other than the kinds of materials traditionally found in an art supply store (an example is the construction made from materials gathered outdoors). As discussed previously, all sorts of interesting items can be collected for use, and the process relies heavily on the artist's identification and accumulation of a ready supply of raw materials.

Exploring Found Objects

Remember that the objects themselves, their juxtaposition, and the ways they are attached and presented all contribute to the visual impact and meaning of the work. As you assemble your collection of items, think about the different ways in which each might function—for example, conceptually (flea market finds may suggest various historical time periods, recyclable items might point to environmental issues), structurally (very small items can be attached close together to cover the entire surface of an underlying form), and formally (using many of one item creates visual repetition). Also, as always, consider the ways in which the materials you are collecting can be altered and transformed.

Table 6-2 contains a list of suggestions to begin your search, and as you gain experience with this way of working you will discover many sources for interesting construction materials. Many of the sources for collage materials discussed in Chapter 5 are also excellent for finding items for found object sculpture.

Table 6-2 Materials for Found Object Constructions

kitchen utensils	corks
toys and toy parts	plastic and paper bags
books	sewing patterns
jar lids	dice
bottle tops	holiday decorations
kitchen utensils	craft supplies
artificial flowers	furniture items
stuffed animals	hardware items
Styrofoam packaging	hand tools
balls of all kinds	ladders and step stools
old CDs and LPs	plastic dishes
shoes and boots	clothing items
produce containers	spools
circuit boards	umbrellas
cardboard packaging	windows and screens
game pieces	picture frames
flip flops	gardening tools
plastic bottles	shells
plastic and wire coat hangers	eyeglasses
mops and brooms	party decorations
dolls	carrying cases
keys	natural materials from outdoors
industrial remnants	

Note: As with the classroom organization of collage materials, it's a good idea to sort found objects for construction by some sort of system, such as object type (toy, kitchen utensil), colors or color families, size, and so forth.

Materials:

A selection of items from Table 6-2

A bag of small items that relate (and can be used) to cover the entire surface of a larger solid form from your collection

Book to transform

Scissors

X-Acto knife and self-healing cutting mat

White glue and tacky glue, plus specialty glues as needed based on your materials: china and glass (Elmer's China + Glass Cement), stone, metal, and other assorted materials (Elmer's ProBond Advanced)

Low temperature hot glue gun with nontoxic glue sticks

Wire

Needle and thread
Masking tape
Hand tools and hardware as needed for altering and attaching materials—
  drill, hammer, nails, screws, screwdriver, pliers, wire cutters
Acrylic paints, assorted colors including black and white
Paint palette, brushes (including flat short handled bristle brushes for glazes),
  and water container
Paper towels
Newspaper for covering work surface

Getting Started:

1. Study your collection of objects and think about how individual items might
  be used together, based on item type, color, shape, size, material, and possible associative meeting. For each construction that you make, consider the
  following questions: Do you want to camouflage or create a particular order
  by working with materials that are similar in some way? Do you want to
  create dissonance, irony, or humor by juxtaposing materials with meanings
  or visual characteristics that are opposite or dissimilar? What ways can you
  think of to alter the materials, given the tools with which you have to work?

   a. Transform a book—How might you use the cover and pages of the book
     from your collection as an art material to transform? Use scissors, an
     Exacto knife, other tools, needle and thread, and/or glue—and consider
     different actions such as folding, slicing, tearing, pleating curling,
     scratching, rolling, shredding, recombining—as you reconstruct the
     book as a found object sculpture.

   b. Select some objects from your collection to combine into a standing
     structure. Which objects will you use as they are and which ones will
     you alter? How will you use the available tools to change the materi-
     als? How will you place and juxtapose the objects? Once you have a
     beginning plan for an arrangement, start to attach the parts together,
     choosing the best approach based on the types of materials you are
     joining and the ideas you want to suggest in the work (for example,
     nails and screws "mean" differently from needle and thread). Consider
     how the construction will support itself at the bottom, and at what
     points it will touch the table surface. As you work, consider the space
     around the structure and voids you might want to create inside for
     visual interest. Walk around or turn the piece periodically to make
     sure it is the way you want it from different vantage points.

   c. Take the large solid object that will serve as a form on which to create
     a layer or "skin" of smaller objects. Consider the relationship between
     both the small objects themselves and the larger form. What ideas do
     you want to suggest, and how will you arrange and juxtapose the
     various elements to do this? Alter the materials as needed, and attach
     the small pieces to the surface of the large object using whatever
     attachment methods best suit your purpose.

   d. Try other ways of altering objects and of combining and attaching
     objects in various configurations. Can any of your items be stretched or
     stuffed? Knotted together? How might you deconstruct some of your ob-
     jects? What kinds of ideas do these actions suggest in the finished piece?

2. In what ways is working with objects that suggest functions and associations
  from nonart contexts different from more traditional studio techniques?

Artist Profile: **SANDRA EULA LEE**

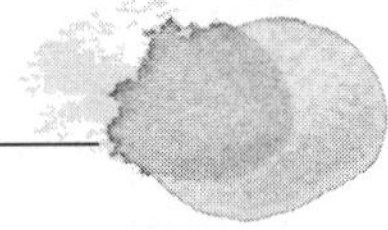

Sandra Eula Lee collects familiar objects and alters and combines them to construct sculptures and installations. According to Lee, the works suggest political and social issues that frame daily life (see Figure 29 in the color insert). She writes:

Beginning with material reality, I take familiar objects I encounter and recombine them into sculptures and installations. I construct wider meanings from the found materials and events in my life, finding the uncanny aspects or details of my physical surroundings that can be recombined to reveal the social issues within daily life. I begin with things considered commonplace and make decisive changes to arrive at more complex readings. I believe meaning can be culled from the personal objects we use, the materials we leave behind, and the neighborhoods we inhabit. I'm concerned with the individual's struggle on a day-to-day basis; the politics and the humor that make up everyday life.

What kinds of objects and materials are present in this work? What are some different associations these objects might bring to an interpretation of the piece? How do the materials' transformation and juxtaposition influence your reading and response?

What did you discover about this process that you did not know or had not considered before? How might you engage your students in working in this fashion?

CLAY

In my experience, most students love to work with ceramic clay, to the extent that they repeatedly request the opportunity to do ceramics projects in class. What is it about this material and its processes that gets kids so excited? First, they like the feel and responsiveness of clay, and the immediacy of being able to model and build things like animal and human figures, buildings, and functional objects such as plates, cups, and containers to hold things. They also like the techniques that ceramic clay affords, ways of working that are very different from those of other media—pinching and hollowing out, rolling and coiling, constructing with slabs and using molds, joining pieces by scoring and using slip, embellishing surfaces with textures and glazes, and firing in the kiln.

Although there are many techniques in ceramics, the basic stages in the work process are building and shaping with wet clay, letting the formed clay dry for about a day then detailing the "leather hard" (stiffened) clay, letting that air dry for a few more days then decorating on "bone-dry" clay, then firing the piece in a kiln. The firing is usually done twice, with the first firing (bisque) preparing the clay for the application of liquid glaze. Glaze adds a protective and waterproof sealing of the clay surface, making it safe for food and drinks.

Students also enjoy working with nonceramic clays (not hardened by heat) such as air-dry clay and modeling clay and dough. And they enjoy using polymer clay, which is baked in an oven to harden. Explore a variety of clays in response to the suggested activities that follow. If you have access to a kiln, be sure to use ceramic clay for some of your work, finish those pieces with slips or glazes, and fire the pieces according to the directions provided by the kiln manufacturer.

Note: There are many approaches to working with clay and several excellent resources for exploring this medium in more depth than is possible here (see bibliography and resources at the end of this book).

Exploring Clay

What are different types of clay like to work with and what are some different approaches to using them? Explore the techniques that follow to construct a variety of clay forms and objects. As you are working, note how the properties of clay both lend themselves to particular construction techniques and present interesting challenges in the process.[5]

Materials:

White low-fire clay, available in a 25 lb. bag or larger quantity from clay suppliers (if you have access to a kiln)
Air-dry clay
Modeling clay and dough in a few colors
Polymer clay in a few colors
Large bucket of water (for cleaning clay tools)
Wooden board covered with canvas to use under clay, piece of canvas, or Masonite board (sized to individual work area)
Small boards for storing work between stages
Wire clay tool for cutting
Small sponges
Bowl of water
Plastic knife and fork (you can also use clay tools)
Squeeze bottle of slip (clay mixed with water for joining parts)
Rolling pin
Plastic coated paper clip
Two wooden boards ¼ to ½ inch thick, 1 to 2 inches wide, around 2 feet long
Ruler
Nontoxic low-fire glazes (if you have access to a kiln)
Tempera, watercolor, and acrylic paints and palettes
Water-soluble pastels and pencils
Mod Podge, gloss medium, or matte medium
Nontoxic shoe polish
Paintbrushes
Container of water for surface treatments
Spray bottle filled with water
Canvas mats or canvas-covered boards
Plastic bags (dry cleaning bags are great) or plastic wrap for protecting in-process work
Newspaper for covering work surface for supporting hollow and slab pieces
Paper towels
Rags

---

[5] I am indebted to Kevin Nierman, Elaine Arima, and Curtis Arima, creators of the very excellent book, *The Kids 'N' Clay Ceramics Book: Handbuilding and Wheel-Throwing From the Kids 'N' Clay Pottery Studio*. Several of the projects in this section are adapted from the book.

Getting Started:

1. The basic hand-building activities that follow are intended for you to become familiar with different types of clay products and their properties and processes, and to begin to think about how you might use both ceramic and nonceramic clays with your students.

Holding the wire tool taut horizontally, cut off a piece of white ceramic clay or air-dry clay from the block by putting the wire behind the part you want to cut away and pulling the wire toward you, like using a cheese cutter. Working on a canvas mat or board, explore different ways of changing the clay with just your hands (pulling, pinching off pieces, rolling, twisting, patting/pounding, poking holes and textures, bending folding, coiling). Also explore ways of arranging and combining pieces. How can you make the clay rise up tall from the table surface? How can you make it extend sideways? What happens when you press things into it?

Next, practice some basic joining techniques, such as scoring. Use a fork to scratch the ends of two pieces where they will be joined, apply slip from the bottle, press the two pieces together firmly, and use your fingers to smooth the creases of the joint until they are no longer visible.

Note: For class distribution of clay, precut hunks from the block and roll into balls about the size of a grapefruit. Put the balls of clay back in the plastic bag with a damp paper towel and close tightly until you are ready to distribute them. The clay balls will remain soft and moist in the bag.

If the clay starts to dry out while you are working with it, dip your fingers in water and add a little to the clay, kneading it to mix (don't use too much water or the clay will become too mushy and sloppy). If you need to leave your work in the

F 6-10: Jen Rifkin, clay figure in process. (below, left)

F 6-11: Jen Rifkin, clay figure glazed and fired. (below, right)

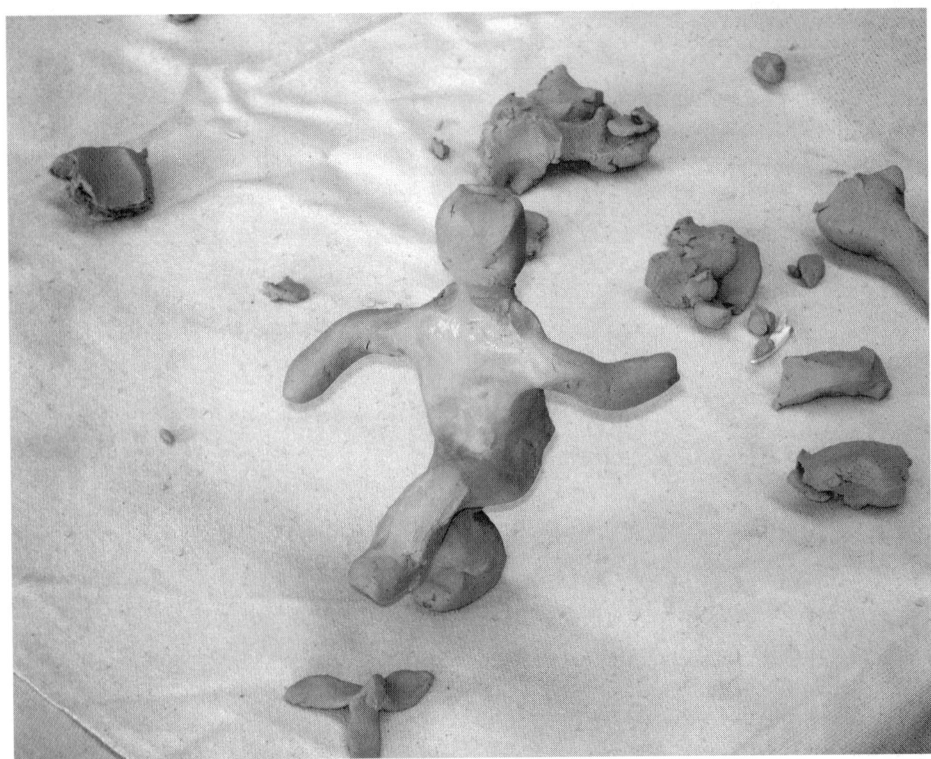

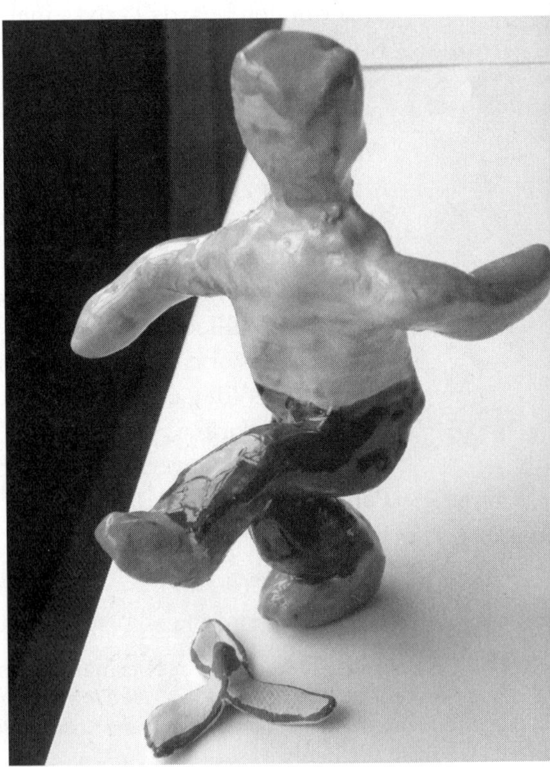

middle of the forming stage, cover it closely with plastic (insert a damp paper towel inside the plastic) so the air does not dry it out.

To recycle scraps of soft clay, press the pieces into a ball, spray with a little water, and wedge the clay by throwing it on the canvas with as much force as you can. Repeat this about 20 times, turning the ball each time.

a. Solid modeling—Students are usually eager to make clay figures of people and animals, among other things, and these are excellent places to start with clay because figures can be formed easily through modeling the material directly. Because they are usually portrayed in the process of doing different activities, human and animal figures also offer great sculptural challenges having to do with showing action and movement, and with body positioning, weight, and balance as the sculpture is being formed. Prompts for students can lead from simple standing figures to what people/animals might be doing when they are bending and reaching or don't have all feet on the ground, to seated figures, to multiple figures interacting with one another in a setting. In this way, the prompt is open-ended to allow for as many narrative themes as there are students, while presenting increasingly sophisticated construction and technical challenges (see Figures 6-10 and 6-11).

Use clay to create a series of figures, animals and/or people that represent some of the construction challenges discussed above. Pinch off pieces of clay to roll and shape into torsos, arms, legs, and heads, and use scoring and slip to join the parts together. Make your figures in a variety of positions showing different types of action, and challenge yourself with increasingly complex balance issues. When you have the basic figures, use scoring and slip to add additional pieces of clay that suggest clothing, hair, ears, tails, props, and other details. Finish the surfaces to your liking, leaving them the way they are or smoothing them in particular areas. When you are satisfied with the works, leave them to dry out according to the clay manufacturer's suggestions.

Note: You can use props to support parts of wet clay works while they dry—for example, pieces of Styrofoam can be placed under areas that sag or need propping up (like animal torsos on top of short or thin legs). Just be sure that when the sculpture dries in your chosen position it will be balanced to stand upright without tipping over. Clay pieces that are more than an inch thick will need to be hollowed out so that they fire properly in the kiln.

b. Pinch pots—Pinching is a very simple technique that can be adapted to make many kinds of pot and dish forms. Using a ball of clay about the size of your fist, push your thumb into the center, stopping about ½″ from the bottom (you can use a straightened out paperclip to poke through to the bottom, then measure that distance on the paperclip with a ruler, pushing the clay back in place when you're done). Next, holding the clay in the palm of one hand, use your other hand to pinch the wall of the clay between your thumb and fingers, rotating the pot in your palm (the walls will become thinner as you progress). Place the bottom of the pot on your canvas surface to flatten it so that it is stable and does not roll, and continue to pinch and rotate the pot until the walls are between ½″ and ¼″.

This basic pinch pot technique can be adapted to create larger forms (add clay by pinching small bits in as you turn the form) and bowls (start with a larger ball of clay for bowl forms and pinch the walls thinner and press out at the top to widen it as you rotate). When you are done exploring pinch pots, leave them to dry out according to the clay manufacturer's suggestions.

Note: Because clay works are not easily identifiable at this stage of wet work, always have students use a pencil or other tool to write (incise) their names or initials on the bottoms of their clay pieces.

c. Coils—Long rolls of clay can be used to build a variety of forms, including dishes, cups, bowls, and tall structures. To begin, press a fist-sized piece of clay into an oblong shape with your hands and place it horizontally on your canvas surface. Using both hands, roll out a long coil as evenly as possible, until the clay is about ½" thick.

To make coaster and plate forms, wind the clay in a flat spiral from the center out, making sure the coil edges are touching at all points. Add additional coils as necessary by joining ends, until your piece is the size you want (cut off any excess coil). Using your thumb, smooth and seal the cracks (this makes the piece watertight) and repeat on the bottom if you wish. To make a lip or edge for a plate, add a coil to the top all the way around and use scoring and slip to attach, then smooth the inside and outside seams.

For taller pieces or pieces that have curved walls (extending out from the base in the middle and then coming back in at the top), you can use the coaster and plate forms above as bases and stack several coils that are just long enough to go around the base once (this will create a straight cylinder form). Score and use slip on both the rim of the base and the coil that will attach to it, then roll and stack additional coils until your piece is the height you have in mind. Using one hand as a support and the other to work the clay, carefully smooth and seal the seams on the inside, being sure to not make the walls too thin. To make pieces that have curved walls, use progressively longer coils and stack them on the outer edge of the coils beneath the shift (this will widen the form). To bring the form back in as you approach the top of the piece, progressively shorten the coils and stack them on the inner edge of the coils beneath as you reach the top.

To create handles for cups and bowls, lay a piece of ½" coil on the table and press it to flatten slightly. Bend the handle to the shape you want, and attach it to your piece by scoring and using slip. When you are satisfied with the pieces, leave them to dry out according to the clay manufacturer's suggestions.

d. Slabs and hollow modeling—Rolled slabs of clay can be used to make tile, plate, bowl, and box forms, and they can be draped or leaned on any number of objects or laid in molds to capture their forms, or pressed around armatures (which burn out during kiln firing) to make all kinds of hollow sculptural work. While very young children like to use their hands to pound and pat clay into slabs for building and shaping, older students can use rolling pins (and wooden boards, if available) to create slabs with an even thickness.

To create a slab, begin with a brick sized piece of clay and use a rolling pin to pound and flatten it. Roll evenly with the rolling pin, until the clay is about ½″ thick. You can use wooden boards set flat against the long sides of the clay if you wish—this will keep the rolling pin level as you roll and ensure the evenness of the slab and its ½″ thickness.

To make a tile, use a knife to cut the clay to the shape you want. To make a plate, cut the slab in the shape you want and then roll out a coil to apply to the rim of the slab (attach by scoring and using slip, and smooth the seams as with coil work above). Experiment with laying and draping—after about a day of drying, a slab can be placed in a space where a shelf or table meets a wall to make a folded 90 degree angle form, or laid over a rounded object to capture its curve. You can also use plates, bowls, pie and cake pans, and platters as press molds— just put down a layer of plastic wrap so that the clay does not stick to the mold. Once you have laid and carefully pressed the slab into the mold, trim the excess clay from the rim with a knife and smooth the edges with a damp sponge.

You can also use slabs to make parts of figures, architectural forms, and other sculptural works by rolling them into hollow tube shapes on their own (and smoothing the seam where the edges meet) or wrapping them around rigid cylindrical forms to shape them. Another strategy is to stuff hollow forms with newspaper to support the clay form while it dries. Once different parts are dry enough to move, they can be attached to build the sculpture.

e. Surface texture—The pliability of clay makes it ideal for applying surface textures and other embellishments. You can press objects into soft clay, attach small clay shapes to the surface by scoring and using slip, draw lines in the clay with a stick or pencil, or wait for it to become leather hard and then use a clay tool to carve a design or image into the surface.

f. Surface color and finish—If you are using ceramic clay that will be fired in a kiln, you can paint several coats of underglaze in selected areas of a wet or leather hard piece, or wait for the piece to become bone dry and cover all visible surfaces (never apply glaze to the bottom of the piece, as doing so will cause it to stick to the kiln during firing). You can use as many colors as you want and overlap colors if you wish.

Kiln-fired clay pieces (that are already bisque fired) can also be decorated with low-fire glazes (the glazes seal the clay and make it safe for holding food and beverages). Underglazed pieces should be finished with clear glaze. For pieces without underglaze, apply colored low-fire glazes with a paintbrush, sponge or crumpled paper to create patterns and textures, or a toothbrush to achieve a spattered effect—you can also use stencils to create surface designs with glaze. Another option is to dip the piece in a bucket of glaze, using one color for the whole piece or multiple colors for different parts of it (you will need to use dipping tongs for this technique, and remove dried glaze from the bottom of the piece with a damp sponge before firing).

Bisque-fired ceramic clay and air-dry clay pieces can also be finished with tempera, watercolor, and acrylic paints, water-soluble pastels and pencils, and nontoxic shoe polish, then sealed with Mod Podge, gloss medium, or matte medium (these pieces will not be safe for food and drinks). Experiment with these surface treatments on your clay pieces, using drawing and painting ideas and techniques from Chapters 2 and 3. What kinds of effects can you achieve? How might you plan for your students' work in clay forming and surface treatments?

Artist Profile: **JENNIFER McCANDLESS**

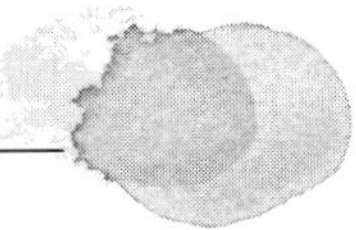

Jennifer McCandless works in stoneware to create figurative works that address issues of "movement, gravity, balance, and displacement" and "the narrative issues that define the story of one's life" (see Figure 30 in the color insert). She writes:

Clay is such a fluid, plastic medium. I like for the sculptures, even though they are very hard when fired, to retain that fluid feeling of the wet clay.

Each piece has a certain life of its own, its own personality, from the sublime and elegant to the whimsical and humorous. The work is painted in many layers instead of glazed. The paint surface and the three-dimensional textures help to animate the work as well. I am ultimately aiming to clarify, expose, and bring these forms to life. They are explorations of the liminal zone between abstraction and representation.

Note: I have found that students need to be invited to really think about how they will finish their clay pieces, so I present the surface development phase as related to the clay forming phase but substantive in its own right. The clay object should be treated as a surface for all kinds of potential mark making, image making, and design—through open-ended questioning and discussion about approaches that can be taken with the materials available. Otherwise, students may simply finish the piece using the simplest means available, without carefully considering (and actively inventing) multiple approaches and strategies.

F 6-12

Mary Hafeli, Weathering, 2007 (detail).

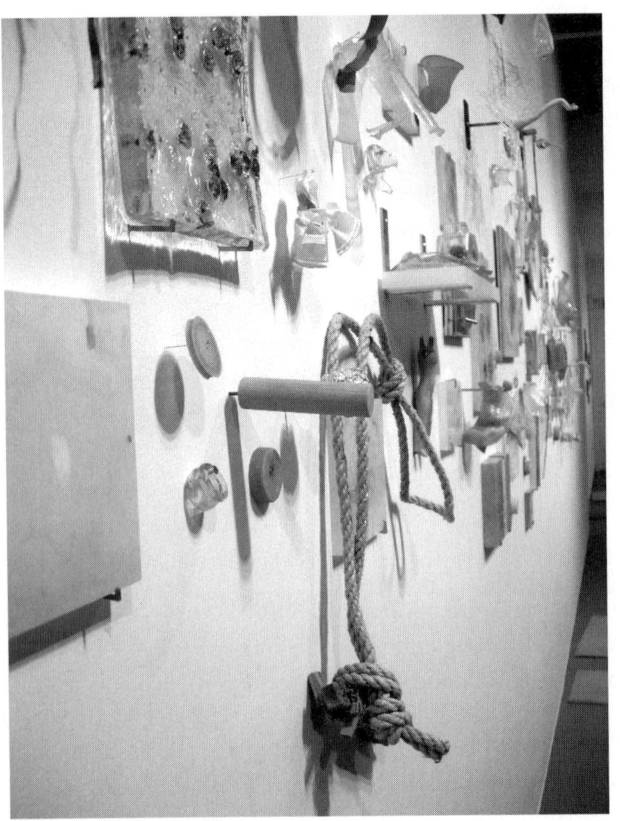

g. Modeling clay and dough and polymer clay—Experiment with several colors of modeling clay, modeling dough, and polymer clay. With the modeling clay and dough, form solid figures and objects using some of the hand building techniques from working with ceramic clay. How is the feel of these materials different from one another, and from ceramic clay? How can the colors be used together, and mixed to form new colors?

Form small objects with the polymer clay, experimenting here also with different techniques (this clay is especially good for bead making and other jewelry applications). How is the polymer clay different from the other modeling materials? Which ones are easiest to work with? Which ones allow for the most detailed work? How might you use these materials with students of different ages?

Note: Brands of polymer clay have different specifications for baking—follow the baking instructions for your brand of clay.

2. Out of all of the clay experiences presented here, which ones did you find most interesting? Why? Which ones are most challenging? How might you integrate regular clay experiences into your curriculum for students of different ages and levels of experience?

MIXED MEDIA WITH CONSTRUCTION
AND OTHER MATERIALS

In addition to focusing on one or more works that are designed to be freestanding sculptures, some artists create installations. These artworks often involve a number of component parts and are hung on parts of walls or entire walls, or are placed in a large area of a room or gallery (floor, ceiling, corner), or outdoor site. Installations are often designed to respond in some way to their sites, and to highlight or change perceptions of the spaces they occupy (see Figure 6-12 and Figure 31 in the color insert).

Installations can be done with groups of students, with each student contributing multiple components of the overall work—components can be three-dimensional or two-dimensional. Students should be given the opportunity to look at and discuss different examples of installation works so that they have a good idea of what is possible and what installation entails. Once you and your students have identified a theme and identified a space in the school or other site (be sure to get permission, and check fire code regulations if you plan to suspend things from the ceiling), you can brainstorm the kinds of component works that will be made, the materials and techniques necessary for creating them, and the ways in which the parts will be displayed as a cohesive construction. A good way to organize and manage mixed media work for installation is to set up workstations so that students can work in small groups by medium/technique, rotating through multiple stations as needed.

Other approaches to mixing two- and three-dimensional media include using drawing, painting, printmaking and/or collage to create environments for three-dimensional works and using two-dimensional materials to make constructions designed to fit the human form. Both of these approaches extend students' thinking about what sculpture is and can be.

Exploring Mixed Media with Construction
and Other Materials

Explore combining materials, working with two-dimensional and three-dimensional forms simultaneously, and making wearable works from nontraditional materials in response to the suggestions that follow.

Materials:

Materials needed for a selection of three-dimensional construction techniques
A selection of collage elements, supports, and attaching materials
Colored garbage bags, newspaper, wrapping paper, several rolls of toilet tissue, and/or plastic wrap
Colored duct tape
Needle and thread
Scissors
Tempera, watercolor, gouache, and/or acrylic paints and mediums
Paintbrushes
Containers of water
Palettes, containers, and trays for dispensing paints
Graphite pencils and colored pencils, oil pastels, water-soluble pastels
Ink pens

Getting Started:

1. Make a series of small, exploratory works that combine one or a few of the materials featured in this chapter. How might you make a construction from wire and cardboard, wire and paper strips, or wire and cellophane? From natural materials and found materials? Fabric and wood?

2. Take one of your constructed objects and create a two-dimensional work that relates to it as a surrounding environment. Or take a large two-dimensional work and create a three-dimensional construction in response to it. As you are planning your work, think about the characteristics of the piece you are starting with, which of those you want to carry forward into the second piece, and the ways in which the two will contrast with one another. How does combining these works change the process of creating? How does the pairing of the works support new visual interest and meaning?

3. Design and construct an article of clothing—Working with a partner and choosing from such materials as colored garbage bags, newspaper, wrapping paper, several rolls of toilet tissue, plastic wrap, colored duct tape, and needle and thread, design a dress or pants/skirt with a top that can be worn. Use draping, cutting, pleating, fringing, weaving, braiding, twisting, wrapping, and other strategies to alter materials and create the piece. What kind of form will your clothing construction have? How will you use the materials both functionally and artistically? What kinds of embellishments might add visual interest?

4. Experiment with a small installation—You may want to use some of the three-dimensional objects you made and create two-dimensional works that relate to them in some way. Or start with two-dimensional pieces and create three-dimensional constructions in response. How will the various materials and formal elements (color, shape, texture, etc.) work together? How will the different meanings of the pieces and their materials interact?

5. Creating an installation on a wall is very much like composing a collage—you will need to consider the space itself, how to arrange the components in the space, which pieces will be placed next to each other, and how the works will be attached to the wall (remember that attachment methods can offer another layer of meaning and interest to the work). How far out from the front plane of the wall will your components extend? How will you consider and integrate the bottom and top of the wall? What will be the overall shape of the installation? How will you consider the ceiling and floor spaces? For installations that don't involve a wall, you'll need to figure out how to arrange objects on the floor and/or suspend them from the ceiling.

STUDIO REFLECTION: FORMING AND BUILDING

Looking at your construction experiments and considering the range of visual effects you were able to achieve, what are the characteristics of the materials and processes that draw you to them? Which materials and techniques do you think produced the most interesting results? Why? Which approaches are most challenging? Which ones would you like to spend more time exploring? How would you go further using these techniques? Compare your responses to what the artists below have to say about their choices and use of materials.

More Artists on Media

Artist Profile: **DEIRDRE FOX**

Deirdre Fox's "object drawings" are "visual poems" that merge drawing, painting, and mixed media construction in their use and expansive alteration of "identifiable discards" (see Figure 6-13). For Fox, both the objects themselves and the multiple actions taken to transform and combine them contribute to a narrative identity for each piece that shifts between past functions and present reincarnations. She writes:

I began using toss away containers, conduits, coverings and connectors as a primary material for drawing visual poems because these physical objects are modern artifacts that hold to a prior functional identity that must be shed, yet need not be fully let go, to serve as points, lines, areas and volumes of a nonfunctional drawing. I connect and straddle the identities of the physical objects by collapsing, inflating, stretching, folding, marring, staining and otherwise altering them to function as points, lines, areas and volumes in wall based assemblages, completed by light and site position. The combinations inevitably embody male and/or female aspects.

Conceptually, the work begins in Paleolithic rock art, which had been preserved largely because it lay undiscovered for thousands of years and upon discovery has had to be actively protected, and in the ubiquity of vessels as artifacts. It extends to the question exemplified, for example, by Eva Hesse's Studio Leavings, of when an object begins to be art. Visually, the work begins in analytic cubism, and once extended to physical materials, expands upon Eva Hesse, Robert Morris, and others who worked with physical material. The language of the physical material and real physical volume must be accommodated or countermanded.

The use of identifiable discards as artifacts encourages a pause, in which to contemplate and confront both what it means to be accounted for, present and acted upon and culpability over what often gets physically and metaphorically tossed away without thought. Making preservable work that appears disposable counters the modern, wasteful paradigm to build in obsolescence.

How does Fox's work draw you in? What ideas and associations are suggested by her choice of materials and their physical properties? What kinds of actions have been used to alter materials and give them new function and meaning?

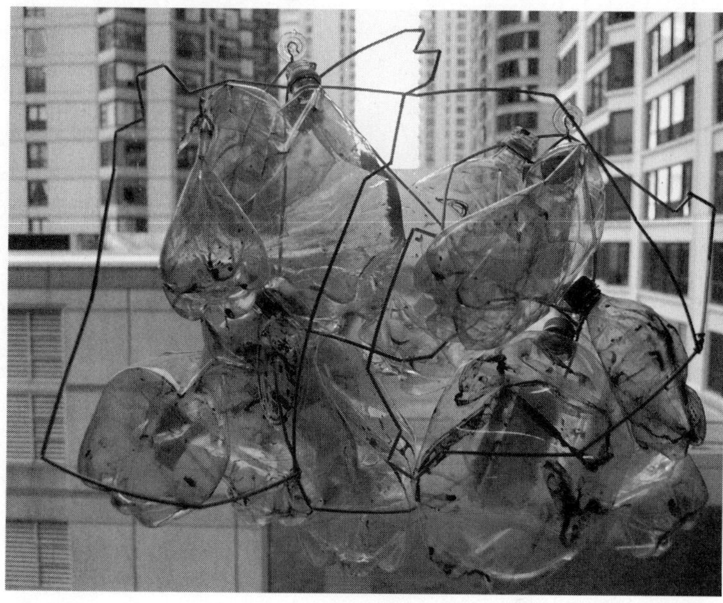

F 6-13
Deleterious Vignette Pocket, 2010, assemblage on window, 26" × 30" × 8". © 2010 Deirdre A. Fox.

Artist Profile: **LOIS SCHKLAR**

Toronto artist Lois Schklar's drawing installations combine wire and found objects with graphite and paper or wall drawing surfaces (see Figures 6-14a and 6-14b). How does the artist's combination of sculptural materials, light and shadow, and drawing contribute to the feeling and mood of the work? What ideas does the interplay between these elements suggest or convey? Schklar comments,

Tethered Memories Hung Low Beneath the Void is from "Familiar Territory," an ongoing series of mixed media drawing installations. The installations reflect my interest in manipulating diverse and often-disparate materials, the relationship objects have with one another and the physical and psychological space these objects occupy.

Working directly on the wall, I explore the formal qualities of line, space and movement. I use materials gathered from the urban and natural environment, objects from my personal collection, recycled remnants of old work and graphite drawings transferred directly to the walls as mark making tools.

Words flow into and out of the working drawing. Shadows, both real and illusory, shift on the walls. Graphite traces the process while text identifies a personal relationship to the objects in an effort to document and remember their significance. Words become testimony to the power of memory and its inevitable decline.

Each drawing installation builds on the ideas of the proceeding installations or experimentation I have undertaken while working in my studio and/or previous exhibitions. This process encourages a sense of play, being in the moment and a nonlinear approach to documentation while also providing an opportunity to adapt each drawing installation to a specific environment.

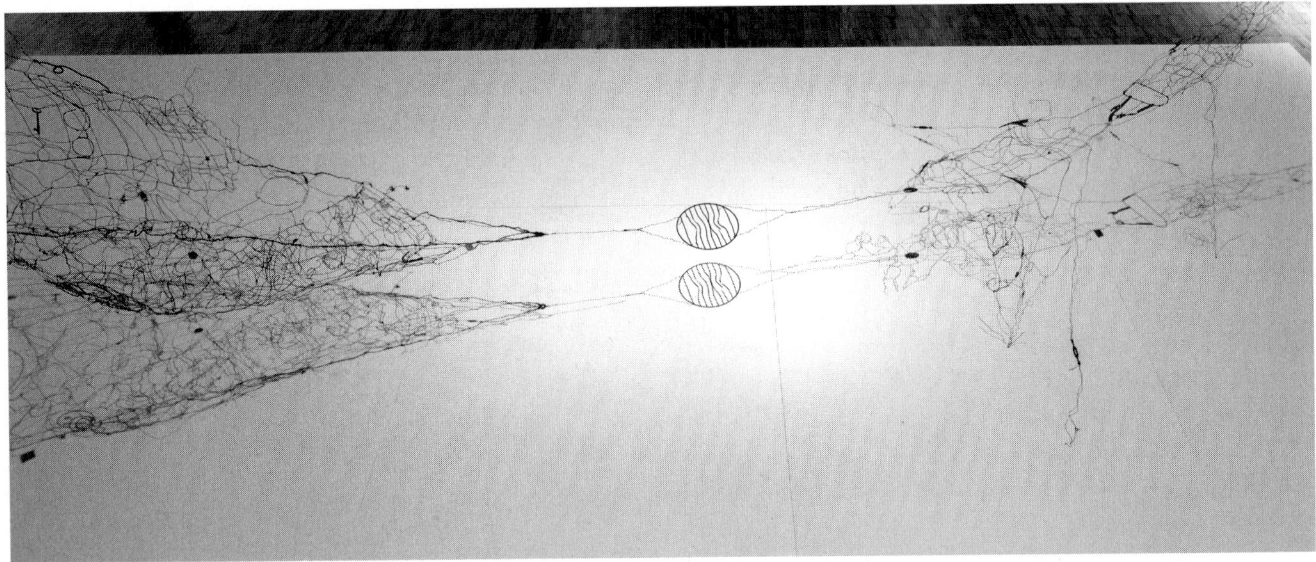

F 6-14a
Tethered Memories Hung Low Beneath the Void, 2011, mixed media, wire, 20' × 12' × 12'. Desgined and made by Lois Schklar. Photo by Peter Legris.

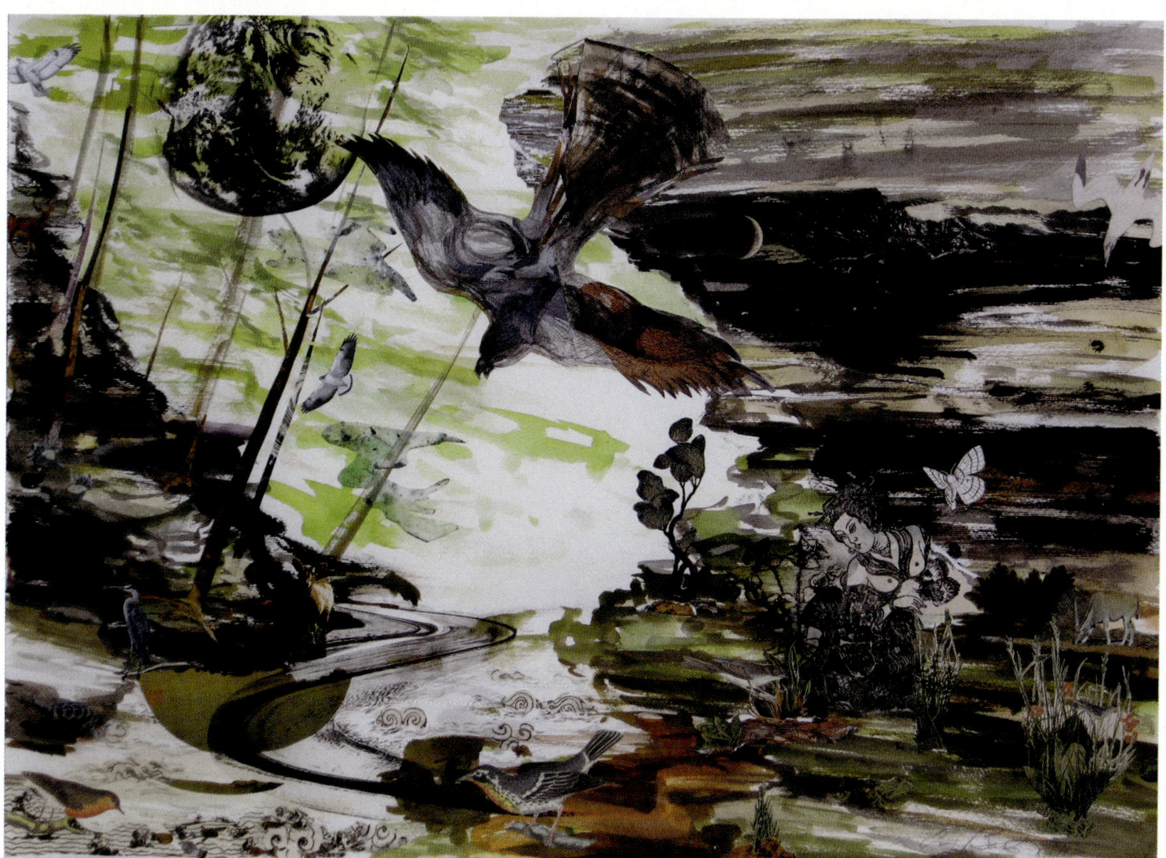

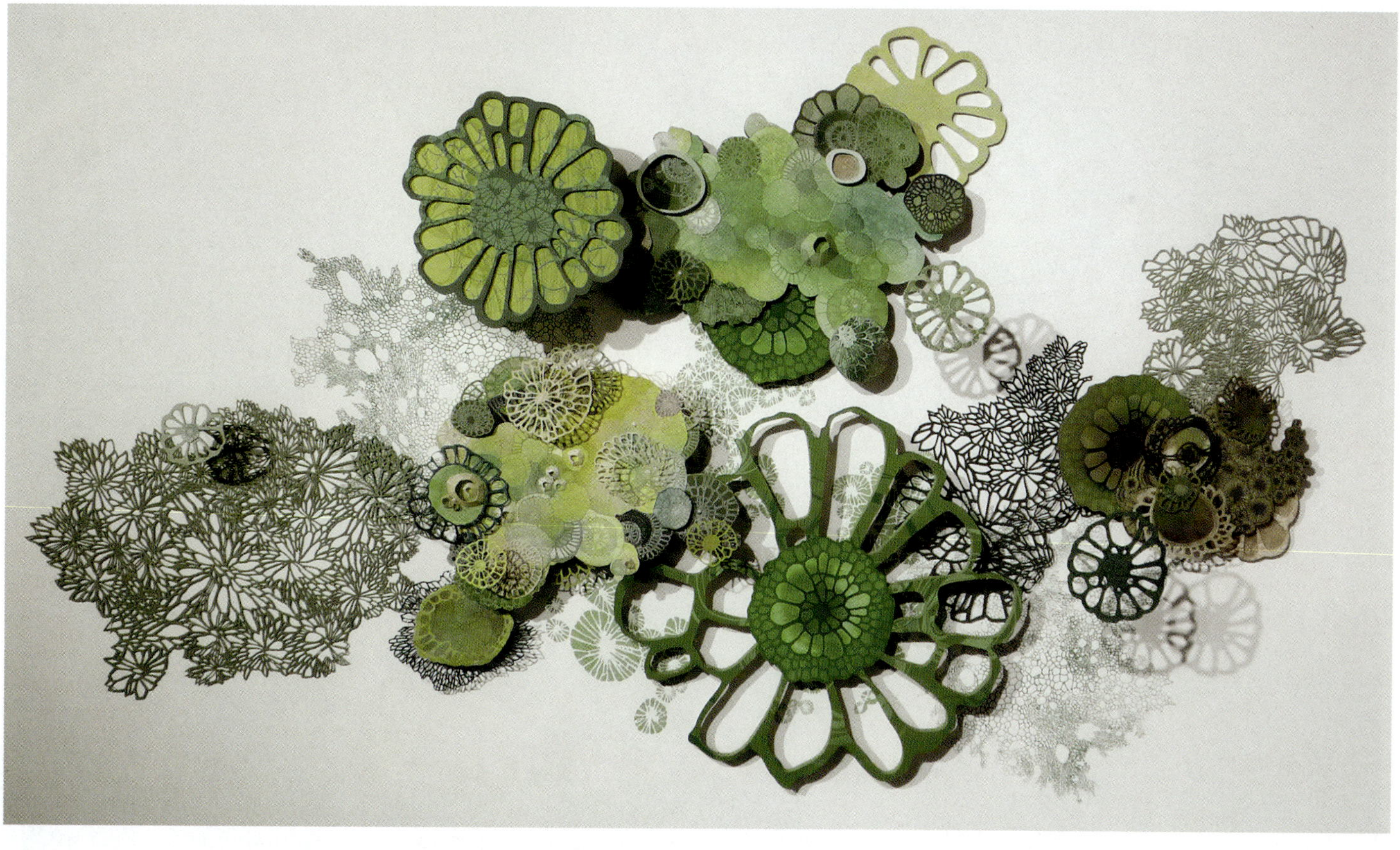

F 18
Lauren Kussro, Coral Confection, 2013, etching, silkscreen, monotype on paper, wood, paint, cut paper, and beads, 4' × 4'.

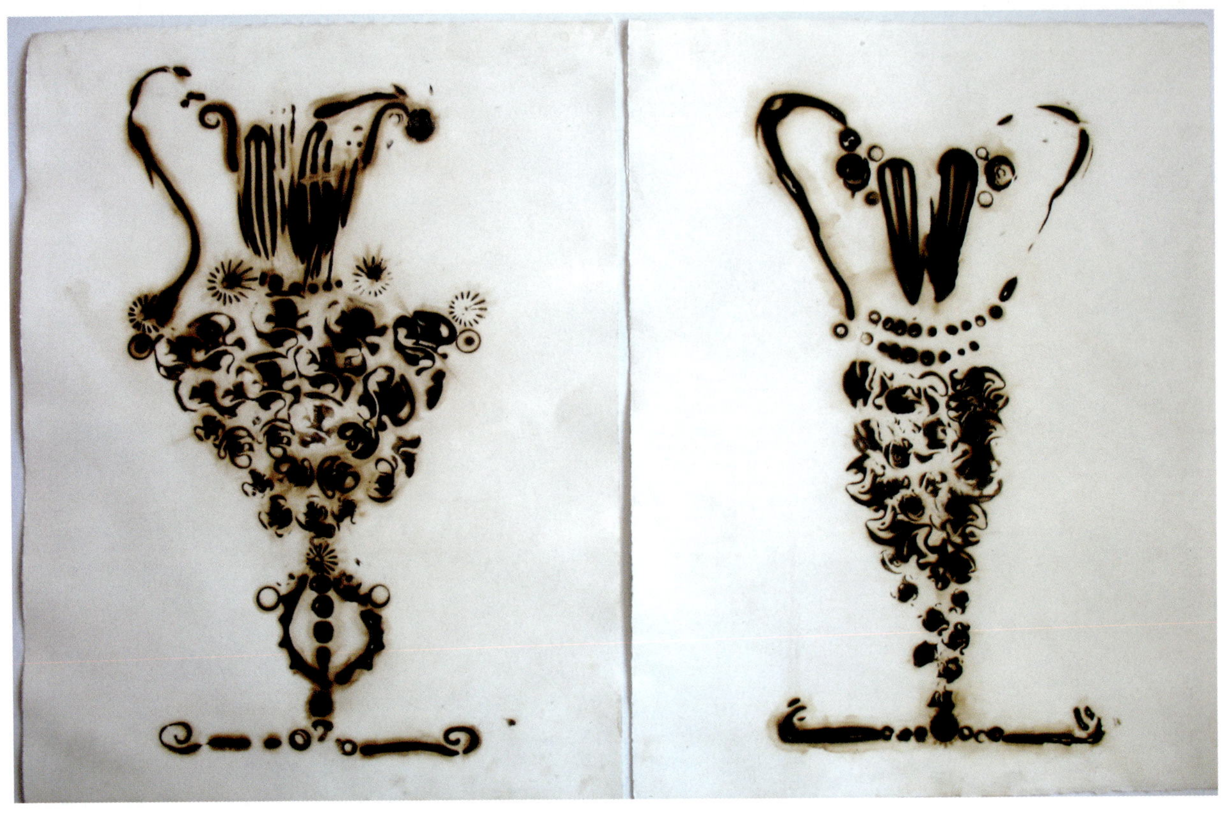

F 19
Anne Gant, Pair of Vases, 2013, hot glass on Rives BFK paper, 18" × 30" each.

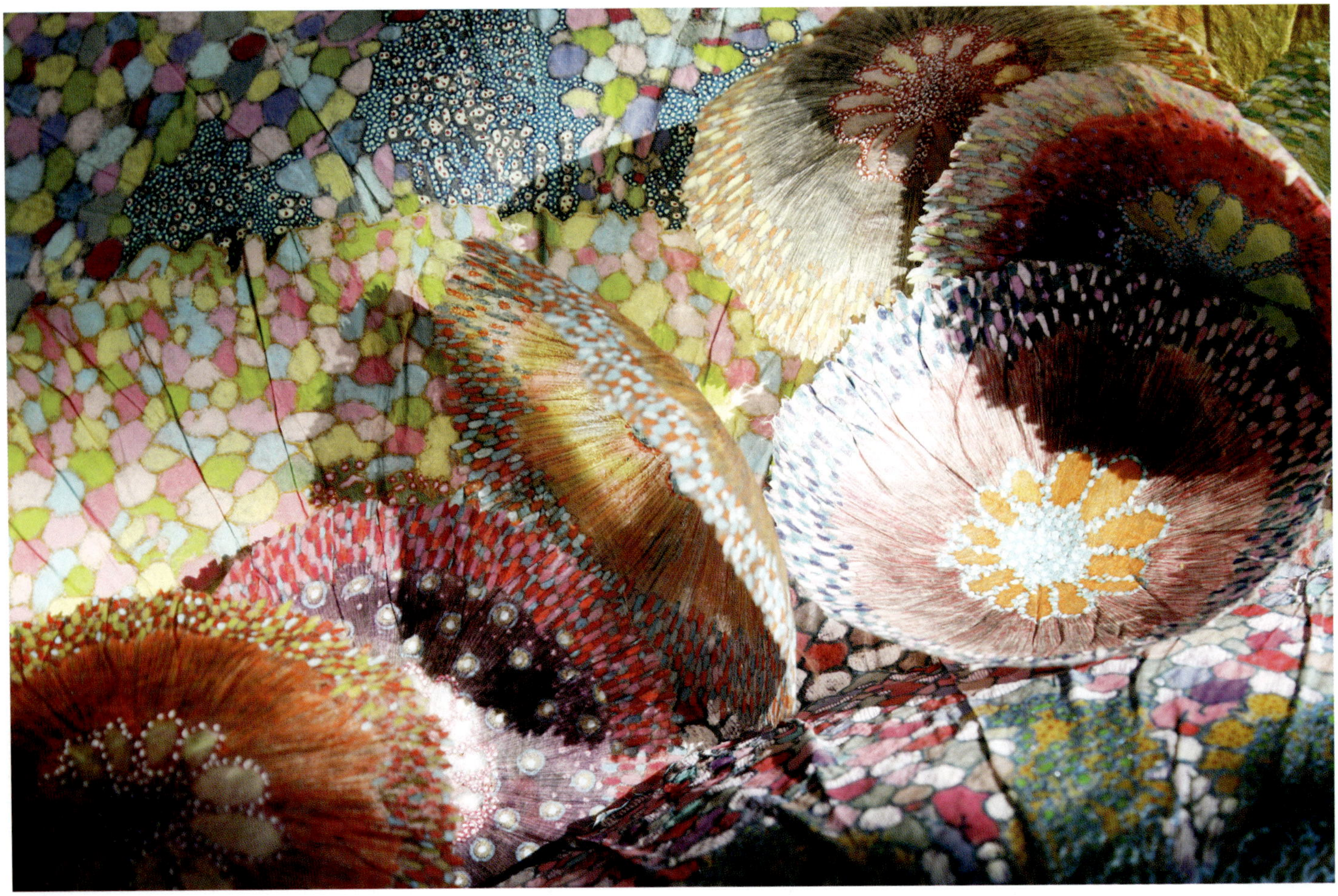

F 20
Jill Parisi, Cascade, 2008, Outdoor installation, handcolored etchings, dimensions variable. Photographer Jill Parisi.

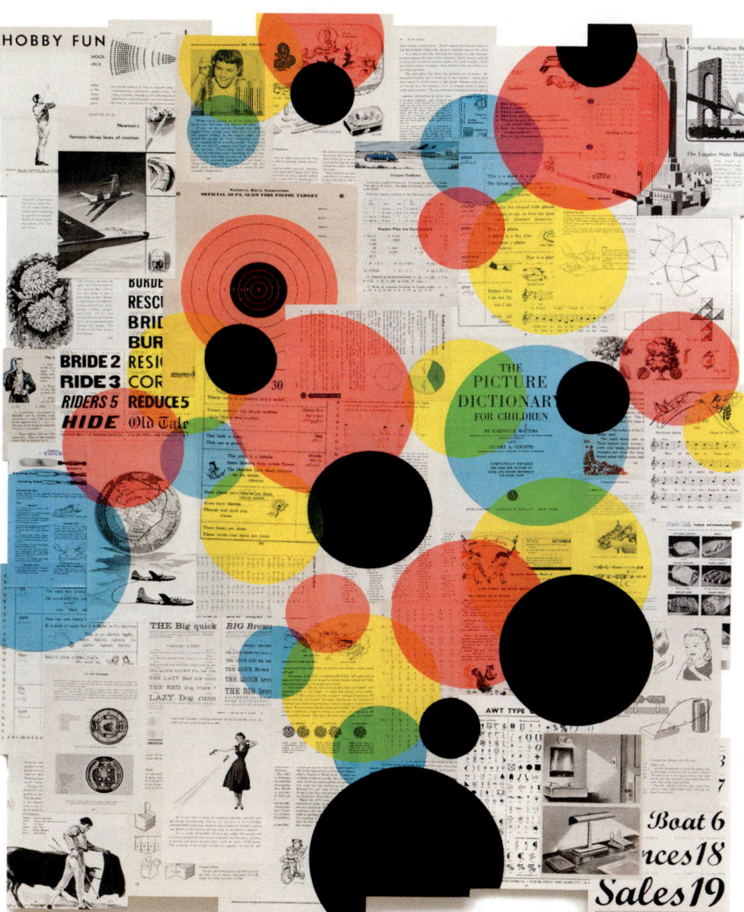

F 21

Tamar Cohen, The Big Quick, 2010,
silkscreen on newspaper collage,
40" × 50". 2010 © Tamar Cohen.
All Rights Reserved.

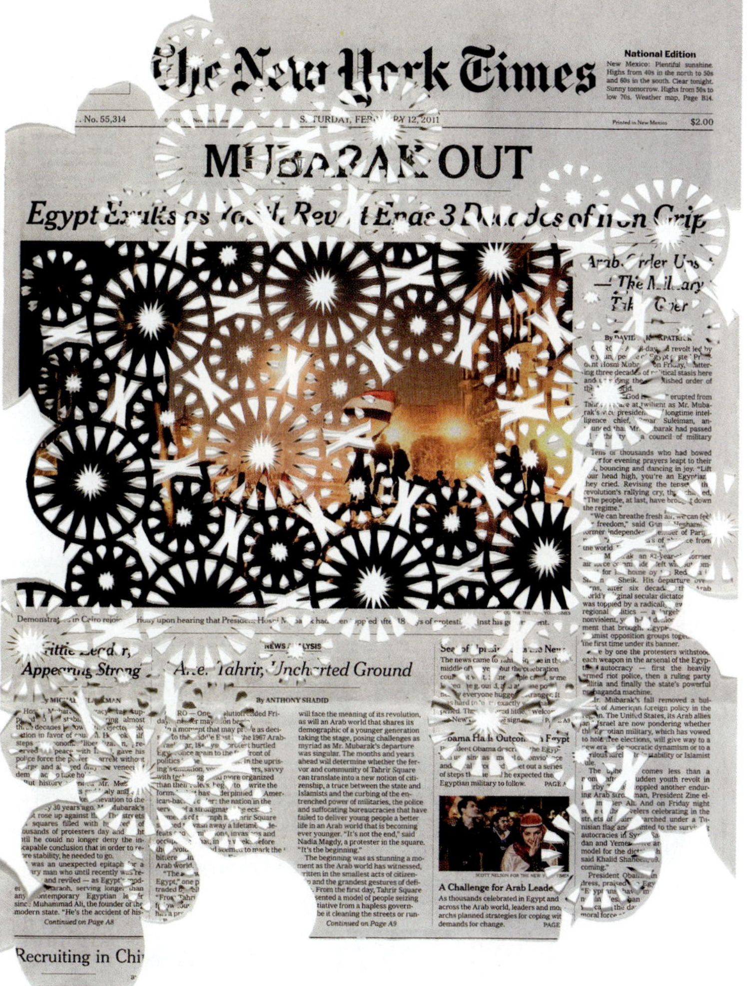

F 22

Donna Ruff, 2.12.11,
2011, cut newspaper, 16" × 11.5".
© 2011 Donna Ruff Collection,
New Mexico Museum of Art.

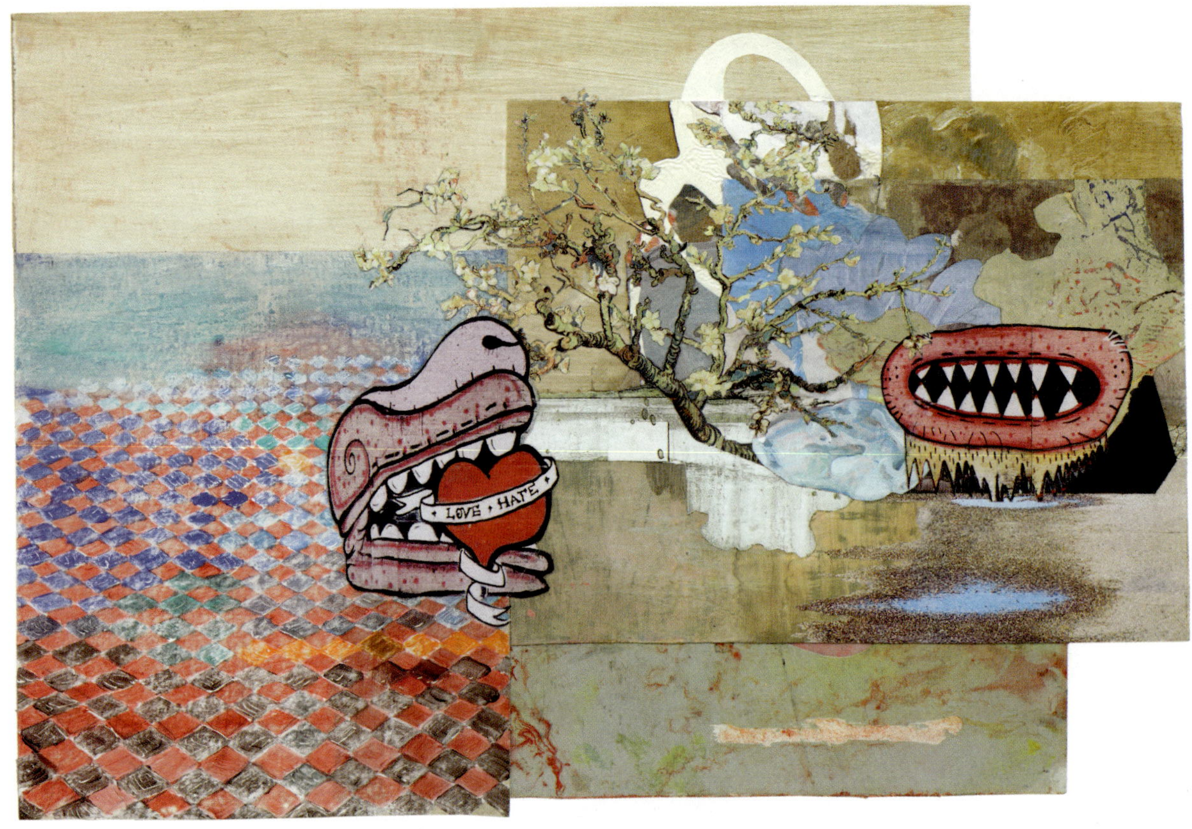

F 23
*Sophie Aston, A
Love Story, Part 6,
2011, collaged
paper, 19.25" ×
28.25".*

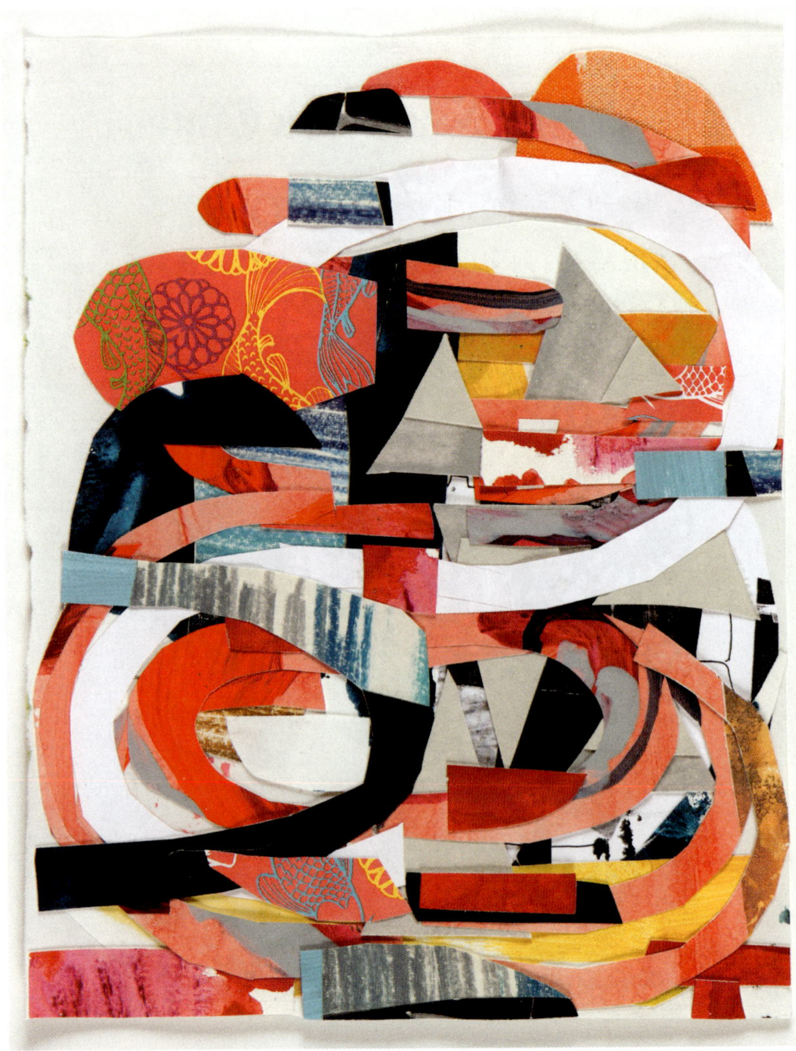

F 24
*Barbara Campbell Thomas,
Orange/Blue Loop Rhythm, 2012,
acrylic, ink, and collage on paper,
11" × 8.5".*

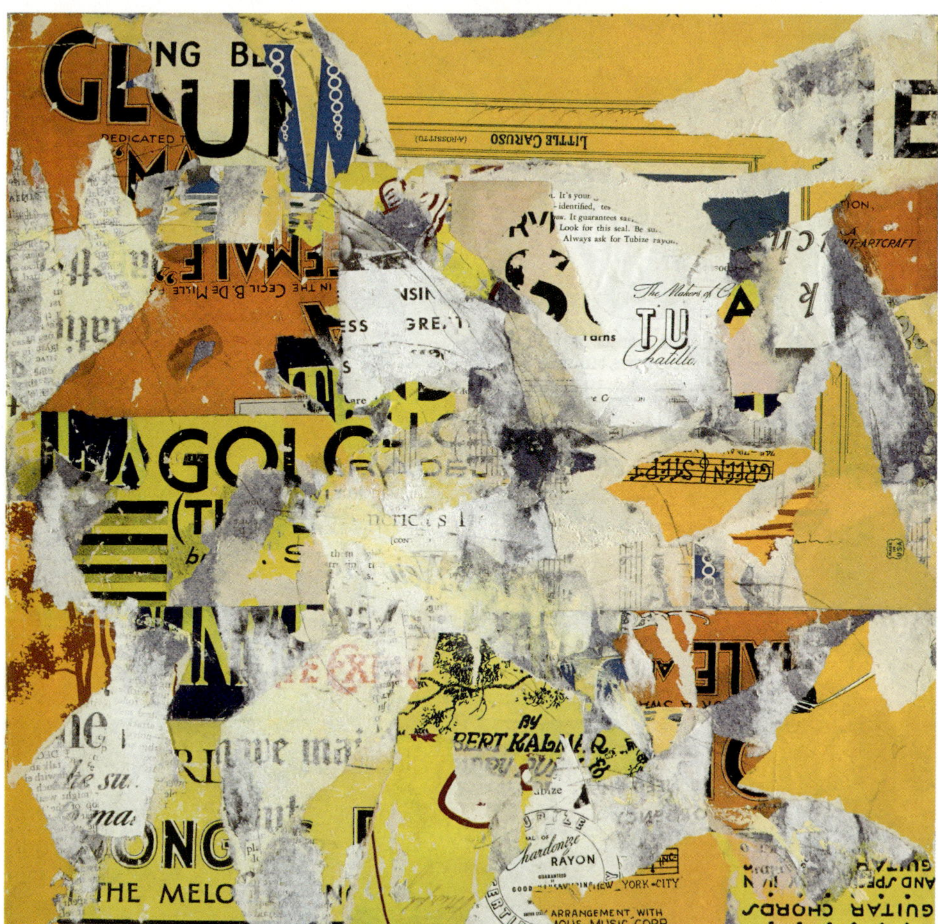

F 25

Susan Reedy, Urban Soliloquy 3, *2009, vintage sheet music and magazines, acrylic, graphite pencil on canvas, 12″ × 12″. Courtesy the artist. Photo credit IMG_INK.*

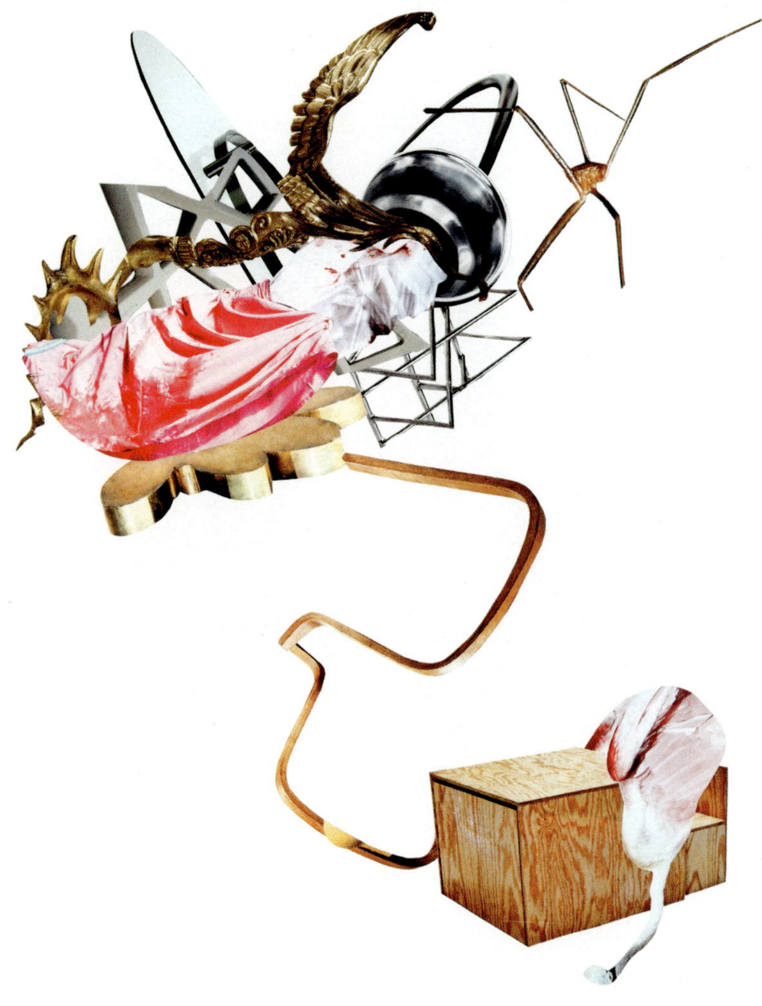

F 26

Barbara F. Kendrick, Evangelus with Sleeping Flamingo, *2012, collage, 25″ × 18″. © Barbara F. Kendrick.*

F 27
*Anat Shiftan,
Garden View
series, 2012,
porcelain with
cobalt blue,
manganese
brown, and black
brushwork,
12″ × 18″ × 4″.*

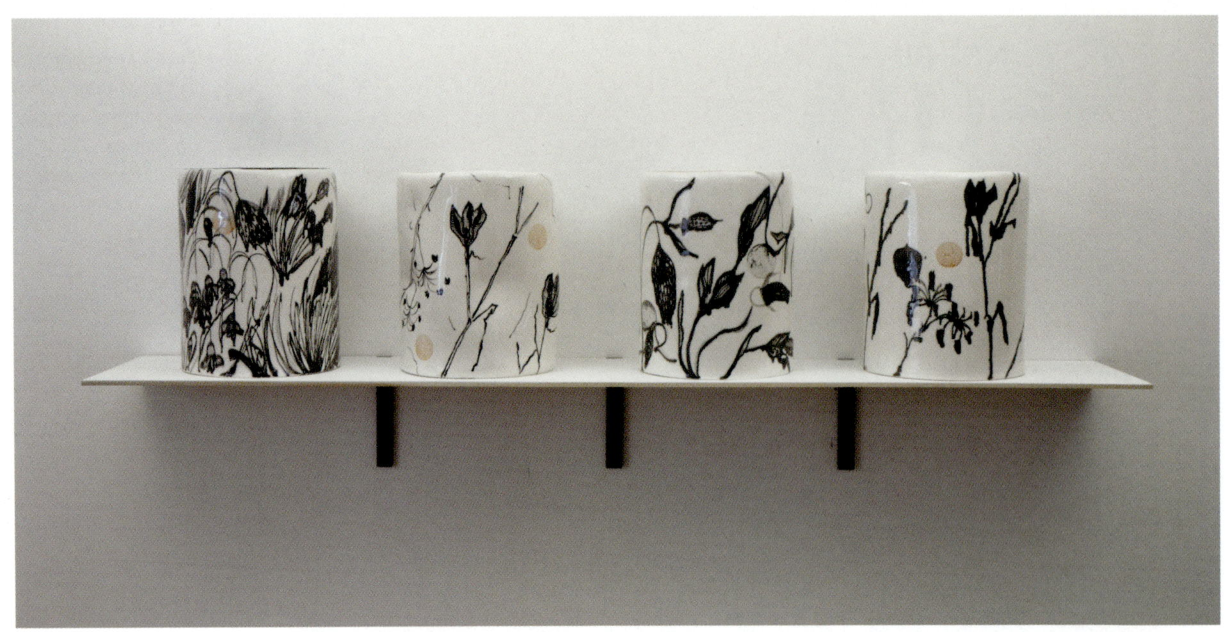

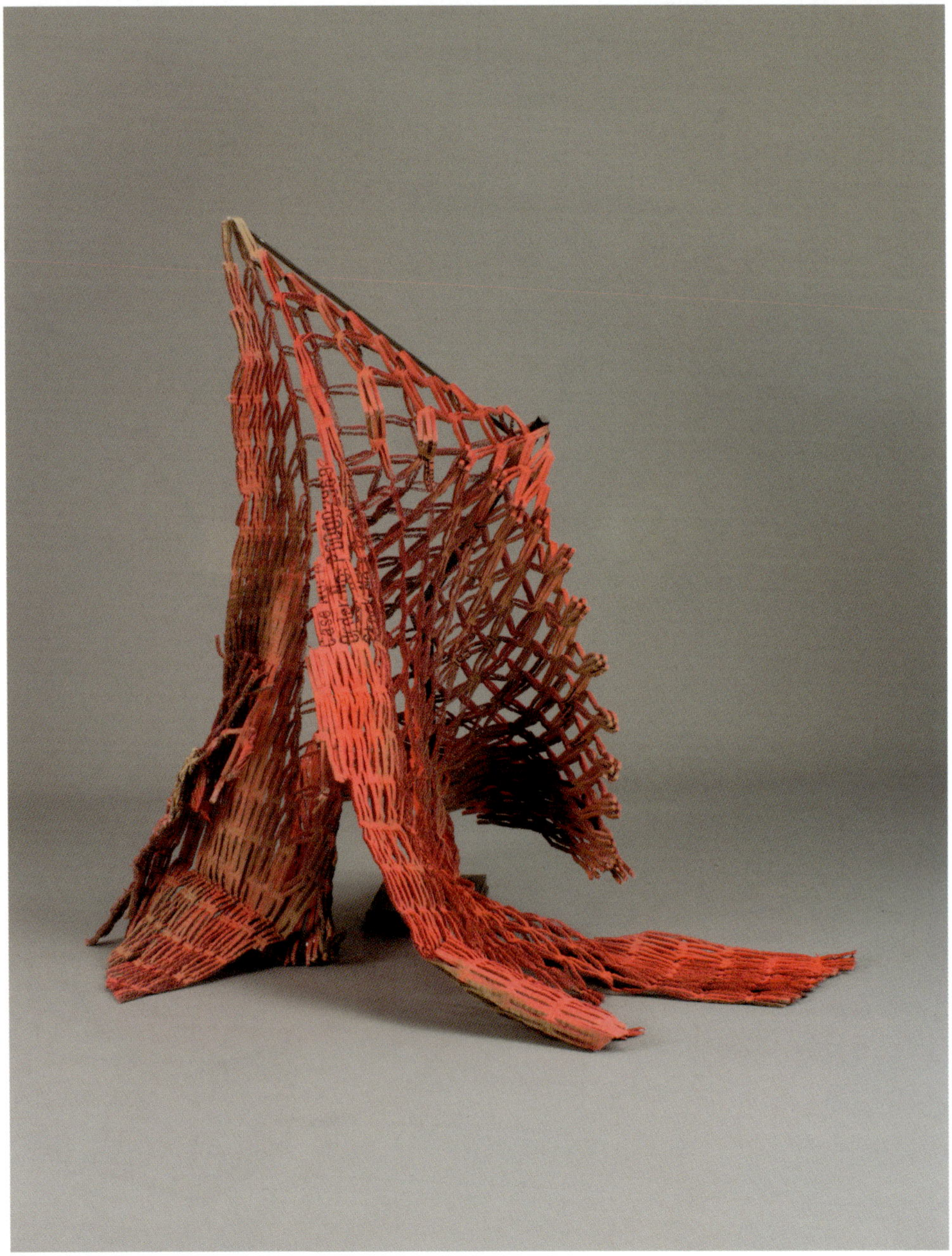

F 28
Todd Baldwin, Untitled, steel
and cardboard, *2011,
29″ × 28″ × 30″. Artist
collection. Image courtesy of
the artist © 2011 Todd Baldwin.*

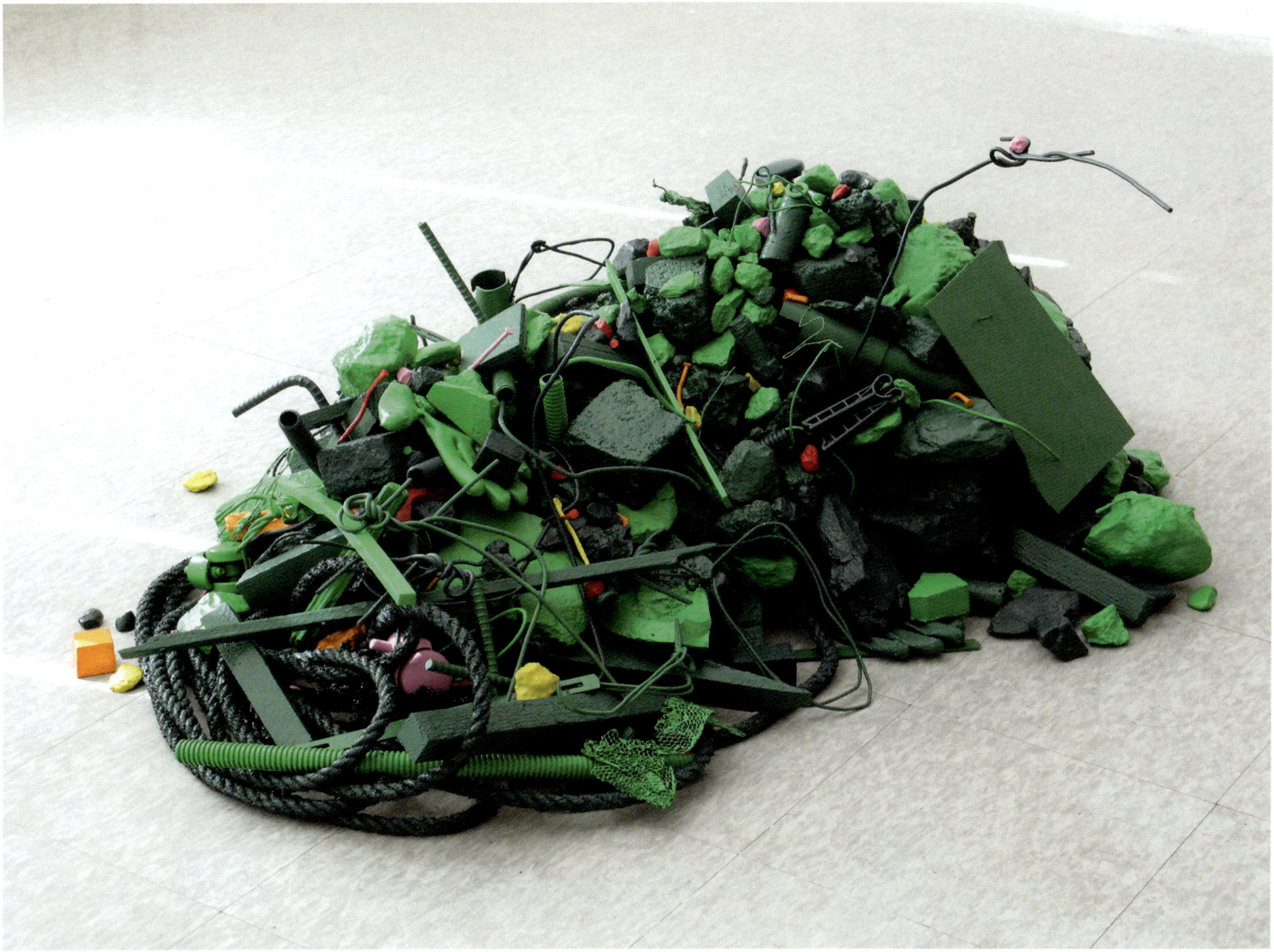

F 29
Sandra Eula Lee, Seeds in a wild garden, 2010, rubber collected from construction sites in Korea, house paints in colors from local gardens, variable dimensions. © Sandra Eula Lee.

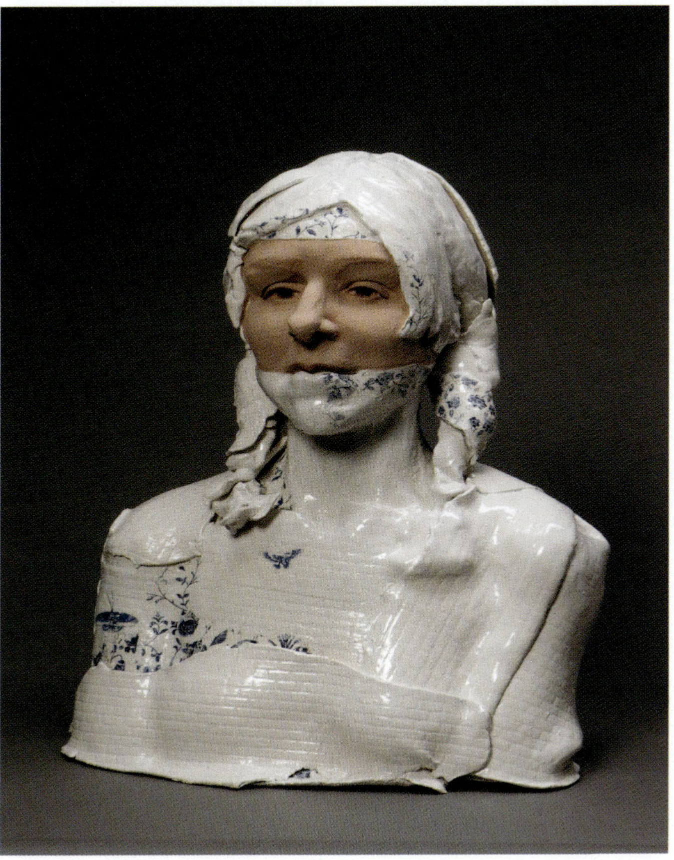

F 30
Jennifer McCandless, Teen Layers, 2012, red and white stoneware, glazed, 28" × 28".

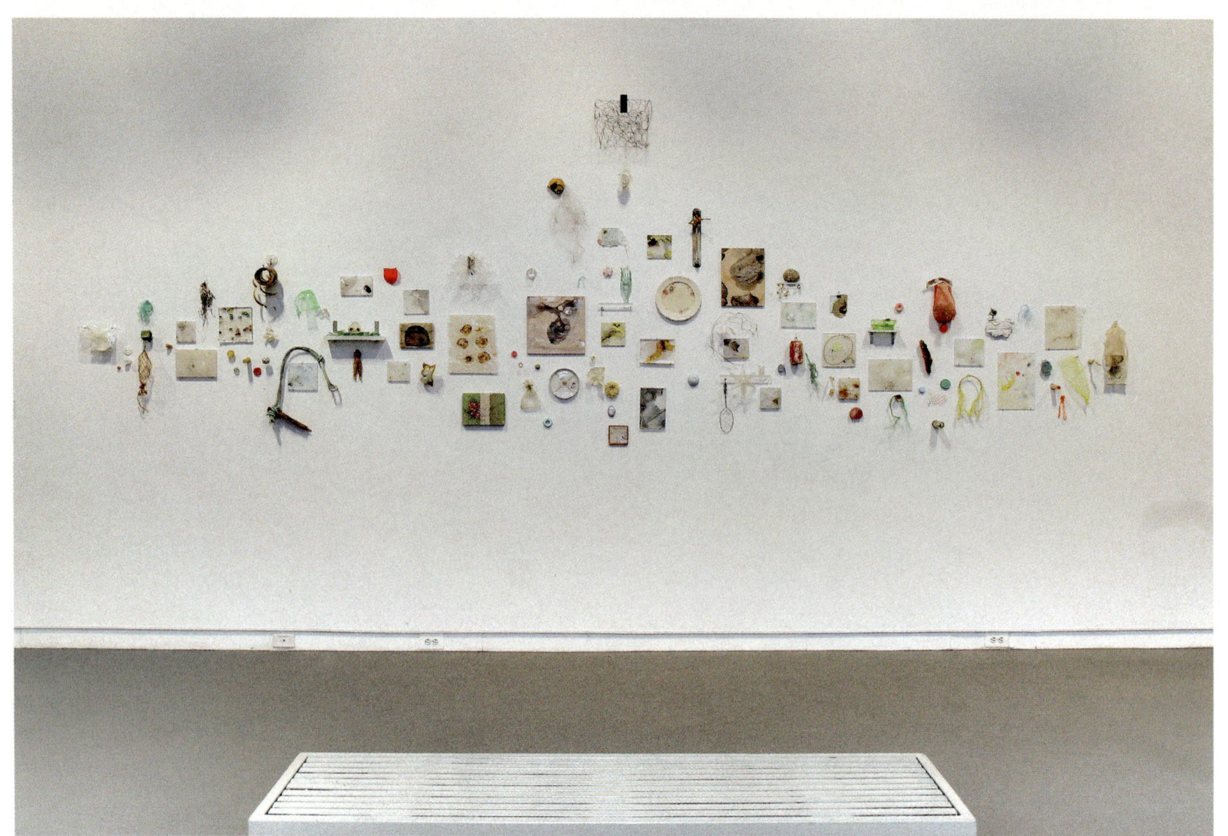

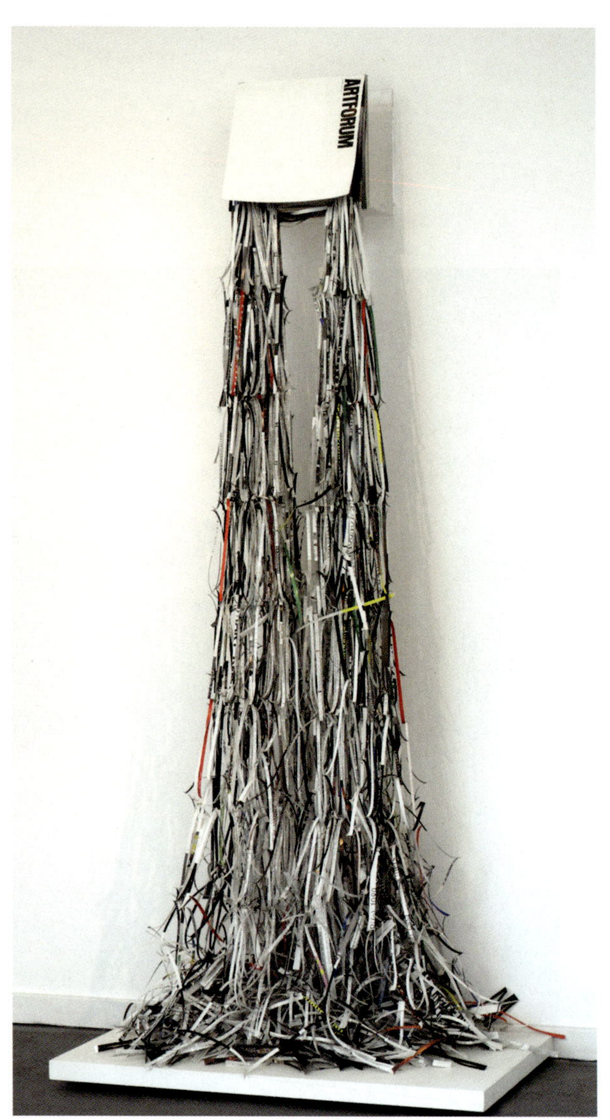

F 32
*Francesca Pastine, ArtForum 43,
Ghost, 2012, artforum magazine,
Plexiglas, screws, wood, 8″ × 10.5″.*

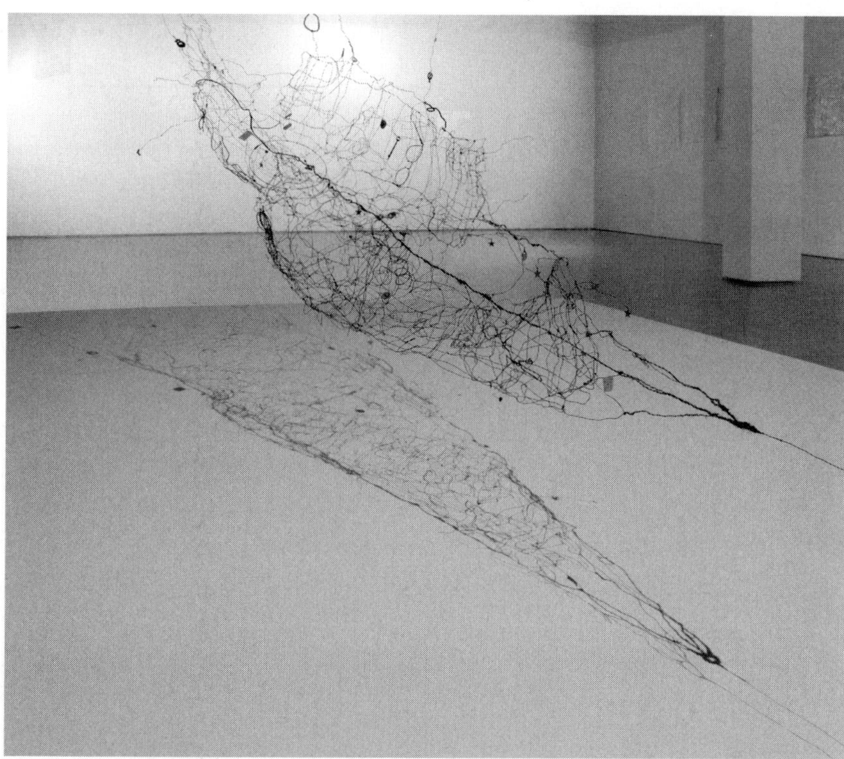

F 6-14b
Tethered Memories Hung Low Beneath the Void, 2011 (detail). Desgined and made by Lois Schklar. Photo by Peter Legris.

Artist Profile: **FRANCESCA PASTINE**

According to Francesca Pastine, the series *Artforum Excavation* uses a variety of material manipulations to "map out a tangle of associations, unique contradictions and paradoxes through curious juxtapositions" (see Figure 32 in the color insert). She aims to "recontextualize content and subvert it" and sees her work as a "meditation on materiality which results in a palpable complexity between form and information." Pastine writes:

I am excited by the potential of material and its transformation through the process of handwork. My work speaks to the physical act of the hand creating—not in the sense of 'gesture', but through intimate care and attentiveness to detail. Informed by time-intensive traditions such as folk art, sewing, and folding, I like to think of my work as falling somewhere between drawing, sculpture, and collage.

I began using ArtForum magazines as a medium for my work in 2008. I had noticed that they were familiar fixtures in my friends' *homes. Apparently, because of their glossy nature, nobody wanted to throw them away. I was intrigued by their square format, particularly when the bloated art market was reflected in their one-inch thickness, and I began asking my friends for their unwanted magazines. Starting with the covers, I cut, bend, manipulate, pull, and dig my way through the magazines, revealing a visceral topography of art trends. The finished work becomes an unsolicited collaboration with the magazine and the cover artist. Maintaining a strong connection to the physicality of drawing, my X-acto blade mimics a pencil, subtracting rather than adding. I eschew glue or other manipulations that change the inherent character of the magazines. In this way, they retain their association to what they are, carriers of information that have been handled, earmarked and scuffed over time. Through physically intervening with these familiar icons of the art establishment, I suffuse the inanimate with emotional power, creating a palpable complexity of form and information.*

Artist Profile: **LEOPOLD VAN DE VEN**

Leopold Van De Ven's work combines wood, papier-mâché, and many other materials to make drawings, collages, and three-dimensional objects (see Figure 6-15). In his work with these assorted media, Van De Ven is interested in both "sensory confrontation" and narrative meaning or story through "forms that brace themselves and as such constitute the visibility of space." Van De Ven writes:

My work is based on the concept of space; to show space and rediscover it, sometimes even in two-dimensional form, but always with the same idea in mind. This is how I see it: two qualities of a drawing are representation and the imagination of depth. An object has a three-dimensional, physical presence and can therefore be an inconvenience. It is tangible, has substance and can hence constitute a drama/tell a story.

What stories, ideas, or references might be suggested in this piece? How do the qualities of the materials themselves and Van De Veld's arrangement and presentation of them in this form contribute to your interpretation?

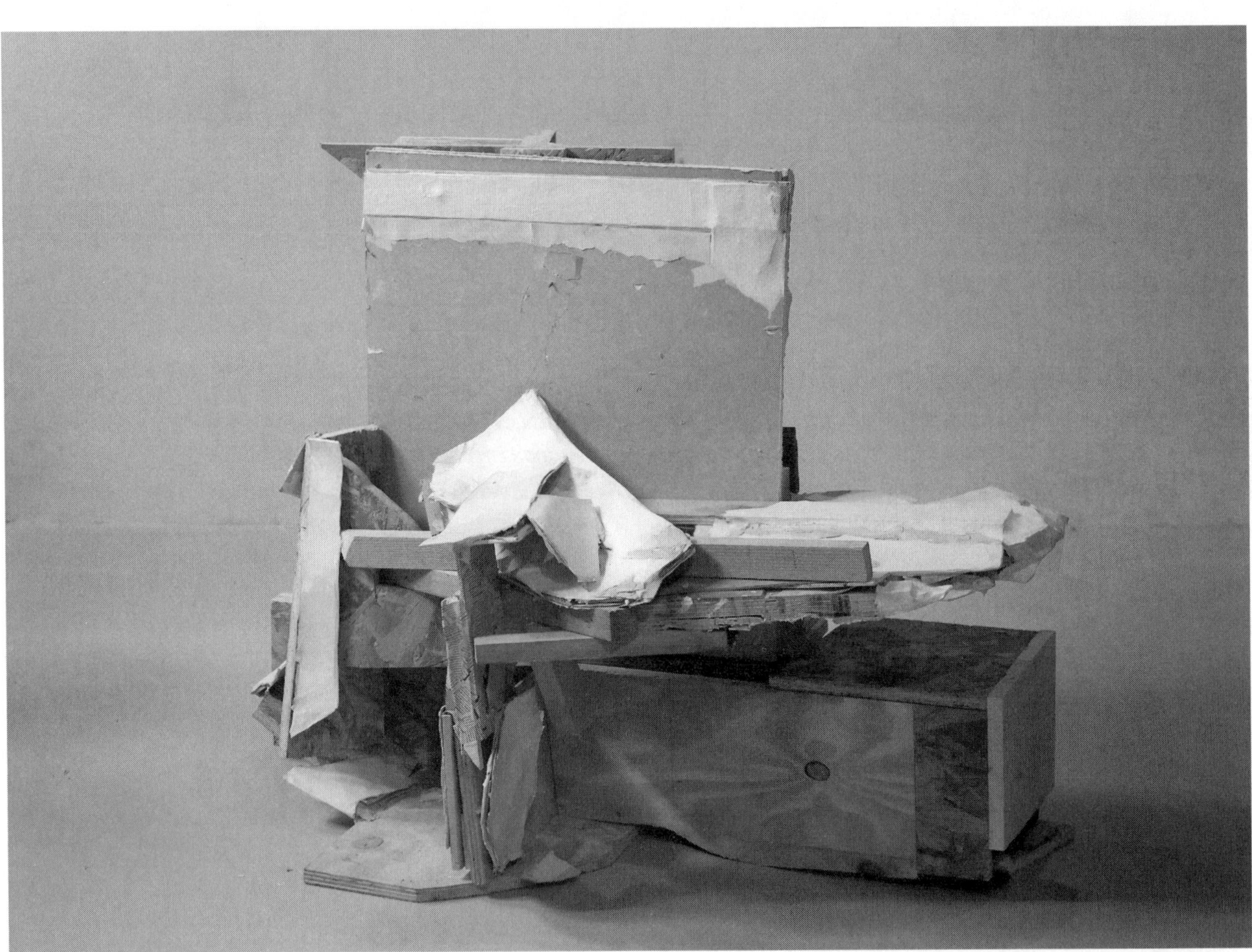

F 6-15

Leopold van De Ven, Untitled, 2013, papier-mache, wood, plaster board, 42" × 35" × 34".

Artist Profile: **ANAT SHIFTAN**

Anat Shiftan's *Still Life* series, part of her larger project titled Looking at Nature, investigates the painterly traditions of the still life in light of globalization and cross-cultural influences (see Figure 6-16 and Figure 27 in the color insert). According to Shiftan, along with other works that also examine nature through lenses of art, history, and global politics, these works are "a springboard for artistic expression; an effort to awaken a sense of wonder in nature; in the magic of looking at reality; the beauty and the ambivalence enfolded in nature; and the political aspect of 'packaging' nature in the art object." She writes:

In her essay On Flowers in Contemporary Art, *curator Edna Moshenson writes that "the flower motif, re-legitimized in art, has an economic aspect today—evidence of a flourishing art market," and that "the addiction to beauty, to the decorative, to pleasure, is a privilege of an affluent society, mainly of the commercial art world." She argues that the flower is also a highly critical and subversive image, and says that the flower image depicted in art today is, rather than a metaphor for the natural cycle of life, a metaphor for the life cycle of art.*

In the Still Life *series, I refer to botanical drawings and historic Still Life paintings. The process of creating impacts the form and meaning of the final object. I use traditional ceramic techniques to create a volumetric ceramic still life rendering that is a response to the history of two-dimensional renderings of that subject in drawing and painting.*

The goal of the process of LOOKING AT NATURE is to awaken wonder and show the fine line between beauty and corruption and the alluring magic of and in nature.

What ideas come to mind as you view this piece? Why do you think this is? How has the artist used form, color, surface treatment, and arrangement of the objects to suggest these ideas? What are the ways that clay has been manipulated to represent very different objects and materials in the piece?

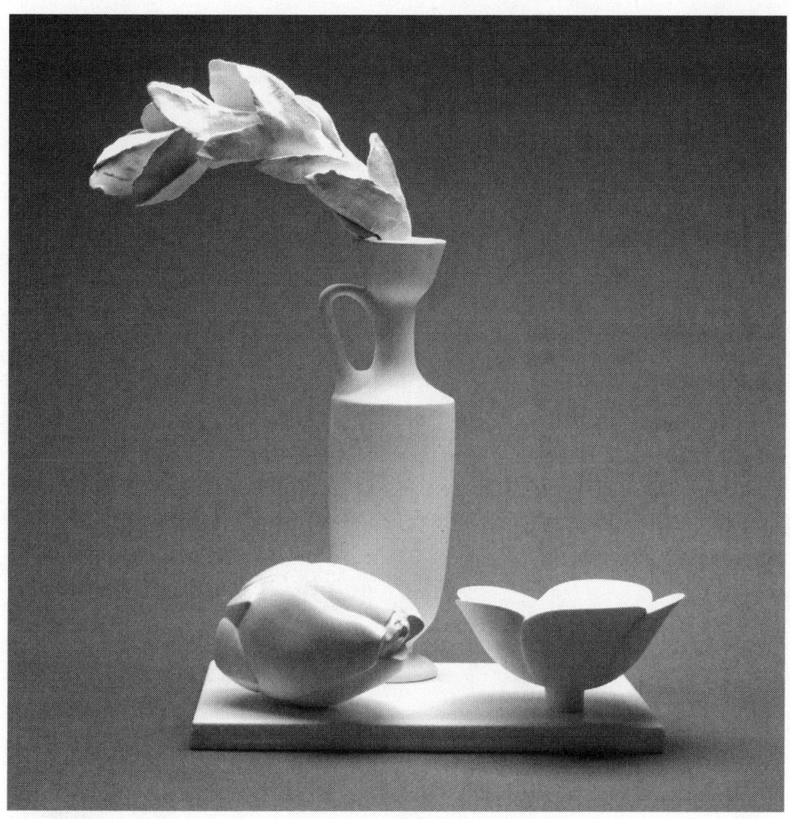

F 6-16
Anat Shiftan, Still Life, 2010, unglazed porcelain, burnished, 16" × 7" × 12".

Artist Profile: **MOREL DOUCET**

Morel Doucet's work is based in part on fantasy and dreams—"whimsical forms resulting in a diary of my personal mythology" (Figure 6-17a and 6-17b). The work is inspired by an interest and respect for "indigenous tribal cultures of the Amazon, Aboriginal natives of Australia, and the Yoruba tribe of West Africa." Doucet is also "fascinated with garments and textiles of Native Americans and Afro-futurism." He says about his work:

My work spans the exquisite spectrum of clean and simple, to the grotesque accumulative take-over of the body. Through writing, drawing and sculpting, I seek to create a dialogue with the natural world while exploring elements of my cultural identity. Examining different exotic cultures of the world has enabled me to connect the dreaming experience as a universal theater of fantasy, nightmare, desire and prophecy. Each work of art is the result of my personal interaction with my dreaming experience. I explore different themes of ambiguity as a means of subverting the borders between my subconscious and the mundane restrictions of society. I work with fragmented narratives and their morphologies to merge them in order to reflect the holistic nature of life.

How does Doucet shape and work the surfaces of clay to convincingly represent human and natural forms? How do the small forms interact with one another, and with the large form from which they emerge? What ideas can be interpreted in both the objects represented and the ways in which the artist has worked with clay to form them?

F 6-17a

Morel Doucet, Leshy and the Traveler, *2013, clay and oil paint, 12″ × 8″ × 10″. (below, left)*

F 6-17b

Morel Doucet, Bloom, *2013, clay, 23″ × 16″ × 18″. (below, right)*

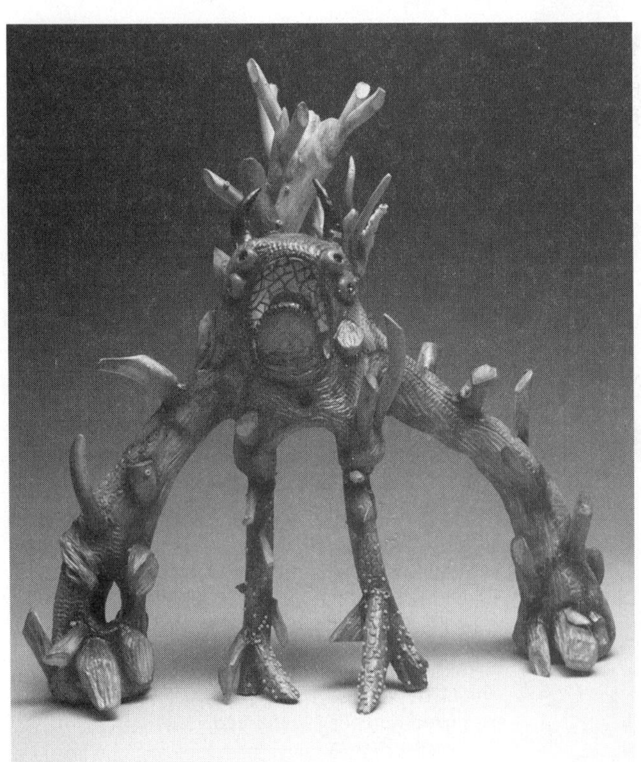

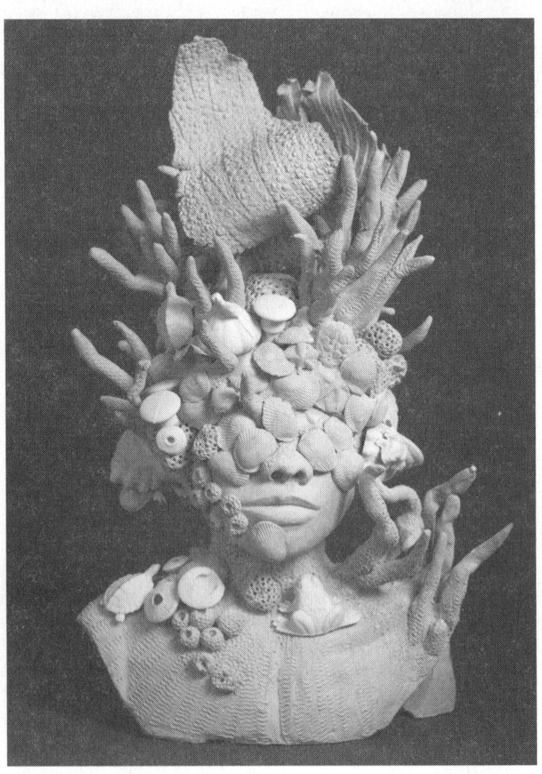

Thoughts about Forming and Building as a Studio Practice

This chapter's focus on constructing objects and forms that have volume features a variety of materials and ways in which to work with them. You have noted throughout the chapter how you might you use some of these techniques in your own lessons for students of different ages. What concepts and skills will you emphasize in your three-dimensional work with students? What broad themes might you ask your students to respond to in their constructions? Consider how you might invite kids to create constructions based on working from observation and imagination, and how you will encourage them to develop narratives of their own experiences in the pieces they create. Also think about how you might sequence construction experiences so that they follow and extend learning in other media. How might a three-dimensional construction lesson build upon a lesson featuring drawing, painting, printmaking, or collage? Discussed in what follows are practical considerations for presenting to kids the techniques for building and forming featured in this chapter.

Setting up for Working with Construction Materials

ESTABLISHING A CLIMATE OF EXPERIMENTAL INQUIRY

In a climate of experimental inquiry in three-dimensional construction, students are invited to consider a large number of materials and asked to imagine how particular things could be used (see Figure 6-18). For example, with clay, I invite the class to brainstorm all of the ways in which the material can be changed with hands and/or tools and ways that parts can be arranged in a construction. We also talk about how different clay shapes can be used in a building a form—what shapes could be arms and legs, torsos and heads, containers and handles, and so on. With wood, pieces, we brainstorm how differently shaped pieces might function—discs might be wheels of a car or bicycle, flat pieces could be walls of a building (see Figure 6-19).

Students both experiment with established technical approaches and are encouraged to invent their own techniques. Here again, they are actively involved in brainstorming, sharing, and demonstrating divergent approaches to building with materials and they collectively troubleshoot ways to solve construction challenges. This exploration of construction techniques, the testing out of different approaches, and group brainstorming of broad themes that encourage individual interpretation builds and encourages ongoing experimental inquiry in the class.

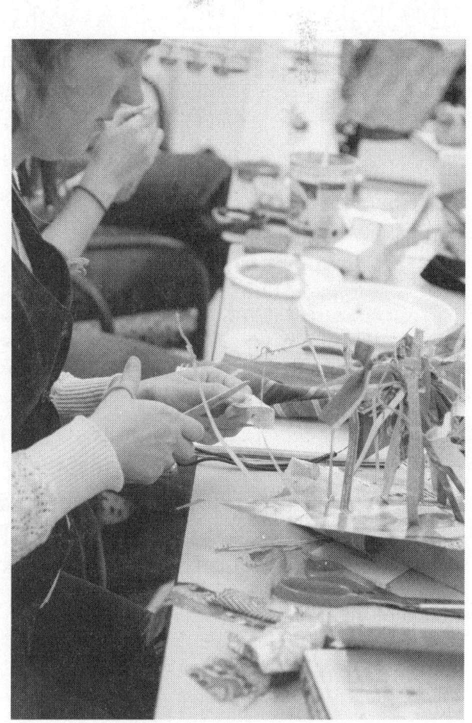

F 6-18: Constructing with assorted materials

MATCHING TIME ALLOTTED AND PROCESSES OF WORKING WITH MEDIA

Three-dimensional construction involves both the processes used to build forms and a consideration of surface treatments and embellishment. Both the building and finishing of the surface can take several class periods to complete. As with other media, it is helpful to think of the process as phases (introduction and initial idea generation, research and media exploration, form construction, and surface embellishment). In this way, lesson content can be designed and planned so that each phase is given ample time and attention to support students' mastery of the materials, techniques, and processes.

CONSIDERING STUDENTS' AGE, PHYSICAL CHARACTERISTICS, AND PRIOR EXPERIENCE

Once again, students' age, strength, coordination, and prior experience with construction will help to determine the techniques and approaches to use with particular classes. While all of the approaches presented in this chapter can be scaled and adapted for different abilities and ages, starting with limited materials and tools and gradually introducing new options ensures continued exploration in three-dimensional construction just as it does in other media.

BALANCING EFFICIENCY WITH STUDENT AUTONOMY

As with collage, sorting materials by type and setting up their distribution so that students can easily select materials and tools with which they would like to work invites independent judgment and artistic autonomy. At certain points throughout the construction activity, having students work in pairs on each other's work can provide an extra set of hands to support forms as they are constructed and encourage additional solutions to structural problems.

ANTICIPATING MESS AND PLANNING FOR CLEANUP

As with other media, have students wear smocks when working with messy materials, cover work surfaces, and communicate processes for cleaning spills. For cleanup at the end of the class period, clearly establish how works in progress and finished works will be collected and where they will be stored, how tools will be cleaned, if necessary, and collected, how work spaces will be tidied, and how students will wash their hands if needed.

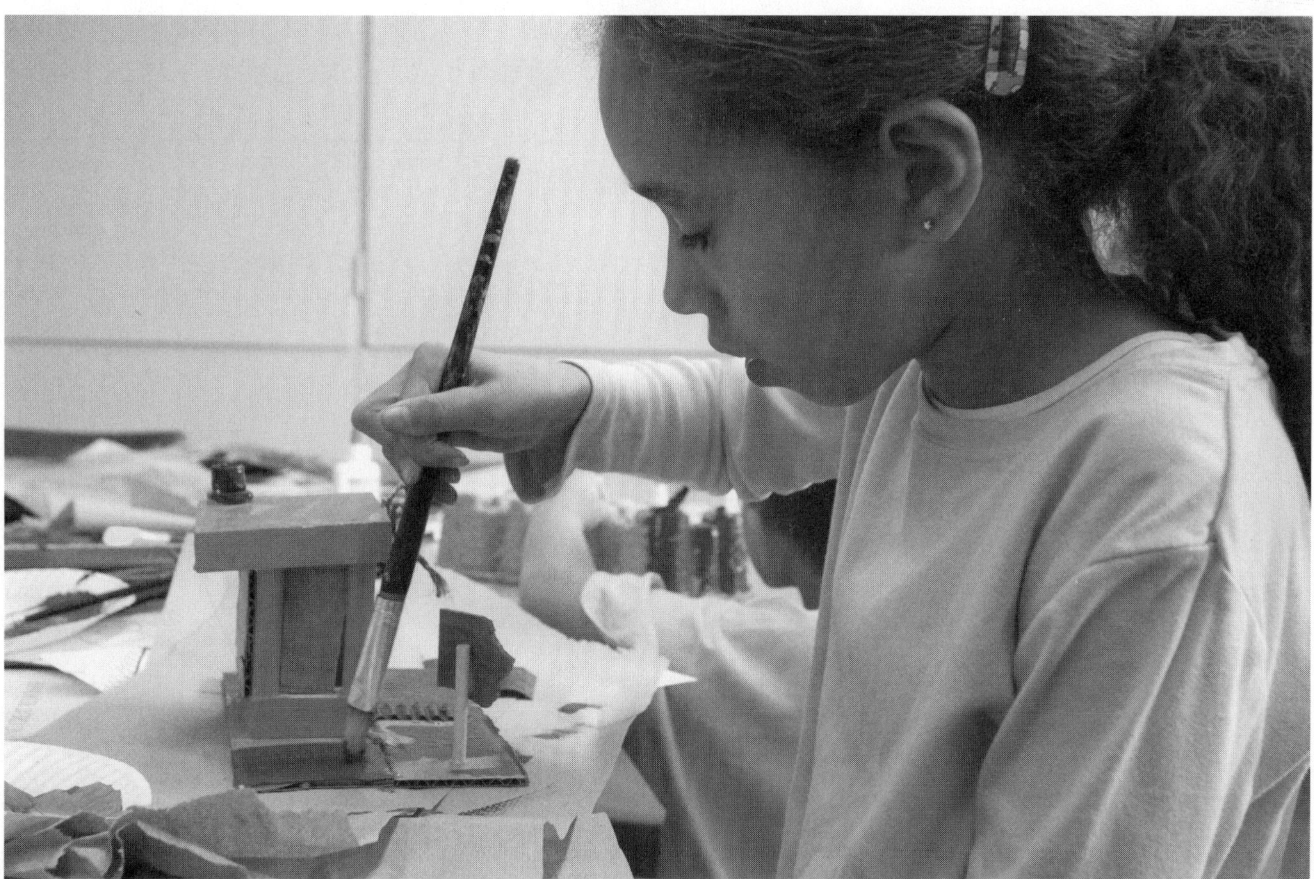

REFLECTING ON AND ARTICULATING LEARNING

F 6-19: Painting mixed media construction

At different points in the lesson, invite students to share what they are discovering and learning how to do throughout the working process. At the end of each work period, ask them to share how they selected, altered, and attached materials, the interesting effects they were able to achieve, the problems they encountered and solved, and the thematic ideas in their work. As with all other media, brief written explanations about the goal of the construction experience and what was learned in individual approaches creates an archive of skills, concepts, and ways of thinking that can be used as a resource in other lessons and in displays of students' finished works.

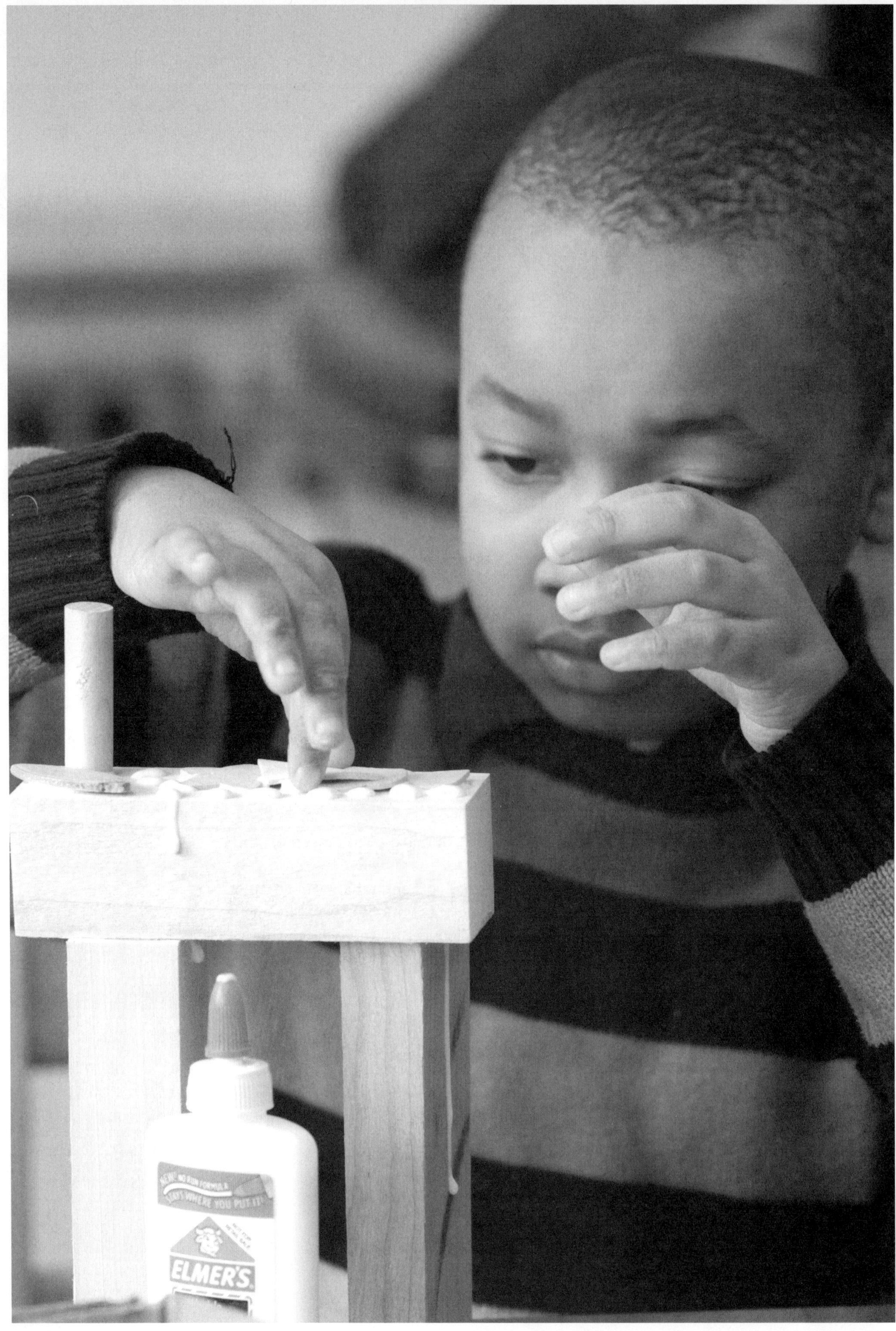

Building with wood

7

Articulating Studio Learning Outcomes and Planning for Meaningful Instruction

It seems so evident that we, as teachers, must keep our questions open—the thronging questions about particular art forms and about art itself and about the place of art in human life.

—**Maxine Greene**[1]

---

[1] M. Greene (2001). *Variations on a blue guitar: The Lincoln Center Institute lectures on aesthetic education* (p. 37). New York, NY: Teachers College Press.

THIS CHAPTER IS ABOUT SOME of the concepts and skills that can be taught through studio activities, both within this book's emphasis on the expressive potential of materials and within the broader arena of art making. It also revisits the dispositional elements of artistic thinking and practice as these play into planning lessons and curricula. With these considerations in mind—and with a focus on students as artists and learners, themes and approaches in historical and contemporary art, ways of structuring and sequencing lessons, and the instructional practices that encourage students to engage in creative studio practice—we now put your new insights about materials into practice in planning for studio teaching.

In the following sections, you are invited to apply and synthesize your insights about the properties of materials—as well as your understanding of their uses and expressive potential—as you design studio-based lessons. Rather than dictating visually and conceptually uniform outcomes, your lessons will encourage and support young people to construct artworks based in their intentions, their inventions, and their meanings (see Figure 7-1). Hopefully, the studio explorations featured in the preceding chapters have helped you to develop a broad understanding of different materials and clarified some processes, techniques, and expressive ends for which they can be used. These insights about materials, although essential, are but one component of the pedagogical knowledge needed to plan for substantive and meaningful art experiences for students. As art teachers, we also need to identify the concepts, skills, and ways of thinking we will teach (related to materials, formal content, narrative ideas, representation, and art ideas from historical and contemporary practices) and understand our students as artists and learners so that we can develop effective instructional approaches. Finally, we need to design lessons and curricula that provide purposeful direction for our work with students—and we need to foster vibrant and productive studio classroom environments and assess both the learning of our students and the effectiveness of our own teaching.

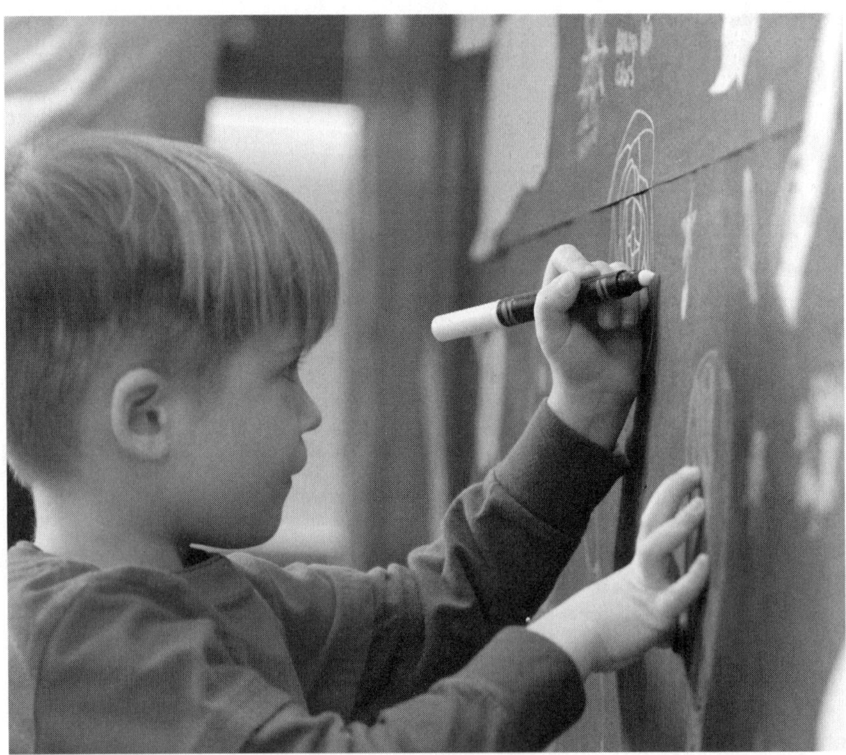

F 7-1: Mural drawing in art class

Young Artists as Learners

In my own studio teaching, selecting content begins with my understanding of who my students are as artists and learners. This global understanding of my students includes insights about their development over time and with respect to particular needs and characteristics (cognitive, social, emotional, language, physical, artistic).[2] It also includes my knowledge of their lives, cultures, and individual interests. Finally, and most important for me, my understanding of my students as artists and learners includes both an awareness of the kinds of ideas that can emerge from all of these considerations—ideas students may be interested in making art *about*—and my understanding of the different sources students draw upon in forming images and expressing ideas in their artwork. Insights about the ways in which young people grow and develop as artists are critical to my ability to appropriately calibrate my teaching—in other words, to identify the capacities my students already have as artists and anticipate the new skills, understandings, and ways of thinking they are ready to learn and practice. While it is beyond the scope of this book to provide a comprehensive analysis of young people's artistic development, the following overview presents some of the developmental considerations teachers need to take into account when planning art experiences for young people.[3]

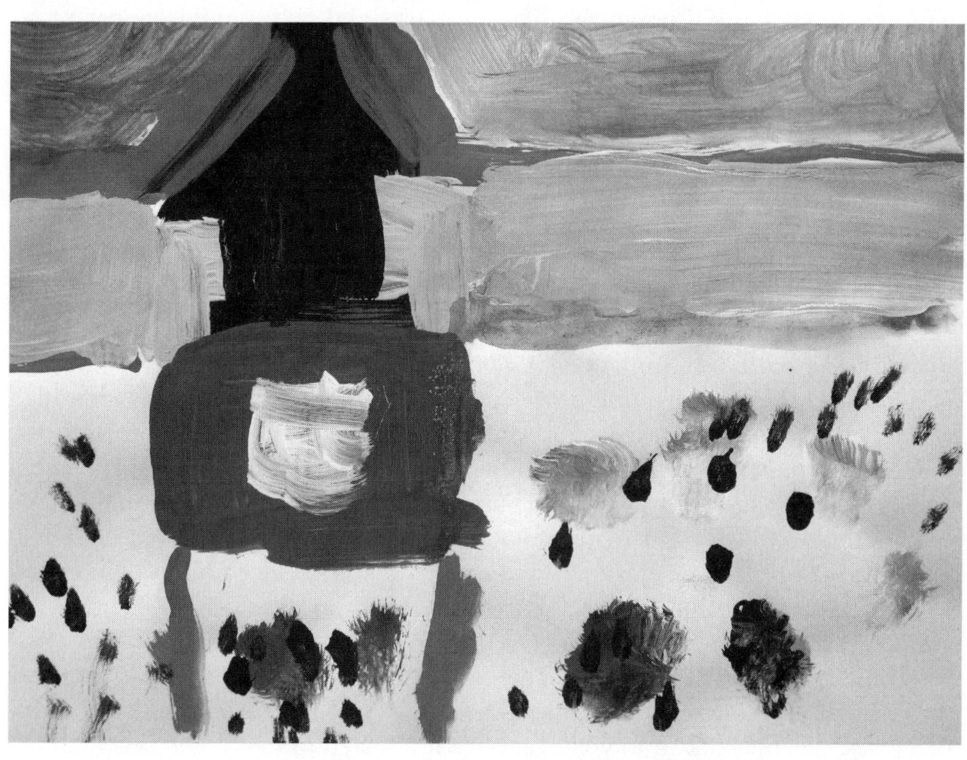

F 7-2: Tempera painting

---

[2] For a detailed description of young people's cognitive, emotional/moral, social, language, physical/perceptual, and aesthetic development, see Kerlavage's (1998) chapter, "Understanding the Learner," in Simpson et al., *Creating Meaning through Art* (pp. 23–72).

[3] This abbreviated account draws from a summary of artistic development presented in Burton and Bildstein's (2010) *Challenging Thinking: Possibilities and Potentials for Teaching and Learning in the Visual Arts*. For additional sources, see Burton (2000), Kindler (1997, 2004), Smith (1993, 1998), and Thompson (1995).

OVERVIEW OF ARTISTIC DEVELOPMENT

This brief synopsis of issues in artistic development begins with young children and their encounters with art materials. Early learning comes from discovering through play that materials like pencils, markers, and crayons can be used to make marks on a surface. Different actions of the hand or arm holding the material—sweeping, tapping, arcing, looping, moving up and down or side to side, pressing firmly or lightly—result in correspondingly distinctive lines and shapes. Other kinds of materials such as clay, paper, and paint promote different kinds of actions. Clay can be mushed and molded and pulled apart into shapes of various kinds, while paper can be folded, rolled, crunched up, or torn into pieces. Paint can be spread across an entire surface or used only in particular places, and can look different ways on the paper depending on how much is on the brush. Along with actions and the marks and forms that come from them, young children invent increasingly elaborate organizations, or arrangements, of marks. They create enclosures that serve as distinct places for organizing marks on a surface—marks can be made inside and outside of enclosed areas. And young children divide up the surface in a variety of other ways, creating designs with several, often repeating, parts. What children learn through their early explorations of different materials is that each material has certain physical properties (dry/wet, smooth/sticky, thick/thin), visual qualities (transparency/opacity, color, texture), and plastic or manipulative characteristics (pliability, movement, stackability). From using materials to create and organize different marks and forms children learn that lines and shapes, and the ways in which they are arranged, have relational possibilities (big/small, top/bottom, light/dark, near together/far apart). As they continue to gain experience with materials, young children learn that all of these qualities can suggest or express different ideas and feelings—and that drawings, paintings, and three-dimensional constructions can be "about" some part of their experience in or thoughts about their worlds (see Figure 7-2).

At some point, depending on the amount and types of experiences they have had with materials, young children start to name their images and constructions. This often happens after the work is made, but may happen while the work is in process and eventually naming will happen at the outset. While it may be difficult for adults to see the connection between the artwork and its subject as identified by the child, naming is based on a connection the child has made between the image or construction, the qualities of its materials, and a familiar idea, person, object, or other aspect drawn from immediate experience (for example circle shapes may be wheels of a car, even though the body of the car may not be shown in the image). Since these early representations are about children's emotional experiences of things, people, and places—not how they "see" them—elements of the images are often sized according to their prominence in the child's life.

Children's experiences with people and activities expand as they grow older and these direct experiences and observations, as well as remembered and imagined ones, become central to what they are interested in making artwork about. At the same time, children include more and more narrative and design details in their artworks. This leads to new ways of organizing, both in two-dimensional painting and drawing (defining areas such as ground and sky, for example, and placing figures and other subjects accordingly) and in three-dimensional constructions. These new ways of organizing in drawing and painting also support children's developing ideas about and interests in accounting for three-dimensional space in their visual narratives—for example, figures and objects that are meant to be at some distance may appear higher on the page.

For younger children, sizes of figures and objects may be relative to their emotional importance or to their centrality to a visual narrative. As they grow older, young people's works show increasing attention to presenting things as they appear—adult figures are larger than figures of children, houses are larger than people, and so forth. As their range of experience and interest continues to expand, visual narratives grow in potential topics and subjects. In addition to topics focused on people and activities in their immediate environment children become interested in things happening in other places and at other times. In painting and drawing, their works become more detailed and include an increasing number of elements. New ways of thinking about three-dimensional space on the two-dimensional surface and inventing strategies for representing larger amounts of information become an important part of children's art practice.

As young people's learning about the world expands with age and experiences, so too does their source material for making works in clay, paint, ink, and other media. Interests move from self and immediate worlds to self in relation to others, people's relationships with one another and with their environments, how things work in the world, the context of social rules and the conventions that guide human behavior and action, and issues of truth, justice, and morality.

Older children also become interested in how others perceive them and this extends to their artwork in a variety of ways. They often are intent on creating images that are convincing to others in their presentation of narrative ideas or themes. They are also frequently concerned with making (and they sometimes struggle to create) visual representations that they deem "accurate" depictions of things they observe, imagine, believe, or feel. Older students' capacity to judge their own work in relation to a concern for rightness and realness leads to a desire to learn art conventions like perspective, human and animal proportions, and foreshortening. Students' desire for creating convincing portrayals also leads them to want to learn more refined techniques with materials—such as chiaroscuro, a use of light and dark to achieve a sense of volume in three-dimensional objects depicted in a drawing or painting, or ways of altering the surface of clay to suggest hair, skin, fur, clothing, and so on in human and animal figures.

During this time as they grow throughout childhood and adolescence, changes in physical characteristics and developing cognitive, social, emotional, linguistic,

F 7-3a
Haydee Naula, Untitled, 2013, mixed media on paper, 18" × 20". (below, left)

F 7-3b
Haydee Naula, Untitled, 2013 (detail). (below, right)

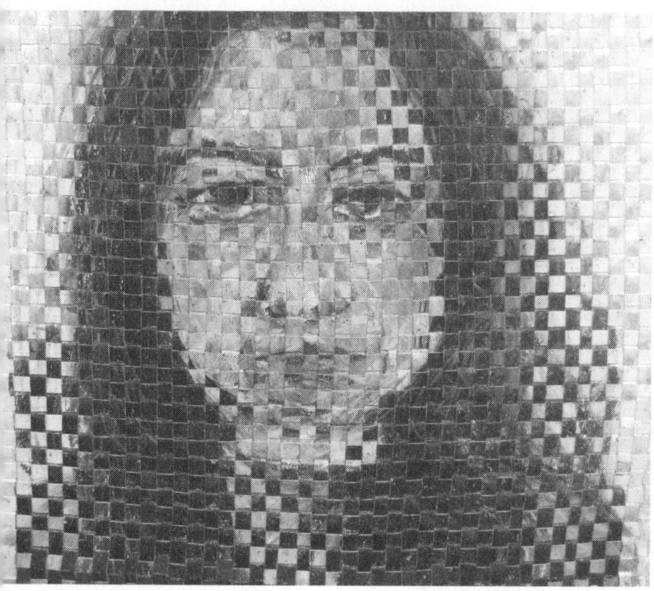

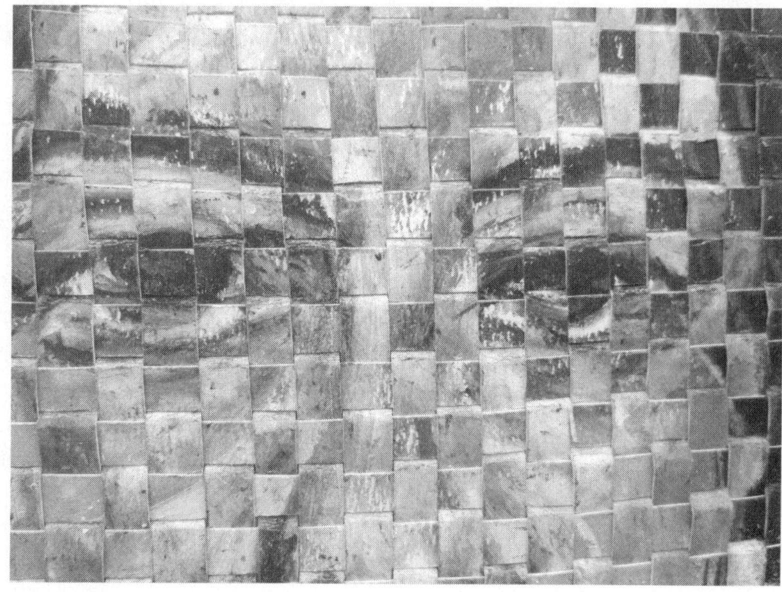

and moral capacities lead young people to experience art making in new ways. They approach materials from new vantage points, develop new insights about formal issues such as line, color, texture, space, and volume, and expand upon their sense of what art is and can be about (see Figures 7-3a and 7-3b). We turn next to sources and inspirations for young people's art ideas and the contexts from which they draw as they make studio works.

SOURCES OF AND CONTEXTS FOR YOUNG PEOPLE'S ART IDEAS AND PRACTICES

Young people's inspirational focuses for their artworks are based in not only their own developing experiences in and of the world but also their growing capacities to observe and imagine events and topics that are further away from everyday experience.

Many of Burton and Bildstein's (2010) examples of different kinds of lessons and Chapman's (1978) "sources of inspiration" for art offer a useful sampling of the ways in which artists, both children and adults, form ideas for art making. In turn, these considerations can lead to lessons that are framed or oriented to address and support students' natural inclinations for making art. For example, within 11 different focuses for lessons, Burton and Bildstein's orientations include exploratory (playing with a material, practice, or idea), observation (translating close and careful looking to material representation), memory (recalling or speculating about past events or experiences), imagination (reinterpreting ideas and events), material (vigorously exploring possible uses and combinations of materials), inventing (trying out, combining, recombining ideas and materials), fine art (understanding ideas that change over time and the work and practices of artists), and popular culture (investigating contemporary images, objects, and ideas, including their powers of influence) (pp. 22–23). All of these suggestions for framing lessons fit with young people's artistic interests and with their goals for their artwork at different ages and levels of experience.

Alternatively, Chapman (1978, pp. 46–57) describes several "sources of inspiration" and "means of elaborating ideas" that guide the practices of adult artists—and these, too, can be applied to young people's studio work. Chapman's inspirational sources include *natural and constructed environments, inner feelings and imagination, quest for order,* and *ordinary experience.* Her description of varied artists' practices includes *observing and making visual studies, changing habits of work* ("shifting gears" in service of the work at hand), *exploring meanings and symbolism,* and *considering purposes and means* (identifying what is to be expressed or created and how it will be accomplished).

In my own research interviewing teens about their approaches and ideas as artists (Hafeli 2002, 2012), I found that young people bring to their studio experiences a long list of sources for developing content in art making, including several that are inherent in the process itself. For example, teens may understand their art to be about such concerns as:

1. formal aspects (line, shape, color, etc.) and their expressive effects,
2. properties of art materials and their expressive effects,
3. representing people, objects, etc. through observation,
4. representing real or imagined experiences and events,
5. representing ideas, feelings, and beliefs,

6. representing ideas through symbolism,
7. development of skill and ability, or the artwork as a record of and opportunity for getting better at doing something,
8. contexts of school and learning, including learning in art class and learning in other subjects,
9. contexts of art worlds, including contemporary and historical practices and ideas, and
10. contexts of cultures, including personal, family, local, and world cultures.

Many of the sources and influences on students' artwork that I found relate to the Burton and Bildstein's (2010) lesson ideas and Chapman's (1978) inspirational sources for art making. In preparing to select lesson content and design learning experiences for young people, it is important for teachers to both consider the sources of children's and teens' ideas for creating art and explicitly plan for students' meanings, interests, and prior knowledge and experience to be part of the studio experience. It is also essential to have a full understanding of children's artistic development at different ages and levels of experience. In doing so, teachers will effectively meet student artists where they are at in their studio thinking and practice. More important, they will teach content that not only fits with but also extends artistic skills, interests, dispositions, and capacities—with an awareness of and respect for students' own concerns for their work (see Figure 7-4).

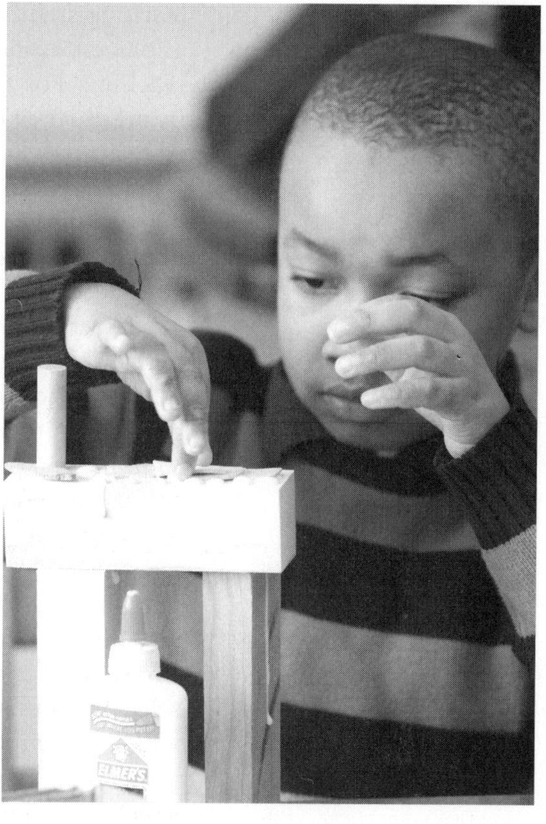
F 7-4: Building with wood

Note: Aligning instruction with students' ideas, interests, and developmental capacities as artists: Think back again to some of your early art making experiences and the ideas, themes, and topics in which you were interested as a young artist. What kinds of personal ideas do you remember making drawings, paintings, and three-dimensional works about? In what ways did the kinds of art projects you were invited to do fit with and encourage your own ideas for making art? If you have access to children, ask them about their ideas as artists and what subjects and themes they like to address in their work. If you are observing art classes in a school, compare kids' interests as artists, as you understand them, to the kinds of studio activities you see presented in art class. In what ways are students' ideas and expressive interests invited, supported, and extended through the content of lessons presented in the art class?

Developing Content for Art Lessons

Art making, with its wide-ranging practices spanning cultures, geographical locations, historical periods, and contemporary approaches, has no shortage of potential content for teaching. If you have conducted field observations of teaching and learning in a variety of educational settings, you have undoubtedly noticed that lesson and curriculum content, styles of teaching, and teachers' ways of interacting with students can look very different from one art class, and one teacher, to another. Many teachers align their instruction with national, state, or local learning standards or a curriculum shared within a school or district, but this alignment usually is not considered a constricting force in planning content for teaching. For the most part, art teachers have the opportunity to shape and frame their work with students based on highly individualized ideas—about what art is, what art making entails, who students are as artists and learners, the knowledge, skills, and ways of thinking (dispositions) that are essential for students to develop and practice in art class, and the instructional approaches that are best for accomplishing goals for student learning that are shaped from these considerations.

Describing the specific learning outcomes for curriculum and lesson plans is both an exciting and daunting task for beginning art teachers and those preparing to teach. The process is one of (1) content selection, (2) analysis, in which you break down art processes and experiences to identify concepts, skills, and ways of thinking and practice that will be taught and learned, and (3) synthesis, in which you use carefully chosen words to clearly and concisely describe the particular learning that you have identified as a focus. The wide range of art content for teaching and learning presents both opportunities and challenges for art teachers. For while a high degree of curricular flexibility is a welcome benefit of teaching art, this lack of specific requirements means that teachers have an enormous world of ideas and topics from which to choose. As an art teacher, how do you select from this vast pool of possibilities the instructional content on which you will focus your teaching? And as curriculum and lesson plans call for some sort of rationale or reasons for the content contained in them, how will you justify your selections as being essential, relevant, and appropriate learning for your particular students at a given point in time?

As we have seen, in planning curriculum art teachers take into account students' characteristics as artists and learners at various points in their development. The knowledge, skills, and ways of thinking that are deemed important for young people to develop and practice in art class, and the instructional approaches that are best for accomplishing these goals for student learning, spring from these considerations. In my practice as a studio art teacher, the elements outlined above form the core and purpose of my work with students. Concretizing the elements—clarifying and articulating my own understanding about art, students, and teaching—provides me with a "big picture" of what I want to accomplish with my students over time. I periodically revisit these elements because my views about these considerations change over time as contemporary art content changes, and as students and what they bring to the learning experience also change. The questions that guide the formation and ongoing revision of my extended goals for teaching are:

1. What should students know?
2. What should they be able to do?
3. What should they "be like"?

All of the other parts—broad curriculum frameworks, individual units/segments and lessons, instructional approaches and strategies, the fostering of a particular kind of art class ambiance, and other considerations—follow from there.

There is no right or wrong place to start in forming your own big picture and overarching goals for student learning. I find it helpful to begin with the particular ways of thinking and studio practices that I want to instill in my students—the "What should student-artists be like?" question—in contrast to the

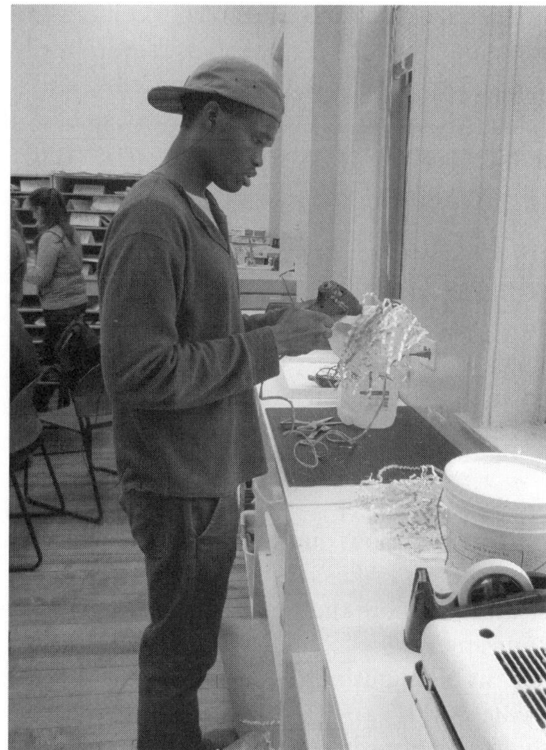

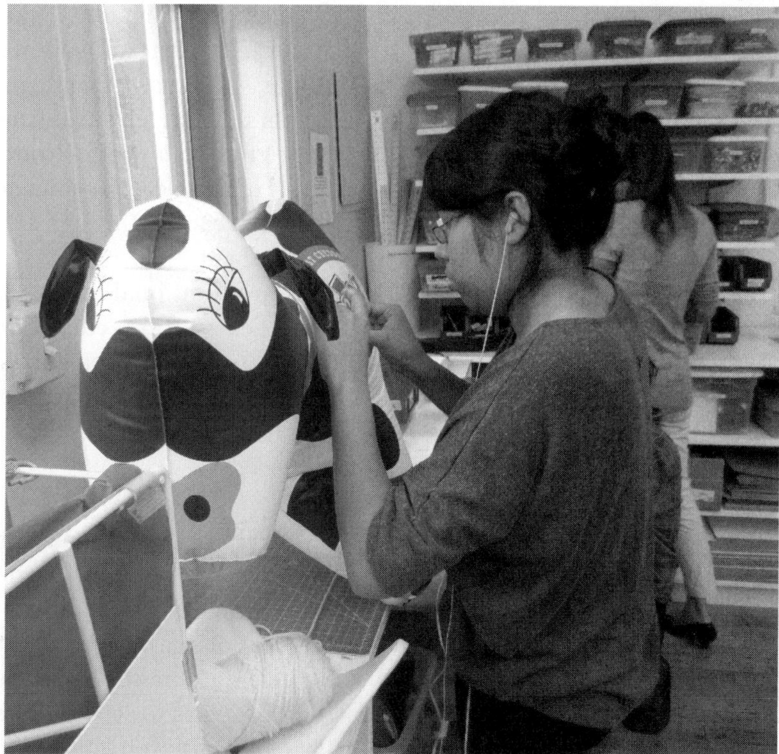

conceptual knowledge and skills on which I will ultimately also focus our lessons and curriculum. I do this because starting with essential artistic dispositions and practices and using them collectively as a filter for other content helps me to select from the vast, unwieldy, and constantly growing pool of art knowledge and skills those learning outcomes that will encourage and advance the ways of thinking I want my students to develop. I also believe that teachers tend to focus too narrowly on knowledge and skills—because they have been taught or may be mandated to do so—and as a result artistic ways of thinking are not sufficiently made explicit or are left out altogether. Finally, artistic dispositions are often thought to be more difficult to assess. For me, this is all the more reason to focus on this critical component of studio production and develop ways to effectively document it in student learning.

F 7-5a: Aaron Barksdale, work in progress. (above, left)

F 7-5b: Haydee Naula, work in progress. (above, right)

ARTISTIC WAYS OF THINKING AND PRACTICE

The analysis of artists' statements in Chapter 1 is an excellent place to begin when thinking about goals for student learning that have to do with artistic dispositions and practices. The statements themselves make clear that artists both recognize and value the complexity of thought and action that studio work entails. By understanding what needs to be taken into account, worked through, and resolved as artists create their work—and putting that together with their own sense of what studio work entails and their understanding of students as artists and learners—art teachers can integrate artists' perspectives on studio thinking and action with other important considerations as they envision and plan art classroom experiences (see Figures 7-5a and 7-5b).

The analysis in Chapter 1 highlights essential artistic practices and dispositions—like problem finding and solving, flexible purposing, originality, perseverance, risk taking, tolerance of ambiguity and uncertainty, belief in the process, and willingness to delay closure—that are central to the art making processes of a particular group of artists. From my perspective and experience as an artist and teacher, all of these can be considered as core elements of studio practice, and can be taught and learned through art class experiences that are purposefully designed to promote them.

There are additional considerations that come from the work of other researchers in the fields of art, education, and psychology. For example, Elliot Eisner's (2002, pp. 70–92) list of learning outcomes in the arts, developed over a sustained consideration of this topic (he published an early, related list in 1978), contains the following "lessons the arts teach" that are relevant to this discussion. According to Eisner, the arts:

1. "teach children to make good judgments about qualitative relationships," rather than relying on correct answers and rules, as in other disciplines,
2. "teach children that problems can have more than one solution and that questions can have more than one answer,"
3. "celebrate multiple perspectives," in highlighting the idea that "there are many ways to see and interpret the world,"
4. "teach children that in complex forms of problem solving, purposes are seldom fixed but change with circumstance and opportunity," necessitating "an ability and willingness to surrender to the unanticipated possibilities of the work as it unfolds,"
5. "make vivid the fact that neither words in their literal form nor numbers exhaust what we can know,"
6. "teach students that small differences can have large effects," leading to an understanding of subtlety,
7. "teach students to think through and within a material,"
8. "help children to learn to say what cannot be said," and to "reach into their poetic capacities" to find the words to describe their responses to and experiences with artworks, and
9. "enable us to have experience we can have from no other source" and within this experience "discover the range and variety of what we are capable of feeling."

A third source of artistic thinking and practice can be found in research conducted by Burton, Horowitz, and Abeles (1999). Their large-scale study of over 2000 children examined characteristics of students who had more experiences in the arts along with those of students who had fewer arts experiences. The researchers found a correlation between students with "high arts" backgrounds and the ability to:

> *express ideas and feelings openly and thoughtfully, form relationships among different items of experience and layer them in thinking through an idea or problem, conceive or imagine different vantage points of an idea or problem and to work towards a resolution, construct and organize thoughts and ideas into meaningful units or wholes, and focus perception on an item or items of experience, and sustain this focus over a period of time. (p. 42)*

The study reported other findings related to artistic dispositions, such as high arts students' need to "figure out or elaborate on ideas on their own," "structure and organize thinking in light of different kinds of experiences," and try out or demonstrate "knowledge in new and original ways." Additionally, the study found that for students who had more experience in the arts, "learning involves task persistence, ownership, empathy, and collaboration with others" (p. 42).

Finally, a fourth resource for considering artistic dispositions and practices can be found in Hetland, Winner, Veenema, and Sheridan's (2007) *Studio Habits of Mind*. Based on their observations of art classes in two arts-rich Boston area schools, the researchers identified the following components of learning in the visual arts:

1. Develop Craft (use and care for tools and materials, learn artistic conventions)
2. Engage and Persist (take on problems of relevance within art and personal worlds, develop focus, persevere)
3. Envision (form a mental image for something not available for direct observation, articulate a plan for possible next steps in the evolution of an artwork)
4. Express (construct meaning in a work)
5. Observe (look closely, see things that may not be obvious)
6. Reflect (form and communicate insights about artworks and working process, judge personal work and learning and that of others according to standards in the field)
7. Stretch and Explore (attempt to work beyond one's capacities, be open to following the work as it evolves without a predetermined plan, be comfortable with learning from mistakes/accidents)
8. Understand the Art World (know a broad range of historical and contemporary art ideas, interact with other artists in class, community, and broader art worlds) (p. 6)

A close read and comparison of the kinds of dispositional elements of art making practices contained in these four sources reveals several common findings that, taken together, provide a starting point for teachers to use in forming their own lists of artistic dispositions that are essential to teach. In Table 7-1, I have provided my own priority list that, at this point in my teaching, helps me to focus my work as both an art teacher and teacher educator. As I mentioned before, this list is not fixed—it is open to ongoing revision and change as I gain new insights based on my understanding of the students with whom I work, their ways of approaching art making, and the ever growing content base of contemporary art practices.

Note: Planning overarching dispositional goals: What elements of artistic thinking and practice do you think are important to have as "big picture" goals for student learning? Why are these dispositions so valuable for student learning in art? How will they help students both in making and responding to art and in other areas of their learning and lives? Create your own list of art dispositional teaching/learning goals, drawing from the resources here and from other research you do on your own. This list will help to shape and frame the decisions you make about curriculum and lesson content in the following sections.

Table 7-1 An Evolving List of Essential Artistic Dispositions and Practices

In my work with students, I want them to:

find problems worth solving and ideas worth pursuing in their work

put themselves and their ideas "out there" by developing a personal voice

be flexible and willing to go where the work leads

be experimental in trying out different ways of doing things

be resourceful and inventive

take risks, understand that doing so may at times lead to failure or not achieving what was hoped for

practice discipline and focus

persevere through inevitable challenges in the process

have belief in the process, accept that art making is often ambiguous and that one rarely knows for certain how the work will turn out

be open to hearing others' interpretations of and judgments about their work, and be constructive in their responses to the work of others

develop artistic independence and use it to judge the "rightness" of their own work

understand the art making approaches of other artists and locate their work in communities of practice

---

WHAT STUDENTS SHOULD KNOW AND BE ABLE TO DO

While there may be national,[4] state, or local standards for student learning in art that you are expected to address in your teaching, or a curriculum you are expected to use, you still need to be able to articulate the specific goals and student learning outcomes that your lessons will address. Focusing in this way helps you to think carefully about and plan with purpose the particular activities you will carry out as a teacher to make possible the student learning you have identified.

---

[4] The 1994 *National Standards for Arts Education* were revised by the National Coalition for Core Arts Standards, with implementation by states beginning in 2014. The new visual arts standards are framed by the following "artistic processes" and corresponding "anchor standards": Creating (generate and conceptualize artistic ideas and work; organize and develop artistic ideas and work; refine and complete artistic work); Presenting (analyze, interpret, and select artistic work for presentation; develop and refine artistic techniques and work for presentation; convey meaning through the presentation of an artistic work); Responding (perceive and analyze artistic work; interpret intent and meaning in artistic work; apply criteria to evaluate artistic work); and Connecting (synthesize and relate knowledge and personal experiences to make art; relate artistic ideas and works with societal, cultural, and historical context to deepen understanding).

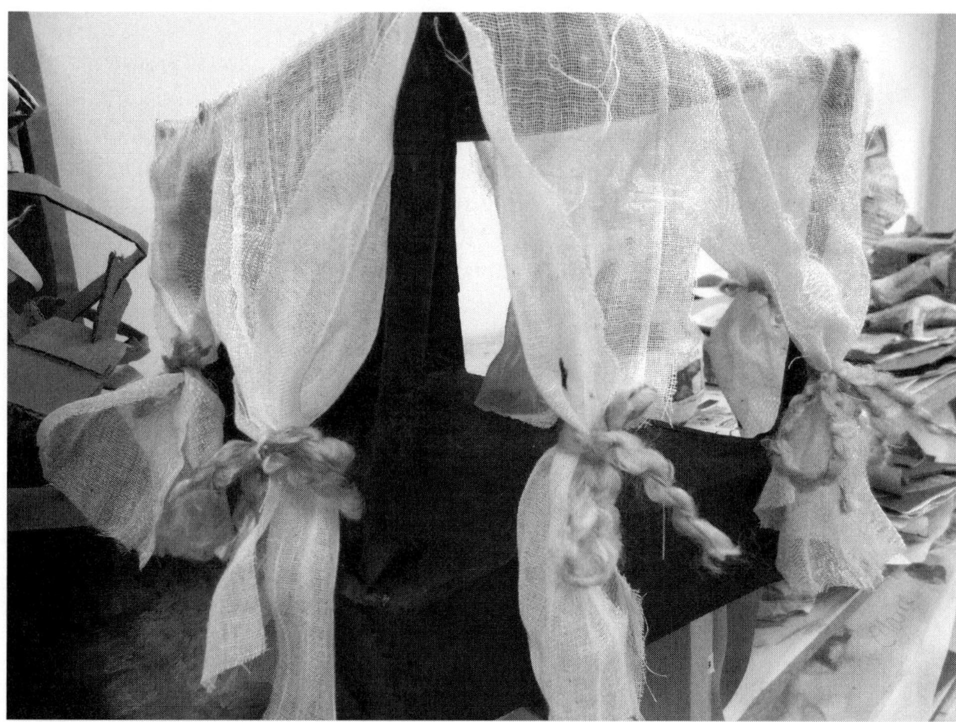

F 7-6
Cecilia Oh, Untitled, 2013, papier-mâché and mixed media, 12" × 13" × 6".

One way of approaching this "drilling down" into art content is to think about different types of learning in art, many of which have already been discussed—for example:

1. learning in, through, and about materials
2. learning about form and composition (line, shape, tone/value, color, texture, space, etc., and their relationships and organization)
3. learning how to portray visual likeness (objects, people, and other things)
4. learning how materials, marks and forms, and their organization can express ideas, feelings, and states of being
5. learning about ideas, topics, and approaches from contemporary and historical art practices
6. learning that integrates art and other areas of learning, such as writing, science, mathematics, and so forth
7. learning that considers cultural, social, political, environmental, and other worlds as content sources for making art

Again, this is just one way in which art content can be broadly considered for the purpose of organizing and planning instruction. In any one of these areas, specific content ideas can be further developed, as briefly illustrated in the following sections. These categories of learning outcomes are not mutually exclusive—lessons that teachers develop will naturally contain multiple focuses, as the process of making art involves attention to multiple, intertwined considerations or dimensions.[5]

---

[5] Listed in the bibliography and resources at the end of this chapter are many additional books for art teachers to consult as they identify content for their teaching and as they articulate specific learning outcomes. See, for example, Smith (1993, 1998), Lord (1996), and Anderson & Milbrandt (2004).

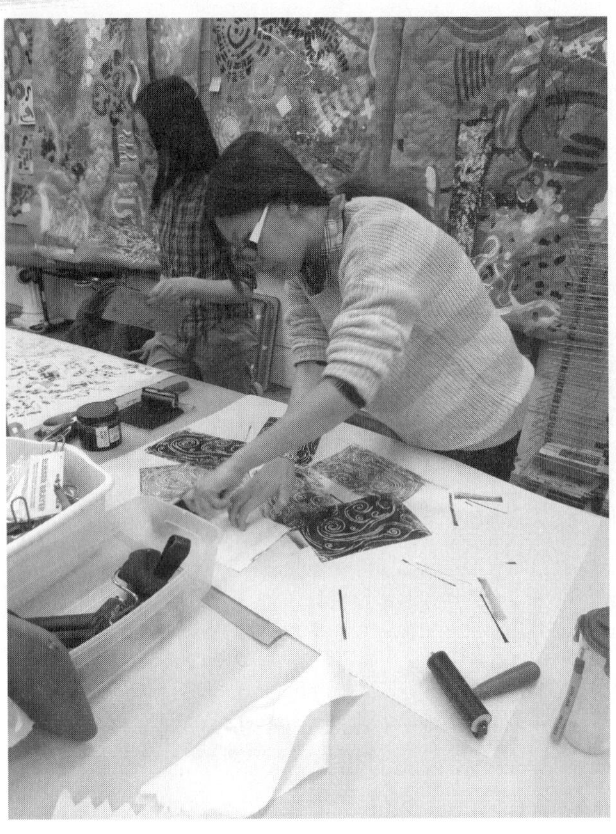

F 7-7: Joanna Chou, printing with relief plates

A Focus on Materials

Your extensive work in exploring materials provides you with an excellent starting point for identifying what can be taught and learned here. Consider, for example, concepts about the physical properties of materials (for example— the fluidity of paint, the plasticity of clay), their technical possibilities (paint can be applied and spread on a surface to create lines, shapes, designs, and images and thinned with water to create transparent effects, charcoal can appear light or dark on the paper according the amount of pressure applied, clay can be molded and shaped to create forms), and their representational and expressive potential (transparent effects can represent such things as water, glass, or ice and suggest moods and feelings like dreaminess or solitude, charcoal can be manipulated to suggest the rough texture of bark or the softness of clouds) (see Figures 7-6 and 7-7).

Note: Identifying concepts and skills related to materials: Using your materials explorations and your notes about working with different media, compile a list of concepts and skills that can be emphasized in your teaching when using individual materials. Make sure to include both physical/technical and representational/ expressive learning outcomes.

A Focus on Form

Formal components and principles of art are defined in various ways by different people. In the book *Graphic Design: The New Basics* (2008), Ellen Lupton and Jennifer Cole Phillips list the following (see http://www.gdbasics.com for descriptions and related design problems):

> point, line, and plane
> rhythm and balance
> scale
> texture
> color
> figure/ground
> framing
> hierarchy
> layers
> transparency
> modularity
> grid
> pattern
> diagram
> time and motion
> rules and randomness

A different collection might be drawn from the following: color, line, shape, value/ tone, texture, form/volume, size, space, direction (elements) and harmony, unity, opposition, balance, gradation, repetition, scale/proportion, movement, pattern,

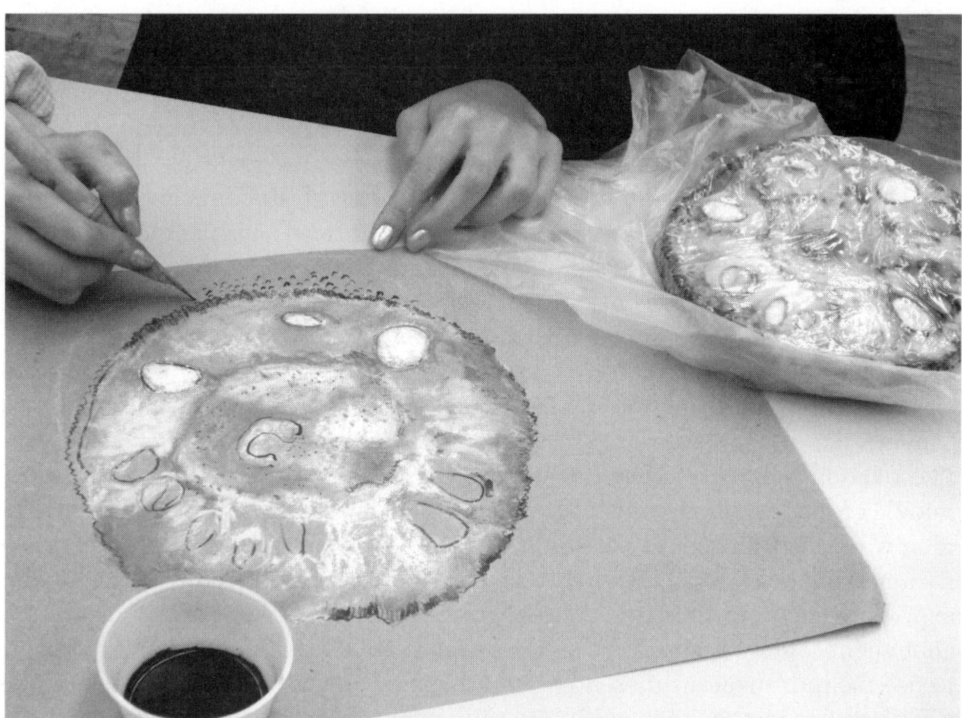

F 7-8: Christine Hsieh, drawing from observation

variety, contrast, dominance/emphasis, unity (principles). Again, these terms are not defined and understood in any singular way (a good idea is to research multiple definitions and arrive at your own that you will use in your teaching). As with the many concepts and skills that can be derived from a focus on materials, formal concerns offer a multitude of concepts and skills for focusing students' learning. Once again, you can consider the properties of different components (lines can be short, long, curved, angled, and straight, and be layered to create built-up areas) and their representational and expressive potential (angled lines and gradations can suggest three-dimensionality or space, a mass overlapping of lines can suggest a tangle or snarl, or a nest—these varied concepts in turn can suggest different expressive ideas, such as tension or protection).

Note: Identifying concepts and skills related to formal concepts: Using your materials explorations and your notes about different media and the marks and forms they make, compile a list of concepts and skills that can be emphasized in your teaching about formal concepts. Make sure to include both learning about properties of formal components and representational/expressive learning outcomes.

A Focus on Representational and Expressive Strategies

While much of the work that students do is satisfying to them in terms of their abilities to work with materials to express ideas, at times they will be interested in learning how to make more visually or expressively convincing portrayals of objects, people, ideas, feelings, moods, and other things (see Figure 7-8). Helping your students develop their skills at representing ideas, concepts, and relationships they are interested in communicating in their work is tricky, for introducing representational conventions (like proportions of the face and body, perspective, foreshortening) too early is not effective and can be confusing. Good teaching involves closely observing students as they work and talking to them about what they are hoping to accomplish. Students may express dissatisfaction with their artwork's capacity to be convincing or to "look real." While this may be about being able to show three-dimensional qualities of volume and space, size relationships or scale, or presenting a consistent vantage point in a two-dimensional work, it also could be about getting a mood right with a particular use of color, portraying a certain attitude of a person through line, or some other expressive goal.

On one hand, this could be a good time to work with students in getting them to observe closely how things appear—and to brainstorm with and demonstrate for each other how they might show those visual effects and details using materials and formal components like line, contrast, color, gradation, and so forth. For example, showing students how a light source shining on an object makes the appearance of the object's surface shift from lighter to darker as it moves away from the light, and capturing this gradation in pencil, charcoal, ink, or paint, can help them to convincingly portray three-dimensional properties. Similarly, having them observe size relationships with regard to near-far distance and discussing foreground, middle ground, and background can help students create the illusion of space in their work. On the other hand, this is also a good time to discuss the more expressive metaphorical possibilities that formal components like color, texture, and expressive effects from materials can be used to create. For example, a discussion about light sources might focus on the dramatic effects of light and dark and how to use them to suggest different moods, feelings, or sensory states. Lines can be discussed not just for their utility in, say, depicting the curve or angle around a three-dimensional object but also from the point of view of expressive effects— materials can be used to make lines that suggest fragility, strength, speed, and slowness, among many other possibilities. This more subtle expressive learning is a central part of studio practice, and leads to sophisticated forms of meaning making with art materials.[6]

Note: Identifying concepts and skills related to representational and expressive concepts: Using your explorations and notes, and your understanding of artistic development, compile a list of concepts and skills that can be emphasized in your teaching about representational and expressive concepts. You can integrate your knowledge of subjects, topics, and themes that are relevant for young people at different ages as well as your understanding of their representational challenges and goals.

A Focus on Art World and Approaches

For lesson content that focuses on themes and approaches drawn from contemporary and historical art, teachers can look to the practices of artists working and exhibiting today and those from the past. There are several sources for identifying conceptual themes in contemporary art. Several years ago, *ARTnews* published an analysis of these trends, which included: art that deals with ritual, meditation, and spiritual healing, installations composed of trash objects, videos that blur fact

---

[6] As you have experienced for yourself in your materials explorations, the studio process does not follow a straight line from idea to physical outcome. Rather, ideas are mediated through work with materials—in other words, materials themselves and their expressive effects influence ideas, suggest meanings in process, and open up conceptual paths not necessarily intended by the artist at the outset. Another way of looking at meaning making in studio learning is through Eisner's (1971) *expressive outcomes*, learning that is made possible within "curriculum activities that are intentionally planned to provide a fertile field for personal purposing and experience" (p. 103). The idea here is that the teacher cannot dictate at the outset the outcomes for student learning when the development of students' meanings for their work is an explicit focus of the lesson.

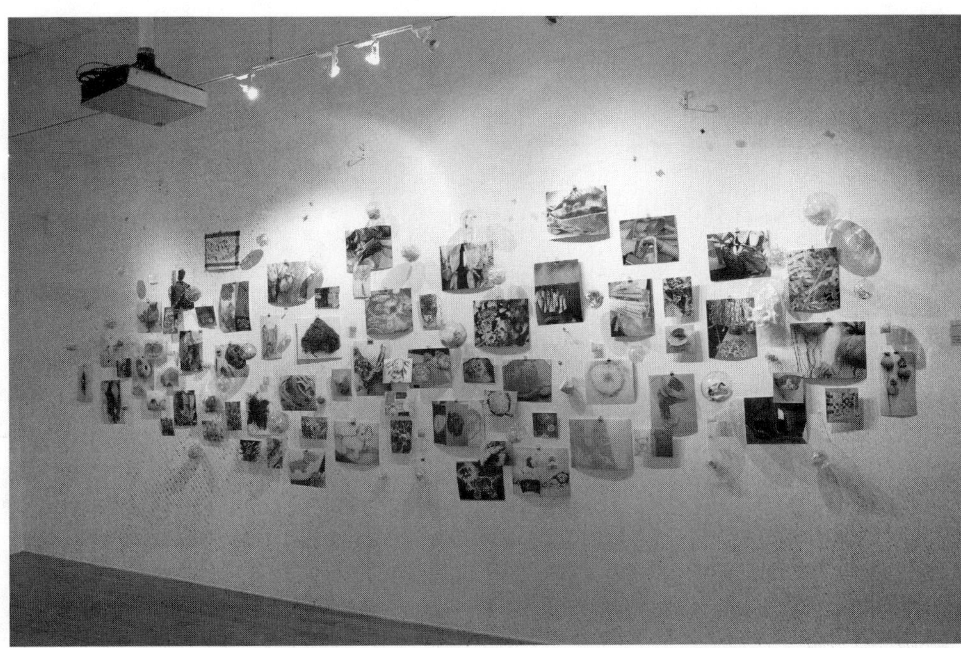

F 7-9: Collaborative installation, 2013

and fiction, postmodern mannerism and twenty-first century romanticism, street art, dark moments in American history, excessive use of common craft materials, utopian skepticism, and psychedelic aesthetic (see Figure 7-9).[7]

Another source of contemporary art ideas and approaches is the website art21 (http://www.art21.org). Across more than a decade art21 has profiled 100 artists whose collective practices address the following themes: identity, consumption, place, spirituality, humor, loss and desire, time, stories, play, structures, memory, power, paradox, ecology, protest, romance, systems, transformation, fantasy, compassion, change, balance, history, and boundaries. Additional sources for curriculum ideas derived from contemporary art are Gude's (2004) suggested practices of appropriation, juxtaposition, recontextualization, layering, interaction of text and image, hybridity, gazing, and representin,' and her suggested experiences (2006) of playing, forming self, investigating community themes, encountering difference, attentive living, empowered experiencing, empowered making, deconstructing culture, reconstructing social spaces, and not knowing. Weintraub's (2003) contemporary approaches for young artists and Ingledew's (2011) comprehensive compilation of "visual ideas" are other sources for planning curriculum around contemporary art. Finally, additional contemporary art topics and approaches include biography and autobiography, language and word meanings, altering, obscuring/obfuscating/blurring, irony and sarcasm, mapping and geographies, animals' rights, and biculturalism.

Note: Identifying concepts and skills related to contemporary and historical art ideas: Using the ideas presented here and those that you find through your own research, make a list of learning outcomes related to themes/topics and studio approaches from contemporary and historical art. Keep in mind your understanding of children's artistic development as you consider learning outcomes that will effectively match the capacities and growth potential of younger and older students.

---

[7] Top ten trends in contemporary art (2006). *ARTnews, 105* (2), pp. 98–124.

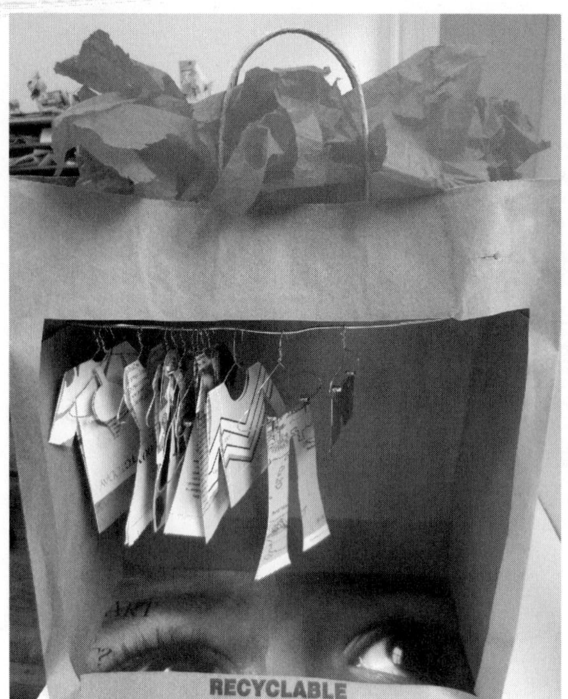

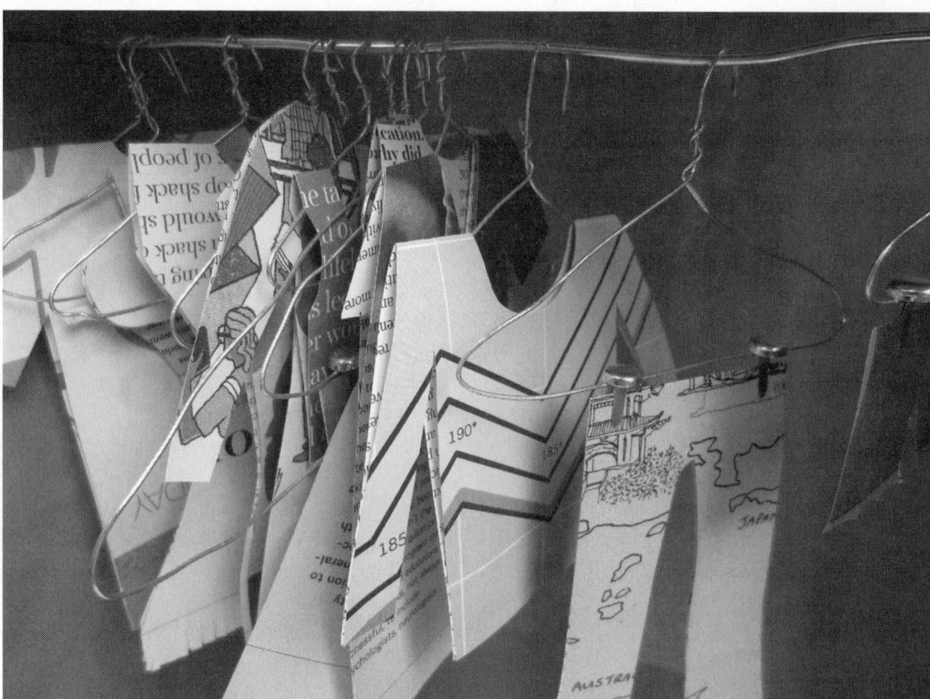

F 7-10a
*Sandy Kuan, Untitled, 2013
mixed media, 16″ × 12″ × 4″.
(above, left)*

F 7-10b
*Sandy Kuan, Untitled, 2013
(detail). (above, right)*

A Focus on Interdisciplinary Learning, Social and Cultural Issues, and Collaborative Art Making Outside the Art Class and School

Students of all ages are often very interested in making artworks that address content and themes that emerge in their learning outside of the art class—for example, in social studies, history, creative writing, science, music, and mathematics. As they grow older and become aware of cultural practices, social issues, and political events and movements, they are also eager to use their studio work as a means to express their knowledge, beliefs, and attitudes about both local and more global cultural topics. At the same time, young people are interested in studying and contributing through art making to the larger visual culture of their worlds—through engaging analyses of advertising products and practices, television shows, toys and games, and many other aspects of their experience. And physically extending beyond the art class and school, art teachers and students may engage in projects that are developed collaboratively with community groups, designed to be created and exhibited or presented in alternative local sites.

There are some excellent resources for art teachers to use in identifying learning in these areas that can be integrated into the art class, including Anderson et al.'s (2010) *Art Education for Social Justice*, Helguera's (2011) *Education for Socially Engaged Art*, Bolin and Blandy's (2011) *Matter Matters: Art Education and Material Culture Studies*, Sweeny's (2010) *Inter/Actions/ Inter/Sections: Art Education in a Digital Visual Culture*, and Desai, Hamlin, and Mattson's (2009) *History as Art, Art as History: Contemporary Art and Social Studies Education*. State and local content standards for student learning in areas outside of art (see, for example, the Common Core standards for English Language Arts and Mathematics—http://www.corestandards.org/the-standards) are also starting points for developing interdisciplinary learning outcomes in art lessons.

Note: Identifying concepts and skills related to interdisciplinary learning, social issues, and cultural themes: Beginning with the resources presented here and those that you find through your own research, make a list of learning outcomes related to interdisciplinary and social/cultural themes and topics.

While it is helpful for the purposes of identifying potential instructional content to isolate and focus individually on the areas above, in reality teaching and learning in art classes weaves together various kinds of content simultaneously. For example, a single lesson featuring collage could support explicit teaching of artistic dispositions (resourcefulness, flexible purposing, willingness to delay closure, problem finding and solving) as well as concepts and skills related to materials (ways of changing and arranging collage elements to express different ideas), form (color, shape, texture, pattern, etc. and their relationships and effects), expression (skills in using materials and forms for representation and expression of students' ideas), and historical and/or contemporary art ideas and practices, among other outcomes (see Figures 7-10a and 7-10b). And circling back on Eisner's (1971) ideas about expressive outcomes, just as creating artworks calls for the artist to be flexible about the endpoint and responsive to different paths the work might take, so, too, should teachers and students be open to the unforeseen and unintended teaching and learning outcomes that have the potential to be significant and meaningful for students. In the next section, we turn to applying this discussion of possible learning outcomes to ways of constructing lessons and developing curriculum in art.

In the Classroom: Planning for Teaching and Learning

There are many ways to structure individual art lessons and myriad approaches to relating lessons to one another in a curriculum or extended plan for teaching and learning. In this section, I briefly describe a range of possibilities and invite you to draw from them as you design your own approach, plan a single lesson with

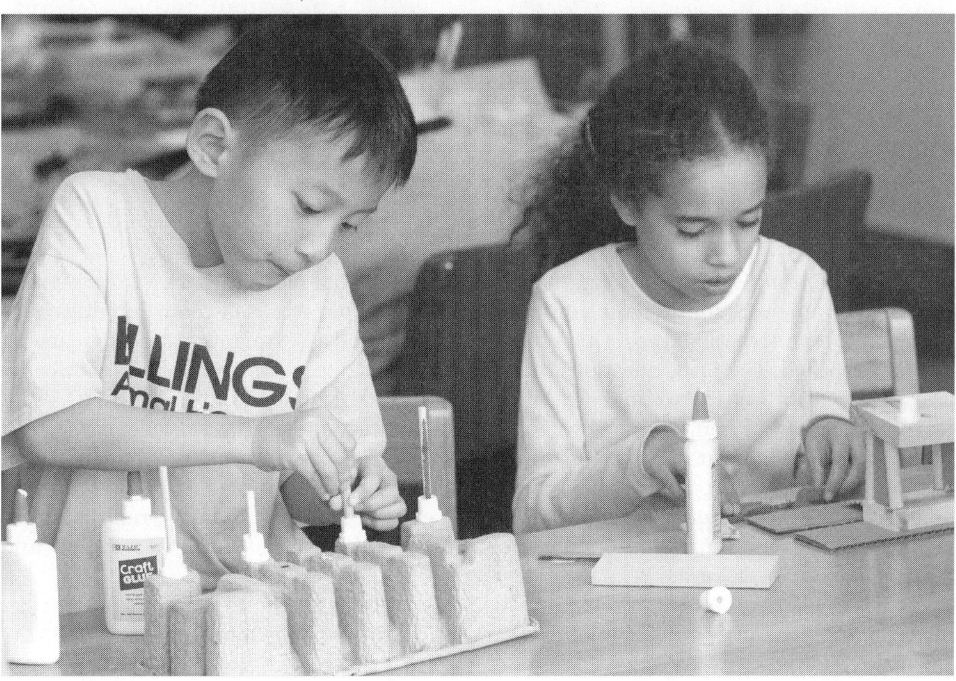

F 7-11: Students building mixed media constructions

engagement with art materials as the starting point, and begin to think about how you might develop a curriculum.

PLANNING INDIVIDUAL LESSONS— CONCEPTUAL COMPONENTS

Among other researchers within and beyond art education, Albers and Murphy (1999), Burton (2013), Burton and Bildstein (2010), Davis, Sumara, and Luce-Kapler (2007), James (2000), Kaye (1997), Sandell (2009), Stewart and Walker (2005), Walker (2001), Wiggins and McTighe (2005),[8] and McTighe and Wiggins (2013) have all put forward models for conceptualizing lessons, many of these specifically geared for studio teaching. Most of these approaches share some core characteristics—for example, for the art-based models, the inclusion of particular types of art-related content. Most of these approaches also share a reliance on a "big," "essential," or "enduring" idea or question that both focuses the lesson and establishes its importance for students to spend time engaging with the content.[9] According to Wiggins (2007), a question is essential when it:

1. causes genuine and relevant inquiry into the big ideas and core content,
2. provokes deep thought, lively discussion, sustained inquiry, and new understanding as well as more questions,
3. requires students to consider alternatives, weigh evidence, support their ideas, and justify their answers,
4. stimulates vital, ongoing rethinking of big ideas, assumptions, and prior lessons,
5. sparks meaningful connections with prior learning and personal experiences, and
6. naturally recurs, creating opportunities for transfer to other situations and subjects.

Following from a large topic area within which critical questions or ideas can be generated, the lesson plan needs to balance open-endedness with structure so that divergent thinking and creative practices are encouraged in students' work and learning (see Figure 7-11). Kaye's (1997) description of "elegant" problems (that will lead to similarly "elegant" solutions, as in the sciences)[10] and Davis, Sumara, and Luce-Kapler's (2008) description of "enabling constraints" share some complementary

---

[8] In *Understanding by Design*, Wiggins and McTighe (2005) present "backward design," a three-part framework for designing lessons in which planning for classroom activities happens only after instructional goals have been articulated and assessments of student learning clearly described. The three questions that guide the design process are: (1) What is worthy and requiring of understanding? (2) What is evidence of understanding? and (3) What learning experiences and teaching promote understanding, interest, and excellence?

[9] Essential ideas and questions can come from many sources, and may spring from such themes as life cycles, power, beliefs and values, reality and fantasy, survival, conflict, ecological systems, interdependence, good and evil, spirituality, identity, relationships, symbolic and metaphorical meaning, adaptation and evolution, and perception and reality.

[10] For Kaye (1997), an elegant problem is "worth solving" and "elicits elegant solutions" by encouraging "flexibility, fluency, elaboration, and originality of responses" (pp. 281–282).

characteristics in this pursuit.[11] In her research on how to encourage older students to create meaning in their work, and not just aim for technical proficiency, James (2000, p. 160) suggests six conditions for the lesson and its structure: (1) flexible but focused constraints, (2) personal, social, and artistic relevance, (3) practice with creative and metaphoric concepts and processes, (5) expectations of complexity, ambiguity, and depth of meaning, and (6) expressive and reflective writing. These conditions dovetail with Gude's (2000) suggestions for designing art experiences that: feature an issue that is important to students, are based on a contemporary social theme, include examples of past and recent artworks that have explored the theme, and teach a conceptual or technical method for making artworks.

Identifying a broad area within which to focus a big idea or essential question and then considering such lesson characteristics as those offered by James and Gude above leads to the identification of relevant and more specific lesson content, often called objectives or student learning outcomes. As described above, these are the concepts and skills that will be learned and the dispositions or ways of thinking that will be elicited and encouraged (like those identified in the previous sections of this chapter). It is also helpful to identify academic language, or vocabulary words, that relate to the lesson content and that students will learn. The lesson plan also needs to articulate prior knowledge and skills students need to have and how the content is justified or aligned with their developmental characteristics, learning capacities, and interests and with any commonly shared learning standards or outcomes. And, the plan needs to explain how instruction will be tailored for students with special needs and abilities—for example English language learners, gifted students, and students with learning disabilities or special emotional and physical needs. Finally, the lesson plan needs to provide concrete criteria and strategies for assessing students' achievement or mastery according to the particular learning objectives or outcomes that have been identified—both while learning is in progress and at the end of the lesson. If you are currently part of a teacher education program, or were in the past, the lesson plan format used in your courses most likely addresses many of these areas.[12]

PLANNING INDIVIDUAL LESSONS— IMPLEMENTATION COMPONENTS

Along with the conceptual part of lesson planning—the goals for teaching and learning and their justification and assessment—lesson plans also usually articulate a sequence of teaching-learning activities in which the students and teacher will engage to bring learning about. These are often organized by each day or class period that makes up the lesson (a lesson may span several class periods). Plans for the in-class activities specify the kinds of teaching and learning that will take place during each class period, such as introductory discussion, demonstration of studio processes, student work time, in-process sharing of students' works,

---

[11] According to Davis, Sumara, & Luce-Kapler (2008), enabling constraints establish limitations for students' actions and activities in a lesson in order to make possible inventive, divergent responses and unanticipated outcomes.

[12] Teacher certification assessment programs and agencies, such as edTPA or state offices of teacher certification, may call for additional considerations that need to be addressed as part of the performance standards for teacher certification.

discussion of related artists' works or examples of other types of visual/material culture, and closing activities such as reviewing what was learned and accomplished during the class. Plans also include any printed materials that will be distributed to students such as project guidelines, assessment activities, and other teaching documents.

Note: Planning a single lesson: Plan a lesson that includes targeted learning in and about art materials and their expressive potential, based on your studio explorations and incorporating your selection of thematic content drawn from possibilities presented so far in this chapter. Make sure your plan includes the components and considerations discussed here and allows for your students to choose their own subjects or topics for what their work will be about and/or accomplish (problem-finding). Also, allow for enough room in the lesson to encourage individuality across students in the images or constructions they create. In other words, ensure that the works will not look the same visually, as if the students have all followed a singular formula dictated by their teacher (review the examples discussed in Chapter 1).

The following questions, while they don't cover all aspects of what needs to be in your plan, may be helpful as you focus your thinking:

1. Does the learning aimed for in the lesson stem from essential questions, focused art content (concepts, skills, ways of thinking), and a consideration of students' artistic development?
2. Does the lesson allow for students to develop themes and ideas connected to their own lives and experiences? Does it teach something that they are (or will be) interested in and able to learn?
3. Are the skills, concepts, and ways of thinking taught through the lesson essential for students' ongoing growth and development as artists?
4. Do the guidelines or requirements for what students will do and make set meaningful limits (not arbitrary but purposeful)? Do they promote divergent responses, individual choices, and interpretations that allow for students to find problems

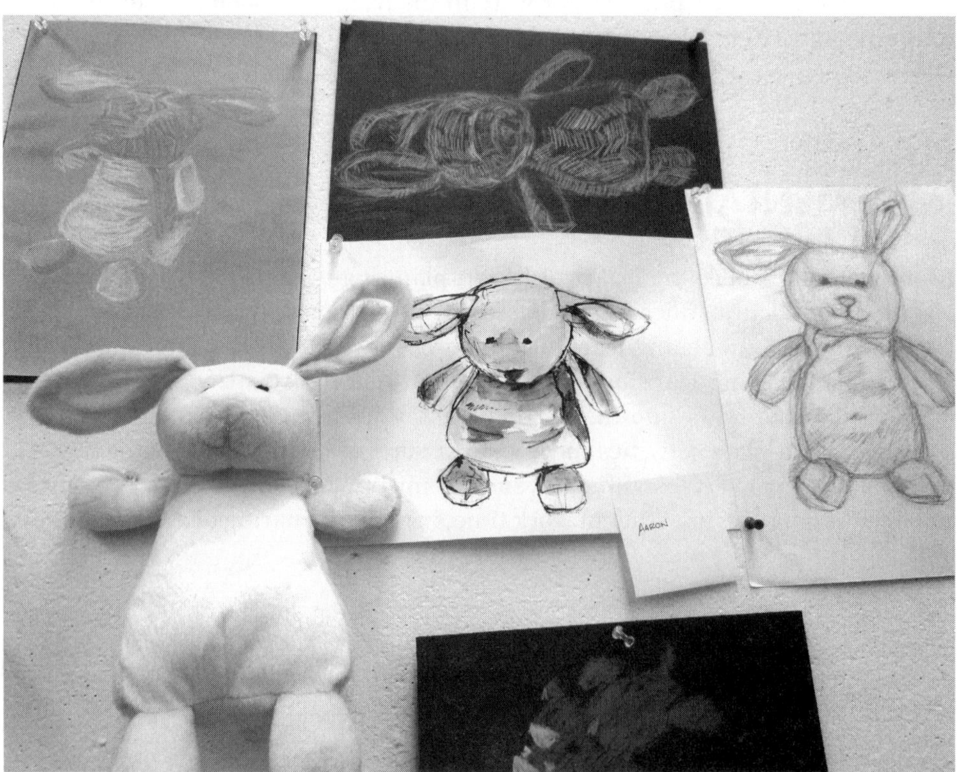

F 7-12

Aaron Barksdale, observation drawings, 2013, mixed media, various dimensions.

worth solving (and not just solve a problem given by the teacher)? Do the guidelines prompt elaboration of students' ideas related to expressive concerns, and to their work with materials and formal components?

5. Does the lesson offer sufficient challenge that will hold students' interest and make them better at doing something? Will the lesson promote curiosity and present or promote new concepts, skills, and/or artistic dispositions?

6. Do the assessment criteria and strategies align with and provide direct evidence related to the learning outcomes identified for the lesson? Do they reflect ways in which artists and young people actually think about and make artworks?[13]

GROUPING LESSONS IN AN EXTENDED CURRICULUM

There are many ways of organizing lessons into a curriculum that spans an extended period of time. Some teachers work within an articulated school or district curriculum that describes learning outcomes for a year's worth of learning in art classes for each grade level or age group they teach. Other curriculum documents are designed for shorter durations, such as a few lessons that are connected in some way. In either case, lessons in a curriculum tend to be sequenced with the intention of expanding and deepening students' understanding about particular art practices, concepts, or ways of thinking (see Figure 7-12).

One way of grouping and sequencing lessons is by using broad themes, as in the big ideas and essential questions described previously. Curricula can also be organized by medium (collage, three-dimensional construction, painting, drawing, video, etc.), genre (portraiture, public art, environmental art, social activism, etc.), chronology (ancient art to current practices), or any number of other approaches. Regardless of the way in which its content is organized, and regardless of its intended duration, a curriculum should provide for students to not only gain new understandings and skills but also deepen and expand upon what they know, the ways in which they approach their work as artists, and the skills learned in prior lessons. A curriculum should also make explicit for students how the content and learning experiences from lesson to lesson are connected. To accomplish this circling back on and pushing forward students' ongoing learning, many teachers design curriculum along a spiral, in which concepts learned and skills gained in any one area (painting techniques, color relationships and effects, graphic design, observational drawing, digital media, public art practices, for example) are reintroduced and expanded upon at designated points in the semester or in progressive years.[14]

Note: Thinking about Curriculum Planning: In my first year of teaching art I was asked by the school principal to develop a written curriculum for grades K–8, because the school did not have one. While I had experience in designing lessons and sequencing them in groups of three or four for specific age groups, I had never thought about what students should

---

[13] For an extensive analysis of different models for assessing student learning, see Hafeli (2009).

[14] A spiral curriculum can connect learning in a multiyear sequence that spans different grades or age groups. Features of a spiral curriculum include revisiting topics with increasing levels of difficulty and challenge and relating new learning to previous learning.

experience in art at each grade level—nor had I ever considered how those experiences should build upon one another each year as students progressed through my classes. While this was an enormous undertaking, and one that required a great deal of focus, it was a wonderfully valuable experience. I now have my students write multiple year curricula as part of their preparation to become art teachers.

Writing a "scope and sequence" for a large scale curriculum as described above involves identifying categories of learning (like those described earlier in this chapter) and then identifying the particular outcomes within each category for students at each grade level or age grouping. This kind of curriculum development does not require detailed plans for each lesson—rather, the document lists the knowledge, practices and skills, and artistic dispositions that will be the focus of teaching and learning. Some curricula also highlight particular activities—such as field trips to art museums, galleries, and centers and collaborative projects with artists or groups in the community—and describe interdisciplinary connections to subject areas beyond the visual arts.

Take some time to think about how you might structure teaching and learning outcomes over a semester or year, or across years in a multiple year curriculum. How will you sequence learning experiences and make explicit connections between them? How will you circle back on and advance students' prior learning on a continual basis?

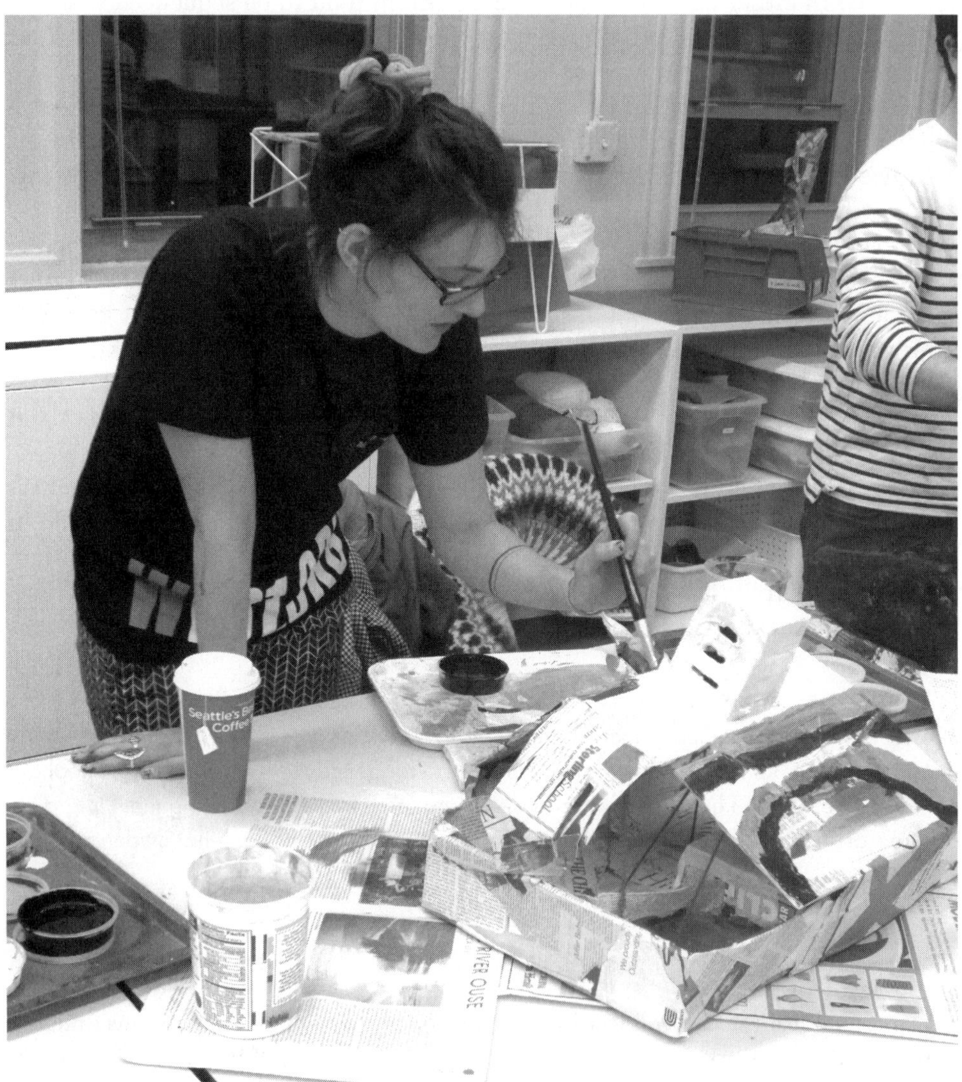

F 7-13: Clarissa Ghelli, mixed media construction in progress

In the Classroom:
Fostering an Environment of Studio Inquiry

A FINAL WORD

This book has focused on inviting you to engage in studio experiences to gain some insights into how you can be the kind of teacher who promotes young people's own studio ideas and approaches. Hopefully, it has helped you to learn more about how art materials can be used by artists to create forms that express ideas—ideas of the maker (see Figure 7-13). It has encouraged you to consider students as artists in their own right, with their own ways of conceptualizing, making, and judging their artwork. What does this kind of classroom look like? How do students interact with other students, and with the teacher, within an environment that expects students to take charge of the kinds of work that gets made?[15]

While it is important to carefully plan for teaching and learning with regard to identifying outcomes (and be flexible to pursue promising outcomes that are unanticipated), and while it is critical to organize the space to, as much as possible, promote student autonomy, setting the right tone for the studio classroom in other ways is also crucial. For example, you can purposefully model for students how people will both approach their work and respond to and interact with one another by revisiting your own ideas about students as artists. If you consider student artists as independent thinkers, then involve them as peer presenters in demonstrations of processes and techniques. Publicly celebrate acts by individual students who exhibit the artistic dispositions you seek to promote through your teaching. When a student takes a risk in her work, perseveres through challenges, tries many different ways of doing something—all of these and other studio practices will gain importance among your students the more you make them an explicit part of your teaching. When students see that the collective work from a single lesson all looks different, instead of the same, their ideas about making art shift and this, too, changes the tone of the class. And when questions like "Is this good?" and "Is this how you wanted it?" are turned back on individual students and their class of peers—because, after all, they are the artists in charge of their artwork, not the teacher—students begin to treat themselves and each other as valid sources of judgment about art. Finally, students who see their stories and meanings as central "content" in the art class have very different perceptions about what it means to be an artist at school than students whose teacher dictates the subjects and themes of the artwork created in class.

Being an art teacher brings with it a certain power (and responsibility) to grow and shape your students' thinking about art, and about themselves as artists, both now and in the future. Keep your hands and mind in materials and the forms and meanings they can create, your eyes looking out at diverse studio practices of artists, and your ears tuned in to your students as learners and the stories and images that make up their artistic culture. If you can integrate these central components of teaching art, the rest will come along, too.

---

[15] For alternative ways of thinking about classroom organization for teaching and learning with student choice in mind, see Jaquith and Hathaway (2012) and Douglas and Jaquith (2009).

Bibliography

Albers, P., & Murphy, S. (1999). *Telling pieces: Art as literacy in middle school classes*. New York, NY: Routledge.

Anderson, T., Gussak, D., Hallmark, K., & Paul, A. (2010). *Art education for social justice*. Reston, VA: National Art Education Association.

Anderson, T., & Milbrandt, M. (2004). *Art for life: Authentic instruction in art*. New York, NY: McGraw-Hill.

Art:21. (2005a). Ellen Gallagher interview—eXelento and DeLuxe. Retrieved July 14, 2013, from http://www.art21.org/texts/ellen-gallagher/interview-ellen-gallagher-exelento-and-deluxe.

Art:21. (2005b). Interview—Susan Rothenberg: The Studio. Retrieved July 19, 2013, from http://www.art21.org/texts/susan-rothenberg/interview-susan-rothenberg-the-studio.

Art:21. (2005c). Martin Puryear interview—Stone Carving. Retrieved July 26, 2006, from http://www.pbs.org/art21/artists/puryear/clip1.html.

Art:21. (2005d). Mel Chin interview— Knowmad. Retrieved July 26, 2006, from http://www.pbs.org/art21/artists/chin/clip1.html.

Art:21. (2005e). Susan Rothenberg interview—Gestures. Retrieved July 26, 2006, from http://www.pbs.org/art21/artists/rothenberg/clip1.html.

Art:21. (2005f). Tim Hawkinson interview—Überorgan. Retrieved July 26, 2006, from http://www.pbs.org/art21/artists/hawkinson/clip2.html.

Art:21. (2003). Trenton Doyle Hancock interview—It came from the studio floor. Retrieved July 10, 2013, from http://www.art21.org/texts/trenton-doyle-hancock/interview-trenton-doyle-hancock-it-came-from-studio-floor.

Art:21. (2002). SHORT (video from the series "Exclusive")—Martin Puryear: Printmaking. Retrieved July 19, 2013, from http://www.art21.org/videos/short-martin-puryear-printmaking.

Atkinson, J., Harrison, H., & Grasdal, P. (2005). *Collage sourcebook*. Gloucester, MA: Quarry.

Ayres, J. (1991). *Monotype: Mediums and methods for painterly printmaking*. New York, NY: Watson-Guptill.

Babington, J. (2006). Against the grain: Helen Frankenthaler woodcuts. Retrieved July 26, 2006, from http://www.nga.gov.au/exhibition/Frankenthaler/Default.cfm?MnuID=4.

Bain, C. (2009). Untangling legal issues that affect teachers and student teachers. *Art Education, 62*(5), 47–53.

Barker, S. (1997). *Children can build: Building with wood for ages 3–9*. Maineville, OH: Laughing Star Press.

Barlow, M. (2001). Memories in the material: An interview with Patricia McKenna. *Sculpture Magazine, 20*(3). Retrieved July 26, 2006, from http://www.sculpture.org/documents/scmag01/april01/mckenna/mckenna.shtml.

Bautista, T. (2006). *Collage unleashed*. Cincinnati, OH: North Light.

Bayles, D., & Orland, T. (2001). *Art and fear: Observations on the perils (and rewards) of artmaking*. New York, NY: Image Continuum Press.

Beardsley, J., Arnett, W., Arnett, P., & Livingston, J. (2002). *The quilts of Gee's Bend*. Atlanta, GA: Tinwood Books.

Berger, J. (1974). *The look of things*. New York, NY: Viking Press.

Bolin, P., & Blandy, D. (2011). *Matter matters: Art education and material culture studies*. Reston, VA: National Art Education Association.

Brown, C. (2010). *The sculpture techniques bible*. London: Quarto.

Burton, J. (2000). The configuration of meaning: Learner-centered art education revisited. *Studies in Art Education, 41*(4).

Burton, J. (2013). *A guide for teaching and learning in the visual arts*. Unpublished manuscript, Teachers College, Columbia University.

Burton, J. (2000). The configuration of meaning: Learner-centered art education revisited. *Studies in Art Education, 41*(4), 330–345.

Burton, J., & Bildstein, I. (2010). *Challenging thinking: Possibilities and potentials for teaching and learning in the visual arts*. Teachers College, Columbia University—Program in Art and Art Education.

Burton, J., Horowitz, R., & Abeles, H. (1999). *Learning in and through the arts: Transfer and higher order thinking*. Center for Arts Education Research, Teachers College, Columbia University.

Causey, A. (1998). *Sculpture since 1945*. New York, NY: Oxford University Press.

Clough, P. (2007). *Clay in the primary school*. London: A & C Black.

Clough, P. (2007). *Sculptural materials in the classroom*. London: A & C Black.

Chapman, L. (1978). *Approaches to art in education*. San Diego, CA: Harcourt Brace Jovanovich Publishers.

Corwin, L. (2008). *Printing by hand: A modern guide to printing with handmade stamps, stencils, and silk screens*. New York, NY: Abrams.

Davis, B., Sumara, D., & Luce-Kapler, R. (2007). *Engaging minds: Changing teaching in complex times*. Abingdon: Routledge.

Davis, B., Sumara, D., & Luce-Kapler, R. (2008). *Engaging minds: Changing teaching in complex times* (second edition). New York, NY: Routledge.

Dawson, I. (2013). *Making contemporary sculpture*. London: Crowood Press.

Desai, D., Hamlin, J., & Mattson, R. (2009). *History as art, art as history: Contemporary art and social studies education*. New York, NY: Routledge.

Dewey, J. (1938). *Experience and education*. New York, NY: Macmillan.

Dorn, C. M., Madeja, S. S., & Sabol, F. R. (2004). *Assessing expressive learning*. Mahwah, NJ: Erlbaum.

Eisner, E. (1971). Media, expression, and the arts. *Studies in Art Education, 13*(1), 4–12.

Douglas, K., & Jaquith, D. (2009). *Engaging learners through artmaking: Choice-based art education in the classroom*. New York, NY: Teachers College Press.

Eisner, E. (2002). *The arts and the creation of mind*. New Haven, CT: Yale University Press.

Eisner, E. (2004). *The arts and the creation of mind*. New Haven, CT: Yale University Press.

Eisner, E. (1979). *The educational imagination*. New York, NY: Macmillan.

Eisner, E. (1978). What do children learn when they paint? *Art Education, 21* (3), 6–10.

Elkind, D. (2007). *The power of play: Learning what comes naturally*. New York, NY: De Capo Press.

Elkins, J. (2000). *What painting is*. New York, NY: Routledge.

Elkins, J. (2001). *Why art cannot be taught*. Champaign, IL: University of Illinois Press.

Elsworth, A. (1998). *Watercolor workbook*. Pleasantville, NY: Reader's Digest.

Emory, L. (1989). Believing in artistic making and thinking. *Studies in Art Education, 30*(4), 237–248.

Goodman, N. (1978). *Ways of worldmaking.* New York, NY: Hackett Books.

Greene, M. (2001). *Variations on a blue guitar: The Lincoln Center Institute lectures on aesthetic education.* New York, NY: Teachers College Press.

Gude, O. (2006). Principles of possibility: Considerations for a 21st century art and culture curriculum. *Art Education, 60*(1), 6–17.

Gude, O. (2004). Postmodern principles: In search of a 21st century art education. *Art Education, 57*(1), 6–14.

Gude, O. (2000). Investigating the culture of curriculum. In D. Fehr, K. Kehr, & K. Keifer-Boyd (Eds.), *Real-world readings in art education: Things your professor never told you* (pp. 75–81). New York, NY: Falmer Press.

Hafeli, M. (2002). Angels, wings, and Hester Prynne: The place of content in teaching adolescent artists. *Studies in Art Education, 44*(1), 28–46.

Hafeli, M. (2001). Encountering student learning. *Art Education, 54*(6), 19–24.

Hafeli, M. (2012a). Following on. In J. Burton and M. Hafeli (Eds.), *Conversations in art: The dialectics of teaching and learning.* Reston, VA: National Art Education Association.

Hafeli, M. (2012b). "If only you could see into me." Interpreting meaning in Mr. Romani's art class. In J. Burton and M. Hafeli (Eds.), *Conversations in art: The dialectics of teaching and learning.* Reston, VA: National Art Education Association.

Hafeli, M. (2000). Negotiating "fit" it student artwork: Classroom conversations. *Studies in Art Education, 41*(2), 130–145.

Hafeli, M. (2011). The intimate chatter of storied objects: Aesthetics and connectivity in "matter out of place." In P. Bolin & D. Blandy (Eds.), *Matter matters: Art education and material culture studies* (pp. 25–35). Reston, VA: National Art Education Association.

Hafeli, M. (2008). "What happened to authenticity? 'Assessing Students' Progress and Achievements in Art' revisited." In R. Sabol & M. Manifold (Eds.), *Through the prism: Looking into the spectrum of writings by Enid Zimmerman.* Reston, VA: National Art Education Association.

Hancock, T. D. Tunnel. Retrieved August 7, 2013, from http://www.ipcny.org/files/NP11_Summer%20brochure%20draft.pdf.

Hartill, B., & Clarke, R. (2005). *Collagraphs and mixed media printing.* London: A & C Black.

Helguera, P. (2011). *Education for socially engaged art: A materials and techniques handbook.* New York, NY: Jorge Pinto Books.

Hetland, L., Winner, E., Veenema, S. & Sheridan, K. (2007). *Studio thinking: The real benefits of visual arts education.* New York, NY: Teachers College Press.

Horodner, S. (2001). The language of stuff: An interview with Richard Wentworth. *Sculpture Magazine, 20*(3). Retrieved August 29, 2013, from http://www.sculpture.org/documents/scmag01/april01/went/went.shtml.

Hughes, A., & Vernon-Morris, H. (2008). *The printmaking bible: The complete guide to materials and techniques.* San Francisco, CA: Chronicle.

Ingledew, J. (2011). *The a-z of visual ideas: How to solve any creative brief.* London: Laurence King Publishers.

James, P. (2000). Working toward meaning: The evolution of an assignment. *Studies in Art Education, 41*(2), 146–163.

Janis, H., & Blesh, R. (1962). *Collage: Personalities, concepts, techniques.* Philadelphia, PA: Chilton.

Jaquith, D., & Hathaway, N. (Eds.) (2011). *The learner-directed classroom: Developing creative thinking skills through art.* New York, NY: Teachers College Press.

Jennings, S. (2006). *The new artist's manual: The complete guide to painting and drawing materials and techniques.* San Francisco, CA: Chronicle Books.

Kerlavage, M. (1998). Understanding the learner. In J. Simpson, J. Delaney, K. Carroll, C. Hamilton, S. Kay, M. Kerlavage, & J. Olson, *Creating meaning through art* (pp. 23–72). Upper Saddle River, NJ: Merrill.

Kindler, A. (2004). Researching the impossible? Models of artistic development reconsidered. In E. Eisner & M. Day (Eds.), *Handbook of research and policy in art education* (pp. 233–252). New York, NY: Routledge.

Kindler, A. (Ed.). (1997). *Child development in art.* Reston, VA: National Art Education Association.

Kino, C. (2005, October 2). A visit with the Modern's first grandmother: Draw it, shape it, paint it. What's there to talk about, asks Elizabeth Murray? *New York Times*, p. 30.

Krug, M. (2012). *An artist's handbook: Materials and techniques.* London: Laurence King Publishing.

Latta, M. (2001). Letting aesthetic experience tell its own tale: A reminder. *Journal of Aesthetic Education, 35*(1), 45–51.

Lerman, L., & Borstel, J. (2003). *Liz Lerman's critical response process: A method for getting useful feedback on anything you make, from dance to dessert.* Takoma Park, MD: Liz Lerman Dance Exchange.

Lord, L. (1970). *Collage and construction in grades 1–4.* New York, NY: Scholastic.

Lord, L. (1996). *Collage and construction in school—preschool/junior high.* New York, NY: Bank Street College of Education.

Lord, L. (1996). *Collage and construction in school—preschool/junior high.* New York, NY: Bank Street College of Education.

Lupton, E., & Phillips, J. (2008). *Graphic design: The new basics.* Princeton, NJ: Princeton Architectural Press.

Marchesseau, D. (1989), *The intimate world of Alexander Calder.* Paris: Solange Thierry Editeur.

Mayer. R. (1991). *The artist's handbook of materials and techniques* (5th ed.). New York, NY: Viking Press.

McTighe, J., & Wiggins, G. (2013). *Essential questions: Opening doors to student understanding.* Alexandria, VA: Association for Supervision and Curriculum Development.

Meyer, J. (2002, May). Grand allusion: James Meyer talks with Ann Truitt. *Art Forum.* Retrieved July 26, 2006, from http://www.artforum.com/archive/id=2756&search=ann%20truitt.

Miller, D. (Ed.). (1959). *Sixteen Americans.* New York, NY: Museum of Modern Art.

Munro, E. (2000). *Originals: American women artists.* New York, NY: Da Capo Press. National Gallery of Art (2006).

National Gallery of Art (2006). Mark Rothko, Introduction. Retrieved July 26, 2006, from http://www.nga.gov/feature/rothko/intro1.shtm.

Nierman, K., & Arima, E. (2000). *The Kids 'N' Clay ceramics book: Handbuilding and wheel-throwing projects from the Kids 'N' Clay pottery studio.* Berkeley, CA: Tricycle Press.

Paley, V. (2005). *A child's work: The importance of fantasy play.* Chicago, IL: University of Chicago Press.

Plowman, R. (2012). *The collage workbook.* New York, NY: Lark Crafts.

Quiller, S. (2008). *Watermedia painting with Stephen Quiller.* New York, NY: Watson-Guptill.

Reyner, N. (2007). *Acrylic revolution.* Cincinnati, OH: North Light Books.

Rockman, D. (2000). *The art of teaching art: A guide for teaching and learning the foundations of drawing-based art.* New York, NY: Oxford.

Romano, C., & Ross, J. (1980). *The complete collagraph: The art and technique of printing from collage plates.* New York, NY: Free Press.

Ross, J., Romano, C., & Ross, T. (1991). *The complete printmaker: Techniques, traditions, innovations.* New York, NY: Simon and Schuster.

Sandell, R. (2009). Form + Theme + Context (FTC) for rebalancing 21st century art education. *Studies in Art Education, 50*(3), 287–299.

Schjeldahl, P. (2010). Between the lines: What has become of drawing? *New Yorker,* November 29, 2010. Retrieved July 10, 2013, from http://www.newyorker.com/arts/critics/artworld/2010/11/29/101129craw_artworld_schjeldahl.

Shay, B. (2010). *Collage lab.* Beverly, MA: Quarry.

Singer, D., Golinkoff, R., & Hirsh-Pasek, K. (2009). *Play = learning: How play motivates and enhances children's cognitive and social-emotional growth.* New York, NY: Oxford University Press.

Smith, N. (1993). *Experience and art: Teaching children to paint* (2nd ed.). New York, NY: Teachers College Press.

Smith, N. & the Drawing Study Group (1998). *Observation drawing with children: A framework for teachers.* New York, NY: Teachers College Press.

Steiner, U., & Herzog, S. (2004). The idea is what matters! An interview with Mona Hatoum. Retrieved July 26, 2006, from http://www.qantara.de/webcom/show_article.php/_c-310/_nr-144/_p-1/i.html.

Stewart, M. & Walker, S. (2005). *Rethinking curriculum in art.* Worcester, MA: Davis Publications.

Stiles, K., & Selz, P. (Eds.). (1996). *Theories and documents of contemporary art.* Berkeley, CA: University of California Press.

Sullivan, G. (2005). *Art practice as research: Inquiry in visual arts* (2nd ed.). Thousand Oaks, CA: Sage.

Sweeny, R. (2010). *Inter/Actions/Inter/Sections: Art education in a digital visual culture.* Reston, VA: National Art Education Association.

Taylor, L. (2011). *The ceramics bible: The complete guide to materials and techniques.* San Francisco, CA: Chronicle Books.

Thomas, L. (1987, December 13). Noted with pleasure. *New York Times,* p. 2. Retrieved July 26, 2006, from http://query.nytimes.com/gst/fullpage.html?sec=health&res=9B0DE0DB163FF930A25751C1A961948260.

Thompson, C. (Ed.). (1995). *The visual arts and early childhood learning.* Reston, VA: National Art Education Association.

Topal, C., & Gandini, L. (1999). *Beautiful stuff: Learning with found materials.* Worcester, MA: Davis Publications.

Top ten trends in contemporary art (2006). *ARTnews, 105*(2), pp. 98–124.

Vaughan, S. (2001, April 1). Making it: Staying true to a unique vision of art. *Los Angeles Times.* Retrieved July 26, 2006, from http://www.graphicwitness.org/coe/latimes.htm.

Walker, S. (2001). *Teaching meaning in artmaking.* Worcester, MA: Davis Publications.

Weintraub, L. (2003). *In the making: Creative options for contemporary art.* New York, NY: Distributed Art Publishers.

Wiggins, G. (2007). What is an essential question? *Big Ideas,* retrieved September 10, 2013, from http://www.authenticeducation.org/ae_bigideas/article.lasso?artid=53.

Wiggins, G., & McTighe, J. (2005). *Understanding by design (expanded 2nd edition).* Alexandria, VA: Association for Supervision and Curriculum Design.

Wilson, B. (1997). Child art, multiple interpretations, and conflicts of interest. In A. Kindler (Ed.), *Child development in art* (pp. 81–94). Reston, VA: National Art Education Association.

Resources

Book Resources

Albers, J. (2013). *Interaction of color: Revised and expanded edition*. New Haven, CT: Yale University Press.

Art class: A complete guide to painting. (1999). San Francisco, CA: Chronicle Books.

Beal, N., & Miller, G. (2001). *The art of teaching art to children: In school and at home*. New York, NY: Farrar, Straus and Giroux.

Berger, J. (2012). *PUSH print: 30+ artists explore the boundaries of printmaking*. New York, NY: Sterling.

Bishop, C. (2011). *Installation art*. London: Tate Publishing.

Braun-Reinitz, J., & Shicoff, R. (2001). *The mural book: A practical guide for educators*. Aspen, CO: Crystal Productions.

Brooks, S. (2002). *Drawing as expression: Techniques and concepts*. Upper Saddle River, NJ: Prentice Hall.

Collins, J. (2007). *Sculpture today*. London: Phaidon.

Craig, A., & Craig, R. (2011). *Block printing: Techniques for linoleum and wood*. Mechanicsburg, PA: Stackpole.

Davidson, M. (2011). *Contemporary drawing: Key concepts and techniques*. New York, NY: Watson-Guptill Publications.

Digby, J., & Digby, J. (1985). *The collage handbook*. London: Thames and Hudson.

Ewing, P., & Louis, L. (1999). *In the paint*. New York, NY: Abbeville Press.

Flood, R., Hoptman, L., Massimiliano, G., & Smith, T. (2012). *Unmonumental: The object in the 21st century*. London: Phaidon.

Giorgini, F. (1994). *Handmade tiles: Designing, making, decorating*. Ashville, NC: Lark Books.

Godfrey, T. (2009). *Painting today*. London: Phaidon Press.

Gottsegen, M. (2006). *The painter's handbook: Revised and expanded*. New York, NY: Watson-Guptill Publications.

Heyenga, L. (2013). *Art made from books: Altered, sculpted, carved, transformed*. San Francisco, CA: Chronicle Books.

Harper, G., & Moyer, T. (2010). *A sculpture reader: Contemporary sculpture since 1980*. Washington, DC: ISC Press.

Jennings, S. (2006). *The new artist's manual: The complete guide to painting and drawing materials and techniques*. San Francisco, CA: Chronicle Books.

Larbelestier, S. (1995). *The art and craft of collage*. San Francisco, CA: Chronicle.

Leland, N., & Williams, V. (1994). *Creative collage techniques*. Cincinnati, OH: North Light.

LeClair, C. (1991). *Colour in contemporary painting: Integrating practice and theory*. New York, NY: Watson-Guptill Publications.

Manco, T. (2012). *Raw + material = art: Found, scavenged and upcycled.* London: Thames and Hudson.

Maslen, M., & Southern, J. (2011). *Drawing projects: An exploration of the language of drawing.* London: Black Dog Publishing.

McElroy, D., & Wilson, S. (2009). *Image transfer workshop: Mixed-media techniques for successful transfers.* Cincinnati, OH: North Light.

Nelson. R. (2012). *What does a hammer do?* Minneapolis, MN: Lerner.

Nelson. R. (2012). *What does a level do?* Minneapolis, MN: Lerner.

Nelson. R. (2012). *What do pliers do?* Minneapolis, MN: Lerner.

Nelson. R. (2012). *What does a screwdriver do?* Minneapolis, MN: Lerner.

Nelson. R. (2012). *What does a wrench do?* Minneapolis, MN: Lerner.

Paint and painting (1993). New York, NY: Scholastic.

Paper works (2012). Berkeley, CA: Ginko Press.

Rockman, D. (2000). *The art of teaching art: A guide for teaching and learning the foundations of drawing-based ar*t. New York, NY: Oxford.

Schwabsky, B. (2011). *Vitamin P2: New perspectives in painting.* London: Phaidon Press.

Sidaway, I. (2000). *Everything you ever wanted to know about art materials.* Cincinnati, OH: North Light Books.

Smith, N. & the Drawing Study Group (1998). *Observation drawing with children: A framework for teachers.* New York, NY: Teachers College Press.

Steinhart, P. (2005). *Why we draw.* New York, NY: Vintage Books.

Stromquist, A. (2005). *Simple screenprinting.* New York, NY: Sterling.

Szekely, G., & Bucknam, J. (2012). *Art teaching: Elementary through middle school.* New York, NY: Routledge.

The art of sculpture. (1993). New York, NY: Scholastic.

The history of printmaking (1996). New York, NY: Scholastic.

Topal, C. W. (1983). *Children, clay, and sculpture.* Worcester, MA: Davis Publications.

Utley, C., & Magson, M. (2007). *Exploring clay with children.* London: A & C Black.

Vergine, L. (2007). *When trash becomes art: TRASH rubbish mongo.* Milan: Skira Editore.

Vitamin D2: New perspectives in drawing (2nd ed.). (2013). London: Phaidon Press.

Vitamin 3-D: New perspectives in sculpture and installation. (2009). Phaidon.

Waldman, D. (1992). *Collage, assemblage, and the found object.* New York, NY: Abrams.

Walker, L. (2007). *Housebuilding for children* (2nd ed.). New York, NY: Overlook Press.

Zakin, R. (1994). *Electric kiln ceramics: A guide to clays and glazes* (2nd ed.). Iola, WI: Krause Publications.

Website Resources

Art21
http://www.art21.org
Art and Learning to Think and Feel
http://bartelart.com/arted/art-ed-home.html
collageart.org
http://www.collageart.org
Common Core State Standards Initiative
http://www.corestandards.org/the-standards
Graphic Design: The New Basics
http://www.gdbasics.com

International Print Center
http://www.ipcny.org/
International Sculpture Center
http://www.sculpture.org/
Spiral Workshop
http://www.uic.edu/classes/ad/ad382/
Teaching for Artistic Behavior
http://teachingforartisticbehavior.org/
The Drawing Center
www.drawingcenter.org
The International Museum of Collage, Assemblage and Construction
http://collagemuseum.com
The Painting Center
http://www.thepaintingcenter.org

Index